American Civilization

This revised and updated edition of the hugely successful *American Civilization* provides students of American studies with the perfect background and introductory information on contemporary American life. The sixth edition examines the central dimensions of American society from geography and the environment, government and politics, to religion, education, sports, media and the arts. This book:

- covers all core American studies topics at introductory level
- contains essential historical background for American studies students in the twenty-first century
- analyzes issues of gender, class, race and minorities in America's cosmopolitan population
- contains color photos, case studies, questions and terms for discussion, bibliographical references and lists of websites central to each chapter
- accompanied by a fully integrated companion website featuring extensive references for further reading, links to key primary sources, filmographies and advice for students on how to approach essay questions.

Featuring new color illustrations and case studies, this edition includes expanded sections on the environment, immigration, foreign policy, media and the arts, sport and leisure cultures as well as a new section on the LGBT community and detailed coverage of the 2012 election and shifting economic situation.

David Mauk is Associate Professor of North American Area Studies at the University of Oslo and is the author of *The Colony that Rose from the Sea: Norwegian Maritime Migration and Community in Brooklyn* and many articles on American politics, immigration and ethnicity.

John Oakland is the author of *British Civilization* (now in its seventh edition), *Irish Civilization* (with Arthur Aughey), *Contemporary Britain* and *British Civilization: A Student's Dictionary*. He is a former Associate Professor in English at the Norwegian University of Science and Technology.

American Civilization

An introduction

Sixth edition

David Mauk and John Oakland

Routledge
Taylor & Francis Group

LONDON AND NEW YORK

First published in 1995 by Routledge
This edition published 2014 by Routledge
2 Park Square, Milton Park, Abingdon, Oxon OX14 4RN

Simultaneously published in the USA and Canada by Routledge

711 Third Avenue, New York, NY 10017

Routledge is an imprint of the Taylor & Francis Group, an informa business

British Library Cataloguing in Publication Data
A catalogue record for this book is available from the British Library

Library of Congress Cataloging in Publication Data
Mauk, David, 1945–
    American civilization : an introduction / David Mauk and John Oakland. —
    Sixth Edition.
        pages cm
    Includes index.
    1. United States—Civilization. 2. United States—Civilization—Study and teaching—
    Foreign countries. I. Oakland, John. II. Title.
    E169.1.M45 2013
    973—dc23
    2013005182

ISBN: 978–0–415–82201–5 (hbk)
ISBN: 978–0–415–82202–2 (pbk)
ISBN: 978–0–203–79697–9 (ebook)

Typeset in Berling
by Keystroke, Station Road, Codsall, Wolverhampton

Printed in Great Britain
by Bell & Bain Ltd, Glasgow

Contents

Plates

Figures

Figures

Tables

Preface and acknowledgements

This book examines central structural institutions of American (US) civilization, such as politics and government, the law, the economy, social services, the media, education and religion. Chapters on the country and the people also emphasize the geographical and human diversity of the US. Each chapter adapts public opinion polls to illustrate the attitudes of Americans towards the society and cultures in which they live and operate.

Methodologically, the book combines descriptive and analytical approaches within a historical context and also provides information on debates and recent developments in the US. The comprehensive nature of the book is intended to encourage students and teachers to determine their own study needs, to assess their personal responses to American society and to engage in critical discussion. Essay and term exercises at the end of each chapter can be initially approached from material contained in the text. Additional information may be found in relevant websites, "Further reading" sections in each chapter, and a recommended dictionary for terms (Alicia Duchak (1999) *A–Z of Modern America*, London: Routledge).

A book of this type is indebted for many of its ideas, facts and statistics to a range of reference sources, which cannot all be mentioned here, but to which a general acknowledgement is made (see also "Further reading"). Particular thanks are due to public-opinion poll sources and media, such as Gallup, Harris, Polling Report, Pew Research Center, the Roper Center, *The Economist*, YouGov, CNN, *USA Today*, *Fox News*, CBS, NBC, ABC, PRRI (Public Religion Research Institute), *Newsweek*, *Time*, the *New York Times*, *Los Angeles Times* and the *Washington Post*.

The term billion in this book follows the internationally-approved standard, i.e. 1,000,000,000.

Chronology of significant dates in American history

20,000–12,000 BC	Asian and Mediterranean peoples migrated to the Americas
c.3000–2600	Mayan civilization flourished in Central America
c.350–1250 AD	Anasazi built puebo "apartment" complexes in the American Southwest
1001	Vikings established "Vinland" settlement in Newfoundland
1050–1250	Mississippian culture dominated the Midwestern and Southeastern United States
1300s	Aztec civilization rose in Mexico
1492	Columbus came ashore in the Bahama Islands
1492–1542	European explorers visited and mapped parts of the Americas
1497	Europeans began fishing in the Great Banks off the East Coast of North America
1519–21	Hernán Cortéz invaded and conquered Mexico
1518–1620	Smallpox and other European diseases decimated Native Americans
1607	Jamestown, Virginia settlement established
1619	The first African workers arrived in Virginia, not as slaves
1622	Native Americans and Virginians waged war
1620–30	Pilgrims and then Puritans founded New England colonies
1637	Native Americans and Puritans waged war
1624–81	New Amsterdam (New York), Maryland, New Sweden, Carolina, New Jersey, and Pennsylvania were founded
1636, 1647	Harvard College and then public schools started in Massachusetts
1680–1776	The first wave of non-English immigrants arrived in the North American colonies
1732	Georgia, the last of the 13 English colonies, was founded
1730s–1740s	Religious ferment reached a peak during the first Great Awakening
1757	New Yorkers rioted against British policies

1770	British troops fired on Boston protestors
1775, 1776	The American Revolution began; the Declaration of Independence
1783	The Treaty of Paris recognized the independence of the United States and granted it the territory south of Canada to the Mississippi River
1787	A strong federal government under the US Constitution replaced the loose league of states under the Articles of Confederation
1789	George Washington took office as president; federalists and anti-federalists competed in Congress
1792	The New York Stock Exchange opened
1803	The Louisiana Purchase from France added a huge slice of the continent's mid-section to the US; the US Supreme Court claimed the power to declare laws unconstitutional
1808	Congress outlawed the import of African slaves
1810	New York passed Philadelphia in population at third US census
1808–13	The Shawnee leaders, Tecumseh and the Prophet, organized the eastern tribes to resist US expansion beyond the Appalachians
1812–15	The US won no major battle in the war with Britain on American soil
1815–25	Industrialization started in the New England and mid-Atlantic states
1820s–1840s	A religious revival swept across the frontier in the second Great Awakening; social and utopian reform movements spread
1820s–1880s	About 16 million Europeans and smaller numbers of Asians and Latinos immigrated in the second wave
1825	Opening the Erie Canal secured the economic power of the East
1831–8	Native Americans removed from the South along the Trail of Tears to Indian Territory in Oklahoma
1830s	The Democratic Party emerged and competed with the Whigs
1845–8	Conflict and war with Mexico; annexation of Texas, California and the Southwest
1848	The first women's rights convention at Seneca Falls, New York
1850s	Anti-foreign "nativist," abolitionist and pro-slavery movements dominated US politics; the Republican Party emerged
1861–5	Civil War raged over slavery and states' rights
1862	The Homestead Act granted land to people who lived on and farmed it for five years, spurring massive settlement of the inland west
1865–75	Constitutional amendments and a civil rights act were passed to secure the citizenship and rights of former slaves
1877	Reconstruction of the South ended; Southern race laws progressively denied blacks rights in the 1880s and 1890s
1869, 1882–83	Transcontinental railroads completed
1890	The "battle" of Wounded Knee ended centuries of open warfare against Native Americans; the US Census Bureau announced the "closing of the frontier"

1890–1930	About 23 million "third wave" immigrants arrived, mostly from south and east Europe but also from Asia, Canada, and Latin America
1898	Anti-imperialist debate in Congress; the Spanish American-Cuban Filipino War
1890–1920	Progressive Era reforms in social institutions, politics and government
1917–18	America fought alongside the Allies in the First World War
1919	The first tabloid newspaper, the New York *Daily News*, appeared
1919–33	Prohibition of alcoholic beverages became the law under the Eighteenth Amendment to the Constitution (repealed by the Twenty-First Amendment)
1920	Women won the right to vote through the Nineteenth Amendment
1921	The Red Scare and general restriction of immigration started
1929	The Wall Street Crash signalled the start of the Great Depression; the size of the House of Representatives was set at 435
1920s–1940s	Hollywood's classic period of film production
1920s–1970s	Progressively more of the Bill of Rights applied to state law and cases
1932	Franklin D. Roosevelt was elected president and implemented the New Deal to bring the US out of the Great Depression
1937	The Supreme Court accepted New Deal powers of federal government
1939	Commercial television introduced at the World's Fair in New York
1941	On December 7 Japan bombed the Pearl Harbor naval base in Hawaii, and the US entered the Second World War
1946	The post-war baby boom began
1947	The National Security Act transformed American government for the Cold War; the Truman Doctrine sets path of US foreign policy
1950–3	McCarthy era "Red scare" and Korean War
1954	Racial desegregation began with the *Brown* v. *the Board of Education* US Supreme Court decision
1955	The American Federation of Labor (AFL) and the Congress of Industrial Organizations (CIO) combined in a union of US unions
1958	The National Defense Education Act funded scientific competition with the USSR
1953–74	US involvement and war in Vietnam, massive protests at home and abroad against the war in the 1960s; African Americans, Native Americans, Chicanos, women, and gay Americans fought for civil rights
1963	President John F. Kennedy was assassinated; Lyndon B. Johnson assumed the presidency
1960s	Great Society and War on Poverty social reforms; the high point of the youth "counter culture" and of religious ecumenism in the US
1964	The Civil Rights Act outlawed discrimination in housing and jobs
1965	The Voting Rights Act protected voter registration, especially in the South; the Elementary and Secondary Education Act provided massive funding for education reform

1966–2012	In the continuing fourth wave of immigration, more than 38.5 million people arrived, most from Latin America and Asia, but also from the former USSR, Africa, and the Middle East
1968	Martin Luther King, Jr. and Robert Kennedy assassinated; 168 cities erupted in race riots
1969	The Stonewall Riots, when gay men fought back for the first time after repeated police raids
1970	More Americans lived in suburbs than in cities or rural areas
1972	Nixon's "new federalism" began the return of power to the states
1973	*Roe* v. *Wade* decision legalized limited abortion rights for women
1974	President Nixon resigned as a result of the Watergate scandal
1981	AIDS first identified in the US
1970s–1980s	The rise of Christian fundamentalism and conservative religious political activity
1986–8	Mikhail Gorbachev and Ronald Reagan cooperated to bring the Cold War to an end; the Iran–Contras scandal cast a shadow over the second Reagan administration; George H.W. Bush won the presidency
1991	The US led the Persian Gulf War to drive Iraq out of Kuwait
1993–2001	President Clinton presided over the longest economic boom in US history
1996	The devolution of policymaking power to the states occured through the Welfare Reform Act
1999	Congress impeached but did not convict President Clinton
2000	George W. Bush won the presidential election after a 5:4 divided decision of the US Supreme Court stopped Florida vote recounts and calls for uniform vote-counting procedures
2001	The No Child Left Behind Act set in action the most far-reaching national educational reform since the 1960s; terrorists destroyed the World Trade Center and attacked the Pentagon; the US initiated a global war on terrorism in Afghanistan
2002	The Help America Vote Act was passed to standardize voting procedures within states; the USA Patriot Act and the authorization of the Department of Homeland Security transformed American government for the War on Terror
2003	The US-led "coalition of the willing" invaded and occupied Iraq; the Supreme Court decision, *Lawrence* v. *Texas*, ended the criminalization of homosexual relations between consenting adults
2004	No weapons of mass destruction found in Iraq; George W. Bush won a second term as president and the Republicans secured larger majorities in both houses of Congress
2006–13	Legal immigration to the US capped at 675,000 immigrant visas a year
2006–8	In the longest and most expensive presidential election in US history, ten or more men and women announced their candidacy for each major party's nomination; by the early spring of 2008 John McCain emerged as the presumptive Republican candidate

2008	On the Democratic side of the contest, in the first seriously competitive campaign mounted by a woman, former First Lady and then New York Senator Hillary Clinton fought a close contest with Illinois Senator Barack Obama, the first immigrant, mixed-race African American to mount a similarly competitive campaign. In June, Obama won the nomination of the Democratic Party, and in November he won the presidency with unprecedented use of social media, becoming the nation's first black president
2008	In *District of Columbia* v. *Heller* the US Supreme Court decided that the ban on the private possession of handguns in Washington, DC was an infringement of the Second Amendment
2008	The worsening economic crisis, called the Great Recession, became the worst financial breakdown since the 1930s
2009–10	The Obama administration's financial policies rescued Wall Street firms and the Detroit automobile industry, extended unemployment insurance and initiated a jobs and economic stimulus package
2010	In *Citizens United* v. *the FEC* the Supreme Court ruled that corporations have the same rights to freedom of expression as individuals, also regarding contributions to campaign contributions
2010	The Patient Protection and Affordable Health Act (PPACA) was passed with no support from Republican members of Congress. The Act survived constitutional challenges and was upheld in most of its provisions by the Supreme Court in 2012. In the mid-term congressional elections, the Democrats lost their majority in the House of Representatives (and with it united legislative support for Obama's agenda) in part due to Tea Party movement support for conservative Republican candidates
2012	In the next presidential election cycle a dozen Republicans, including a libertarian conservative, a black businessman, a woman supported by Tea Party groups, and several present and former state governors, among them evangelical social conservatives, competed for their party's nomination. Mitt Romney, successful corporate business consultant and former Massachusetts governor, won that contest and faced incumbent Obama in the general election. In November the sitting president won a clear electoral college and popular vote victory. In the congressional elections the Democrats improved their majority in the Senate, but the Republicans kept a (reduced) majority in the House
2012	SMS declined and gave way to smartphones and social networking sites such as Facebook and Twitter
2012–13	Another school mass killing occured at Newtown, Connecticut, when 20 young children and six teachers were killed before Christmas. Gun control was moved to the top of the president's reform agenda in 2013

Chapter 1

The American context

- Ethnic culture
- Religious culture
- Political-legal culture
- Economic culture
- Media cultures
- Arts, sports and leisure cultures
- National identity
- Social and institutional change
- American attitudes to US society
- *Exercises*
- *Further reading*
- *Websites*

This chapter examines foreign and domestic attitudes to the US and places the country within broad historical developments. It describes six major cultures that comprise American civilization and influence debates about national identity, and social and institutional change. The final section deals with how Americans themselves respond to their country.

The term "American civilization" describes an advanced human society, which occupies a specific geographical space (the US) and has been populated historically by many different migratory populations. Its contributory "cultures" now collectively represent a distinctive way of life. Although previously associated with notions of superiority and imperialism, "civilization" generally today has a neutral connotation.

People inside and outside the US have very varied and conflicting views about the country and its inhabitants. Some opinions are based on quantifiable facts. Others are conditioned by ideology, hatred, prejudice, or envy. Many American self-images often stress the nation's supposed "exceptionalism" (its unique mission in the world, idealism, high aspirations and sense of destiny.) But there have also been internal disagreements about the country's values, institutions, policies and national identity, and whether its vaunted ideals equate with American reality. US society is divided politically, religiously, socially, economically and ethnically, although considerable attempts are made to reconcile differences and to unify the people under common beliefs and structures.

Opinion polls report that, under the impetus of national and international events, Americans alternate between feelings of positivism and dissatisfaction about their country. Periods of doubt and conflict, such as the Civil War (1861–5), two world wars (1914–18 and 1939–45), the 1930s Great Depression, the 1945–89 Cold War, the 1950s–60s civil rights campaigns, the 1960s–75 Vietnam War, the 2003–4 Iraq War with its chaotic aftermath and the Afghanistan conflict from 2001, have often resulted in adaptation and renewal.

The US and its foreign policies are still significantly conditioned by the September 11, 2001 attacks on New York and Washington (9/11). In response, the US Administration sought to protect its domestic and worldwide interests; declared its opposition to terrorism; and initiated coalition military action in Iraq and Afghanistan. Resulting strained relations between the US and other nations continue and were illustrated by a Gallup poll in 2007 in which US citizens identified the following countries as the greatest threats to global stability: Iran (35 percent), China (19 percent), North Korea (10 percent), Iraq (9 percent) and interestingly the US itself (8 per cent). US foreign policy is thus frequently criticized by its enemies, allies and domestic commentators alike.

PLATE 1.1 Visitors (August 14, 2011) watch construction work at Ground Zero, the site of the September 11, 2001 terrorist attacks on the World Trade Center, New York City. The twin towers of the Center were destroyed when hijacked planes were flown into the buildings. The site has been redeveloped with a Freedom Tower, Memorial Plaza and fountains in memory of the 2,979 people who died at Ground Zero and the Pentagon, and aboard another hijacked plane. *(Dan Callister/Rex Features)*

In terms of America's standing in the world, a Pew Research Center poll in June 2012 found that European approval of US anti-terrorism policy was low during the final years of the George W. Bush presidency, but recovered initially with President Obama's election in 2008. By 2012, despite claims that American foreign policy was wavering and uncertain, support for the US and its actions was relatively high in Europe, with Britain at 57 percent, France at 75 percent, Germany at 60 percent, Spain at 53 percent, Italy at 65 percent, and Russia at 53 percent. However, largely Muslim nations such as Turkey, Egypt, Jordan and Pakistan were negative about US tactics. In India, 55 percent favored American actions, but only 33 percent in China and 44 percent in Japan. Among Latin American countries, 66 percent of Brazilians supported the US, but only 36 percent of Mexicans. On the other hand, a majority of Americans (76 percent) agreed with US anti-terrorism efforts.

However, many of the nations in the poll (Muslim, European and Asian) disapproved of US drone campaigns against militant leaders and organizations in Pakistan, Yemen and Somalia. The attacks were supported by 62 percent of Americans, with 28 percent opposed. Globally, most people believed that the US acts unilaterally in world affairs and does not adequately consider their views. But 77 percent of Americans believed that their country does in fact take into account the interests of other nations when it comes to making decisions about foreign actions. Despite negative views on US foreign policy, the survey's evaluations of the US and its people were generally favorable in Europe, Brazil and Mexico, but not in Greece. However, the US received low ratings in largely Muslim nations such as Egypt, Turkey, Pakistan, and Jordan, with divided views in Tunisia, Lebanon, China and India.

Some central factors have conditioned US historical development, such as:

- early migrations of diverse peoples to the Americas from worldwide origins;
- colonial and military settlement by Europeans from the late fifteenth century and the establishment of specific social values, religious faiths and institutional structures;
- the treatment of Native Americans and other minority ethnic groups (particularly African Americans) over time;
- the War for Independence from Britain (1775–83);
- the westward expansion of the new nation;
- principles of human dignity and rights to freedom, justice and opportunity contained in the Declaration of Independence (1776) and the US Constitution (1787);
- ideologies of egalitarianism, individualism and utopianism;
- large-scale immigration into the country, especially in the nineteenth and twentieth centuries;
- the Civil War to end slavery, and southern-state secession from the Union (1861–5);
- the development of capitalism with its corporate management and business philosophies;
- increasing government regulation and bureaucracies that have arguably undermined individual autonomy;
- American isolationist and interventionist attitudes towards the rest of the world, particularly during the two world wars, the Cold War period and the early twenty-first century;
- the development of the US as a dominant economic, military and cultural force since the nineteenth century;
- the influence of contemporary globalization (worldwide interdependent economic, political and cultural forces) on the US and other nations.

These (and other) historical developments have created six major cultures in the US, which may conflict with each other and operate on levels of idealism, pragmatism and rhetoric. The first is a diverse ethnic culture founded on Native American civilizations, European colonial settlement, African American slavery and later waves of immigration. The second is a multi-faith or pluralist religious culture, which reflects the many beliefs of colonists and immigrants and is still very prominent today. The third is a political-legal culture based on individualism, constitutionalism and respect for the law. It tries to unite the people under ideal versions of "Americanness," such as egalitarianism, morality and patriotism, which should be practically reflected in political and legal institutions. The fourth is an economic and consumer culture driven by corporate and individual competition and production, which encourages profit and the consumption of goods and services. The fifth consists of media cultures (communication, information and entertainment), which have become technologically complex and dominant in the twentieth and twenty-first centuries. The sixth represents very varied cultural expressions in the arts, sports and leisure, which have traditionally reflected the diversity and inventiveness of US life.

US society has been directly and indirectly conditioned by these cultures. However, although their presence may be generally acknowledged, considerable numbers of people—such as political activists, radicals, intellectuals, the youth, the disadvantaged and minorities—may be alienated from them. Conflicts about assumed national values, harmony and unity have occurred throughout US history. Topics such as taxation, the economy, religious and political polarization, gender roles, the gaps between poor and rich, international military intervention, abortion, gay marriage and the roles of federal and state governments are sources of contemporary debate.

Nevertheless, the major cultures have, since the Declaration of Independence in 1776 and the 1812 war with Britain, collectively helped to create what is seen as a unique national identity in the US for the majority of its inhabitants. The difficulty lies in determining what this may actually consist of in practice. Some critics argue that the nation has recently strayed from its traditional foundations and suffered from crises of self-image and direction. Others maintain that a unified sense of American nationalism and unity is in fact growing stronger.

Ethnic culture (see Chapters 2, 3 and 4)

Initial colonial settlement after 1607 was largely composed of British arrivals, who shared North America with Native American communities and other Europeans, such as the French and the Spanish. Until 1776, more than half of the population came from the British Isles and contributed to a white, mainly Anglo-American, Protestant dominant culture. They promoted many of the new nation's political, social, constitutional and religious institutions. Their political principles were based on democracy, grassroots sovereignty (independence of the people) and skepticism about government. Their social values were conditioned by a belief in individualism; a Protestant work ethic (working hard in this life to be rewarded here and in the next); and the rule of law (acceptance of legal rules applicable to all individuals and institutions irrespective of status or wealth). Other European settlers were integrated in varying degrees into this culture and a mainstream American identity and values developed.

After the colonial period and American independence from Britain (1776), northwestern Europe supplied over two-thirds of US immigration for most of the nineteenth century. There were also many Asian immigrants (particularly Chinese) during this time. At the end of the century there was a shift towards newcomers from southern and eastern Europe. Much of this immigration was neither Anglo by descent nor Protestant in religion, and it significantly altered the demographic composition of the country. Despite greater immigration restrictions, the twentieth century saw a large variety of other nationalities from worldwide origins immigrating to the US. In total, some 60 million immigrants entered the US between 1820 and 2000. In the 1980s–1990s and the early twenty-first century, large numbers of immigrants came from Asia, South and Central America and the Caribbean, with the biggest groups being Mexicans and Latin Americans. But declining immigration from Mexico, weakness in the US job market and less illegal entry has resulted in Asians now becoming the largest group of new immigrants. In 2012, an American Community Survey (ACS) Report based on US Census Bureau statistics estimated that the total foreign-born share of the population in 2010 was about 13 percent (40 million people).

Traditionally, immigrants have often been analyzed in terms of "ancestral groups." The ACS (US census 2008) reported that more Americans traced their roots to Europe than anywhere else in the world, such as 16.5 percent German, 11.9 percent Irish, 9 percent English, 5.8 percent Italian, 3.3 percent Polish, 3.1 percent French, 1.9 percent Scottish, 1.6 percent Dutch, 1.5 percent Norwegian, 1.4 percent Swedish, 1.2 percent Scotch-Irish, 1 percent Russian and 0.7 percent Welsh. Non-European ancestries were also self-identified in 2008, such as African American, American, Mexican, West Indian, French Canadian and American Indian. However, such groups are declining and ancestral claims may be vague, subjective or demographically wrong and individuals may claim more than one such identity.

The effects of colonial settlement, importation of African slaves (from 1619) and later large-scale immigration on US culture have been substantial, in numerical and origin terms. This background (and Native American experiences) is different in size and scope from that of other nations; arguably defines American history as special; and provides the US with a distinct, ethnically-based identity as a nation of immigrants and their descendants.

The US Census Population Estimates 2010 reported that, out of a total population of 308,745,538, there were 196,817,552 whites (a decreasing 63.7 percent of the population), 37,685,848 black or African Americans (12.2 percent), 2,247,098 American Indians and Alaskan Natives (0.7 percent), 14,465,124 Asians (4.7 percent), 481,576 Native Hawaiian and other Pacific Islander (0.15 percent), 50,477,594 Latinos (16.3 percent) and 6,570,530 people composed of two or more ethnic groups (2.1 percent).

A US Census Bureau report in 2009 estimated that whites will become a minority of 48.5 per cent of the total population by 2042 (revised to 2043 in 2012). Non-whites and Latinos together will account for 51.5 per cent of the population, while increasing numbers of people will be self-defined as mixed race. By 2050, non-whites and Latinos will account for 54 percent of the population and whites for 46 percent (dropping to 43 percent by 2060). These demographic changes will result from immigration, higher birth rates among ethnic minorities, intermingling of ethnic communities and an ageing white population with lower birth rates. They are already influencing US social, economic and political life.

Immigrants and imported black African slaves have considerably affected public life at different times in US history. But they have also experienced difficulties of integration into the host society. There have been conflicts and racial tensions between settled groups, Native Americans, African Americans and immigrants, which have sometimes erupted into violence. These factors have revealed nativism (discrimination towards others by the indigenous population) and racism in many areas of American life, often in institutionalized form.

Ethnic diversity has brought advantages and disadvantages over time. It has also gradually reduced the dominance of the original Anglo-American Protestant culture, which had to take account of a growing social pluralism. It is argued that the US has historically managed to integrate its immigrants successfully into the existing society at varying levels, and newcomers have generally adapted to American life. However, despite significant structural and cultural improvement from the 1950s, racial and ethnic divisions still continue to affect American society in both covert (indirect) and overt (open) forms; attitudes to immigration remain volatile; opinions about the existence of racism in the US vary considerably between blacks and whites; small minorities in polls admit to having racial prejudice; and blacks and whites arguably still largely live in different worlds.

A 2009 *Washington Post*-ABC News poll reported that 44 percent of blacks and 22 percent of whites saw racism as a large social problem, as contrasted to 70 percent of blacks and 52 percent of whites in 1996. People still recognized racism in their local communities and African Americans said they experienced racial discrimination in housing, employment and treatment by the police and courts. The poll showed differences in how people of both races saw the problem. For example, three-quarters of whites and just over half of blacks thought that African Americans have reached or will soon achieve equality in the US.

A *Newsweek* poll in April 2012 showed that only 32 percent of Americans thought that race relations had improved since President Obama's 2008 inauguration; 30 percent believed they had become worse; and 60 percent thought they had deteriorated or stagnated. Race still divides America and change has been slow. The poll reported that 89 percent of blacks and 80 percent of whites agreed that racial stereotyping still occurs in America. But they disagree significantly about how it specifically affects people's lives. While 74 percent of blacks have personally felt they were discriminated against because of their race and color, only 31 percent of whites have felt the same way.

Tensions concerning the nature of racism, ethnicity and immigration were reported in a CBS News/*New York Times* poll in January 2004, where 45 percent of respondents believed legal immigration should be reduced and 16 percent thought it should be increased. An *Economist*/YouGov poll in December 2007 found that 55 percent of respondents felt that immigrants were a threat to traditional American values and customs; 69 percent thought that immigrants take jobs away from American workers; 55 percent believed that skilled workers are harmed by immigration; 70 percent felt the same about unskilled workers; and 45 percent considered that consumers are harmed by immigration.

These findings suggest that many Americans see legal immigration as a problem and want illegal immigration stopped. There still seems to be a nativist or xenophobic current in American culture. Diverse ethnic groups have had to both coexist and struggle for individual expression in the US. Today, they must live together in spite of inequalities and tensions between them. Immigration can have a potential for political and social instability with either rejection of immigrants by settled Americans, or rejection of Americanization (adaptation to mainstream American culture) by immigrants. However, these conflicts (arising out of social pluralism) and the problems of assimilation and integration by new groups are not distinctively American, but occur in other nations that have diverse populations.

Religious culture (see Chapter 5)

Religion is the second major American culture and has its roots in ancient Native American belief structures and in the many faiths that colonists, slaves and immigrants later brought to the US over the centuries. Some early settlers escaped religious persecution in their homelands and hoped to establish communities based on what were often nonconformist beliefs. Others brought established native denominations with them. The religious motivations of many initial arrivals were clear and provided institutional and moral bases for the new nation. Many immigrants in later centuries have often strongly identified with their home faiths and preserved them and their ancestral origins in the new country.

Not all settlers or immigrants were religiously inspired. Some travelled for adventure, freedom, new experiences, material gain, land acquisition, and to escape from European habits or oppression. Religious observance fluctuated in later centuries. The US had periods when religiosity was very low and periodic Great Awakenings and missionary activity were needed to restore the faiths. Generally, however, strong religious belief, substantial observance at ceremonies and church services, and a diversity of faiths became defining features of American society, when compared with other countries.

Although religion is a private, personal matter and constitutionally separate from the state, it informs and may condition social, economic and political life beyond the purely denominational. The precise influence of religion (and its limits) on many areas of American life, such as education, politics and ethics, continues to be hotly debated. Despite a desire to keep religion out of politics by legislative and constitutional means, some critics question whether it is realistic or necessary to deny religion a full and active part in public life.

Political-legal culture (see Chapters 6, 7, 8 and 9)

The third major American culture consists of political-legal elements. Its nature has been largely shaped by

- the central place of law and the Constitution in American life;
- the restrictions that the Constitution places upon politics;
- the fact that Americans believe in minimal government, especially at the federal level;
- the perceived need to produce consensual (widely agreed) national policies.

The Constitution is central to this structure, but it has to be interpreted by the judiciary (particularly the US Supreme Court in Washington, DC) to determine whether actions of government and other bodies are constitutional or not. The political system has institutional checks and balances at various state and federal levels, which can sometimes result in stalemate. However, these features do help to solidify the society and move it towards consensus or centrist policies. Idealized versions of "America" constructed through its federal and state political organs and a general respect for the law can potentially minimize conflict.

The need in the political-legal culture for balance and compromise illustrates the degree of abstraction that is involved in defining "the US" and "Americanness." The notion of what constitutes "America" has had to be revised or reinvented over time and reflects the tension between a materialistic practical reality, with its restrictions, and an idealistic, abstract and rhetorical image of the nation. Words such as "hope," "democracy" and "traditional values" are part of election campaigns and the US conversation.

Racial or ethnic differences, immigration and social diversity have been barriers to national unity, and are still problematic. Consequently, it is often argued that the American political-legal system consists of both hard-nosed manipulation of group and ideological interests and an exaggerated rhetoric that might hopefully promote common resolutions. Americans are also aware of corruption, fraud and incompetence in the political and legal systems and that claims to "liberty" and "freedom" are not always respected in reality.

Responses to pluralism have often resulted in consensus politics based on political and judicial compromise. US politics are not usually considered to be as oppositional as in other nations, and historically there has been a variable 60 percent support for the center-left "liberal" Democratic Party and 40 percent for the "conservative" Republican Party. In the 2012 presidential election, on a 120 million voter turnout of 57 percent, Democrats received 51 percent of the popular vote (61.7 million votes), while Republicans gained 48 percent (58.5 million votes). A Gallup poll in January 2012 reported that 40 percent of Americans described their socio/political views as conservative, 35 percent as moderate and 21 percent as liberal. But a Pew Research Center poll in July 2010 found that both liberals and conservatives described themselves as closer to the political center than to the extremes.

However, differences between party policies on minorities, the economy, education, employment, religion and social issues have increasingly played a divisive and polarizing role in US society and at bitterly fought elections. Voters may also register support and opposition across party lines on many single issues such as abortion, gay marriage, the death penalty, education, taxation and gun control. American politics, reflecting the federal nature of US government, often tends to be more influenced by special or state interests than national matters. Politicians in the febrile atmosphere of Washington, DC, promote their own constituency legislation as a response to local and regional pressures. Such concerns, as well as national issues, often persuade Americans to vote simultaneously in election lists for political representatives from different political parties who support specific issues.

Academic critics debate whether or not there has been apathy and low political participation among US voters in recent decades. While some 70 percent of the eligible population may register to vote, others do not register and there can be a low turnout even of registered voters (estimated at a 54 percent average) actually voting in elections. Low turnout and registration suggests alienation from the political process, a feeling that power is in the hands of a political elite at state and Washington levels and that politicians do not consider the concerns of ordinary voters (see Table 1.2 on alienation in the US, 2007–11).

Economic culture (see Chapter 10)

The fourth major US culture is the economic framework, which is also idealistic/abstract and materialistic/practical. Americans generally have a belief in individualism and a free enterprise system, which is supposed to deliver (or supply) goods and services demanded by the consumer market. The people historically have had to fight for their economic and social survival, a process which can result in exploitation of others, excesses and a Darwinian "survival of the fittest" mentality. The competitive nature of US life leads to great disparities of wealth, social inequalities and varying life opportunities. In 2012, for example, 46.4 million Americans were dependent upon government food stamps (debit

PLATE 1.2 Interior of the landmark Time Warner Center, New York City. It is located at Columbus Circle in Manhattan and contains archetypal American malls, restaurants, shops, offices, entertainment venues and residential housing in a transformed urban neighborhood. *(Jon Hicks/Corbis)*

cards) at a cost of $76.7 for their daily needs and 49 million (18.5 percent of those under age 65) in 2011 could not afford, or did not pay for, healthcare insurance.

Although free enterprise and corporate domination of US economic life may claim to deliver what the market requires, the system can also produce inferior products, bad service, incompetence, corruption and little variety or real choice for consumers. Americans have historically been skeptical of big business as well as big government and tend to support the principle of small businesses. However, debates about the capitalist model often ignore significant economic cooperation, charitable organizations, volunteerism and a substantial public sector in the national economy.

Both private and public economic sectors are subject to considerable fluctuations, whether due to market and global influences, speculation, human error or incompetence. For example, the US economy has been considerably influenced since 2007–8 by a worldwide financial crisis, which resulted in recession, a national deficit, job losses and unemployment, corporate closures, bank collapses and individual suffering. According to data from the Federal Reserve in 2012, the typical US household is much poorer since the recession in 2007. The net worth (the difference between assets and liabilities) of the median family fell by some 40 percent from $126,400 in 2007 to $77,300 in 2010, driven partly by the collapse of the housing market. Blame for this situation was placed on the banks and financial institutions for lending too much money in dubious sub-prime transactions, although individuals also borrowed beyond their capacity to repay loans and mortgages. Average incomes consequently dropped 7.7 percent from $49, 600 in 2007 to $45,800 in 2010.

Media cultures (see Chapter 13)

Media cultures have historically grown from simple methods of production and communication to complex modern technologies, online interactive programs and a very diverse media audience and market. They have been tied to political and social concerns, concentrated ownership, class identification, mass literacy, a dominant communication and social role and the expansion of entertainment. The written word was succeeded by broadcasting; television followed the cinema and radio; mass cultures developed more outlets and markets for the media; and the internet and social media (such as Facebook and Twitter) have increased further technological possibilities, communication and leisure opportunities.

The media have provided quality products, instant news, public participation, widened knowledge and a watchdog role under the First Amendment. But they have also sometimes abused their position, appealed to the lowest denominator of taste, encouraged a "celebrity culture" and allegedly participated in a "dumbing down" of social and educational values.

Arts, sports and leisure cultures (see Chapter 14)

Cultural expression in the arts, sports and leisure have historically been very diverse and influential in the US and have reflected class, national and economic conditions and determinants. They have consequently been described in terms of elite or popular culture and high, middlebrow and low cultures. These divisions have expanded and changed over time, but some of the traditional defining limits (and social exclusions) still remain.

The arts have been characterized partly by output from theaters, opera companies, orchestras, film studios and ballet and dance companies, which today can provide both classical and more popular offerings. A wide range of music, from classical to urban and street music and jazz, is available, as is a range of dramatic plays and musicals. Museums and art galleries have also become increasingly popular and appeal to more sectors of society, although subject to economic downturn and fluctuation. Many artistic activities are still carried out by individual participants themselves through different recreational, media and online outlets, as well as by public and commercial organizations.

Sports and leisure activities are also marked by a diversity of types, participation and attendance, although some of the historical distinctions between high and low culture still remain. These illustrate not only the class, economic and cost determinants of participation, but also the complex composition of the population and its interests.

National identity

The above cultures interact among themselves and influence other parts of American life, such as education (see Chapter 12), the people (Chapters 3 and 4), the environment (Chapter 2) and social services (Chapter 11). They also condition debates about what it means to be American ("Americanness") and what constitutes national identity.

A historical dilemma for the US has been how to balance a need for civic unity against the reality of ethnic diversity and to avoid the dangers of fragmentation and conflict. Emphasis was initially placed on "Americanization," or the assimilation of different ethnic groups into a shared, Anglo-American-based identity or "melting pot." But this aim was seen as pressurizing immigrants to move into an Americanized dominant culture, with a possible resulting loss of their ethnic identity. "Assimilation" implies absolute national unity, whereas "integration" occurs at levels of partial and more "natural" blending or mixing.

Debates on national identity have centered on questions of unity (Americanization) as opposed to diversity (ethnic pluralism or multiculturalism), and have reflected political and ideological views. In the 1950s, ethnic differences and issues seemed to be losing their urgency, but revived in the 1990s and early 2000s, particularly with the growth of Latino and Asian ethnic groups.

Debates about social balance have stressed either American values (often represented by consolidationist conservatives) or the preservation of ethnic or minority group interests (supported by reform liberals). On one hand, it is suggested that the unifying American ideal of *e pluribus unum* (out of many, one) is an abstract concept, which does not reflect reality and cannot be practically achieved. On the other hand, emphases on ethnicity and difference arguably weaken the possibility of achieving a set of values that could represent a distinctive "American way of life." Some critics feel that American society is at risk because of competing cultures and interest groups, with each claiming a right to special treatment. They maintain that these conflicts have weakened the sense of an overarching American identity.

From the late 1970s and into the 2000s, there was a reaction against liberal policies and affirmative action programs for minority groups, which allegedly discriminate in the latter's favor in areas such as education and employment. Conservatives assert what they consider to be traditional American values, and many are opposed to liberal policies on abortion, gun control, education quotas, same-sex marriage, religion, the death penalty and immigration. These debates over supposed fundamental American values have further increased anxieties about national identity and where the country is headed.

Such splits in opinion led critics to argue that the US should more realistically be regarded ethnically, culturally and ideologically as a "mosaic," "salad bowl," "pizza" or "stew mix," rather than a "melting pot." However, while the "melting pot" model of America has been rejected in some quarters, the metaphors of salads and stews nevertheless imply that variety and difference should somehow be incorporated into a larger "American" whole. The difficulty lies in defining what the common core identity might or should be.

These metaphors do suggest a certain acceptance of cultural and ethnic pluralism in American society. The reality of heterogeneity (difference) and an adherence to roots have continued despite pressures and arguments in support of homogenization (sameness). It is argued that degrees of separateness and integration vary between ethnic groups, and that absolute social assimilation is both undesirable and impossible. But this can lead to hybrid cultural identities on the one hand and the breakdown of strong national links on the other.

It is argued that while there are extremes of opinion, unfairness, diversity and vested interests in US society, underlying moral and political commitments to freedom, justice, tolerance and equality under the law can succeed in limiting divisions and do promote unity, homogeneity and stability. However, these ideals may not always be achieved in the complex real world and the US has to live resiliently with conflicts and anxieties. Economic, political, religious, ethnic and class conflicts have become more evident in recent years.

Arguably, the tension in the struggle to achieve national and civic identities is between pluralism (or multiculturalism, where the interests of separate ethnic groups or minorities are equally valid) on the one hand and an acceptance of diversity under an umbrella American identity on the other. The latter solution has to be achieved within defining national structures, which acknowledge ethnic identity and roots. Levels of integration (such as citizenship for immigrants, education, home-ownership, language acquisition, intermarriage, economic opportunities and upward mobility) are then achievable, while differences are seen as valid. The 2000 US census indicated that natural forces of integration had grown and that a sense of civic commonality or a distinctive American nationalism had increased. But increased immigration and the growth of ethnic groups indicate potential future problems for a national identity. Liberals maintain that a multicultural, multiethnic society should be the ultimate national goal and demographers argue that terms such as "white" or "Latino" will lose their meaning and people will define themselves increasingly as multiethnic, multiracial or mixed race.

Others question whether this development will provide for representative civic institutions and an American national identity or result in fragmentation and separatism. It is alleged that some Latino arrivals in the US since the 1980s have rejected Americanization. Bilingualism (English and Spanish) in California, the Southwest, Florida and Texas, and a supposed immigrant reluctance to reject old national identities suggested for some critics a contemporary model composed of one nation with at least two contrasting cultures.

But immigrants do integrate on various levels into American society. Historically, Irish, Jewish, Chinese and Italian groups, among many others, have initially lived partially separate lives and been subjected to suspicion and hostility before achieving degrees of integration. The fear of a decline in national unity may therefore seem exaggerated and overlook the US ability to Americanize immigrants. Nevertheless, attitudes to immigration (both legal and illegal) have become increasingly negative in recent years.

Americans have historically tried to construct a sense of overarching national identity and institutional unity by binding the ethnically diverse population to central images of "Americanness," such as the national flag (also known as the Stars and Stripes, Old Glory or the Star-Spangled Banner), the pledge of allegiance to the flag, the Declaration of Independence, the Liberty Bell, Abraham Lincoln's Emancipation Proclamation and Gettysburg Address, the "Star-Spangled Banner" (the US national anthem) and the Constitution. These are meant to provide common cultural signs that promote loyalty to ideal notions of what American citizenship, "America" and "Americanness" might be. Their representative qualities are tied to institutions, appeal to hope and progress and try to avoid the potentially divisive elements of economic, social, class or ethnic differences.

Certain identifying values of "Americanness" have also been traditionally associated with these symbols, particularly those rights stemming from the Declaration of Independence, the Constitution and the Bill of Rights. Elements such as self-reliance, individualism, independence, utopianism, liberty, egalitarianism, freedom, opportunity, democracy, anti-statism (distrust of government), populism (grassroots activism), a sense of destiny and respect for the law are stressed. They stem from the ideas of Puritan religion and the European Enlightenment, which influenced the framers of the Declaration of Independence and the US Constitution. Thus, there are layers of idealism and abstraction in American life that coexist, and may often clash, with reality. Yet this situation is not unique. It echoes the experience of other countries, particularly those that are unions, federations or collections of different peoples with contrasting roots and traditions, who need to erect new national identities while preserving some aspects of their origins.

The degree to which such values are propagated in US society is significant, irrespective of whether they are individually or nationally achieved. They are attractive and valid for many people and may be revealed both in times of normality and crisis. A key feature of American life, therefore, is how individuals manage to combine traditional ideals of the nation with the actual realities of society and how they cope with the resulting tensions.

Other critics have tried to explain the US, its people and its national identity by "American traits." Features such as restlessness, escape from restraints, change, action, mobility, quests for new experiences, self-improvement and a belief in potential supposedly constitute typical American behavior. They are often attributed to immigrant and frontier experiences and a belief in progress for the individual and society. Americans allegedly refuse to accept a fixed fate or settled location, but seek new jobs, new horizons and new beginnings in a hunt for self-

PLATE 1.3 Latino boy dressed in American flag colors and patterns on the Fourth of July (Independence Day). This official US holiday commemorates the day in 1776 when the Continental Congress in Philadelphia gave its approval to the Declaration of Independence from Britain and is now celebrated with processions, speeches, flags and fireworks.
(Erik Isakson/Corbis)

fulfillment and self-definition. The huge sales of self-improvement books based on popular psychology suggest that such attitudes (or the desire to attain them) are widespread.

On the other hand, many Americans seek roots and stability in their lives, their institutions and a national identity. While the alleged informality of American life is supposedly founded on individualism, egalitarianism and a historical rejection of European habits, many Americans respect and desire formalities, hierarchy, order and conformity.

Americans may stress their individualism, distrust of big business and big government and their desire to be free. But communalism, voluntary activities, charitable organizations and group endeavors are also a feature of US life. Individuals have to cope with corporate, political, social, economic and employment bureaucracies with their associated power bases, which reflect the tension between ideal aspirations and everyday facts of life.

One cannot define a single set of traits which are shared by all Americans. Diversity, individual differences and departures from consensual norms limit possibilities and can result in contradictions or tensions rather than unified beliefs. The supposedly American traits are universal characteristics, which are also present in other societies and are neither exceptional in themselves nor distinctively American.

Nevertheless, the six major cultures and various subcultures have produced a composite Americanness and distinctive US image, which are recognized internationally and have influenced a globalized culture, whether simplistically and stereotypically or in more sophisticated forms. They are expressed through Hollywood films, television and radio, music and art, newspapers and magazines, sports, consumption patterns, well-known chain stores and brand names, corporate and financial institutions, business and management philosophies, political activity, ethnic concerns, religion and popular culture.

The 2000 US census suggested that more people now identify themselves and their ethnic/ancestral background as simply "American" or "US," without the need for a qualifier such as Irish American. According to the *Christian Science Monitor* in June 2002, this does not represent a denial of roots but rather an increased sense of commonality, patriotism and American nationalism. However, it is also argued that natural forces of integration over time, such as intermarriage, education and upward mobility, have weakened many Americans' bonds with their immigrant roots, particularly in the later generations. It seems that newer immigrants retain stronger ancestral ties, while other groups, such as many African Americans, now seem more willing to employ both a hyphenated identity and a sole "American" label. But these observations may change significantly in the relatively near future under new demographic pressures.

Some critics argue that the meaning and definition of a more unified national and civic US identity remain elusive. They maintain that a candid debate about the essence of American identity is needed in the current fluid and polarized situation. Opposed and partisan positions between the unifiers and the pluralists/ multiculturalists still operate. Many Americans may generally appear to believe in the inherent validity of apparent American values, but they continue to question what is meant by these values, how consensual they are and, consequently, what it means to be American.

Social and institutional change

The major US cultures are not static. They may influence other countries, just as external pressures can modify the American cultures. But although the latter are conditioned by increasingly globalized forces, they must also remain responsive to specific US political, minority and consumer demands. A national mass culture and economic system are inevitably integrationist forces as they cater for the American market.

US social organizations or institutions have been constructed over 400 years since 1607 and reflect a variety of values and practices. Some are particular to the US and others are similar to those of other nations. All have developed to cope with, and adapt to, an increasingly complex, diverse and dynamic society. They take many different forms and sizes, operate on federal, state and local levels, and may be public or private in character.

The larger elements, such as federal and state governments, are involved with public business, but there is also a diverse range of smaller social and cultural activities tied to sports, local communities, neighborhoods, religion, the theater and expressions of ethnic identity. These may take on more individualistic forms than the larger public institutions.

For some critics, it is the localized life and behavior of people in small-town America that typically define their society, rather than centralized federal institutions and the big cities. However, the larger frameworks do serve as cement that holds local activities and people together. They also contribute to an umbrella sense of American identity and "Americanness." The US, like other countries, gains its identity from a mixture of the local and the national, which inform and influence, as well as conflict with, each other.

The "American way of life" is defined by how citizens function within and respond to local and national institutions and cultures, whether positively or negatively. The large number and variety of such institutions, subcultures and social groups means that there are many different "ways of life" and values and all contribute to the diversity and particular characteristics of American society.

The following chapters stress the historical context of US growth and suggest that the contemporary owes much to the past. Social structures are adaptable, provide frameworks for new situations and their present roles may be different from their original functions. They have evolved over time as they have been influenced by elite and government policies as well as grassroots impulses and reactions. This process of change and adaptation continues and reflects current anxieties and concerns in American life. Social structures contribute to a culture of varied and often conflicting habits and ideals, as well as being practical organizations for realizing them.

This book presents a range of critical viewpoints and opinion polls on US society and its frameworks in an attempt to describe what may, or may not, be regarded as distinctively American. It first considers the physical geography, cultural regions and peoples of the US. It then examines the central social structures within which Americans have to operate, analyzes their historical growth and modern roles, and considers their underlying values.

American attitudes to US society

Social structures and policies affect individuals directly in their daily lives. Despite their diversity of origins and values, Americans do have many common concerns. They identify in public opinion polls what are for them the major issues facing the country. Items such as the economy, politics, government, crime, ethnicity, religion, morality, healthcare, immigration and racism have regularly appeared in lists of problems. Historically, there was skepticism about the accuracy and interpretation of polls. But they are now regarded as valuable indicators of how respondents are sensitive to changing conditions and how their priorities may change or remain static over time.

Polls in recent years have registered declines in ratings for the condition of the country and the performance of US administrations. A Gallup poll in January 2010 found that 75 percent of respondents could trust the government in Washington to do what is right for "only some of the time" and 6 percent said "never." Gallup and the Pew Research Center/Princeton Survey Research Associates International in January–March 2008 showed that between 70 and 80 percent of respondents recorded dissatisfaction with the way things were going in the US. A CBS News poll in September 2011 reported that 23 percent of respondents thought that the country was headed in the right direction, but that 72 percent thought that it was on the wrong track. Prior to the 2012 presidential election campaign, a Rasmussen Reports survey of June 20, 2012 was slightly more optimistic. Thirty percent of likely US voters thought that the country was heading in the right direction, while 64 percent considered that it was on the wrong track.

In the first half of 2004, American polls (according to PollingReport.com) showed that the economy (including taxes and the budget deficit), unemployment, jobs and foreign competition were primary concerns for people, together with education. However, by the time of the presidential election in November 2004, the campaign against terrorism, domestic (homeland) security, foreign policy and Iraq had become increasingly important. The economy and jobs were still prioritized but education had slipped in the ratings. Concern about Medicare (medical program for people over 65 years of age), Medicaid (medical care for low-income people under 65), the cost of prescription drugs, social security (federal payments to people who are unemployed, poor, old or disabled), abortion and same-sex marriage were also prominent. Corporate corruption and immigration had climbed up the poll ratings, whereas worries about gun control, drugs, the death penalty and crime had declined. Prior to the 2008 presidential election campaign and reflecting the 2007–8 financial crisis, a February 2008 CBS News/*New York Times* poll reported that the most important problems facing the country were the economy/jobs, healthcare, terrorism, immigration, the budget deficit/national debt and the gas/heating crisis.

These emphases on the economy, financial issues and healthcare were also leading issues two years later in 2010 when a March Gallup poll reported that respondents thought that the most important problems facing the country were unemployment (31 percent); the economy in general (24 percent); healthcare (20 percent); dissatisfaction with government (10 percent); the budget deficit (8 percent); and lack of money (5 percent). Respondents thought that the most important problems in the near future would be the budget deficit (14 percent); the economy in general (11 percent); healthcare (8 percent); energy (7 percent); and unemployment (6 percent). There was relatively high dissatisfaction with the government in this poll, suggesting that respondents thought that the Obama administration had not dealt satisfactorily with the financial crisis, the recession and health concerns.

Respondents to a June 2012 Gallup poll, prior to the presidential election campaign, classified the most important problems facing the country in terms of a) economic and b) non-economic issues. In the first category, the largest issue was the economy in general (31 percent); followed by unemployment/jobs (25 percent); the federal budget deficit/debt (11 percent); lack of money; and 1 percent each for the gap between rich and poor; fuel/oil prices; corporate corruption; taxes; and wage issues. These responses agreed with other polls and accurately reflected the challenging conditions facing the US and its people. They suggested that the US was still suffering from the financial credit crisis and recession of 2007–9; that the economy was central to people's worries and experience; and that adequate government financial initiatives to solve the problems were lacking. A Gallup poll in September 2011 found that 44 percent of respondents thought that the Republican Party would do a better job of handling national problems than the Democrats (37 percent).

The second non-economic category in the Gallup 2012 survey included other problems that had appeared regularly in polls over the past 20 years and continuing concern about the state of the country. The top ten issues were a dissatisfaction with government performance; healthcare; ethical/moral/religious decline; education; immigration/illegal aliens; foreign aid; lack of respect for each other; war/fear of war; energy/lack of energy sources; poverty/hunger/homelessness (see Table 1.1).

TABLE 1.1 Top ten of the most important non-economic problems facing the country, 2012

Problem	%
Dissatisfaction with government	12
Healthcare	6
Ethical/moral/religious decline	4
Education	4
Immigration/illegal aliens	2
Foreign aid/focus overseas	1
Lack of respect for each other	1
War (non-specific)/fear of war	1
Energy/lack of energy sources	1
Poverty/hunger/homelessness	1

Source: adapted from Gallup poll, June 7–10, 2012. Figures do not total 100%.

These were followed by familiar concerns, which have moved up and down the lists of problems, such as welfare; the judicial system/courts/laws; international problems; environment/pollution; lack of military defense; unifying the country; the media; and care for the elderly/Medicare. Other traditional problems in both categories did not show up significantly in percentage terms, such as cost of living/inflation; foreign trade deficit; crime/violence; race relations/racism; abortion; drugs; terrorism; wars; gay rights; and guns.

Given the optimism of Americans, their faith in their society and belief in an individual ability to achieve the American dream, it is instructive to consider the results of polls that reported on alienation in US society (see Table 1.2) between 2007 and 2011. The responses indicated increasing alienation over the years. They suggest a degree of individual powerlessness felt by ordinary Americans in the face of political, economic, bureaucratic, corporate and institutional forces, and dissatisfaction with social elites.

A further statement was included in the poll, but not in the Alienation Index. In 2011, 87 percent of respondents agreed that "The people in Washington are out of touch with the rest of the country."

TABLE 1.2 Alienation in the US, 2007–11

Americans tend to feel that . . . %	2007	2008	2009	2010	2011
. . . the rich get richer and the poor get poorer	73	71	66	68	73
. . . what you think doesn't count for very much any more	55	57	56	52	66
. . . most people with power try to take advantage of people like yourself	57	59	57	53	63
. . . the people running the country don't really care what happens to you	59	62	53	50	73
. . . you're left out of things going on around you	36	41	35	37	41

Source: adapted from Harris Alienation Index, the Harris Poll, September 2011.

Exercises

Explain and examine the significance of the following names and terms:

the Civil War	secession	"Americanness"	Native Americans
utopianism	the Enlightenment	rule of law	Latino
slavery	individualism	alienation	Constitution
populism	ethnic	anti-statism	exceptionalism
diversity	consensus	corporate	the Cold War
Big Business	Big Government	bureaucracies	"melting pot"
grass roots	culture(s)	consumerism	civil rights
work ethic	frontier	salad bowl	9/11
traits	pluralism	assimilation	the Vietnam War
nativism	egalitarianism	Americanization	Washington DC
ideology	brand names	multiculturalism	integration
globalization	regulation	Old Glory	racism
race relations	inauguration	stereotyping	Awakenings
recession	ancestral	drone campaigns	turnout

Write short essays on the following questions:

1. What are some of the characteristics that you would associate with the American people and their society? Why?

2. Why are questions of "national identity" and "Americanness" important in the US?

3. Is the study of the major cultures an adequate way to approach American society?

4. Do you find that the public opinion poll findings in this chapter give a valid picture of the US? Give your reasons after carefully examining the poll results.

5. Discuss whether multiculturalism and national identity can coexist?

6. Attempt a definition of "racism" and explore its presence in the US.

Further reading

Addington, L. (2000) *America's War in Vietnam: A Short Narrative History*, Bloomington, IN: University of Indiana Press.

Alba, R. and Nee, V. (2003) *Remaking the American Mainstream: Assimilation and Contemporary Immigration*, Cambridge, MA: Harvard University Press.

Bloom, A. (1988) *The Closing of the American Mind*, New York: Touchstone.

Breen, L.A. (2011) *Converging Worlds: Communities and Cultures in Colonial America*, London: Routledge.

Campbell, N., Davies, J. and McKay, G. (2004) *Issues in Americanization and Culture*, Edinburgh: Edinburgh University Press.

Campbell, N. and Kean, A. (2006) *American Cultural Studies: An Introduction to American Culture*, London: Routledge.

Crowther, J. and Kavanagh, K. (eds) (1999) *Oxford Guide to British and American Culture for learners of English*, Oxford: Oxford University Press.

Cullen, J. (2003) *The American Dream: A Short History of an Idea That Shaped a Nation*, New York: Oxford University Press.

Datesman, M.K., Kearny, L. and Keyerleber, J. (2005) *American Ways: An Introduction to American Culture*, White Plains, NY: Pearson Education.

Dubois, L. and Scott, J.S. (eds) (2009) *Origins of the Black Atlantic*, London: Routledge.

Ferguson, N. (2004) *The Rise and Fall of the American Empire*, London: Allen Lane.

Hacker, A. (2003) *Two Nations: Black and White, Separate, Hostile, Unequal*, New York: Scribner.

Hall, J.A. and Lindholm, C. (1999) *Is America Breaking Apart?* Princeton, NJ: Princeton University Press.

Huntington, S.P. (2004) *Who Are We? America's Great Debate*, New York: Simon & Schuster.

Jenkins, P. (2003) *A History of the United States*, London: Palgrave Macmillan.

Leach, E.E. (2004) *Interpreting the American Dream*, London: Palgrave Macmillan.

Lipset, S.M. (1996) *American Exceptionalism: A Double-Edged Sword*, New York: W.W. Norton & Company.

Mancall, P.C. and Merrell, J. (2006) *American Encounters: Natives and Newcomers from European Contact to Indian Removal, 1500–1850*, London: Routledge

Micklethwait, J. and Wooldridge, A. (2004) *The Right Nation: Why America is Different*, London: Allen Lane.

Moen, P., Dempster-McClain, D. and Walker, H.A. (eds) (1999) *A Nation Divided: Diversity, Inequality, and Community in American Society*, Ithaca, NY: Cornell University Press.

Morehouse, M.M. and Trodd, Z. (2012) *Civil War America: A Social and Cultural History with Primary Sources*, London: Routledge

Pope, D. (ed.) (2001) *American Radicalism*, Oxford: Blackwell.

Sandel, M.J. (1996) *Democracy's Discontent: America in Search of a Public Philosophy*, Cambridge, MA: Belknap Press of Harvard University Press.

Sargent, L.T. (ed.) (1995) *Extremism in America*, New York: New York University Press.

Schrag, P. (2011) *Not Fit for Our Society: Immigration and Nativism in America*, Berkeley, CA: University of California Press.

Woods, R.B. and Gatewood, W.B. (2000) *The American Experience: A Concise History*, New York: Harcourt Brace.

Zinn, H. (2003) *A People's History of the United States: From 1492 to Present*, London: Longman/Pearson.

Websites

Gallup opinion polls: www.gallup.com

Pew Research Center: www.people-press.org

www.washingtonpost.com

www.census.gov

www.cnn.com

www.firstgov.gov

www.csmonitor.com

www.lib.duke.edu/reference/polls.htm

www.ropercenter.uconn.edu

www.economist.com/yougov

www.nytimes.com

www.harrispollonline.com

www.harrisinteractive.com

www.pollingreport.com/prioriti.htm

Chapter 2

The country

- Political ecology
- Natural resources, economic development and environmental concerns
- Climate
- The regions: cultural geography
- Native American cultural regions
- Cultural regions in the contemporary US
- Changing public attitudes: where do we go from here?
- *Exercises*
- *Further reading*
- *Websites*

With an area of 3,615,122 square miles (9,363,123 square kilometers) the United States is exceeded in size only by Russia, Canada and China. Of the 50 states, 48 lie between the Atlantic and Pacific Oceans, and between Canada and Mexico, while two, Alaska and Hawaii, lie in the northwest corner of the continent and the Pacific Ocean, respectively. Island possessions in the Caribbean and the Pacific add another 11,000 square miles (28,500 square kilometers) to American territory.

Political ecology

The most pronounced feature of the country is its variety. Its natural environment varies from the arctic to the tropical, from rainforest to desert, from vast plains to rugged mountains. Exploiting its natural resources has depleted reserves, caused extensive pollution and shown a wastefulness that has led to dependence on resources from other nations, although the country's own natural riches remain a main support of its economic life. Recently, energy independence has become a major goal for economists, politicians and national security advisers. Environmentalist movements and public concern since the mid-1800s have successfully lobbied for a huge national system of nature preserves and government monitoring and regulation of the environment. The use of natural resources has become a matter of balancing priorities among overlapping environmental, economic and cultural interest groups. The chapter therefore often focuses on political ecology, that is, on attempts to understand the complex distributional issues involved in Americans' involvement with the environment.

Natural resources, economic development and environmental concerns

Approached from the Atlantic Ocean or the Gulf of Mexico, the country's first land formation is the Atlantic Plain, a coastal lowland stretching from New England to the middle of Texas. A narrow coastal strip in the North, the plain gradually widens to include large parts of the southern states. Its soil is mostly poor but includes a fertile citrus-growing region and the Cotton Belt in the South, which have both been intensively developed for commercial farming. The Plain's most important natural wealth is found along and in the Gulf of Mexico, where much of the nation's crude oil and natural gas reserves are located. Water pollution from industrial development in the North and commercial fertilizers and oil-drilling in the South have posed the most serious threats to the Plain's environment.

The Gulf's wetland wildlife and rich fisheries suffered greatly during the disaster on the BP Deepwater Horizon rig that poured enormous amounts of raw oil into that ecosystem for months in 2010. Drilling for petroleum further north off the Atlantic coast has become a more serious alternative despite environmentalists' protests. As the nation strives for energy independence, politicians consider exploiting an "all of the above" approach and distributing the environmental costs across the country.

Inland from the Atlantic Plain, the land rises to the Piedmont, a gently rolling fertile plateau. Along the eastern edge of the Piedmont is the fall line, where rivers running down to the Atlantic form waterfalls. When water power was used for lumber, grain and textile mills, America's first industrial cities grew up along the northern fall line near the coast. The Piedmont rises to the Appalachians, much-eroded mountains from Canada to Alabama that separate the eastern seaboard from the interior. These mountains, the Appalachian Plateau, and the rugged ridge and valley country to their west delayed European invasion and settlement (see Figure 2.2). Although the Appalachians and the upland sub-regions contain minerals, only iron, building stone and coal are found in large quantities. The coal deposits in Pennsylvania and West Virginia, in the area called Appalachia, are among the world's largest and once provided fuel for developing industry in the Northeast and the Great Lakes regions as well as for heating homes across the nation. Today, Appalachia is among the nation's most depressed areas because "cleaner" gas, oil and atomic energy have partially replaced coal. Producing and using these newer energy sources, however, have also been identified as the main sources of air pollution and acid rain. "Clean" wind and solar energy are among the environmentally friendly technologies the Obama administration supports.

West of the Appalachian highlands lies the Central Lowland, a vast area stretching from New York state to central Texas and north to Canada, which resembles a huge, irregular bowl rimmed by the Great Lakes and highlands. The iron ore in one of these, the Mesabi Range at the western edge of the Lakes, transported inexpensively over the Great Lakes to the coal of Appalachia, made the development of America's industrial core possible. This industrial ecology was the backbone of the nation's economic expansion and claimed priority over environmental concerns until many of its "smokestack" factories proved unable to compete on the global market in the 1970s. The Central Lowland is not entirely flat. The glacial moraine, an area of rocky territory with many lakes, runs along a line just north of the Ohio and Missouri rivers. On both sides of the moraine, the lowland has a table-like flatness except near rivers that have dug gorges. The lowland also varies in rainfall and temperature. Rainfall decreases towards the west, resulting first in a change from forests mixed with fields to the prairies,

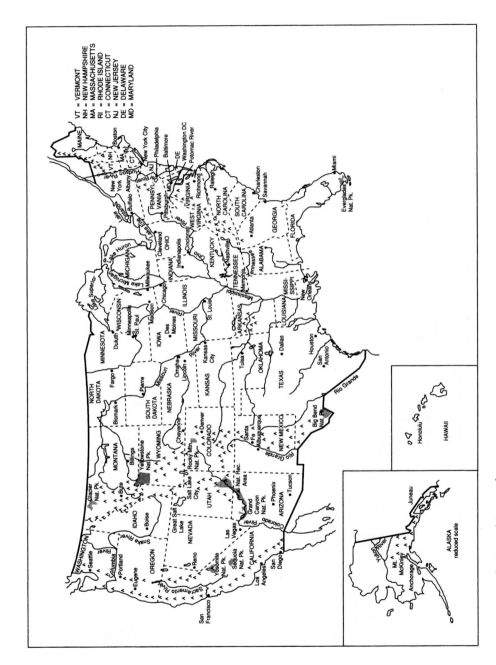

FIGURE 2.1 The United States of America.

PLATE 2.1 A smoggy morning in downtown Los Angeles, where topography, climate, massive traffic flows and population density make pollution a problem.
(Izzy Schwartz/Getty Images)

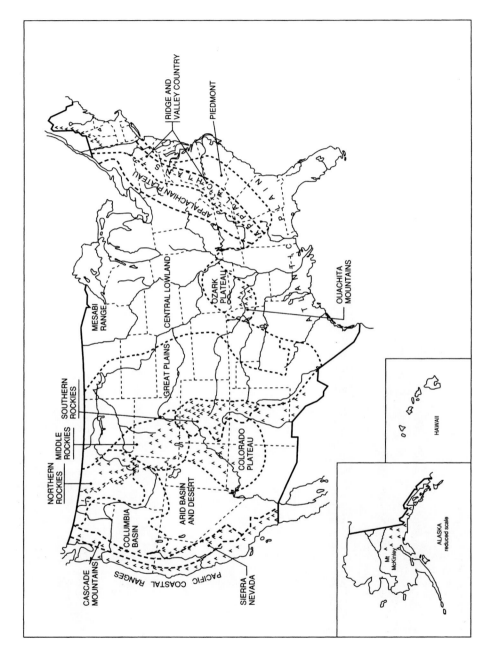

FIGURE 2.2 Physical geography of the US.

where trees are rare. Farther west, the high prairie grass changes to short grass at the 20-inch (50-centimeters) annual rainfall line where the Great Plains begin (see Figure 2.2). From north to south, the long winters of the Upper Midwest change to the snow-less winters of the Gulf states.

The natural resources of the Central Lowland, which is often called the nation's breadbasket, are its soil and fossil fuels. The fields of oil and gas in Texas, Oklahoma and Kansas were the nation's most important domestic supply until reserves in the Gulf and Alaska were tapped. Today oil wells have sprouted up in farming areas and housing districts throughout the region as local residents try to supply their own energy from small deposits. Across the lowland the increase in large-scale agribusinesses in recent years has produced intense efforts to deal with unwanted side effects, including polluted water supplies from plant fertilizers and insecticides and the leakage of concentrated animal feed and sewage from industrial pig, chicken and freshwater fish farming.

The Great Plains is a band of semi-arid territory almost 500 miles (800 kilometers) wide between Canada and Mexico. The plains rise so gradually towards the west that large parts of the region appear to be utterly flat. Most of the plains, however, are broadly rolling, and parts of the northern plains are cut up into spectacular gorge and ridge country called "badlands." The buffalo grass of the plains makes them excellent for ranching, but some areas, watered by automated

PLATE 2.2 Crop spraying in Idaho.
(Sipa Press/Rex Features)

artesian wells or irrigation, are now high-yield farm country. The Plains' mineral wealth, mainly low-grade brown coal, is extracted through environmentally damaging strip-mining, which grows in economic viability as the world price for oil rises and the vulnerability of off-shore energy supplies to hurricanes such as Katrina becomes increasingly apparent. Shale oil deposits in western Colorado with perhaps five times the energy reserves of Saudi Arabia now seem profitable to extract and eventually could make the United States an energy exporter.

From the western edge of the Great Plains to the Pacific coast, a third of the continental United States consists of the Cordillera mountain chains (the Rockies and the Pacific ranges) and the basins and plateaus between them. Near the Southern Rockies' western slopes is the Colorado Plateau, a maze of canyons and mesas, the most famous of which is the Grand Canyon. Surrounding the Plateau is the desert Southwest. Valleys and plains rather than mountains occupy much of the Middle Rockies. The Wyoming Basin has provided a route through the mountains, from the Oregon Trail that pioneers followed to the interstate highways of today. In the northern Rockies are vast wilderness areas and the Columbia Basin, which is etched by the remarkable canyons of the Snake and Columbia rivers.

The western arm of the Cordillera consists of two lines of mountains with a series of valleys between them. In from the coast are the highest peaks, including active volcanoes. The inland valleys contain much of the West Coast's population and economic activity, from Washington's Puget Sound to the Willamette Valley of Oregon and California's Central Valley. All these valleys are blessed with rich soils, and the more southerly were relatively easy to irrigate. Since the invention of refrigeration, these valleys have supplied the nation with fruit and vegetables. The mountains between the valleys and the coast include major earthquake zones, such as the San Andreas Fault, which caused the 1906 quake that leveled San Francisco. Distributing limited water resources fairly, however, rather than earthquakes, seems to be the most serious environmental challenge to a majority of Westerners.

In Alaska, the Cordillera divide into three parts that include North America's highest peak, Mount McKinley at 20,320 feet (6,194 meters). Largely fragile tundra, Alaska's interior is comprised of mountains, broken plateaus and fairly flat valleys with a cold inland climate. Much of coastal and island Alaska has a temperate climate because of warm ocean currents. The building of the trans-Alaska pipeline, coastal oil spills and, as recently as the 2008 presidential election campaign, the debate over plans to open the Arctic National Wildlife Refuge to oil exploration have tested the nation's will to protect Alaska's nature. Republican Vice-Presidential Candidate Sarah Palin, the governor of the state, joined her party and a large majority of Alaskan voters in supporting the opening of the ANWR.

The American Cordillera are world famous for veins of precious metals, such as the gold of the Sierra and Yukon and the Comstock silver lode of Nevada. More recently, industrial metals such as copper and lead have been mined. Large occurrences of oil and gas are found in California and Wyoming, and the Colorado Plateau contains not only coal shale but uranium and soft coal. To extract the oil and coal, say mining companies, open-pit and strip-mining are necessary. Conservationists, on the other hand, argue that this mining devastates parts of the plateau as thoroughly as it destroyed areas of the Great Plains and Appalachia.

The natural riches of Hawaii are vegetable rather than mineral. The state contains almost a million acres (405,000 hectares) of commercial forest and twice as much land suitable for tropical farming. Trade winds give the islands a temperate climate. The volcanic mountains catch much rain on the windward side of the islands so that the leeward side has only moderate rainfall.

Coastlines and river systems

Among the most important physical features and resources of the country are its coastlines, harbors, ocean currents and network of lakes and rivers. The shallow waters of the continental shelf off the North Atlantic coast known as the Great Banks contain many kinds of fish and attracted fishermen from Europe even before European settlers established their first colonies in the New World. By the 1990s the famous cod stocks there had collapsed from international over-fishing, however, and made the need to manage these maritime riches clear to the US and Canada. The East Coast has a warmer climate because of the Florida Current. Fine harbors and estuaries made the sites of New York City, Philadelphia and Baltimore excellent locations for trade.

The great eastern water systems are those that drain the Central Lowland: the Mississippi with its major tributaries and the Great Lakes–St. Lawrence system. One of the world's great inland water networks, the Mississippi system carries freight from New Orleans north to Minneapolis and east to Pittsburgh. Western tributaries of the Mississippi are mostly unfit for navigation, but since the 1950s the Missouri has carried heavy barge traffic as a result of dams, locks and dredging. Because canals connect it to the Mississippi, the Great Lakes–St. Lawrence system functions as the second half of one vast network of inland waterways. The biggest group of freshwater lakes in the world, the Great Lakes carry more shipping than any other inland lake group. The fertile farmland surrounding the lakes and the iron, lumber and fossil fuels near their shores supported the rapid urbanization and industrialization of the Midwest in the 1800s. The opening of the St. Lawrence Seaway in 1959 made the lake cities international seaports by bypassing the obstacles to ocean-going freighters in the St. Lawrence with huge locks.

On the West Coast, limited rainfall and scant mountain run-off dry up all but three river systems—the Columbia, the Colorado and the San Joaquin–Sacramento—before they reach the sea. They do not support shipping, but the West's largest rivers have brought prosperity by providing hydroelectric power and irrigation. The Columbia, once a wild white river, now runs down through dams and calm lakes, turning the arid plateaus of Washington state into vegetable gardens and supplying electrical power as well as drinking water to several states and Native American cultures. The Colorado serves the same purposes on a smaller scale. Proposals for its further development have met with opposition because more dams would destroy the beauty of the Grand Canyon and other canyon lands.

Conservation, recreational areas and environmental protection

Although the country's population is now over 315 million, most of these people live in relatively small areas. Some parts of the country are not suitable for urbanization because of climate or difficult topography. Others have been set aside as recreation areas or wildlife preserves. These and other factors give the US a great variety of national, state and local parks and open spaces. In the US, conservation of natural beauty and resources through national parks gained acceptance in the late 1800s, with vocal support from Theodore Roosevelt, among others. Yellowstone National Park, the first nature preserve created by Congress, was put under federal control in 1872. Congress established the National Park Service in 1916 and gave it the difficult double duty of making the areas entrusted to it accessible for industry and public enjoyment, and of preserving them for future generations. The Park Service now administers more than 200 different sites, whose combined territory exceeds 40,000 square miles (104,000 square kilometers) of land and water. There are national parks in all parts of the nation, but the largest and most famous are located between the Rockies and the Pacific.

Government protection of the parks means controlled development. The federal Department of the Interior and its Land Management Bureau have long granted licenses or leases allowing private economic interests to use the parks' resources at low cost. According to federal law, the government must balance the interests of developers, holiday-makers, environmentalists and Native Americans. Some say this ideal of "multiple use" may have worked when the West was under-populated, but that today it satisfies no one and could lead to the loss of irreplaceable resources.

In the 1960s, a remarkable period of protest and reform in the US, conservationist and environmentalist organizations grew in strength in response to exposés of pollution, such as Rachel Carson's best-selling book *Silent Spring*, and a series of environmental disasters, including a gigantic oil spill off the California coast and the chemical explosion and burning of the Cuyahoga River in downtown Cleveland, Ohio. The high level of public concern became obvious in 1970 when 20 million people took part in the first Earth Day, a nationwide "teach-in," focused on the dangers of pollution. Concerted lobbying of Congress by grassroots groups and highly organized environmental organizations such as the

Sierra Club and National Audubon Society soon resulted in a series of landmark federal laws. In the same year an independent regulatory body, the Environmental Protection Agency (EPA), took on the national government's responsibility for monitoring and protecting America's natural environment, and the Clean Air Act gave the EPA the duty of identifying and reducing airborne pollutants. By 1980 the Clean Water Act, the Safe Drinking Water Act, the Endangered Species Act, the Toxic Substances Control Act, and the Superfund statute—which provides emergency federal funding for eliminating the health hazards of toxic-waste sites across the nation—were in effect. These laws have been repeatedly strengthened and extended in the decades since their enactment due to the environmental damage caused largely by sprawling urban development, new and outmoded industrial sites, and innovative commercial forms of farming and food processing. Federal laws enacted from the 1980s to 2000s have protected rivers, beaches and estuaries from toxic dumping and the public from nuclear wastes and poisonous sprays and residues on foods and cosmetic products.

Climate

Arctic and tropical climates are limited to high mountain-tops, inland Alaska, Hawaii and the southern tip of Florida. The middle latitudes are, however, known for wide variations in temperature and rainfall, and the great size of North America reinforces these differences. In general, the more distant a place is from an ocean, the more it has temperature extremes in the summer and winter. Near the inland center of the continent in North Dakota temperatures have varied from a summer high of 121°F (49°C) to a winter low of -60°F (-51°C). Most climates in America are distinctly inland because, with the general eastward movement of air across the country, the Cordillera mountain system limits the moderating influence of the Pacific to a narrow strip along the West Coast. Thus, San Francisco experiences only a small differential between winter and summer temperatures, but coastal cities in the Atlantic Northeast have the same range of temperatures that extend from the Rockies to the East Coast. The easterly direction of weather systems across the country also means the Atlantic Ocean has only a weak moderating influence.

Rainfall

Rainfall from the Pacific Ocean is so confined to the coastal strip by the Cordillera that the areas between the mountains and the Great Plains are arid or semi-arid. Farther east, rainfall increases because warm, moist air moves up over the nation's middle from the Gulf of Mexico, producing rainfall. This rain often comes in cloudbursts, hailstorms, tornadoes and blizzards, with rapid temperature changes as cold Canadian air collides with warm, humid air from the Gulf of Mexico.

PLATE 2.3 The skyline of downtown Seattle with its famous "space needle" tower. *(F1 Online/Rex Features)*

The seasons

In winter, dry frigid Canadian air moves south, spreading cold weather to the plains and lowlands and causing storms at its southern edge. In summer, that stormy edge moves north as gulf air brings hot weather that eliminates much of the temperature difference between the North and South.

Along the Pacific, seasonal changes follow another pattern. Winter in the Pacific Northwest is overcast and drizzly as a result of warm, moist air from the Alaskan coast. Southern California is a climatic refuge in winter because of its mild temperatures and long periods of sunny weather. In summer, the Pacific Northwest has mild air from the Pacific, and, except in the mountains, is nearly rainless. Farther south, summer means dry, hot air and high temperatures. Autumn in the Northeast and upper Midwest is marked by mild days, frosty nights and crystal-clear skies. Spring here brings temperate weather, but autumn and spring are also the seasons when the gulf and Canadian air masses lurch most violently together, spawning hurricanes along the gulf and Atlantic coasts in the fall and tornadoes in the Mississippi valley in the spring.

The regions: cultural geography

The definitions and boundaries of American regions vary according to the uses they are put to and according to the people making the divisions. Recent developments in the study of geography emphasize how political the subject is because mapping the physical world divides it in ways that decide where people belong and how resources are managed and distributed. More than one meaningful division of the country into regions is possible, and cultural regions defined as groups of states give only approximate borders because cultural boundaries rarely coincide with political units. Individual Native American cultures, geographic areas and states, moreover, often show a unique mixture of traits that makes their inclusion in regional cultures inaccurate at best.

Native American cultural regions

Many distinctive Native American cultures existed when Europeans arrived in the mid-1500s. An estimated 10 million Native Americans then lived in cultures with several hundred mutually incomprehensible languages and widely varying social structures. Any survey of cultural regions in such a diversity of groups must focus on broad similarities (see Figure 2.3).

PLATE 2.4 Waits River, Vermont, with autumn foliage.
(Andre Jenny/Stock Connection/Rex Features)

In the woodland eastern half of the country were areas now known as the northeastern and southeastern maize regions, where a variety of native cultures depended on hunting, fishing, farming and gathering. These are called maize cultures because maize, or corn as it is called in the US, was the most important staple of the Native Americans' diet. The longer growing season in the southeastern maize region resulted in more extensive and highly developed agriculture. In the East as a whole, most housing was constructed of wood, bark and thatch. Women and children usually farmed and gathered wild foods while men hunted and fished. Well-known cultural groups here were the Iroquois, Huron, Mohican, Delaware and Shawnee in the north, and the Powhatan, Creek, Cherokee, Seminole and Natchez in the south.

The Native American cultural area in the prairies and Great Plains is known as the plains or bison region. For thousands of years the population of this area was sparse compared with other parts of the continent. People lived along waterways and depended on riverbank farming, small-game hunting and gathering. Lacking any other means of transportation, they went on a communal buffalo (bison) hunt once a year on foot. Then, between 1700 and 1750, they discovered how to use the horses that reached them from Spanish-controlled areas to the south, and plains cultures were transformed. The population grew because the food supply increased dramatically when bison were hunted on horseback. Learning of this, some tribes, such as the Dakota, migrated from nearby woodlands to the open steppes farther west. Plains peoples exchanged their settled farming customs for the nomadic culture of year-round buffalo hunters, discarding sod lodges for the portable *tipi* and evolving a society dominated by a warrior hunting class. The groups transformed by the arrival of the horse (the Blackfoot, Crow, Cheyenne and Dakota) are among the best-known of Native Americans, largely because of their fierce resistance to white settlement on their hunting grounds.

The Native American cultural region called the Southwest once encompassed a diversity of native cultures, nomadic hunters and gatherers as well as farmers, but most of its people relied on advanced forms of irrigated agriculture. Hopi, Zuni and Acoma people, among others, lived in the two- to three-floor adobe, or stone buildings called pueblos, and farmed nearby land. These cultures all traced ancestry through the female line, and men did the farming while women owned the fields. The Navajo and Apache were latecomers to the region, hunters and gatherers who migrated south from the Canadian plains between 1000 and 1500 AD and who adopted farming from the pueblo-dwelling peoples. The Navajo later learned sheep-raising, peach-growing and silver-working from the Spanish, while some Apache groups took up aspects of nomadic plains cultures, such as the *tipi* and hunting buffalo on horseback, and copied cattle-raising from Spaniards and Americans.

The California-intermontane cultural area included the barren territory around the Colorado plateau and most of California. The nomadic hunters and

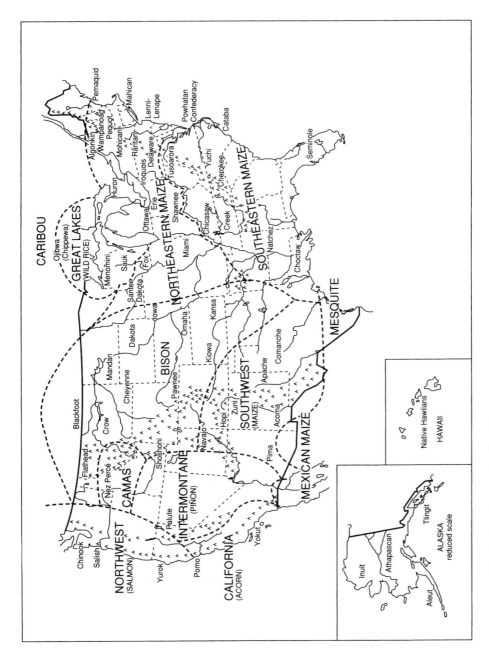

FIGURE 2.3 Native American cultural regions.

gatherers that lived here are often considered materially the poorest of the continent's native cultures. On the other hand, their loosely organized family bands are often praised for their democratic political traditions and peaceful way of life.

The plentiful nature available to the coastal cultures from northern California to southern Alaska made them a stark contrast to highland cultures of the nearby inland areas. Among the most advanced groups of related cultures north of Mexico, the Northwest peoples lived in coastal villages similar to independent city states. Well supplied with wild plants and game, the Chinook, Tsimshian, Kwakiutl, Haida and Tlingit did not need to farm. Fishing for salmon represented their primary economic activity, but saltwater fishing and whaling were also important. They made long seagoing canoes and massive wooden lodges, decorating these, as well as household items and totem poles, with symbolic carving. These peoples of plenty are well-known for the *potlatch*, several days of feasting during which a leading family gave its guests extravagant gifts. The family's wealth was demonstrated by the richness of its generosity, and the guests' degree of satisfaction determined their hosts' prestige in the community. The Northwest coastal peoples were among the few non-agricultural societies to practice slavery, which was common in Native American farming cultures.

PLATE 2.5 The Bitsie family on their ranch in the Navajo Indian Nation Reservation, Monument Valley, New Mexico. Today both men and women among the Navajo practice the sheep-herding learned long ago from the Spanish.
(Patrick Frilet/Rex Features)

The various Inuit groups (including the Aleuts) are the native peoples of Alaska and the Aleutian Islands. The Inuit arrived relatively late and wanted to distinguish themselves racially from the Native Americans living farther south. The coastal peoples are skilled sea-hunters, while the inland cultures are based on hunting big game. The stereotype of the "Eskimo" as a nomadic sea-hunter living in an igloo comes from the Inuit culture of far north Canada. The Inuit of Alaska are settled villagers who build underground sod-walled houses. Fast and efficient dog sledges and kayaks made it possible for them to live in one place and supply themselves with food.

Indigenous Hawaiians gathered food from the tropical forests, terraced mountain sides and irrigated their fields to grow crops. Expert open-sea fishermen from outrigger canoes, they also built semicircular fish ponds along the seashore. The priesthood, aristocracy and royal family owned most of the land, which was divided into strips that extended from a mountain-top to a distance under coastal waters to meet all the owners' needs. The common people lived in small areas where they had limited rights to fish, water, wood, wild foods and farming.

Attitudes toward the land

Attitudes toward land and landownership in Native American cultures varied. Group possession and communal use of land were most common. Almost all native groups had a concept of their own territory that was theirs by long residence and whose boundaries they defended or extended as circumstances demanded. Picturing native cultures as idealized societies in which land had only spiritual value is invariably wrong because it romanticizes and oversimplifies the realities of life in North America before European settlement. The Native Americans were aware of their dependence on the land, which led most native cultures to deify or revere nature. On the other hand, some cultures exploited their environment until it became depleted. Others over-hunted until some animals became extinct. If resources became scarce, groups moved to meet their needs, and conflict with other cultures resulted.

Cultural regions in the contemporary US

Political geography

Today's cultural regions result from varying mixtures of increasingly global antecedents, with Native American elements, at their most noticeable, representing one of several ingredients. The main American regions are much-used concepts for understanding subdivisions of American culture and society. Still, US regions tend to be less distinct than those in older, more demographically stable countries. The high mobility of the American population adds to the homogenizing effects of popular mass culture, modern transportation, urbanization, mass media and the centralization of the economy and government.

The Northeast

The Northeast often seems to be one unit when viewed from other sections of the country. Stretching from Maine, south through Maryland and west to the border of Ohio, the whole region is known as densely populated, highly urban and suffering from becoming post-industrial (changing from older heavy industry to a high-tech service economy). In fact, the Northeast is arguably still the nation's economic and cultural center, and is two regions (New England and the Mid-Atlantic) rather than one.

New England itself is often divided into two parts. Southern New England (Massachusetts, Connecticut and Rhode Island) has long had a cultural importance out of proportion to its size, natural resources and population. Massachusetts received a very large number of early colonists from Britain and rapidly developed stable institutions, cohesive communities and an expanding population that strongly influenced the rest of New England and the northern half of the country during the eighteenth and nineteenth centuries.

Americans trace several aspects of the nation's traditional core culture to southern New England. The original settlers' goal of founding a model religious community that would inspire reform in England was generalized to "American exceptionalism," a belief that the nation has a special mission and ability to set an example for the rest of the world. The region supposedly also bequeathed the country's belief in the so-called Puritan work ethic, the faith that hard work and good morals are rewarded in this world and the next. In the mid-nineteenth century, New England authors such as Ralph Waldo Emerson expressed central values that were taught for more than a century in US schools as the foundation of the entire nation's culture. In the schools' popularized version, the American creed was an optimistic individualism expressed in introspective self-reliance and self-improvement, thrift, hard work and a belief in progress.

In the 1800s New England Yankees became famous for their economic ingenuity, as traveling peddlers, clipper-ship captains and mill owners. The fall line near the coast, by providing cheap water power close to trade routes, made the region the cradle of American industry. When industry converted to steam and electricity, the region lost manufacturing jobs to other parts of the country. One of New England's greatest strengths in its economic competition with other regions today is its concentration of quality institutions of higher education and research. New England is now a leader in innovative business methods, publishing and high-technology industries. The region's tourist industry flourishes because of its scenic qualities and status as a repository of the nation's history. The northern zone of the region (Maine, Vermont and most of New Hampshire), with its woodland mountain areas, has developed a lucrative industry providing

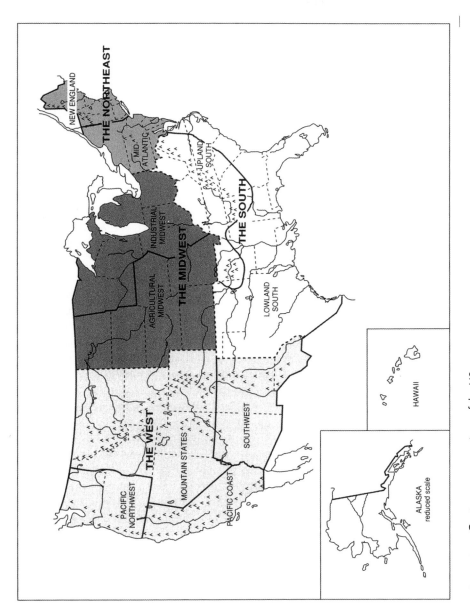

FIGURE 2.4 Contemporary regions of the US.

summer cottages and second homes for people who want to escape East Coast cities.

With a larger, more varied population, better soil and a greater share of natural resources, the Mid-Atlantic region surpassed New England in trade and manufactures during the 1700s. During the next century, these advantages helped the Mid-Atlantic region grow into the nation's commercial-industrial hub. Its harbors became the country's premier port cities, and here too the fall line provided cheap water power. The Mid-Atlantic also has passages through the Appalachian Mountains. First roads, then canals and later railroads followed these east–west routes as they opened western New York, Pennsylvania and the Great Lakes states to settlement and carried farm products to the coastal cities of the Mid-Atlantic. The Erie Canal, joining Lake Erie with New York City, made the cost of shipping a ton of freight from the lake to the city nearly 24 times cheaper, and thus the pattern of transportation down the inland rivers to New Orleans rapidly shifted towards New York, which became the nation's largest and wealthiest city.

By the later 1800s, transportation and trade welded together New England, the Mid-Atlantic region and the big cities of the Great Lakes and inland rivers. This was the urban industrial core that attracted people to jobs in a variety of "smokestack" industries. Although it includes agricultural areas, the distinguishing aspect of the core is still the size and closeness of its racially and ethnically mixed industrial cities. They contain many Latino and Asian groups as well today, but in popular opinion Boston seems Irish, Buffalo is Polish, and New York City mostly Jewish, Italian, African, Asian and Caribbean. By the 1970s, the migration of heavy industries abroad and "high-tech" companies to the South and Southwest resulted in the core being rechristened the "Rust Belt." Like New England, this region has had to develop new jobs, diversify its economy and recruit employers with tax breaks and social services. But the economic tug of war between the regions continues, and the South and West still attract more jobs and people than the urban core.

The South

Traditionally, this region includes the 11 states from Virginia to Texas that formed the Confederacy during the Civil War. In addition, the "border states" from West Virginia to Oklahoma are arguably Southern. Far from homogeneous, the South has two sub-regions, the lowland South on the Coastal Plain and the upland South in the Piedmont, southern Appalachians and Ozarks. The lowland South's diversity includes the Creole and Cajun areas of Louisiana and the Caribbean-African influenced Sea Islands off the Atlantic coast. Many observers argue that much of the South, rural and urban, has lost a great deal of its traditional character because of economic transformation and migration from other parts of the nation and abroad.

The distinctiveness of the Southern lowland developed with the earliest settlement along the Atlantic coast. The first colonists, Englishmen who came for economic rather than religious or political reasons, did not find the gold and silver that Spanish discoveries made them dream about, but the climate and soil proved suitable for growing and exporting cash crops such as tobacco and cotton, that required much manual labor but offered huge profits. Soon estates larger than the family farm (called plantations) became common and resulted in dispersed settlement with a few small urban centers. To meet the need for fieldworkers, plantation-owners imported white indentured servants (people who sold themselves into virtual slavery for four to seven years to pay for their passage to North America). By the late 1600s, however, planters turned to Africans sold into permanent slavery for labor. African slavery existed in all the American colonies, but became the main source of workers only in the plantation South.

As late as the 1830s, a proposal to end slavery failed by only one vote in the Virginia legislature. It was cheap fertile land to the west, improved machinery for harvesting cotton and high prices for the crop from Northern and British textile mills that made cotton the backbone of the early Industrial Revolution. This development confirmed the contrasts between the industrializing North and the slave-dependent South that led to the Civil War. The need to justify slavery and the shared memories of secession, war, defeat and occupation by Union armies reinforced Southerners' regional ties. Although slavery ended with the Civil War, cotton remained the region's main cash crop into the 1930s, and most African Americans remained dependent on their former masters for work and a place to live.

Agriculture is still important, but today the region's products are much more varied. Industry moved south because of low energy and labor costs and natural resources such as iron ore, bauxite, oil, gas and vast pine forests. An increasingly urban-industrial South forms the eastern arm of the so-called "Sunbelt," a swath of the southern and southwestern US that attracts financial, high-tech and media industries to growing population centers from Atlanta, Georgia, to Dallas, Texas. Since the Civil Rights laws and voter-registration drives of the 1960s, the important roles of African Americans in public life and their support for the Democratic Party have driven most conservative white Americans to the Republicans, making the South a two-party region for the first time in a century. In response to these changes, African Americans' migration out of the region reversed in the late 1900s. The rapidly growing Latino population further complicates the picture by voting largely as Democrats. Still, surveys indicate that Southerners as a whole remain less educated, more religious, more conservative and more predominantly old-stock American than the population of the other regions.

The Midwest

The Midwest includes the states bordering the Great Lakes and two tiers of states west of the Mississippi river from Missouri and Kansas north to Canada. The Great Lakes states with their many manufacturing centers are called the industrial Midwest, although they are also important farm states. In similar fashion the two Western tiers of states are called the agricultural Midwest, in spite of industrial cities such as St. Louis and Minneapolis. In the national consciousness, the Midwest is one region: the American heartland of family farms and small towns, perhaps naïvely provincial and optimistic, but still the moral and social center that mediates between the other regions.

The early routes of Western migration through the Appalachians met in the Great Lakes states, making them the first place where the cultures of New England, the Mid-Atlantic and the South combined. By 1860 the Great Lakes Midwest was well integrated into the markets of the Northeast, and during the Civil War it gained a proud sense of its identity from having sacrificed men and wealth for the preservation of the Union. After the war, the settlement of the trans-Mississippi agricultural Midwest was completed as steel-plated ploughs tore up the deep-rooted buffalo grass of the prairies and Great Plains and turned them into farmland. In the 1900s, machinery and new strains of winter wheat made these areas some of the most productive farmland in the world. Eventually this same technology rendered the American ideal of the independent small farmer obsolete, as "agribusinesses" replaced the family farm.

In recent decades Midwestern industrial cities have made great strides towards economic and environmental recovery, despite persistent problems with the loss of manufacturing jobs, slums and urban blight that follow in the wake of de-industrialization. Today Indianapolis, Pittsburgh, Cleveland and St. Louis, for example, can boast of glamorous downtown convention centers, museums and resurgent industries that no longer pollute the air and water. Chicago, the national hub of the commodities market, an important international seaport, and the home of widely diversified industry and cultural institutions, remains the region's premier city.

Midwestern political traditions show a mixture of pragmatic caution and organized protest. While the region has the reputation of being conservative, it was the birthplace of the Republican Party, which opposed the spread of slavery and nominated Lincoln for the presidency. Later, the agricultural Midwest was home to the Populist and Farmer-Labor parties, which protested the economic domination of the Northeast, and a center of the Progressive Movement, which strove to make American governments more honest, efficient and democratic. Midwestern states, such as Minnesota and Wisconsin, have since then been leaders in social and environmental reform. The region's population grows increasingly diverse due to arrivals from Africa, Asia and Latin America.

The West

"The West" is a myth, a popular set of values, and a region of the country. It represents possibility, freedom, self-reliance, the future. As a region, it is made up of three parts: the Southwest, the mountain states, and the Pacific coast. The Southwest consists of New Mexico, Arizona and parts of surrounding states with a similar climate and culture. Seized during the Mexican–American War of 1848, this area now has a mixture of old, unusually strong Spanish-Mexican and Native American communities—and a blend of people from many parts of the country and world who came in large numbers after 1945. Today cattle- and sheep-ranching are important for the economy, but dams on the major rivers and wells have transformed deserts into irrigated farmlands and metropolitan areas, such as Phoenix and Albuquerque. The warm, dry climate has proven attractive to retirees and people with respiratory ailments, as well as to electronics and aerospace companies. Mining, the petroleum industry and tourism in the Southwest's stunning national parks are also important economic supports.

The federal government is the largest landowner in the Southwest and even more clearly dominates the economy of the mountain states. The importance of its decisions about the leasing of federal lands becomes obvious when one learns that the government owns more than four-fifths of Nevada, two-thirds of Utah and vast areas of the sub-region's other states. In Colorado, for example, the national government owns 80 percent of the shale oil deposits. The traditional independence of long-time residents is increasingly frustrated by their lack of control over local resources. Newcomers from other regions, environmentalists, business people, Native American groups and government officials debate how resources should be used. During World War II and the Cold War the federal government used desert areas of the Southwest as test sites for a range of nuclear and conventional weapons with effects that are still hotly debated. The population density is low but appears to be growing so rapidly that some Westerners think in-migration and development are nearing their acceptable limits.

Mining the mountains' mineral riches provided the basis for migration to the sub-region and continues to be an economic mainstay. The mines brought the outside investment, transportation infrastructure and business that laid the financial foundation for urban areas such as Denver and Butte. Agriculture depends on ranching and forestry because other forms of farming require irrigation, and water rights have become as precious as rare metals. Las Vegas and Reno found wealth through the gambling and entertainment industries. Salt Lake City is the heart of the Great Basin Mormon center that is more homogeneous in population than any other cultural area in the US. Today it prospers by expertise in computer software and technology as well as by mining and irrigated agriculture.

European settlement of the Pacific coast began with the establishment of Spanish missions in California in the 1700s and included Russian and British domination of the Pacific Northwest before the US gained sovereignty over the area in the 1840s. The coastal territories attracted sizeable populations and qualified as states before the interior West because of the 1849 gold rush and reports of the lush greenness of the Oregon and Washington valleys. The San Francisco area was the first to experience rapid development because it was the port of entry for the gold rush "Forty-Niners." By the 1870s it was an industrializing metropolis that produced finished goods that successfully competed with imports from the East. Today the city is the hub of a larger area that includes Berkeley and its famous university, Oakland with its many industries, the Silicon Valley complex of computer firms, Stanford University and the Napa Valley wine district. Los Angeles has experienced rapid population growth ever since it became the terminus of a transcontinental railroad in 1885. The LA metropolis, a group of cities connected by a maze of superhighways, is home to the Hollywood film and media conglomerates as well as major energy, defense and aerospace companies. California's two largest urban areas contain every major racial and ethnic group in the nation, with especially large Asian and Latino elements. Politically, southern California has the reputation of being conservative while the northern part of the state is considered liberal.

In the Pacific Northwest the population and culture show less Latino and more New England and northwest European influence, while Asian American groups are as well established as farther south. During the past 30 years, so many people and businesses have relocated to Washington and Oregon that state authorities have attempted to limit growth. Their avowed goal is to preserve the environment and quality of life through a mixed economy based on agriculture, forestry and tourism, as well as on heavy and high-technology industries.

Resource and land-management are major issues in Hawaii and Alaska, as they are in the continental West. Hawaii's government instituted a detailed land-use system soon after it became a state in 1959. The law not only provided areas for commercial, industrial and residential building, but also protected farmland, nature reserves and tourist attractions. In the nineteenth century, settlers from the mainland recruited large numbers of Asians to work on plantations. But after 1900, when the islands became a US territory, these contract labor arrangements became illegal, and high immigration has resulted from better knowledge of the islands' attractions and easier transportation in the age of aviation. Today, the people are highly urban and have a make-up that is unique in the nation. The majority is Asian American, with people of Japanese extraction comprising the largest nationality group. Whites make up the largest minority, followed by smaller groups of Latinos, African Americans and native Polynesians.

The federal, state and Native American tribal governments own more than 99 percent of Alaska. Much of its history has involved struggles between resource-hungry developers, who lease land from government and create jobs for local residents, and conservationists, who lobby public authorities to restrict land-use because they view Alaska as the last chance to preserve an American wilderness.

PLATE 2.6 Vineyard in Napa Valley, California, one of the inland agricultural areas between the western arms of the Cordillera.
(Cosmo Condina/Stock Connection/Rex Features)

Until Alaska won statehood in 1959, settlers and natives there subsisted primarily through fishing, hunting and logging. Except for the short-lived Klondike gold rush of 1898, the area seemed destined to prove right the skeptics who said the country had, in 1867, bought a ridiculously expensive Russian icebox containing only sealskins and salmon.

During the 1950s and 1960s, Alaska received a wave of immigrants who wanted to escape the congestion and pollution in the 48 contiguous states. At the end of the 1960s, oil strikes off the state's northern coast increased interest in developing this "empty" land. The negotiations over how the environment should be preserved and the profits from the oil shared were the most critical in Alaska's history. The huge amounts of land and money Native Americans received in compensation gave them an entirely new status. The state profited so much that it replaced its income taxes with an annual oil dividend of about $1,000 per resident. To safeguard wildlife and the tundra, the trans-Alaska pipeline was insulated and lifted several feet above ground.

The results of oil development have been mixed. The population grew rapidly, reaching more than half a million by 1990, but, though the per-capita income for Alaskans is the highest in the nation, so is the state's unemployment rate. Much of Alaska's employment boom was temporary. In 1989 the super-tanker *Exxon Valdez* ran aground and spilled millions of gallons of oil on Alaska's coasts. The demand for a clean-up united environmentalists, the fishing and tourist industries, Native American organizations and ordinary citizens. Still, because the nation's economy remains largely dependent on fossil fuels, the fleets of tankers plying local coasts seem likely to grow, especially if drilling begins in the Arctic National Wildlife Refuge.

Changing public attitudes: where do we go from here?

In the Gallup poll of March 2012, 91 percent of Americans believed that the nation's energy situation was very (42 percent) or fairly serious (49 percent). Half foresaw a critical energy shortage in the next five years. These results show Americans to be only slightly more optimistic about their energy situation than they were in 2008, despite much media attention to the great potential of shale oil, small oil deposits and alternative sources of energy. Few Americans are ready to give up modern lifestyles and technology, but many have understood that the quality of life in the future is dependent on reconciling environmental and pro-development interests to manage the nation's natural resources wisely. In polls since early 2008 an increasing portion of those polled think greater production is more important than conservation for the nation's energy situation. In these years Detroit automakers' "gas guzzling" sports utility vehicles have been hugely popular, and since March 2010 small majorities of the public have prioritized energy production over preserving the environment. Politicians in Congress and the states have therefore mostly made political gestures, not followed through on major proposals and, as a Gallup report put it, have tried "to avoid alienating either side of the energy-versus environment debate."

Presidential figures have taken stands in this debate and have received a varied response. At the beginning of Democrat Barack Obama's second term, small opinion poll majorities still thought that the Kyoto Protocol was likely to hurt the US economy, and at the same time praised his somewhat limited action to energize American involvement in international efforts to deal with global warming and search for alternate energy sources. In the 2012 presidential campaign, the field of Republican candidates for the party's nomination, including Mitt Romney, strongly favored increased energy production over environmental concerns. Voters again gave Obama a decisive victory but perhaps not primarily for his policy on energy. His rescue of the automobile industry in the industrial Midwest may have weighed more heavily in their minds as economic indicators slowly grew more positive. When polled in 2012, members of the public offered mixed signals regarding how the US should deal with dilemmas regarding the environment and energy needs (see Table 2.1).

TABLE 2.1 Government policies for America's energy supplies

"As I read some possible government policies to address America's energy supply, tell me whether you would favor or oppose each. Would you favor or oppose the government . . ."

	Favor %	Oppose %	Unsure %
allowing more offshore oil and gas drilling in US waters	65	31	4
increasing federal funding for research on wind, solar and hydrogen technology	69	26	5
promoting the increased use of nuclear power	44	49	7
giving tax cuts to energy companies to do more exploration for oil and gas	46	50	4
requiring better fuel efficiency for cars, trucks and SUVs	78	19	3
spending more on subway, rail and bus systems	65	31	4
right now, which ONE of the following do you think should be the more important priority?	Wind, solar hydrogen % 52	Oil, coal natural % 39	not sure gas % 5

Data derived from Pew Research Center survey, March 7–11, 2012. N=1,503 adults nationwide. Margin of error ± 3.

Exercises

Explain and examine the significance of the following names and terms:

political ecology
National Park Service
fall line
Appalachians
Appalachia
Central Lowland
glacial moraine
Great Plains
urban industrial core

attitudes to energy use
the Southwest
Native American cultural regions
Northwest coastal cultures
Environmental Protection Agency
Hawaiians
attitudes toward land
the Northeast
global warming

Write short essays on the following questions.

1.   Outline the main physical features of the US, describing the country's most important natural resources and commenting on the environmental cost of their use.

2.   Discuss the causes of differences between Native-American and contemporary American cultural geography.

3.   Describe US pollution problems and conservation efforts with the attitudes shown in the text and Table 2.1 in mind.

Further reading

Statistical Abstract of the United States, US Printing Office, annual.
The World Almanac and Book of Facts (2012), New York: World Almanac Books.
Time, weekly magazine.
US Bureau of the Census, occasional series and reports.

Websites

www.pollingreport.com/energy.htm
The United States Geological Survey: education.usgs.gov
The United States Environmental Protection Agency: www.epa.gov
The federal commission on the Deep Horizon Oil Spill: www.oilspillcommission.gov
American environmental laws and regulations: www.epa.gov/epahome/lawregs.htm
Geographical and environmental information from the federal government: www.firstgov.gov

Chapter 3

The people
Settlement and immigration

- Mother of exiles
- Early encounters between Europeans and Native Americans
- The founders
- The first wave: colonial immigration, 1680–1776
- The second wave: the "old" immigrants, 1820–90
- Settlement patterns and nativism
- The third wave: the "new" immigrants, 1890–1930
- A renewed immigration debate and immigration restriction
- Wartime policies and the search for principle in immigration policy
- The fourth wave: 1965 to the present
- Attitudes to immigrants: the contemporary debate
- *Exercises*
- *Further reading*
- *Websites*

Mother of exiles

Immigration is a central aspect of US history. It is a major reason that the nation's total population grew to more than 313 million by 2012. Believing in the American dream, many tens of millions of people have come to live in the US. They thus changed their homelands, America and their family histories forever. They strengthened the nation's commitment to "the dream" and to its ideal of being a refuge for the poor and oppressed, a nation of nations. Gradually, over the centuries of massive immigration and the struggles of newcomers and Americans to adjust to each other, the view that the nature of the nation was and *should be* a composite of many national backgrounds, races and cultures gained popular acceptance. This view continues to face the opposition of those who believe newcomers should leave their homeland cultures behind and the dilemma of deciding what is necessary to hold the country and its increasingly diverse population together.

Americans' (and the immigrants') core idealism, pride and naïvety are embodied in Emma Lazarus' sonnet "The New Colossus," which is displayed inside the base of the Statue of Liberty (see Plate 3.1). There is some truth to the dream. Settled peoples have been able to climb a "ladder of ethnic succession" as new waves of immigrants arrive. For most of the foreign-born, life in the US has meant an improvement over their situation in the "old country," the realization of modest hopes for land or home-ownership, for example. Later generations have enjoyed more significant socio-economic progress, although "rags to riches" careers are rare indeed.

"The New Colossus"

Not like the brazen giant of Greek fame,
With conquering limbs astride from land to land;
Here at our sea-washed, sunset gates shall stand
A mighty woman with a torch, whose flame
Is the imprisoned lightning, and her name
Mother of Exiles. From her beacon hand
Glows world-wide welcome: her mild eyes command
The air-bridged harbor that twin cities frame.
"Keep ancient lands, your storied pomp!" cries she
With silent lips. "Give me your tired, your poor,

PLATE 3.1 Profile of the Statue of Liberty in New York Harbor against the sunset.
(Jian Chen/Rex Features)

> Your huddled masses yearning to breathe free,
> The wretched refuse of your teeming shore.
> Send these, the homeless, tempest-tost, to me,
> I lift my lamp beside the golden door!"

However, the meetings of newcomers and native-born have also contributed to America's history of social disorder. The contacts, conflicts and mixing of cultures have fuelled widespread discrimination, economic exploitation, anti-foreign movements and debates over equality, opportunity and national identity. In a country whose history began with the meeting of Native Americans and European colonists and continued through the importation of African slaves and several waves of immigrants, there has never been a single national culture, although for centuries a majority of Anglo-Americans made vigorous efforts to establish one.

The search continues for a metaphor that captures the character of American society. Is it best understood as an Anglo-American core culture to which newcomers sooner or later merge into as they assimilate? Or should it be some form of cultural pluralism as suggested by, among other images, the metaphors of a "melting pot," a "salad" or a "stew" and who is to decide who is included or excluded from these mixtures? Some commentators reject both the claims of a unitary culture and of cultural pluralism, preferring instead forms of multi-culturalism, in which multiple traditions are the ideal, and no cultural group, however old or influential historically, receives priority. Americans disagree over the nature of the process and what the ultimate goal should be: the integration, assimilation, even homogenization, of newcomers or the acceptance of a permanently pluralistic society.

Early encounters between Europeans and Native Americans

When European explorers and settlers encountered Native Americans in the late 1400s, a long history of mutual incomprehension and conflict began. These encounters amounted to a collision of worlds. Contacts between the Americas and other continents had been so rare that plants, animals, diseases and human societies evolved into different forms in the "new" and the "old" worlds. Europeans and Native Americans caught diseases from each other. Europeans survived the first contacts better, but for most of the seventeenth century well over half of them died from difficulties in adjusting to the new environment. The Native Americans fared far worse: epidemics annihilated entire native cultures. North America's pre-Columbian population of 10 million shrank to between 2 and 3 million. The exchange of plants and animals had effects that were just as far-reaching. Horses, donkeys, sheep, pigs and cows were alien creatures to Native

Americans. Potatoes, maize and tobacco were discoveries to Europeans. The potato played a key role in the great population growth that brought millions of European and smaller numbers of Asian immigrants to the US in the 1800s.

European societies were so diverse that Spaniards and the English could hardly imagine living in the same place in peace. Some Native American cultures viewed other indigenous peoples with a dislike no less intense. Yet, each continent's diversity of cultures were related, even quite similar in broad outline, when compared with cultures from the other continent. Thus, all Europeans tended to look alike to Native Americans, and most Europeans seemed incapable of seeing Native Americans as anything but a single people. To Europeans, Native Americans seemed lazy and wasteful of nature's potential. Viewing time as fluid, they had only vague concepts of the past and the future, and so seemed utterly unreliable. Because they viewed nature as a great mother, they could not comprehend how pieces of her could be sold and owned by individuals. From the first European settlement until today, the main focus in conflicts between these continental culture systems has been landownership.

The founders

The people who established the colonies are considered founders rather than immigrants because they created the customs, laws and institutions to which later arrivals (the first immigrants) had to adjust. The Spanish occupied coastal Florida, the Southwest and California in the 1500s and 1600s. After trying to enslave the natives, they worked to convert them to Christianity, farming and sheepherding. As many natives rejected this way of life, the Spanish colonies faced border attacks for more than 200 years.

The English established their first permanent settlement at Jamestown, Virginia in 1607. Their monarch had no desire to rule distant colonies, so instead the Crown legalized companies that undertook the colonization of America as private commercial enterprises. Virginia's early residents were so preoccupied with a vain search for gold and a sea passage to Asian markets that the colony floundered until tobacco provided a profitable export. Because of the scarcity of plantation labor, in 1619 the first African laborers were imported as indentured servants (free people who contracted for five to seven years of servitude). Supported by tobacco profits, however, Virginia imported 1,500 free laborers a year by the 1680s and had a population of 75,000 white Americans and 10,000 Africans in hereditary slavery by 1700.

In the 1630s, Lord Baltimore established Maryland as a haven for Catholics, England's most persecuted minority. Maryland's leadership remained Catholic for some time, but its economy and population soon resembled Virginia's. In the 1660s, other English aristocrats financed Georgia and the Carolinas as commercial investments and experiments in social organization. Within a generation, these colonies too resembled Virginia, but their cash crops were rice and indigo. The Southern settlers warred with the natives within a few years of their arrival and by the 1830s drove the Native Americans from today's South.

To escape religious oppression in England, the Pilgrims, a small group of radical separatists from the Church of England, founded the first of the Northern colonies in 1620 at Plymouth, Massachusetts. The Puritans, who established the much larger Massachusetts Bay colony in 1630, wanted to purify the Church of England, not separate from it. Mostly well-educated middle-class people, they believed they could create a "city on a hill" in America to show how English society could be reformed. To that end, more than 20,000 emigrated in around ten years. By the latter 1600s, the bay colony had expanded to the coast of present-day Maine, swallowed up Plymouth, and spawned the colony of Connecticut. Flourishing through agriculture and forestry, the New England colonies also became the shippers and merchants for all of British America. Because of their intolerance towards dissenters and other religious groups, the Puritans' New England became the most homogeneous region in the colonies.

The founding of the middle colonies (New York, New Jersey and Pennsylvania) was distinctive. The earliest European communities here were Dutch and Swedish outposts of the fur trade that almost accidentally grew into colonies. New Netherlands, along the Hudson River and New York Bay, and New Sweden, along the Delaware River, recruited soldiers, farmers, craftsmen, clergymen and their families to meet the needs of the fur traders who bought pelts from the natives. New Sweden lasted only from 1638 to 1655, when the Dutch annexed it. New Netherlands itself fell to the English fleet in 1664. The Dutch maintained their culture in rural New York and New Jersey for more than 200 years. They also set the precedent of toleration for many ethnic, racial and religious groups in New Amsterdam. Before it became New York, the city had white, red, brown and black inhabitants; institutions for Catholics, Jews and Protestants; and a diversity that resulted in 18 different languages being spoken. Although the dominant culture in colonial New York and New Jersey became English by the end of the 1600s, the English authorities continued the tolerant traditions of the Dutch in the city.

Pennsylvania's founders were Quakers who flocked to the colony after Charles II granted the area to William Penn, an aristocratic Quaker, in 1681 as a religious refuge. As with the Pilgrims and Puritans, official English tolerance for Quakers took the form of allowing them to emigrate. Penn's publicizing of cheap land and religious freedom brought some 12,000 people to the colony before 1690. His toleration attracted a population whose diversity was matched only by New York's.

King Powhatan *comands C:Smith to be flayne his*
daughter Pokahontas beggs his life his thankfullnes
and how he Subiected 39 of their kings reade§ hifto.

PLATE 3.2 King Powhatan ordering the English adventurer John Smith (1580–1631) to be executed while the king's daughter Pocahontas begs for his life to be spared. *(Bridgeman)*

The first wave: colonial immigration, 1680–1776

The founders had come for economic gain and religious freedom, but their descendants gave the first large wave of European newcomers a warm welcome only if they were willing to conform to Anglo-American culture and supply needed labor. The reception that immigrants received varied according to location and the individual's qualities, from the extremes of largely hostile New England, to the more tolerant, diverse middle colonies. It was with mixed rural New York settlements of northwest Europeans in mind that St. Jean de Crévecoeur, an immigrant farmer from France, first stated in 1782 the idea that in America "individuals of all nations are melted into a new race of man." The only people who mixed in his vision, however, were northwest Europeans, and he required that the people in this first version of the melting pot had to turn their backs on their homeland cultures. Like the colonists everywhere at the time, he thought that the white people along the wilderness frontier, like the Native Americans, soon descended into savage barbarism, and he tolerated them primarily because they provided a protective buffer against the natives.

Although conditions in their homelands also played a decisive role, this first wave was possible only because after 1660 the Crown opposed emigration from England and Wales but encouraged it from other nations. In 1662, King Charles II licensed the Royal African Company as the supplier of slaves to English colonies, and during the next century about 140,000 Africans arrived after surviving the appalling conditions and brutal treatment on slave ships.

The largest group of immigrants (voluntary newcomers) was the Scots-Irish. With encouragement from the English, their ancestors left Scotland for Northern Ireland in the 1500s. Yet, roughly a quarter of a million of them left Northern Ireland after 1680 because of economic discrimination by the English. Most paid their passage across the Atlantic by becoming indentured servants (contracting to labor without wages for four to seven years in the colonies). When their term of service was finished, they usually took their "freedom dues" (a small sum of money and tools) and settled on the frontier where land was cheapest. Constantly looking for better land, the Scots-Irish are the source of the stereotype of frontier folk, who feel it is time to move if they can see the smoke from a neighbor's chimney. This moving scattered their settlements from western New England to the hill country of Georgia and made it difficult to preserve their cultural heritage.

The period's 200,000 German immigrants aroused more opposition than the Scots-Irish. The largest non-English speaking group in the colonies, they believed their descendants had to learn German if their religion and culture were to survive in North America. For mutual support, they concentrated their settlements. In the middle colonies, German families lived so closely together in some areas that others found it hard to settle among them. Like the Scots-Irish, the Germans lived on the frontier, but they usually stayed behind when settlement moved farther west. Developing German-speaking towns, they kept to themselves and showed little interest in colonial politics. For some, the last straw was the Germans' prosperity. Renowned for their hard work, caution, farming methods and concern for their property, they were too successful, according to their envious neighbors. Benjamin Franklin expressed what many feared when he said they might "Germanize us instead of us Anglicizing them." In a period so near the religious wars of the Reformation, the reception Germans met also varied according to whether they were non-conformists, reformed Lutherans or Catholics.

Other smaller groups in the first wave showed contrasting ways that immigrants could adjust to new and varied conditions. England sent some 50,000 convicts and perhaps 30,000 poor people as indentured servants to ease problems at home while supplying the labor-starved colonial economy, and these people formed an underclass that quickly Americanized. Immigration from Ireland included thousands of single, male Irish Catholic indentured servants, who assimilated even more rapidly than the Scots-Irish, because of religious discrimination and the difficulty of finding Catholic wives. The Scots, perhaps because of their hatred of English attempts to suppress their culture at home, followed a pattern more like that of the Germans, using compact settlement, religion, schooling and family networks to preserve their culture for generations in rural areas. A Catholic French enclave persisted in South Carolina, but the French Huguenots and Jews, who settled in port towns, illustrated a contrasting tendency. English colonists severely limited their civil rights and sometimes attacked their churches or synagogues, but accepted marriage with them as long as they changed their religion. As a result, their communities nearly vanished.

This first wave of immigration transformed the demography of the colonies. By 1776 English dominance had decreased from four-fifths to a bare majority (52 percent) of the population. The great diversity of the peoples in the country led Thomas Paine, the colonies' most famous political agitator, to call the US a "nation of nations" at its founding. African American slaves composed 20 percent of this population and were a majority in large parts of the southern colonies. Most Native American cultures had been forced inland, to the Appalachians or beyond. Non-English peoples were a majority in most coastal towns, Pennsylvania, the South and parts of all the other colonies. The cultural, political and economic dominance of Anglo-Americans was clear, but the first wave had played a major role in bequeathing America a tradition of pioneers on the frontier, a new vision of itself as diverse, religious tolerance, and a federal system of government that reserved most power to the new nation's quite dissimilar 13 states.

The second wave: the "old" immigrants, 1820–90

Between 1776 and the late 1820s, immigration slowed to a trickle. The struggle for independence and the founding of the nation Americanized the colonies' diverse peoples. The dominant Anglo-American culture and time weakened the old ethnic communities. Dutch and German areas of influence remained locally strong, but most ethnic groups assimilated. In the 1820s most Americans and newcomers therefore thought the situation was unprecedented when the second wave gathered strength.

A range of factors pushed Europeans from their homelands. Religious persecution drove many German Jews to emigrate, and political unrest forced out some European intellectuals and political activists, but economic push factors were decisive for most of the so-called "old" northwestern immigrants. Europe's population doubled between 1750 and 1850. In Ireland and parts of Germany rural people depended on the potato, which yielded more food per acre than grain. The rapid growth of cities encouraged farmers to switch to large-scale production based on farm machinery, the elimination of smallholdings and enclosure of common lands. With these changes, such a large population could not make a living in the countryside. As early immigrants wrote home about their experiences in the US, the alternative of solving problems at home by following routes to specific destinations where friends and relatives had settled became commonplace, and emigration rates soared.

During the 1800s, the industrial revolution and an international trade boom spread from Britain to the Continent and the US, but reached different regions at different times. If nearby cities offered industrial work or jobs in shipping, emigration rates were lower. But the population surplus from the countryside was so large that huge numbers of people left anyway. Stage migration (moving first to the city and, after some years, from there to a foreign country) became common. Following changes in the Atlantic labor market, people moved to where the jobs were. Steamships and trains made migration abroad safer, faster and cheaper, and "America letters" from family and friends in the US gave a remarkably accurate picture of changing economic conditions there. Of the 60 million people who left their homelands between 1820 and 1930, two-thirds settled in the US. During the "old" immigration, 15.5 million people made America their home.

The largest immigrant groups, in order of size, were Germans, Irish, Britons and Scandinavians, but many other peoples, including French Canadians, Chinese, Swiss and Dutch also came in large numbers. The factor that pulled most people to the US was an apparently unlimited supply of land. Few seriously considered the claims of Native Americans. Another pull factor was work. The US needed both skilled and unskilled labor. American railroad companies as well as state and territorial governments sent immigration agents to Europe to recruit people with promises of cheap fertile farms or jobs with wages much higher than they could earn at home. News of boom times in the US, land giveaways such as the Homestead Act of 1862, and the discovery of gold in California brought peaks in the rising immigration.

Settlement patterns and nativism

While the newcomers settled everywhere, they were most numerous in the manufacturing centers of the Northeast and the recently settled farmlands and frontier cities of the Midwest and Pacific coast. Immigrants found many economic niches, supplying much of the market for domestic servants, mill and factory workers, miners, loggers, sailors, fishermen and building workers. Most came with enough funds to travel to places where countrymen could help them adjust to American society, but after potato rot ruined the crop that supported Ireland's rural population, huge numbers of Irish immigrants arrived in the 1840s and 1850s with so little money that they stayed where they landed until they improved their situation.

British immigrants seemed nearly invisible because they spoke English and the Anglo-American culture was much like theirs. White and Protestant, Scandinavians had language problems that made them seem slow to comprehend, and at times they were ridiculed for their homeland ways. Nativism (the dislike of people and things foreign) plagued many "old" immigrants in spite of their apparent similarity to native-born Americans. Germans were welcomed for their technical knowledge and industry, and admired for a culture that was Europe's most respected at that time. But they were also stereotyped as Prussian marionettes or Bavarian louts, criticized for clannishness, and became the targets of temperance movements that attacked their habit of drinking in beer halls after church on Sundays. German Jews were excluded from education and professions, and were shunned in many social circles.

The Irish suffered many forms of discrimination and were often stereotyped as dirty, violent drunks. The most serious opposition they faced, however, came from anti-Catholic bigots, who burned convents and churches as early as the 1830s. All the large immigrant groups found themselves involved in controversies over the control and content of the public schools, but none were so critical of the schools' attempts to Americanize immigrant children as the Irish (usually through the reactions of Irish-American priests).

Anti-foreign agitation reached its first peak in the 1850s. Along with anti-Catholicism, this nativism focused on popular versions of ideas made famous by Alexis de Tocqueville's *Democracy in America*, which claimed that the basic social and political character of the US was transplanted to New England from the mother country. The Know Nothing or American Party believed that not only the Irish, with their alleged loyalty to the Pope in Rome, but also all non-British immigrants, threatened this precious heritage, and so proposed tripling the time needed to gain US citizenship and restricting immigrants' voting rights. On that platform, Know Nothings won dozens of seats in Congress and numerous state and local offices, especially in the Northeast. Internal divisions and the coming of the Civil War defused this nativist movement. Another arose in the 1860s in the West and achieved its goal, the Chinese Exclusion Act, which ended Chinese immigration in 1882. Racism and the fear of unemployment and depressed wages motivated the labor organizations that spearheaded the campaign.

The third wave: the "new" immigrants, 1890–1930

The "new" immigration marked a change in the origin of most immigrants. Around 1890 immigration from northwestern Europe declined sharply (but did not stop), while arrivals from southern and eastern Europe rose. By 1907, four out of five newcomers were "new" immigrants. Between 1890 and 1914, the volume of immigration also soared, topping a million annually several times and equaling the 15.5 million of the old immigration in just 24 years. In numerical order, the largest "new" groups were Italians, Jews, Poles and Hungarians, but many Mexicans, Russians, Czechs, Greeks, Portuguese, Syrians, Japanese, Filipinos and others also immigrated.

To most Americans, the change mostly involved the feeling that the typical immigrant had become much less like them. The religions, languages, manners and dress of the Slavic peoples seemed exotic or incomprehensible. But this tidal wave of people was in several ways similar to its predecessors. The basic economic push and pull factors had not changed. The new immigrants had the same dream of bettering their own and their children's future. Like the Puritans, eastern European Jews emigrated because of religious persecution, chiefly the bloody Russian pogroms.

By the late 1800s falling train and steamship ticket prices (often prepaid by relatives in America) made migration affordable even for the very poor and the young. Cheap travel also permitted people to see immigration as a short-term strategy, and many new immigrants were sojourners, "birds of passage," who stayed only long enough to save money to buy land or a small business in the old country. In general, the new immigrants were younger, more often unmarried, and more likely to travel as individuals rather than in family groups. The opportunities in America had changed too. The closing of the frontier around 1890 signaled the end of the era of government land giveaways. Less than a quarter of the newcomers found employment in agriculture. The Japanese in California are the best example of those who succeeded by buying unwanted land and making it productive. Four-fifths of immigrants went where the jobs were: to the industries in the big cities of the Northeast and Midwest. America had an enormous need for factory workers, but due to mechanization, most jobs were unskilled and poorly paid.

A renewed immigration debate and immigration restriction

The size of the new immigration and the altered job market resulted in larger urban immigrant quarters than Americans had ever seen. Crime, overcrowding, unsanitary conditions and epidemics in immigrant ghettos caused alarm and reform before the Civil War. Now these problems seemed insurmountable, and many Americans became convinced that the more "exotic" foreigners could not be assimilated or even integrated into society. Reactions to the situation in the cities were various. Reformers established "settlement houses" and charities to help immigrants adjust, worked to Americanize them and fought for better housing and parks. Some thought that the ghettos were important buffer zones where immigrants could use their mother tongues and follow old-country traditions while gradually adjusting to the US. Others concluded that the ghettos proved that restrictive immigration laws were needed.

In 1908, Israel Zangwill's play *The Melting Pot* popularized the idea that the diverse groups in the US would eventually fuse many races and cultures through intermarriage and become a new people. To many a native-born reformer, that was a more radical version of the melting pot than they could accept, and to them the metaphor meant that the immigrants should conform to Anglo-American culture, for their own good. Nativists of the time could not imagine a greater calamity than such a melting pot "mongrelization" of the white race. An opposing, progressive view was that the US should be an example of what Horace Kallen called "cultural pluralism," the belief in a collection of cultures united by loyalty to the same political and civic ideals. But pluralists had long split over the issue of race. The founding fathers, for example, made the national motto "e pluribus unum" (out of many, one), but in the Naturalization Act of 1790, they permitted foreigners to become American citizens only if they were white.

Restriction, even regulation of immigration, was slow to develop in the US, which encouraged immigration and, until 1875 only asked local authorities to count immigrants. Foreigners could become citizens in five years and vote as soon as they applied for citizenship. In 1891, the federal government took responsibility for regulating immigration and the next year opened Ellis Island, the famous screening depot for immigrants in New York Bay. Starting in 1910, the federal government operated a detention center to interrogate Asian immigrants before they won approval to enter the country through San Francisco Bay. In the 1920s those who believed the US could not successfully integrate so many immigrants won the passage of severely restrictive, racist immigration laws. The National Quota Acts represented the climax of a campaign for restriction that achieved its first result in 1875, when the federal government began a piecemeal listing of banned groups that, in time, included contract laborers, the Chinese, convicts, prostitutes, lunatics, idiots, paupers, polygamists, political radicals, the Japanese and illiterates.

The influence of eugenics, the pseudo-scientific racism of the early 1900s, which purported to prove experimentally the superiority of Anglo-Saxons over all other "races," was evident in the list and later legislation. So was the combination of First World War super-patriotism that demanded 100 percent Americanism, and the ideological insecurity that grew after the Russian Revolution of 1917. Finally in 1921, Congress passed the first general limitation on immigration, the Emergency Quota Act that drastically reduced the annual number of European newcomers to 358,000 (less than one-third of pre-war

PLATE 3.3 The registration room at Ellis Island in New York Bay in 1912, where government officials decided on the eligibility of most new immigrants to enter the US.
(Underwood and Underwood/Corbis)

levels), and introduced nationality quotas. Each European nation's allotment of immigrant visas per year equaled 3 percent of the foreign-born in the US from that country at the federal census of 1910.

The dissatisfaction of restrictionists with this law revealed the groups they feared most, Asians and the new immigrants from Europe. In 1924 the Asian Exclusion Act ended all immigration from Asian nations, and a National Origins Quota Act reduced European nationality quotas to 2 percent. More important, it moved the census for counting the foreign-born of each group back to 1890, when only small numbers of "new" immigrants were in the US, so that their quotas became much smaller. The 1924 Act also introduced a new concept, national *origins* quotas, based on the accumulated part of the American population of each European national background and the increase of each between 1790 and 1920, which cut the quotas for all European nations but the United Kingdom by one-half to two-thirds. In 1929, when the national origins quotas went into effect, Britain's was 65,361, while Italy's, for example, was 5,802 and Syria received the minimum of 100 visas. This narrow, specifically Anglo-American definition of the national identity remained the legal framework for immigration to the US until 1965.

Wartime policies and the search for principle in immigration policy

Writing immigration law that functions as intended has proved difficult. The Quota Acts did end the new immigration, and arrivals from northern and western Europe did fall sharply, but immigration from the United Kingdom also declined. Even the western European nations with much reduced quotas left those unfilled. Nor did Congress guess that arrivals from "non-quota" nations in the Western Hemisphere, such as Mexico and US territories and the Philippines and Puerto Rico, would soar into the millions by 1960. Events during these years defied governmental plans. The depression of the 1930s put a stop to mass immigration. Local authorities and "vigilantes" forcibly deported about half a million Mexican Americans, many of them US citizens, during that decade. Nazi and fascist regimes caused an enormous flow of refugees, 250,000 of whom Congress admitted as non-quota immigrants under special laws. Many more, including 20,000 Jewish children, were turned away because the US was unwilling to put aside national origins quotas during a time of high unemployment and rising anti-Semitism.

The Second World War and the Cold War caused several contrasting shifts in policy. The government imported temporary farm labor from Mexico under the "*bracero* program" due to wartime labor shortages and lifted the ban on Chinese immigration because of foreign policy considerations. Yet it also bowed to panicky racists on the West Coast, who feared foreign spies, and confined 115,000 Japanese Americans in "internment camps," confiscating most of their property. After the war, federal law provided for the entry of families formed by US service people abroad, and several hundred thousand displaced persons (those so uprooted by the war that they had no homes to return to) were admitted by Acts of Congress. Between 1948 and 1959, Cold War refugees from communist countries, such as Hungary and Cuba, also came. The total of non-quota immigrants for those years reached 750,000, and made a mockery of the idea of regulating immigration according to national origins quotas.

Moreover, during the Cold War, when the US competed with the USSR for the allegiance of non-aligned nations, the racist principles underlying the quotas were a foreign policy embarrassment. In 1952, the McCarran–Walter Act stated that race was no longer a reason for refusing someone an immigrant visa. Instead it started the so-called "brain-drain" to the US by reserving the first 50 percent of visas for each country for people with needed skills. But the law kept the national origins principle, gave many Third World countries tiny quotas, and made communist or socialist associations a bar to immigration. Pressure for an entirely new approach grew.

The Immigration Act of 1965 provided this new approach, but also had unforeseen consequences. It replaced national origins quotas with hemispheric limits to annual immigration. To emphasize equal treatment, all nations in the eastern hemisphere had the same limit of 20,000 immigrants annually. A system of preferences set principles for selecting immigrants. Reunifying families, the most important principle, reserved nearly three-quarters of immigrant visas for relatives of American citizens or resident aliens. Spouses, minor children and parents were admitted outside the limits. Grown children as well as brothers and sisters were given special preferences. The second principle continued the "brain-drain" by reserving 20 percent of visas for skilled people. Refugees received the remaining visas. Legislation made the national limit and preference system global in the 1970s.

Congress intended to make up for past injustices to southern and eastern Europeans through family reunification visas for siblings and grown children, which it hoped would lead to the reappearance of the "new" immigrants. For ten years the plan worked, but by 1980 it became clear that the family preferences benefited people from other nations much more. In 1965 Europe and Canada provided the majority of immigrants to the US, but by 1980 less than one-sixth came from those places and four-fifths were almost equally divided between Asia and Latin America. Expecting Western nuclear families, American law-makers did not anticipate, for example, how foreign students from Third World countries, especially Asians, would adjust their legal status upon graduation and become immigrants who used the family reunification clauses to bring in extended families.

The fourth wave: 1965 to the present

The 1965 law ushered in the fourth major wave of immigration, which rose to a peak in the late 1990s and produced the highest immigration totals in American history by the end of the decade. In addition to the many immigrants allowed by the hemispheric limits (changed to a global total of 320,000 in 1980), the wave has included hundreds of thousands of immediate relatives and refugees outside those limits. It has also contained millions of illegal aliens, who cross borders without papers (or with false ones) or arrive at airports on student or tourist visas and then overstay.

Between 1961 and 2010 more than 34.5 million people secured legal permanent resident status in the US. The Census Bureau estimated that 10.8 million more were in the country as undocumented or illegal immigrants in 2010. The list of the ten largest nationality groups among these is shown in Table 3.1 for 1960, 2007 and 2011. The table shows only one Latino and no Asian immigrant groups but many European nationalities in 1960. The prominence of Mexicans around halfway down the list, however, foreshadowed future trends. At the peak of the fourth wave in the 1990s, some 9.5 million more newcomers arrived. The second list of groups, from 2007, well *after* the peak brought by the 1965 Act, reveals the law's unexpected benefits for the Third World immigrants of the fourth wave. In 2007 no Europeans were in the ten largest immigrant groups. Three-quarters of the legally resident foreign-born (more than 38 million people) were Latino (51 percent) or Asian (25 percent). Remarkably, another 42 percent of the immigrant population in 2007 consisted of people whose nations contributed less than the ten nationalities listed in the chart. In other words, although this wave is predominantly Latino and Asian, it is also the most diverse wave the US has seen. Another striking feature of the table is the Mexicans' rise in prominence from a mere 6 percent in 1960 to a presence approaching a third of the entire group in the 2007 and 2011 lists of immigrants.

Central Americans and Asians have long been the chief global regions sending the US people in the fourth wave. Yet important shifts have occurred in migration to the US between 2007 and 2012–13. Mexican immigration began to fall sharply in 2007 and within three years it and even the combined immigration from Latin America—including those coming in illegally—was surpassed by increased arrivals of newcomers from Asia. By mid-2012 Asian Americans had replaced Hispanics as the largest and most rapidly growing racial group in the country.

Like the earlier waves of newcomers, the fourth includes a broad range of socio-economic groups. One result of saving visas for needed occupations is that a very noticeable minority are highly skilled workers, professionals (especially engineers, doctors and nurses), and entrepreneurs with capital. The large majority of *both* legal and illegal immigrants are similar to those who have arrived since the

TABLE 3.1 The effects of the fourth wave on the ten largest immigrant groups, 1960 contrasted with 2007 and 2011

1960	%*	2007	%	2011	%
1 Italians	(13%)	1 Mexicans	(31%)	1 Mexicans	(29%)
2 Germans	(10%)	2 Filipinos	(4.4%)	2 Chinese**	(5%)
3 Canadians	(10%)	3 Chinese ***	(4.3%)	3 Indians	(5%)
4 British	(9%)	4 Indians	(4.1%)	4 Filipinos	(4%)
5 Poles	(8%)	5 Vietnamese	(3.0%)	5 Salvadorans	(3%)
6 USSR residents	(7%)	6 Salvadorans	(2.8%)	6 Vietnamese	(3%)
7 Mexicans	(6%)	7 Koreans	(2.7%)	7 Cubans	(3%)
8 Irish	(3%)	8 Cubans	(2.5%)	8 Koreans	(3%)
9 Austrians	(3%)	9 Dominicans	(2.3%)	9 Dominicans	(2%)
10 Hungarians	(3%)	10 Canadians	(2.3%)	10 Guatemalans	(2%)

* = percent of the total foreign-born in the US

**excluding Taiwan but including Hong Kong

*** including Taiwan and Hong Kong

Sources: Migration Policy Institute, 2012; American Community Survey (ACS, 2011); Yearbook of Immigration Statistics 2007, Office of Immigration Statistics, US Department of Homeland Security.

1820s. They are above average educationally and economically at home but, with the exception of Asian immigrants, are below average in these areas in the US. They have come because commercialization and industrialization (now revolutionizing the Third World) have disrupted their traditional economies.

At the socio-economic bottom of this wave are often recently arrived groups of refugees from wars and other disasters. In the 1960s and early 1980s huge groups of people fled southeast Asia to the US as a result of America's involvement in the Vietnam War. The poorest also include people who obtain visas because they are near relatives of recent, more skilled immigrants or who take jobs Americans do not want. Among the latter are Latino women recruited by agencies as live-in domestic servants and nannies. Spreading the word about these jobs and moving into better-paid work once they have acquired more English, they bring their families and forge the links in "chain migration" based on a network of female contacts.

The limits on authorized immigration to the US are very liberal. In 2012 the annual global cap for legal immigration was 675,000. That is, the government issued that many immigrant visas each year. Immediate family members are not counted in the cap and come in as additional legal immigrants. Family reunification rules allotted 480,000 visas. People with needed skills, 140,000 of them, entered through employment visas. Another 55,000 got their "green card" as legal immigrants through the diversity lottery, which was planned to distribute visas among nationalities that have not immigrated in large numbers recently. No individual country could receive more than 7 percent of the total visas.

The nationalities and skin colors of most people in this wave are different and more various, however, and they arrive in different ways and settle in different places. There are colonies of Hmong in Minneapolis, Vietnamese on the Mississippi Delta, East Indian hotel-owners across the Sunbelt, Middle-Eastern Muslims in Dearborn, Michigan and New Jersey and large concentrations of Latinos not only in the Southwest and the nation's big cities, where their communities are large and

PLATE 3.4 Unauthorized Latino immigrants crossing the high metal barrier fence along the Mexican border, Tijuana, Mexico.
(Les Stone/Sygma/Corbis)

long established, but also across the rural districts and small towns of the South and Midwest, where their population has grown by 70 to 80 percent between the last US federal censuses. These large foreign-born settlements have given rise to contemporary forms of racism and nativism. Groping for ways to adjust to the changes in their country's population, some Americans are again resorting to broad stereotypes.

Attitudes to immigrants: the contemporary debate

In 1982, when the Gallup Organization asked Americans whether specific ethnic groups had been good or bad for the US, on the whole, the longer the group had been the country, the more favorable was the public response. Thus, by then large majorities thought Irish Catholics and Jews, who earlier suffered from widespread discrimination, had been good influences on the country. Racial attitudes, however, appeared to be decisive in creating long-term low opinions of non-white ethnic groups. Less than half of the Americans questioned in 1982 thought Japanese, Chinese and African Americans had favorably affected the country, and only one in five or less approved of having recent non-white groups, such as Puerto Ricans, Vietnamese and Haitians in the US.

PLATE 3.5   A multiethnic, multiracial crowd enjoying a recent Macy's Thanksgiving Day Parade in New York City.
(Joseph Sohm/Corbis)

Large numbers of Asian immigrants in the fourth wave arrived with more capital and a higher level of education than most Latinos. Those facts and popular attitudes towards some Asian cultures' emphasis on respect for parents, education and hard work have led some media commentators to lump all Asian Americans together under the label of the "model minority." This ignores the large majority of Asian immigrants who come with little money and education; the problems of Asian refugees who have experienced wartime traumas; and job discrimination and violence against Asian Americans. For its own convenience, the federal government invented the word "Hispanics" to put in a single category all the Central and South American Spanish-speaking cultures arriving in the US in the fourth wave. A handy label for official statistics, the word became identified with illegal immigrants in the popular mind because of the large number of immigrants unlawfully crossing the border with Mexico. It thus contributed to prejudice against hugely diverse Latino populations. About 52 percent of "illegals" are Mexicans, but the "undocumented" come from countries as diverse as China, Nigeria and Iran.

Illegal immigration causes heated debate over government policy to control entry to the US. One segment of public opinion stresses that tolerating illegal immigration encourages a general disregard for the law, lowers wages for other workers, and undermines the 1965 law that gives all nationalities an equal chance for immigrant visas. Other Americans emphasize that illegal immigrants take jobs that US citizens do not want, are paid less than the legal minimum wage, work in substandard conditions, and, while needing the benefits of social welfare programs, dare not reveal their situation for fear of being deported.

The federal government responded to this ongoing debate in 1986 by passing the Immigration Reform and Control Act (IRCA). The law attempted to minimize illegal immigration while expressing acceptance and giving rights to people already inside the US. It set fines and penalties for employers who hire illegal aliens and also attempted to prevent employment discrimination through rules that outlawed firing or refusing to hire people because they look foreign. The law offered "amnesty" (legal immigrant status) for illegals who had stayed in the US for four years and for many temporarily resident farm workers. Almost 3 million people became legal immigrants through the IRCA. Their improved situation was the one great success of the legislation. It proved difficult to document that employers had broken the law, and the number of illegals, which declined at first, rose again to between 9 and 11 million in a few years.

In spite of rising reactions against immigration in the 1980s, national policy became more liberal through the Immigration Act of 1990. It raised the annual total of immigrant visas, the limit for individual nations and the number of asylum seekers who could remain in the US. It also removed restrictions on the entry of many groups, including homosexuals, communists, people from nations adversely affected by the 1965 law, and additional family members, including the spouses and children, of illegals given amnesty. During the economic boom of the 1990s,

Chapter 4

The people
Women and minorities

- The reason for American women's and minority history
- Women in America
- Native Americans
- Lesbian, gay, bisexual and transgender Americans
- African Americans
- Asian Americans
- Latinos
- *Exercises*
- *Further reading*
- *Websites*

The reason for American women's and minority history

Discrimination has given women and some minorities a special status in American society. For much of American history, male-dominated society in the US has forced women, Native Americans, African Americans, Asian Americans, Latinos and people with minority sexual orientations into inferior categories. As a result, these groups have their own histories as subjects of changing opinion and government policy even though their experiences are integral parts of the nation's history. They have molded American history through their struggles for equality and resistance against discrimination. Inequality has led to group differences in attitudes, class, occupation, income, health, housing and crime. The gap between national ideals and the realities of prejudice has agitated the nation's conscience and prompted a very uneven but persistent progress toward greater equality.

There has been constant debate over the proper means of creating a more just society. Neither policymakers nor the subjects of policy have agreed on the course to follow. More than a century of federal civil rights laws has proved that changes in the law often do not function as intended, nor do they assure changes in attitudes. Defining what equality means has proved difficult. Most Americans have supported equality of opportunity (an equal chance to develop one's abilities and to be rewarded for them) but not equality of results (an evening-out of economic, social and political power). In practice, equality of opportunity and most attempts to redistribute wealth have failed or have been short-lived. Affirmative action programs and election districts that arrange for preferential treatment of women and minorities, in order to correct the effects of past discrimination, have faced increasingly strong opposition and been discontinued, in part by Supreme Court decisions. Although Americans favor equality, they are at odds about what it is and about the degree to which government can or should provide it.

Women in America

Numerically a majority, women today experience unequal treatment in significant ways. They are assigned (or are socialized to choose) prescribed roles and do not as often work in the most prestigious occupations, earn as much money or enjoy positions of equal social status as men. Popular attitudes continue to keep too many women in traditional places. Mostly working in poorly paid service jobs, they remain severely under-represented in the highest levels of politics and business management. Nevertheless, great changes in their position have occurred and continue to take place in the twenty-first century.

Historically, women's legal status in America was determined by English common law. Until the mid-1800s, a woman experienced a "civil death" upon marriage, which meant she ceased to exist legally except through her spouse. She had no right to own property, control her wages or sign contracts. Divorce, granted only in extreme cases, was easier to obtain for men than for women. A single woman was expected to submit to her father's or brother's will until she married. Claiming that women were physically frail and mentally limited by nature, men kept women dependent.

There were historical circumstances and attitudes that worked against or contradicted this conventional view of women. On the Western frontier, women's skills were as essential as men's and the scarcity of women meant they could not be pampered. "Back East" the shortage of men meant widows and single women were often courted and needed to fill the occupational roles of men. From the earliest colonial days, most American women have worked. Before the industrial revolution, most handicrafts were practiced at home, and women were expected to be as proficient as men. Women were a majority among the first factory workers when the industrial revolution began in New England textile mills. Before the Civil War they worked in more than 100 occupations, mostly less skilled industrial ones, but earned on average about one-quarter of men's wages. Women were among the first workers involved in strikes for higher pay and better working conditions. They joined the labor movement from its beginning and formed their own unions when men showed little interest in organizing them.

The nineteenth century

Some middle- and upper-class white women were leisured or had no paid work at home. Among these were the founders of girls' schools between 1800 and 1850 and of famous women's colleges, such as Vassar and Mount Holyoke, in the latter 1800s. These social classes also produced most of the century's female reformers, who were prominent in the crusade against alcohol abuse and in movements to improve conditions in prisons, insane asylums, hospitals, schools and immigrant ghettos. The first movement for women's rights was closely related to female reformers' experiences in abolitionist (anti-slavery) campaigns. Women abolitionists publicized parallels between discrimination against African Americans and women after they were attacked as "unwomanly" for speaking to mixed audiences of men and women. In 1848 two abolitionists, Lucretia Mott and Elizabeth Cady Stanton, led the first women's rights convention in Seneca Falls, New York. In language taken from the Declaration of Independence, the convention's "Declaration of Sentiments" called for property and divorce rights, educational and employment opportunities, and the vote.

Thereafter, the women's movement held regular conventions and worked to realize its stated goals. Before the Civil War, Susan B. Anthony led successful efforts to improve women's status in marriage and divorce cases, as well as their economic rights, under New York state law. A few years later, however, these liberal provisions were repealed. Women were increasingly accepted as teachers and moved into nursing and government-office work during the war. Feminists joined the successful campaign for the constitutional abolition of slavery through the Thirteenth Amendment, but the movement split in two when it became clear that only African American men were offered the vote in the Fifteenth Amendment.

One faction opposed broadening the franchise if it excluded women, championed a wide range of women's rights and pursued the vote through a *federal* women's suffrage amendment. Another group presented women's voting rights as a separate issue from suffrage for African American men, avoided involvement in other causes that might alienate influential groups and concentrated on winning the vote on a state-by-state basis.

The latter group first tasted victory when Wyoming Territory granted female suffrage in 1869, but of 17 states that considered women's suffrage between 1870 and 1910, only three approved it. Several other states gave women voting rights limited to municipal or school issues and elections. Although men continued to deny women membership in unions for skilled workers, female activists assisted unskilled women's unionization and mounted successful campaigns against child labor. On the other hand, their fight for abortion rights, birth control and membership on juries met with failure until after the Second World War.

The twentieth century

The movement united behind efforts for ratification of the Nineteenth Amendment, which granted women the right to vote in all elections in 1920. Women strongly supported campaigns to deal with political corruption and urban social problems at the turn of the century, so many male politicians thought they would vote for a broad range of social reforms or form a women's party to defeat conservative male candidates.

But women voters divided over issues in much the same way as men. Many women's rights organizations disbanded soon after suffrage was won, and women's economic position improved slowly in part because of disagreement within the movement. Female social reformers who demanded protective measures that treated women as a special category successfully lobbied for laws limiting women's working hours and occupational choices to protect their safety and health. Until the 1970s civil rights legislation for women and court decisions affecting their rights were generally based on such a protectionist approach.

Other feminists insisted that this approach kept women in poorly paid jobs and prevented equality with men because it assumed that women were the weaker sex. These activists proposed another constitutional change as early as 1923, the Equal Rights Amendment (ERA), to remove the remaining legal inequalities between men and women. Some opponents of the ERA feared it would overturn protective legislation for women. Such dissension, but even more the generally conservative mood of the country, led to the relative dormancy of the women's movement between the late 1920s and the early 1960s. The turning point in women's employment came after World War II. Many married women who went to work during the war continued to work after it, and many more joined them in the following decades. While 15 percent of married women were employed in 1940, by 1970 almost 50 percent had jobs outside the home. Many more married women were working, and by 1979 the majority were middle-aged and middle-class. Husbands accepted the change with little protest because most wives did not take jobs until the children entered school and then earned wages that kept the family in the middle class. Not only were larger numbers of women of all classes, married and single, working, but a larger percentage of them were getting a higher education.

Thus, when a new women's movement blossomed in the 1960s and 1970s, challenging the view that women's place was keeping house, many Americans agreed. The reality they lived no longer squared with the conventions of the past. Again stimulated by African Americans' demands for civil rights, the women's movement lobbied effectively for the 1964 Civil Rights Act, which was the first such legislation to explicitly ban discrimination based on sex as well as on race. The more radical feminists of the 1970s rejected conventional gender roles and family life as stifling, patriarchal and frequently dysfunctional. By mid-decade, women's lobbying had helped pass laws that promised women equal treatment in the job market and admission to higher education, equal pay for equal work and equal availability of loans and credit. Advocates of women's rights also pursued their goals through litigation (court cases). In 1973 the Supreme Court allowed for limited abortion rights through the *Roe* v. *Wade* case brought by women lawyers, and since then the court has further limited abortion rights only marginally. In a series of rulings during the 1970s and 1980s, it also supported affirmative action programs that aimed to increase the number of women and minorities among employees or students until it equaled their proportion in the local population. In the 1978 *Regents* v. *Bakke* case, the court struck down a policy of using numerical quotas for affirmative action, but it still supports flexible programs that encourage companies and institutions to actively recruit women and minorities. In the 1990s, however, rising public opposition to affirmative action was evident in a referendum in California and a federal district court decision in a Texas case that ended "positive discrimination" in favor of women and minorities in those states. Since that time affirmative action programs and court cases have usually concerned not gender but efforts to ensure racial and ethnic diversity.

The ERA proved to be the major initiative for women's rights in the twentieth century that ultimately failed. Its text stated that neither the states nor the federal government could limit a person's rights on the basis of sex. In 1972 Congress passed the ERA with little opposition. To become a part of the Constitution, it then had to be approved by three-quarters of the state legislatures. After many states passed it in the early 1970s, however, support lagged and the ERA fell three states short of ratification in 1982.

Explanations for its failure differ. Some believe the conservative swing in public opinion that elected Ronald Reagan worked against ratification. Opposition among women who felt their accepted role would be undermined also weakened the chances for success. Others note that national opinion polls throughout the period showed majorities for ratification, but emphasize the difficulty in winning the three-quarters majority of states required. The National Organization for Women (NOW, founded by a group of older, moderate women in 1966) asserted that the struggle for ratification was well worth the effort because it raised women's awareness of their social position, involved them in the political process on their own behalf, and helped pass equal rights provisions to many state constitutions. Yet others comment that the ERA was not necessary by the 1980s because civil rights laws and court decisions had accomplished the same goal.

PLATE 4.1 The fight for women's rights in the United States. Two suffragists put up a billboard in New York City around 1917.
(C.J. Tavin/Everett/Rex Features)

Evaluating the contemporary situation for women

Today, court action has reduced the legal hindrances to equality between the sexes. "Protective" laws based on sexual stereotypes have been repeatedly overturned. Employment ads cannot ask for applicants of only one sex. Most large private organizations that prohibit female members are banned. Federal Courts support strict laws against sexual harassment (unwanted sexual advances). Polls indicate that since law professor Anita Hill accused Supreme Court nominee Clarence Thomas of sexual harassment during televised Senate hearings in 1991, more women are prepared to take men to court over sexual offences, and more men expect them to do so. Judicial approval of state laws granting unpaid maternity leaves in the late 1980s led more private employers and public authorities to institute maternity leave programs. In 1993 Congress mandated unpaid leave after the birth of a child for some 42 million public workers. By the early twenty-first century, many employers also offered child day-care centers for working mothers, but women in low-wage jobs were seldom offered these facilities and could not afford to take unpaid maternity leave.

Women's groups and public surveys continue to indicate that in these and other ways, the progress made since the 1970s has been limited. For instance, sex

PLATE 4.2 Thousands of pro-choice supporters marched in New York during August 2004, when the Republicans held their national party convention in the city, to show their stance on the issue of abortion.

(Sipa Press/Rex Features)

crime remains unabated, despite efforts at reform. In 2012, three out of four rapes did not lead to an arrest, exactly as was the case at the end of the 1970s. Many times a rape is not only untested legally, it is uninvestigated. The reforms of the last 40 years mean that the victim's sexual history no longer becomes evidence for the defense, the law no longer requires a corroborating witness to the crime, and police medical officers must use a "rape kit" to collect evidence from victims.

Commentators note that an important part of the problem is that most rapes are committed by people familiar to the violated women and that in such cases police and legal officers often act on the assumption that many of these accusations are false or impossible to prove. Critics in women's groups who focus on the easy availability of pornography and media violence as causes of rape as well as child and wife abuse have won few policy changes.

Since the end of the 1970s the rate of women engaged in bachelors or higher degrees has steadily risen over men's higher education. Yet in 2010—nearly a half century after the Equal Pay Act (1963) became federal law to end gender-based differences in pay—women's earnings remained on average only three-quarters of men's. Furthermore, women still earn higher degrees mostly in fields traditional for women that offer lower earnings (such as the fine arts, foreign languages and nursing), even though today women are making unprecedented inroads in highly paid "male" professions (such as engineering, medicine and the law).

Some sense of recent changes in women's educational situation appears evident from yet another affirmative action case. In *Grutter* v. *Bollinger* a white woman went to court against the University of Michigan law school to prove that she had been refused admission in 1997 because of the institution's affirmative action policies that gave preference to underrepresented groups in the student body, such as Native Americans, Latinos and blacks. In 2003 the US Supreme Court decided against her, declaring in a 5–4 decision that racial diversity was a "compelling interest" in the university's efforts to provide the "educational benefits that flow from a diverse student body." In 2006, however, voters ended the university's affirmative action program in a state referendum. See the comments on the *Grutter* case later in the chapter.

The number and size of businesses owned by women has risen rapidly since the late 1990s, but the increase here is also mostly in healthcare services, where female owners controlled between half and three-quarters of facilities in 2010. Women ran for, and were elected to, high public office in record numbers in the 1990s and the first decade of the 2000s. The number of female state governors, members of state legislatures and the US Congress reached new heights. In 2008 Hillary Rodham Clinton, the former first lady, by nearly winning the Democratic Party's nomination for the presidency, became the first seriously competitive female candidate for that office. In 2011 women's representation on big business's Fortune 500 boards reached a new high of 16 percent, an increase of less than 4 percent in the last decade. After the 2012 elections for the first time one in five US senators were women. Still, that fraction illustrates how women remain far outnumbered by men at the higher levels of government and management.

Perhaps most worryingly, women's economic position still seemed to illustrate in exaggerated form the distance between the rich and the poor in the 1980s and 1990s. The "feminization of poverty" continued to increase, especially after the economic boom of the 1990s ended. The income of working single mothers increased at a slower rate to that of other families during the boom and fell more rapidly after it. While the 1996 Welfare Reform Act helped many people find work in good times, from 2004 onward increased numbers of single mothers found themselves without work or without day-care for their children, or both. Women, especially non-white and immigrant women in service trades, were several times as likely to be living in poverty as men, and female-headed families made up nearly half of all poor families.

Native Americans

Native Americans became a small minority as a result of a long history of successful invasion, military conflict and pressure by Europeans and then white Americans. The conflict was always an uneven one. In the very early days, Native Americans outnumbered the invaders at the point of contact, but their opponents possessed insurmountable technological advantages, including metal weapons, textiles, written languages and books. Epidemics caused by a lack of immunity to European diseases, moreover, reduced the Native American population drastically while the influx of Europeans became enormous. European and white American cultures were also more aggressively expansive and acquisitive than indigenous cultures.

Patterns formed in the colonial period

British settlers came in much greater numbers than other Europeans and primarily sought land, rather than trading partners or mineral riches. They presented Native Americans with a threatening front of compact settlement, brought their own women and segregated themselves from the natives. Thus, no large mixed race of "mestizos" appeared in British America.

Relations between the natives and the English were marked by distrust, resentment and disastrous wars. A predictable sequence of events set the pattern for almost 300 years of contact. First was a short period of relative peace when the settlers exchanged technology for land, furs and knowledge of the Native Americans' survival techniques. Then conflicts caused by trade disagreements, expanded white settlement and cultural misunderstanding escalated into full-scale war. In the 1620s and 1630s the natives tried, by war, to expel the intruders and threatened the existence of the Virginia and New England colonies. During the third phase of massive retaliation, the natives were defeated militarily. Often the colonists received help from tribes that were traditional enemies of those that attacked the settlements. During the final phase, Anglo-American policies aimed at easing the expansion of settlement while minimizing the "Indian threat." For the most part, colonists were left to devise their own solutions to this threat until the 1750s. In victory they usually tried to exterminate native opponents, drive them farther inland or enslave and deport them. Often, the settlers negotiated treaties based on a policy of forced separation to free territory for colonial settlement and to end violence. The natives were moved to distant lands that (the colonists promised) would be reserved for them permanently. In short, the "Indian reservation" system dates back to the 1630s and 1640s.

Colonial authorities promised to protect the rights of reservation natives. Some colonists also encouraged them to adopt European ways and Christianity. In New England, villages of Christianized natives were known as "praying towns," for example. But assimilation on distant reservations failed. Native peoples further west attacked the reservations because they objected to intrusions into their territory. Colonists squatted on reservation land when it was no longer distant from colonial settlement, and colonial authorities rarely acted to limit settlement. Native Americans resented and resisted attempts to assimilate them. Thus one cycle of violent conflict followed another, and Native Americans were continually pushed further west. In outline, with the substitution of US for British authorities, this general sequence of developments continued into the early 1900s.

In the eighteenth century, Britain and France competed for power in North America. Both vied for native allies, which led Native American groups to offer their allegiance to the highest bidder. The Iroquois Confederacy in western New York and Pennsylvania, for instance, was especially successful in playing one European power against the other and for a long time was able to channel white settlement to the south of its territory. The French generally won support from more tribes because their trading activities seemed far less threatening. To change this, the British government established a new policy during the French and Indian War (1754–63). It gave gifts to native leaders, bypassed the colonists through direct negotiations with the natives and, most importantly, set a western limit to colonial settlement.

The Proclamation of 1763 made a line west of the Appalachian Mountains the official boundary of British America. To the west of the line was "Indian Country," which settlers had to leave. Parliament had applied the colonists' policy of separation to both settlers and natives and had created a huge Native American reservation. Its action brought enough tribes to Britain's side to defeat the French, who gave up much of their land claims in North America. The line infuriated the colonists, who ignored the proclamation but cited the limit on western settlement as a reason for rebelling against the mother country. When the American Revolution came, most tribes remained loyal to Britain. The US therefore treated several tribes as conquered nations after the war and demanded their lands without payment.

Conquest and removal, 1783–1860

Through the treaty of 1783, Britain ceded to the US all the land between Canada and Florida to the Mississippi River and asked no protection for Native American rights. With the coming of peace, tens of thousands of settlers moved into the area, but more than 100,000 Native Americans blocked their way. In the Great Lakes region a powerful native confederacy would not permit settlers north of the Ohio River. On the Southern frontier, several tribes refused to give up lands, despite pressure from Southern states. First the US sent armies against the Northern confederacy to take its land by conquest. When American forces suffered repeated defeats, however, the US negotiated a treaty after its first major victory. The confederacy ceded huge amounts of land but won annual payments of goods and cash in return. Thus the US government set an important precedent that recognized Native American land claims and the need to pay for lands taken by settlers. Abandoning reliance on military conquest, many American leaders promoted a new version of the assimilation policy. Congress sent teachers and missionaries to the natives to transform them into farmers who could live in American society. The Native Americans were not asked if they wanted to be "civilized," and those who favored harsher policies said their resistance was proof that assimilation was impossible.

Meanwhile, observing the rapid growth of the white population west of the Appalachians between 1800 and 1810, the Shawnee leaders Tecumseh and The Prophet worked to form a grand alliance of tribes east of the Mississippi to limit US expansion. Tecumseh applied to the British for help when he heard that the two nations might go to war. The difficulty of unifying warring tribes defeated the Native Americans' last attempt to control the land east of the river. While Tecumseh was lobbying for support among Southern tribes, Americans defeated his forces in the North and British guns were discovered at his headquarters. A year later Tecumseh and his allies joined the British against the US in the war of 1812, and Tecumseh was killed in 1813. The loss of leadership and British support led many tribes to move further west after the war.

Tribes who remained east of the Mississippi found themselves forced to accept a revival of the old separation policy, now called *removal* and defined as moving Native Americans west of the river. Thomas Jefferson supported the idea as early as 1803, when he argued for buying the area from the Mississippi to the Rocky Mountains (the Louisiana Purchase) from France. Removal gained popularity even with so-called "friends" of the Native Americans who said the policy would give the natives a chance to acquire social and political skills for assimilation away from white squatters, their diseases and their alcohol. In 1830 President Andrew Jackson, famous as a combatant against the Native Americans

Tecumseh.

PLATE 4.3 Tecumseh (1768–1813), Native-American chief of the Shawnee tribe, who was killed in the battle of the Thames in Canada, October 5, 1813, is shown here wearing a British medal and tunic.
(Bettmann/Corbis)

in the war of 1812, signed the Indian Removal Act. Many tribes north of the Ohio River had signed individual removal treaties before that time and had moved to parts of present-day Kansas. Now, federal policy required the removal of all remaining tribes to a permanent "Indian Territory" in today's Oklahoma. State authorities so terrorized Southern tribes that all but two (the Seminoles and the Cherokees) accepted removal as the only alternative to extermination.

The Seminoles held out for seven years through guerrilla warfare in the Florida Everglades. The Cherokees had adopted many American institutions including industries, schools, a newspaper and an American-style government and constitution during the earlier period of federal assimilation programs. Influenced by the society around them, some Cherokees (mostly those who had intermarried with Americans) were slaveholders. The Cherokees appealed to the US federal courts to fight removal plans and the state of Georgia's seizure of their lands. The Supreme Court ruling in this case (*Cherokee Nation* v. *Georgia*, 1831), set a precedent for later decisions concerning Native Americans' rights and status, even though it had little immediate effect. The court said a Native American tribe was neither an independent nation nor a state but a "domestic dependent nation." Within US borders, tribal lands were still outside American political structures. By right of first residence, Native Americans had sovereignty over their lands and could lose them only voluntarily and with just compensation. The federal government alone could negotiate with a tribe. State laws did not apply on Native American lands or reservations, where native laws took priority. American citizens could not enter Native American lands except by permission or treaty right. By implication, the Removal Act and Georgia's actions were declared illegal.

President Jackson and Georgia ignored the court's ruling. Federal troops and state militia in the winter of 1838 "escorted" the Cherokees to Indian Territory. Because of the weather, harassment by Americans, and poor government planning for food and shelter, a quarter of the Cherokees died during the march along the path known as "The Trail of Tears." By 1840 nearly 100,000 Native Americans had been forcibly removed to Indian Territory. Here, the great differences in the terrain and climate required painful adjustments for eastern woodlands peoples. Put on much smaller parcels of land, groups with long traditions of mutual hostility were forced to live side by side. Western Indians resented the newcomers' entry into their lands and raided the territory for food and livestock. Unable to cope with the situation and often not given the protection and material aid promised by the federal government, many Native Americans in the territory sank into the dependence, alcoholism and poverty their "friends" had feared.

War, concentration and forced assimilation, 1860–1934

During the Civil War, several Southern tribes in Indian Territory supported the South by supplying Confederate armies with food, and so, after the war, were asked to give up even more land by the North. At the war's end, removal was replaced with a policy of concentration as Americans occupied the prairies and plains once considered the "Great American Desert" and rushed in to profit from gold and silver strikes in the West. US government support for transcontinental railroads increased settlement and quickened the slaughter of the buffalo on which the plains natives depended. Native Americans were to be concentrated on reservations to free as much land as possible for development.

Between 1850 and 1890 the Native Americans in the West struggled unsuccessfully to keep their land. The familiar pattern of settlement, conflict escalating to war, treaty-making and treaty violation leading to new wars was repeated. At the famous battle of the Little Big Horn, for example, Dakota warriors led by Sitting Bull and Crazy Horse killed Lieutenant Colonel Custer and his men when they attempted to punish the Native Americans for attacking gold prospectors who broke the treaty with the Dakotas by entering their sacred Black Hills. The era of open warfare ended with the so-called battle of Wounded Knee. This bloodbath resulted from clumsy attempts by American authorities to suppress the Ghost Dance religion that promised believers a return to the happy conditions before the appearance of the whites. Accused of promoting the religion, Sitting Bull was arrested and killed by Native American police while in custody. When US soldiers tried to disarm a nearby group of Dakotas at Wounded Knee Creek, they fought back in anger over reservation conditions and the death of Sitting Bull. The panicked troops sprayed the men, women and children with gunfire until all 300 were dead.

From the 1870s to the 1930s the US tried to assimilate the Native Americans quickly. The motives for this ranged from an unselfish wish to free natives from dependence and poverty to a barely disguised aim to acquire reservation lands cheaply. Assimilation programs also caused dissension within native groups. Native Americans who had white relatives or who were already rather Americanized tended to favor adoption of US institutions. Racially unmixed natives were often cultural traditionalists who resisted all forms of assimilation.

The efforts at Americanization took three main forms. The first was the deliberate eroding of tribes' legal authority. On reservations, agents from the US Bureau of Indian Affairs (BIA) made all final decisions. In the 1870s and 1880s Congress removed any appearance of local control by declaring the end of tribal sovereignty and treaty-making and replacing tribal rule with the application of US or state laws. In the same years Congress gave private companies rights to use Native Americans' land without their consent. Granting US citizenship was another way of weakening tribal authority, because it gave Native Americans individual rights they could defend in court and made them responsible as individuals to state and federal law. By 1905 more than half of all Native Americans had US citizenship, and in 1924 Congress extended citizenship to the rest.

Americans who believed assimilation could be achieved in a single generation put their faith in the second major plan for assimilation: educating Native American children at boarding schools far away from their reservations. To break all ties with tribal culture, the pupils were forbidden to wear native clothing, practice native customs or religions or speak native languages. Both academic and vocational, the curriculum stressed American history and government. In the 1880s and 1890s the BIA founded some two dozen of these schools, as well as day and boarding schools on reservations, where the discipline and curriculum were similar. Allotment programs (dissolving reservations into small farms owned by individual Native American families) were the keystone of the third method of assimilation. Tried out before the Civil War, allotment became US policy for all but a few tribes under the Dawes Act of 1887. Typically, allotment plans gave a Native American family 160 acres and single adults half as much. This nearly always left a huge amount of "surplus" reservation land available for sale to non-Native Americans.

Supporters of the Dawes Act believed that Native Americans would experience the American dream of becoming economically self-reliant and politically independent farmers through allotment. The process would as effectively Americanize them as it had millions of European immigrants, in the opinion of many. But critics pointed out that Native American farming was communal, not a collection of individual holdings. Without time to develop an American sense of landownership and farming methods, the results of allotment might be the cheap sale of "Indian family farms" to white Americans and starvation among huge numbers of landless Native Americans. To prevent this, the Dawes Act forbade the sale or leasing of allotted land for 25 years. But when Congress removed these restrictions after just four years, Native Americans' lands changed hands rapidly. By 1934, some 4 million acres (1.6 million hectares) of reservation land had been declared surplus and sold to white Americans or sold by failed Native American farmers to white Americans. Allotment had provided a bonanza for speculators and land-hungry settlers.

Tribal restoration and termination, 1934–70

By the 1930s studies had repeatedly blamed allotment for the extreme poor health, poverty and low educational levels of Native Americans. Franklin D. Roosevelt's "Indian New Deal" attempted to correct the mistakes of the past. The relief and employment programs available for other Americans suffering from the depression were extended to Native Americans. New better-staffed hospitals for Native Americans were built. Most boarding schools were replaced with local schools offering religious freedom, bilingual education and programs to nurture native culture. The Indian Reorganization Act of 1934 was the centerpiece of the reversal of public policy known as tribal restoration. It repealed allotment, supported the return of considerable "surplus" land and allotment farms to communal ownership, and provided federal funds for further adding to tribal lands.

The BIA was now required to help develop self-government on reservations. Money was provided for founding these governments, which were offered federal credit for the conservation and economic development of local resources. Each tribe could accept or reject the Act through a referendum. The Indian New Deal made effective progress towards providing social services, an economic base and self-government on reservations, until funding ended at the start of the Second World War. In response to failing government support and a growing awareness of their common cause, people from a range of Native American cultures joined to form the nation's first large-scale national organization, the National Congress of American Indians (NCAI) in 1944 to monitor federal policies and secure the rights and benefits of all indigenous peoples.

By 1953 advocates of rapid assimilation again constituted a congressional majority, however, and pushed through three new programs. The first aimed to settle Native American claims against the US by offering financial compensation for lost lands and treaty violations. Once claims were resolved, the BIA proposed termination (dissolving the tribe/reservation as a legal entity and making Native Americans ordinary citizens of local and state governments). Then the BIA could complete the process of assimilation, the argument went, by helping former members of the tribe find work in cities. Instead of making natives "regular" Americans by transforming them into farmers, this new policy (called relocation) was designed to accomplish the same end by turning them into industrial workers. By the 1960s most of the progress of the New Deal years had been reversed, and the policy of assimilation again seemed bankrupt. Termination and relocation had increased welfare dependency and social alienation rather than producing self-sufficiency and social integration.

Native American interest groups formed to seek change through lobbying and court cases. Protest organizations, such as the National Indian Youth Council (NIYC) founded in 1961, worked to build Native Americans' self-respect and pride. The more radical American Indian Movement (AIM), started in 1968, focused on mobilizing urban Native Americans through confrontation with the authorities and used direct action to capture media attention. Claiming it as their territory, for example, thousands of AIM supporters occupied Alcatraz Island in San Francisco Bay between 1969 and 1971. In late 1972 and early 1973, AIM activists barricaded themselves for more than 70 days against armored vehicles, federal marshals and the FBI at Wounded Knee, South Dakota, which they declared an independent nation. Near the end of the decade Indian activists marched from San Francisco to Washington, DC, along "The Trail of Broken Treaties," to publicize again the need to review the history of US treaty violations.

The situation of Native Americans in recent history

The activism of the 1960s and 1970s bore fruit in many ways in the late twentieth and early twenty-first centuries. Native American law firms won important victories in US courts. Native American lawyers convinced judges to view tribes according to their early nineteenth-century status as dependent domestic nations, which helped them successfully champion traditional religious practices, tribal independence, mineral, game and water rights and the return of ancient artifacts and skeletons. Court actions also returned or brought payment for vast tracts of land to honor old treaties.

An important goal of the intertribal "self-determination" movement supported by national Native American organizations was to lobby the federal government for equal treatment and self-government. The movement's initial success was confirmed in 1968, when the passage of the Indian Civil Rights Act guaranteed individuals living on reservations all the rights included in the US constitution. That at once protected them from rights violations by American or tribal governments and allowed tribes to qualify for the welfare and poverty benefits available to other citizens. From then to the present, federal laws building on this Act have made US funding and other assistance available for improving the health services, child-care, housing and education of Native Americans, on and off reservations.

In 1975, Congress confirmed this legal status in the Indian Self-Determination Act, which gave tribal councils most powers exercised by state governments. The councils develop both an economy and social institutions that are tailored to their own natural resources and values. At the tribes' request the BIA may offer assistance, but its role is phased out as tribes become autonomous. In response, councils have developed industries (including hundreds of food-processing, oil, gas and mining firms), irrigation systems, tourist resorts, more than 30 colleges (some of them offering both BA and MA degrees), and scores of tribal gambling casinos that earn Native Americans around $1 billion a year. A few tribes have grown rich from mineral deposits. For example, about 20 percent of US oil and two-thirds of the country's uranium are on reservation land.

As life on the reservation has improved, the flight of Native Americans to US cities has been reversed, but as early as the 1990 census, only one out of four Native Americans was a "reservation Indian." The other three lived in urban areas where jobs were more plentiful and varied. The adjustment to the city has not been very successful for Native Americans. About 20 percent live below the poverty line, unemployment is high and those with jobs frequently earn low wages. A small, well-educated urban elite enjoys a much higher standard of living and is frequently well integrated in American society. In 1996, in the hope that it would attract unsuccessful urban Native American people back to the reservations, the Native American Housing Assistance and Self-Determination Act (NAHASDA) updated reservation housing programs with block grants that allow tribes to identify and design suitable housing for themselves.

Despite that effort, in 2012 most of America's estimated 2.7 million "reservation Indians" lived in appalling conditions. Of all American ethnic groups, they had the highest unemployment, alcoholism, poverty and suicide rates. Many cases of malnutrition, mental illness, and incest as well as an exceptionally short life expectancy indicate that much remains to be done to improve the situation. Yet, at the 2010 census, 5.2 million Americans identified themselves as wholly or partly native. That is more than double the 1990 figure and far more than the birth rate alone can explain. One answer is that 2.3 million of these people indicated that their heritage was a mixture of Native American and one or more other ethnicities. Tribal leaders and experts point to a wish to share in gambling revenue and affirmative action programs, widespread interest in family history and, most encouraging, to the decline in the social stigma attached to being Native

American. By 2011, after many claims and counterclaims had been settled, the census estimated that the whole or partly Native American population was 5.1 million and that only half of this population was "American Indian and Alaska Native only."

Lesbian, gay, bisexual and transgender Americans

Not until the 1950s did advocacy organizations appear that publicly represented gay and lesbian Americans as minorities suffering discrimination. Even though state laws prohibited their sexual orientation, categorized it as a form of mental illness, and subjected its practice in private between consenting adults to police prosecution, the social taboo and resulting secrecy attached to these groups, as well as to bisexual and transgender people, delayed their organization and group consciousness. Despite these conditions, gay life was a well-known dimension of city life in places such as Harlem and Greenwich Village as early as the 1920s. The movement and mixing of many millions of people during both world wars, especially the second, made gays and lesbians (like members of other groups) more aware that they shared experiences and concerns with others.

In the 1950s support networks organized by the Mattachine Society and Daughters of Bilitis raised group and individual consciousness through publications and meetings that offered assistance and disseminated information. Social scientists published groundbreaking studies of gay and lesbian life in the United States around the same time that documented the social pressures they faced and how well adjusted they were compared to the heterosexual population.

The LGBT civil rights movement of the 1960s and 1970s built on this foundation. Gay rights demonstrations and marches in San Francisco, Philadelphia and New York, among other cities, made public demands for the rights society and the law denied these communities. Peaceful protest famously turned to active resistance in Greenwich Village on June 28, 1969, when gay men fought back after repeated police raids on the Stonewall Inn, which they considered their local club and bar. Events in the Village served as inspiration for the drag performers, minorities, and gay and transgender people, all of whom took part in the Stonewall Riots, to come together across the nation in defense of their rights. During the 1970s, the "gay liberation movement" served as the umbrella label for the next phase of LGBT protest and a new generation of activists. In 1973 the American Psychological Association stopped categorizing homosexuality as an illness, which to some degree lessened the possibility that these minorities could be institutionalized with the mentally ill or lose their parental rights, jobs and places in schools and civic organizations because of charges of moral turpitude. Activists in this decade developed a wide range of lesbian organizations (including demands for attention in feminist groups such as NOW) as well as more gay associations, worked for inclusion in the nation's religions and clergy, and took public demonstration and direct political action to new heights through the National Gay and Lesbian Task Force and the march on Washington in 1979. The decade also witnessed the ordination of the first openly gay minister and the election of gay political representatives.

The agony of AIDs-related illnesses and deaths in the epidemic that ravaged gay communities in the 1980s and later drew the nation's attention, although tardily, to the great human resources of its LGBT population as well as to the related plagues among those injecting illegal drugs or depending on blood transfusions for survival. In combined efforts gay spokespeople spearheaded efforts to gain funding for treatment and research to control the effects of the epidemic, prolong the health of its victims, and search for a cure. Street theater, most notably in work performed by Queer Nation and the AIDS Coalition to Unleash Power (ACT UP), as well as marches on Washington by hundreds of thousands of LGBT people and their supporters in 1987 and 1993, succeeded in making the medical, economic and civil rights needs of sexual minority groups well known, especially as LGBT people became increasingly recognized as family members, friends and contributors to society.

The rights of gay and lesbian soldiers, whose sexual orientation, if known, had throughout the twentieth century been cause for dishonorable discharge from military service, became a very visible political issue in the 1990s and early 2000s because of high-profile court cases, documentary films and political action. By that time an open lobby and interest group whose votes were courted by many candidates for Congress and the presidency, gay men and women received support from President Clinton, who tried unsuccessfully to reverse the ban on gay members of the military because of opposition from the Joint Chiefs of Staff. The policy of "don't ask, don't tell," enacted in 1993, meant that, as long as it was concealed, LGBT service people's sexual orientation had no effect on their military service or record. The law was an unhappy stop-gap compromise. Yet it remained in force for 17 years and led to the discharge of and loss of benefits for an estimated 12,500 service people. The policy finally ended through action by Congress and President Obama at the end of 2010, despite a Republican filibuster in the senate. Open toleration of gays in the military went into effect in mid-2011, and in early 2013 the American Civil Liberties Union (ACLU) won an agreement with the Defense Department that it would return lost benefits to gay service people participating in the ACLU's case against the government.

From the 1990s to the second decade of the twenty-first century increasing numbers of celebrities and ordinary people have been "coming out" as LGBT individuals, and polls of the public, including straight members of the military, have indicated growing levels of comfort with people of different sexual orientations and identities. The Supreme Court decision, *Lawrence* v. *Texas*, in 2003 ended the criminalization of homosexual relations between consenting adults. Same-sex civil unions, legal under Vermont law in 2000, were recognized by statute in six states

PLATE 4.4 A symbolic rainbow flag waves above men and women marching together in the 43rd Annual Gay Pride Parade in New York City in June 2012.
(Eric Pendzich/Rex Features)

and the District of Columbia by 2012. Near the end of that election year three more approved it through state referenda and one defeated a proposal to ban it. In the large majority of states, same-sex unions remained illegal. Federal law, furthermore, did not recognize gay marriages, which prevented partners in them from getting the benefits of other married couples. At the same time national polls indicated that the majority no longer opposed these unions. Three-quarters of straight service people reported that they were comfortable with gay colleagues, but the harassment of lesbians and gays in uniform continued, according to their testimony. Hate crimes against gays continued, even as the first openly gay US senator was elected in 2012 and lesbian and gay couples more frequently established stable family lives with children. However, enormous strides have been made. Self-identification as LGBT rose to 3.4 percent of Americans in 2012. The pace of public acceptance accelerates. But in some parts of American society the LGBT community still experiences discrimination, rejection and abuse.

African Americans

At the 2010 census, more than 42 million Americans identified themselves as black or black in combination with one or more other races. Due to the rapid growth of the nation's Latino population, they comprised the country's second largest minority group (12.3 percent of the population) in 2012. Mostly old-stock Americans, they include growing populations from Caribbean and African countries. When Africans first arrived in the American South in 1619, they did not come as slaves. By the late 1600s, however, hereditary slavery had become the rule and African Americans were degraded to the status of property. Some owners treated their slaves better than others, but all had ultimate power over what was their property. For black people, slavery meant hard work, poor living conditions and humiliation. Slave labor was especially important on large tobacco and rice plantations in Virginia and Maryland. When the US became independent, slaves made up about 20 percent of the population.

Dependence on slaves diminished as tobacco and rice grew less profitable in the early 1800s. At the same time, moral indignation over the slave trade grew so strong that in 1808 the importation of slaves was banned. New technology, however, then made slave labor more important than ever before. Eli Whitney's cotton gin, which cleaned cotton many times faster than was possible manually, meant greatly increased profits if plantation owners had more slave cotton-pickers to keep their cotton gins in full operation. By 1860 the slave population had grown to just under 4 million. With a booming cotton economy (and cheap land available by "removing" the Native Americans west of the Mississippi), the cotton South expanded westward. This often meant that slave children had to move away from their parents to serve masters who were often the younger sons of slave-owners on newly developed plantations.

Between 1820 and the Civil War, several compromises were reached in Congress to keep the number of slave states and free states equal. Anti-slavery supporters felt this policy condoned slavery, while slave-owners thought each state should be able to decide whether it wished to be "slave" or "free." Compromise finally failed, and the Civil War began in 1861. Lincoln freed the slaves in the undefeated parts of the South in early 1863 through the Emancipation Proclamation and, after Union victory, amendments to the Constitution abolished slavery, granted the former slaves citizenship and gave black men the right to vote. Congress repealed the black codes the Southern states had passed to limit the rights of former slaves. However, with no land or education, most black people had to work as sharecroppers or had to lease land and equipment from their former masters. Rents were so high that they had to give most of their crop in payment and had little to sell to get out of debt.

The new constitutional amendments were enforced in the South by the presence of the Union army from 1865 to 1877 during Reconstruction. Then, however, the troops were withdrawn and the North abandoned the cause of the former slaves. For 80 years the federal government left the South alone. Southerners did not accept black people as equals; they passed laws that denied them social, economic and political rights, and they segregated almost every aspect of public life. These "Jim Crow laws" remained in effect in most Southern states until the 1960s. In the Supreme Court, a Southern majority interpreted the Fourteenth Amendment to mean no *government* should deny equal protection, but private persons could.

The *Plessy* v. *Ferguson* case in 1896 established the court's separate-but-equal doctrine approving segregation. In 1909 a group of black and white people founded the National Association for the Advancement of Colored People (NAACP) to fight for African Americans' civil rights in general and to win repeal of the separate-but-equal doctrine in particular. At the time, Jim Crow laws affected most African Americans because about 90 percent of black people lived in the South. In 1915 the NAACP persuaded the Supreme Court to annul the grandfather clause, which denied the vote to persons whose grandfathers had not voted in the 1860s, but violent intimidation and discriminatory local laws still kept Southern black people from voting. In 1935 the NAACP won the invalidation of some residential segregation laws, but again with little practical effect.

The much smaller black population in the North grew rapidly and developed vibrant urban communities around the time of the First World War. *De jure* segregation (separation of the races by law) was the rule in the South. In the North, *de facto* segregation (racial separation through informal means) was almost universal and forced black people to live in ghettos, such as Harlem in New York City, the country's most famous black community. By the 1920s, black people's bitter disappointment over their limited freedom in Northern centers resulted in protest movements, some demanding integration (like the NAACP) and others, such as Marcus Garvey's, promoting self-help in preparation for a return to Africa. In spite of these developments, the mass migration from the South continued. The rush for jobs in munitions and weapons industries during the Second World War accelerated the move to the North and also brought blacks to West Coast cities. By the 1950s almost half the nation's African Americans lived in restive ghettos outside the South.

From 1938 the African American lawyer Thurgood Marshall, who later became the first black Supreme Court justice, led the NAACP legal defense group. More liberals took seats on the Supreme Court during the following 20 years. These changes helped the NAACP achieve more success in the courts, where it fought the separate-but-equal doctrine by showing the inequalities forced on black students by school segregation. The court did not overturn the doctrine, but during the following decades its decisions made segregation almost impossible to implement in graduate and professional schools. Not until 1954, however, in the *Brown* v. *Board of Education* case, was the separate-but-equal doctrine reversed. The court followed up this historic ruling with the annulment of *de jure* segregation in public places, and thus sent black people a message that the time was right to fight for their cause.

Implementing these changes was difficult. The South offered massive resistance, and the court got no help from the other branches of government. President Eisenhower had publicly supported segregation, and a conservative coalition of Southern Democrats and Republicans dominated Congress. Not until violence broke out in Little Rock, Arkansas, when nine black students tried to attend a white school in 1957, did the president send the National Guard to enforce the court's ruling. The next president, John F. Kennedy, used the Guard or federal marshals several times in other Southern districts to desegregate the schools. Defiant Southerners therefore avoided desegregation in other ways. White people who had the means sent their children to private schools that were not bound by federal law. By 1964 only 2 per cent of black children in the South attended desegregated schools. In 1969 the Supreme Court ordered the desegregation of all public schools, and later approved measures to force integration, such as racial quotas, the grouping of non-contiguous school districts, and bussing in order to achieve racial balance in the schools. Since segregation still determined residential patterns (most black people lived in the inner cities while white people lived in the suburbs), there was strong opposition to bussing. After the court ruled against bussing plans between cities and suburbs in 1974, unless discriminatory districting could be proved, few new attempts to bus pupils were made.

Other forms of *de jure* racial discrimination existed in the South in the 1950s. Black people then were also prevented from voting and were kept out of jobs and white facilities. In 1955, Rosa Parks, a black woman from Montgomery, Alabama, who had attended a seminar encouraging her to defend her civil rights, was arrested and fined for refusing to give up her seat on the bus to a white man. This incident sparked a black boycott against the city's bus system led by the young Baptist minister Martin Luther King, Jr. One year later the federal courts ruled that segregated transportation violated the Fourteenth Amendment. The African American Civil Rights Movement of the 1950s and 1960s was underway. King was one of the organizers of the Southern Christian Leadership Conference (SCLC), which coordinated civil rights activities. His "I Have a Dream" speech to more than 250,000 people at the Lincoln Memorial in 1963 is regarded as one of the most inspiring calls for racial equality in American history.

White officials' brutal suppression of civil rights protests in the South, newly visible on nationwide television, made Americans more conscious of racial injustice. President Kennedy addressed the problem for the first time from the White House and called fighting racism a moral issue. The Civil Rights Act of 1964 outlawed discrimination in jobs and public accommodations, and the following year the Voting Rights Act led to black voter registration drives that transformed politics in the South. This has been called the non-violent revolution. However, peaceful protestors, both black and white, were killed and, while Martin Luther King, Jr. was advocating non-violence, other black people felt change was too slow in coming. African Americans' expectations had been raised enormously, and they were disappointed with how little change civil rights laws brought to their daily lives. The frustrated residents of the black ghetto in Los Angeles exploded in riots in 1965. Detroit and Newark witnessed massive property destruction and dozens of deaths from race riots in 1967.

Some black radicals wanted to establish an alternate African American culture inside the US. Some of these formed the Black Power and Black Panther movements. Malcolm X became one of the most famous black Muslims, a leader of the Nation of Islam, which created its own variant of Islam and rejected America's lifestyle and politics. These movements became involved in violent conflicts with the police. For many black people, non-violence seemed defunct as a means of winning civil rights. Malcolm X was killed in 1965 and three years later, when Martin Luther King was assassinated, 168 American cities erupted in racial conflict.

The message *was* heard, nonetheless, by some inspiring leaders and their supporters in this reform-minded period in US history. President Johnson's Great Society and War on Poverty were contested packages of reforms and took time to reach many of the people who needed assistance, but his dedicated staff spread out across the nation and hired tens of thousands to implement programs of assistance through relief (Supplemental Security Income), education (Head Start and Upward Bound), job training (the Job Core), medical help (Medicaid and Medicare), and public housing. African Americans benefited greatly from these initiatives from the time they were fully operational at the end of the 1960s. In the next two decades these efforts gained wider scope. Following President Richard Nixon, who instituted affirmative action minority preferences for federal contracts in the early 1970s, private industry and business began hiring blacks for professional, managerial and skilled jobs, instituting affirmative action employee searches and on-the-job training as necessary.

Institutions of higher education, such as the City University of New York and other public systems, realizing that more blacks needed higher education, offered "open admissions" to local high school graduates as well as programs of remediation to help young people get that entrance ticket. In the interest of "leveling the playing field," colleges and universities across the nation offered high school and even elementary education to help minorities catch up from the 1970s to the 1990s. The black middle class grew substantially, and real progress seemed underway as tens of thousands took advantage of the new opportunities. In the 1990s, however, the tide of opinion turned. The public backlash against preferential treatment grew decisive as the majority on the US Supreme Count became more conservative. In 1996 Congress strictly limited the length of time the poor could benefit from welfare programs, severely affecting the poorest blacks. Court decisions or referenda limited affirmative action in higher education in several states in the 1990s, among them California and Texas, causing large and immediate declines in minority enrollment at the same time that blacks remained under-represented in such high-status studies as medicine and law.

The contemporary situation for African Americans

In retrospect, it is clear that passing laws was the easy part. Neither the civil rights nor the Black Power movements of the last century succeeded in achieving racial equality. The nation has still not found a way to enforce civil rights laws. In 2005 when the mainly black communities of New Orleans' poorest districts faced death and disease in the floodwaters of Hurricane Katrina, the state and federal authorities were very slow to react. How can one quarter of black people be brought out of poverty and invisibility before disaster strikes? To make use of equal opportunity, African Americans need higher education and the skills to obtain better-paid jobs. That, in turn, should enable them to afford better housing and improved living standards. In 2008, however, their wages remained depressed and their unemployment and poverty rates twice those of white people, as the nation slid into its worst economic slump since the 1930s. Even though a third of black Americans had risen to the middle class, a larger portion still lacked a high school diploma or, at best, stopped their education with an Associate Degree at a junior college. In 2012, 58 years after the *Brown* decision, 46 percent of black school children and 84 percent of their white counterparts went to schools where their own race predominated. Race and socio-economic status together determined where large majorities went to school and kept most blacks in poor inner-city school districts. Despite the Fair Housing Act of 1968, most black people still face discrimination when they buy or rent housing. Residential desegregation has been minimal and equal standards in the schools have therefore not been achieved.

Only half as many blacks *completed* a college degree as whites in the first decade of the twenty-first century. In 2003 the University of Michigan won a narrow 5–4 victory in the protracted *Grutter* v. *Bollinger* case when the US Supreme Court decided that race could be used as a factor in admissions decisions because of the "compelling interest" of giving students the educational benefits that come from a diverse student body. Given the chance, however, a large majority of the Michigan public reversed the court's decision by voting to end affirmative action at the state's universities in a referendum in 2006. By that time national polls indicated that the majority of Americans did not think they or their government should shoulder the responsibility for helping the disadvantaged.

When blacks did have equal qualifications on paper, the appearance of being better qualified often had limited effects if employers doubted the quality of their credentials, assumed that participants in affirmative-action programs got special treatment, or felt alienated from black people because the races continued to have little contact with each other.

Ironically, the 2000 census showed that the most progress in residential desegregation in the 1990s occurred in the South, where black people leave cities for suburbs at the same time as white people, instead of decades later as in the other regions. Between 1990 and 2005 black people migrated into the South in record numbers, reversing their century-long flight from the region. By 2012 the most racially segregated cites in the nation were in the Northeast and Midwest, including Boston, New York, Pittsburgh, Detroit, Chicago and St. Louis.

Blacks winning elective office offered the greatest hope for attaining the dream of racial equality, in the view of some. In 2000 there were more than 7,000

PLATE 4.5 Malcolm X addressing a crowd at a Black Muslim rally in Harlem, New York in 1963.
(Everett/Rex Features)

elected black officials in the US, while there had been fewer than 100 in 1964. Most of these (including 300 mayors) were in local government. At the national level, blacks were concentrated in the House of Representatives. Only three had been elected to the Senate since 1945. By the 2011–13 Congress the number of black members reached a new high (44), but only one senator was among these. The most visible national figures recently have been appointees, such as Colin Powell and Condoleezza Rice. Continued socio-economic inequality and the unkept promises of public policy continued to make mainstream black leaders, such as Jesse Jackson, urge personal responsibility and self-reliance on their community and to increase the appeal of more radical, racist black figures, such as Louis Farrakhan. Finally, in the 2008 presidential election Barack Obama seemed to rise above the prejudice and divisive partisan politics of the past, never running as a black man and winning a clear electoral victory on the theme of being the candidate of all the people in the *United* States. In 2012 Obama won a second term, despite his own unfilled economic promises, with the support of a coalition consisting of considerable numbers of white male liberals, a larger percentage of white women, and overwhelming majorities of non-whites across the nation.

Asian Americans

"Asian American" is a convenient term that lumps together a diverse collection of immigrant and American-born populations. It includes, for example, both Hmong tribes-people who came as refugees after the Vietnam War and the descendants of the Chinese who settled before the Civil War. The principle of continental origins is used to justify putting in one category people with different religions, skin colors, socio-economic backgrounds and historical experiences. The US census compiles information on this diverse composite group together with another such group, "Pacific Islanders," which includes native Hawaiians, Guamanians and Samoans, among others. Between 2007 and 2010 migration to the US from Asia rose somewhat and Latino immigration dropped sharply with the much publicized result that Asian Americans became the nation's largest and fastest growing foreign-born racial minority. These changes came because of a variety of factors, however, and may not be lasting. In 2010 Asian Americans numbered a record 18.2 million people, 36 percent of immigration to the US and 4.7 percent of the country's whole population.

Between the 1970s and 2010 the Asian-born population of the US exploded in size. The Asian American community grew on average by nearly 49 percent per decade and by 200 percent or more in some cities in every region of the country. At the same time both their prominence in the fourth wave of immigrants and their diversity has grown. The six largest Asian ancestry groups (Chinese, Filipino, Asian Indian, Vietnamese, Korean and Japanese) have been joined by hundreds of thousands of people from some 20 other Asian nations. It is only the old-stock American perception that all these people *look* Asian (and the different treatment that this perception has caused) that has given them related experiences in the US.

The first large group of Chinese, some 370,000 people, came with the second wave "old" immigrants between the late 1840s and 1882. One-fifth settled in Hawaii and the rest on the West Coast, mostly in California. About 400,000 Japanese immigrated between the 1880s and 1908 and settled in roughly equal numbers on the West Coast and in Hawaii, where they composed the largest Asian immigrant group. Small groups of Koreans and East Indians (about 7,000 each) came to the islands and West Coast states from 1900 to 1930. During the same period, approximately 180,000 Filipinos immigrated, about three in five of them first arriving in Hawaii.

The situation of Asian immigrants varied greatly between Hawaii and the mainland. In the islands, most were recruited as contract workers on sugar planta-tions, where they did back-breaking stoop labor under military-style discipline and the supervision of often abusive overseers. Nationality groups were segregated in different camps and pitted against each other to keep wages low and prevent a unified labor movement. But plantation owners were dependent on these workers and so provided food, housing and medical care. To get workers to stay when their contracts ended, they helped women immigrate, encouraged family life, supported religious and ethnic customs, and built schools and community centers.

PLATE 4.6 Chinatown in Manhattan with New York's City Hall in the near background.
(Jose Fuste Raga/Corbis)

The discrimination Asian Americans suffered in Hawaii was much milder than that on the mainland because they made up a large majority of the islands' workforce. In 1920, when they worked in every part of Hawaii's economy, Asian Americans comprised more than half of the islands' population, and about two in every five people there were Japanese Americans. Thus, most Japanese Americans on the mainland were put in concentration camps during the Second World War, compared with less than 1 percent of those on the islands. In the 1930s, Asian Americans began to assume prominent positions in Hawaiian politics. Since 1959, Hawaii has been the only state in which they have both played major roles in state politics and represented the state in Congress.

On the mainland the situation of Asian Americans was fundamentally different until the mid-1940s. Always a tiny minority compared to European Americans, they could much more easily be made victims of systematic discrimination. Anti-Asian campaigns in the Pacific West were designed to segregate Asians from white people, prevent them from competing economically and end their immigration entirely. Anti-miscegenation laws against racial-mixing forbade marriages between Asians and white people. Many businesses refused them products and services. The only housing they could find was often in Asian American ghettos. A series of Supreme Court decisions decided that they were non-whites and therefore ineligible for citizenship. Many Western states also passed alien land laws, which prohibited non-citizens from leasing or owning land. In 1882 the Chinese were excluded from immigrating. The 1908 Gentlemen's Agreement, prohibiting the entry of Japanese laborers, was followed in 1921 by the "Ladies' Agreement" that banned Japanese women's immigration. Three years later all Asians were barred from immigrating.

With assistance from sympathetic white people, Asian Americans fought these forms of oppression. They found loopholes in the land laws, circumvented immigration exclusion laws, created their own job opportunities by starting businesses, formed union and protest organizations and, through these, stood up for their rights through strikes and lawsuits. For all Asian American groups apart from Japanese Americans, the Second World War brought decisive social and economic improvements. Public attitudes became positive to the Chinese, Koreans, Filipinos and East Indians, whose homelands were American allies. Members of these groups joined the US armed forces or intelligence networks. Tens of thousands of Japanese American youths left the concentration camps to serve in the American military and prove their loyalty. War industries gave Asian Americans professional and skilled work that previously had been denied them. By the war's end, all four groups could immigrate and all but Koreans had won citizenship rights. Between 1945 and 1965, discriminatory laws against Asian Americans were repealed or struck down by the courts.

Asian immigrants to the US after the Second World War are distinctive in several ways. Refugee laws permitted the entry of Asians who had married American military personnel in that war and the Korean War that followed. In

1965 a new immigration law opened the way for the huge wave of Asian immigration that still continues. Well educated Asian students who took advanced degrees in the US discovered that they could qualify to become immigrants and later bring relatives through the law's family reunification provisions. Often these people have been less prepared for American life. As a result of the Vietnam War, hundreds of thousands of Vietnamese, Laotian and Cambodian refugees settled in the US. The first wave of southeast Asian refugees in the mid-1970s were mostly rather well-off, Westernized people who had cooperated with the colonial French and then the US forces. Later groups in the 1980s and beyond were often poorer and less educated.

As a result of the above circumstances and other factors, a significant minority of fourth-wave Asian American immigrants consists of well-educated professionals, and many more come from urban areas, where they worked in modern industries. More of the recent immigrants also arrive as families rather than as single men and plan to settle permanently. On the other hand, recent refugees are often destitute, poorly educated and unprepared for city life. The Hmong and Mien, pre-industrial upland peoples of southeast Asia, have found adapting to modern conditions particularly hard. The numbers of Japanese newcomers are now small while the totals from other Asian nations have set new records.

Asian Americans today

Since the mid-1960s, the popular media have often depicted Asian Americans as the country's most successful ethnic groups, its "model minority." Their high median family incomes, unusually high level of academic achievement and low rates of unemployment, crime, mental illness and dependence on welfare have been held up as examples to other minority groups. They emphasize traditional family values, such as a stable marriage with children and living in multi-generation family households, more than any other part of the population. In 2012 they were also without parallel in believing in hard work, successful careers and being satisfied with the US as the best place for pursuing these goals.

The media image of Asian Americans' success, moreover, caused resentment that fed a rising wave of anti-Asian activity in the 1980s, when the US Civil Rights Commission reported dozens of cases of racial slurs, violent assaults, vandalism and harassment against Asian Americans. Across the nation, conflicts occurred between Korean store-owners and residents of the Latino or African American communities where many of these shops are located. In the 1992 Los Angeles riots, their shops became the special target of looters, and some 1,800 Korean businesses were destroyed. After reactions to the rapid progress of Asian immigrants and economic competition from Asian nations cooled during the boom years of the later 1990s, however, Asian–African relations in the US improved.

The concentration of Asian Americans in only a handful of states, historically and today, has been a source of both benefits and drawbacks. The first wave of

Asian immigration settled mostly in Hawaii, on the West Coast and in the Chinatowns of large cities, such as New York. In these places Asian newcomers established networks of mutual assistance and an ethnic economy that supported many compatriots, but their visibility also fueled anti-Asian movements based on racism and feelings of economic competition. Around two-thirds of all Asian Americans live in just six states—California, New York, Texas, New Jersey, Hawaii and Illinois. Most Japanese and Filipino Americans live in the West while a majority of Chinese, Indian, Vietnamese and Koreans live in other regions of the country. In California and Texas during the 1990s the high proportion of Asian Americans winning places at prestigious state universities contributed to the backlash against programs that give preferential treatment to minorities, even when the Asian Americans in question had not benefited from affirmative action.

A closer look at their situation shows that, despite their successes, significant numbers of Asian Americans have serious socio-economic problems and still face considerable discrimination. Asian Americans are twice as urbanized as white people. One reason for this is that their high family incomes are more dependent than white people's on living in central cities with large, diverse job markets. Only these places can provide work for the number of family members who work long hours and contribute their wages to one household income, which, taken together, is higher than the family incomes of white households. In *personal* incomes Asian Americans have not caught up with white Americans. An explanation for that is that they are more concentrated in semi-skilled service trades and low-level professional and management positions. Still, despite the large number of refugees from Asia, about half as many people in these ethnic groups lived in poverty in 2012 than was the case among Latin Americans, the other large body of recent immigrants. Asian Americans' educational attainments, moreover, were higher than those of white people, and a higher portion of them worked in management, professional and related occupations, such as financial managers, engineers, teachers and registered nurses. Still, many successful Asian Americans reported that a so-called "glass ceiling" of prejudice kept them out of the higher management levels of industries and professional firms. The slums of major American cities that have a high incidence of poverty, health problems, drug abuse and teenage gangs often overlap with the poorest parts of Asian American communities. By 2012 more Asian Americans lived in racially mixed areas than any other group, fewer in ghettos or areas dominated by one group, and more in better multicultural urban neighborhoods or suburbs.

Latinos

A Spanish language and cultural background is the inexact basis for calling people with ethnic origins in the Caribbean and Central and South America "Latinos" or "Hispanics." Thus the term does not apply to people from countries in the

Americas whose cultural forms have been chiefly determined by other European cultures, such as Brazil, Haiti or the Bahamas. Those commonly called Latinos include the Central or South American descendants of Native American peoples, African slaves, later immigrants from European and Asian nations and mixtures of these groups. In 2010 somewhat more than half of Latinos identified themselves as white. The majority is Catholic, but significant numbers are Protestant or members of other religions. Most are relatively recent immigrants to the US, but Mexican Americans have been coming in large numbers since the beginning of the 1900s and include the descendants of the early Spanish settlers from the 1500s, whose lands were conquered by the US in 1846–8.

The Census Bureau estimated that about 50.7 million people (16.4 percent of the population) were "Hispanic or Latino" in 2012. Those figures represented well over a 100 percent increase in the last 24 years and meant the Latino population continued to be among the fastest growing groups in the nation. Today Latinos are a larger minority than African Americans, and the significance of that fact is even clearer when one remembers that the largest part of the 11 million unauthorized immigrants in the US are Latinos.

Two-thirds of Latinos (33 million people) identify themselves as Mexican Americans. Many live in the Southwestern states, in Los Angeles or in large Midwestern cities such as Chicago. Between 1990 and 2006, however, Mexican American communities have appeared throughout the nation and have grown most in number and size across the rural and small-town South and Midwest. From 2007 through 2012, however, immigration from Mexico, both legal and illegal, has fallen sharply, and in some of those years more Mexicans have re-migrated to their homeland than migrated to the US. The Mexican American population has continued to increase but mostly from children born in the US.

The other Latino groups are small by comparison. Puerto Ricans, the second largest group, make up 9.2 percent of Latinos and live mostly in New York City and other Northeastern urban areas. The two next largest groups, Cubans and Dominican Americans, whose largest communities are in Florida and New York City, comprise 3.7 and 3.6 percent of Latino Americans. The remaining Latinos have about 30 different national origins, the largest of which are Salvadoran, Dominican, Guatemalan and Colombian.

Like Native Americans, African Americans and Asian Americans, Latinos have faced race prejudice and economic discrimination in jobs, housing, education and politics. A combination of forces brought the first large groups of Mexican immigrants to the US in the two decades after 1900. Congress passed a law that provided funding for irrigated farming in the Southwest in 1902, and since the US step-by-step excluded Asian immigration by 1924, a new source of unskilled field workers became increasingly urgent as the region's agribusinesses continued their rapid expansion. Filipino "nationals" provided some new laborers but could not satisfy the demand for fruits and vegetables created by continued population growth, urbanization and the advent of refrigerated transportation. These magnetic factors became irresistible after 1909 when Mexico descended into a decade of revolution and violent political instability.

By 1920 nearly 100,000 Mexicans lived in California alone, and the precedent for some main features of Mexican (and Central American) immigration was set. The need for "stoop labor" to tend and harvest crops across ever wider acreages continued through the 1920s, when Mexicans were also a very large group among the low-wage workers in Southwestern mines and railroad gangs as well as in Midwestern farms and foundries. But in the Depression of the 1930s, hundreds of thousands of Mexican Americans (including many born in the US) were fired and sent home when jobs were scarce. Mexicans were welcome at the bottom of the occupational ladder again during World War II. In 1942 the US and Mexican governments reached an agreement that legalized their temporary status in the US. This *bracero* program arranged for the recruitment of some 4.5 million Mexicans as guest workers before it ended in 1964. The agreement was supposed to guarantee the *braceros* civil rights and working conditions, but fell so far short in Texas that Mexico refused to send more of its citizens there. The program expanded during the Korean War and again in the mid-1950s in response to growing needs for cheap, non-union labor. With the program's end illegal immigration from Mexico, following family chains along the job routes established by the program, soared until the IRCA amnesty in 1986. From then until 2007 both legal and illegal Mexican and Latino immigration generally rose to new heights and fuelled the controversy over the restriction of immigration. See the final section of this chapter.

For many decades, Latino children have been sent to segregated "Mexican" schools in the West and Southwest. When federal courts declared them to be white in the 1940s, the situation improved somewhat, but a decade later local officials used these rulings to "integrate" schools by creating districts where most pupils were Latino or African American, while non-Latino white pupils attended school elsewhere. Today the great majority of Latinos still go to school in segregated districts. To this point race, rather than English language competence, was decisive for their US schooling, even though, like other immigrant children, they were often punished for speaking their native language and met pressure to Anglicize their culture at school.

In the Southwest, Florida and the New York City area Latinos achieved political influence decades ago by being elected to office on all levels of government. In the 1960s and 1970s, they organized "brown power" protest movements that fought for civil rights on the streets and in the courts, enhancing Latinos' pride and stimulating a variety of cultural institutions. Latinos have long been actively involved in union movements of many kinds despite the prejudice of some white labor leaders. The largest occupational group of Latinos was for many years migratory farm workers. César Chávez became the first nationally well-known Latino leader in the 1960s through his successful five-year national boycott and strike negotiations as head of the United Farm Workers Union of California. Still, in the 1980s and even the 1990s civil rights workers and scholars discussed how perhaps it was the element of "proximity" (nearness and ease of returning to Mexico) that explained Latinos' relatively low profile in US politics. Since 2000, however, that has changed. The group's voter participation has grown rapidly, and the Latino vote may well have given Obama a winning margin in swing states such as Florida, Colorado and Nevada in both 2008 and 2012.

Attitudes to Latino America: the nation's largest immigrant subculture

Public opinion regarding Latinos, always mixed, grew increasingly negative as the immigration of Spanish-origin groups skyrocketed at the end of the twentieth and beginning of the twenty-first centuries. Reactions were particularly strong from Texas to California but noticeable across the nation. Proficiency in English understandably became the center of debates over civil rights for Latinos because the nation had never before witnessed a wave of immigration in which so many nationality and cultural groups shared a language. More than 20 states declared English their official language in reaction to the use of Spanish by Latinos in the 1980s. In schools bilingual programs (teaching offered in both the pupil's mother tongue and English) became a major battle in a "culture war" centered largely on whether Latino communities would have to acquire English or have the opportunity of functioning in both English and Spanish. The uneasy compromise reached in many places tolerates bilingual instruction only until proficiency in English is reached. Programs for "cultural maintenance" find little support in most places.

Latinos won an important victory in 1982 when the Supreme Court decided that the children of illegal immigrants were entitled to public education. In 1994, however, California's voters passed Proposition 187, which challenged the ruling and would have denied the state's illegal immigrants all social services except emergency medical attention but for court actions brought by civil rights groups. In 1996 California and Texas voters ended state affirmative action programs knowing well that these helped not only blacks but Latinos secure better education and jobs. In 2003–4 polls in California showed that large majorities opposed allowing illegal immigrants to receive state driving licenses, without which this largely Latino group would find making a living increasingly difficult. The issues of language competence, workers' rights and access to government services came together in the *Sandoval* case that the US Supreme Court resolved in 2001. Citing the Civil Rights Act of 1964, lawyers serving the poor in Alabama helped Martha Sandoval, a Spanish-speaker whose English was limited, sue the state for discrimination based on her cultural background, because it passed a law requiring that all driver's tests be given in English. In a 5–4 decision the court ruled that the law did not have a disproportionately large effect on Sandoval and others in her

PLATE 4.7 César Chávez, leader of the United Farm Workers, speaking to union members in California in 1979.
(Michael Salas/Time Pix/Rex Features)

situation. It further overturned decades of federal court decisions based on Title VI of the Civil Rights Act of 1964 that had declared unconstitutional various examples of discrimination ranging from school law to the location of polluting industries that were viewed as having a disproportionate effect on the basis of race, color or national background.

The census in 2010 showed that educational levels among foreign-born Latinos were the lowest of any group in the nation. A third had completed only a ninth grade education or less, and as a group they ranked as the most likely to drop out of school. On the other hand, in every measure of education the foreign-born among Latinos improved their level of performance between 2000 and 2010. Unemployment and poverty rates for Latinos were also the highest among the foreign-born, which commentators blamed chiefly on their educational situation, the enormous increase in Latino immigration in past years and rising anti-Latino feeling in the regions of their greatest concentration. The high number of Latino newcomers, especially illegal immigrants, continued to feed rising hostility and concern about Latinos even after their immigration started declining after 2007.

In the Southwest, border patrols and local police often stop Latinos on the assumption that they might be illegal aliens. In 2010 Arizona passed a law making it a state crime for the foreign-born not to carry documentation of their immigration status or to seek employment if they were not "authorized." Most controversially, the law allowed state police to stop and arrest people without a warrant if they had reason to suspect they might be unauthorized. In a state where Mexican Americans made up more than 60 percent of immigrants, this seemed to target Latinos, whether they had come to the state only recently or been there for generations. Such "racial profiling" has also led police departments to single out African Americans as suspects. Soon Utah, Indiana, South Carolina, Georgia and Alabama passed similar laws, and a majority of other states considered the possibility. In opinion polls the public supported state legislation when the federal government did not "fix" immigration problems. On the other hand, the federal Justice Department, under President Obama's instructions, successfully filed a lawsuit asking for an injunction to stop implementation of the Arizona law. By 2012 a divided Supreme Court heard the case, struck down the state crimes it created and emphasized that in matters of immigration and deportation the federal government had the primary authority. State authorities could stop people they had reasonable reason to suspect were undocumented but they could not hold them; instead they had to check with federal immigration agents before deciding to hold the suspects.

After 2012 there were also signs of Latinos' growing political influence, which ought to help secure policy changes to improve their opportunities and status. During the presidential election campaign the candidates paid extraordinary attention to the "big" states where most Latinos live. Census Bureau analyses and political commentators indicated that Latinos had become a large minority that could determine majorities in the houses of Congress. Since 2004 unprecedented numbers of Latino Americans have been elected to office, including two members of the US Senate, one from Colorado and the other from Florida. A higher portion of Latinos than of whites or blacks participated in the 2008 and 2012 elections, when they accounted for a larger percentage of voters nationwide than ever before. In short, the group has clearly demonstrated its political clout. Nonetheless, the Latino presence in Congress in 2009 was less than African Americans' despite the larger Latino population, and Latinos remain under-represented in political office at all levels of government.

In the second decade of the 2000s some speak resentfully of the "browning" or "Latinization" of America. Others relish signs of growing Latin visibility in the nation's culture from Spanish-language signs and businesses to new foods, popular music and fashion.

Exercises

Explain and examine the significance of the following names and terms:

equality of opportunity	English common law	abolitionists (regarding women)
Seneca Falls Convention	protectionist legislation	2010 Arizona immigration law
ERA	affirmative action programs	*Roe* v. *Wade*
Stonewall riots	"domestic dependent nation"	forced assimilation
Indian New Deal	Self-Determination Act	Asian contract workers
anti-miscegenation laws	urban ghettos	model minority
"glass ceiling"	black codes	same-sex marriage
Plessy v. *Ferguson*	NAACP	*de jure* segregation
non-violent revolution	illegal immigrants	school segregation
bilingual education	César Chávez	the *Sandoval* case

Write short essays on the following questions:

1. Discuss the factors that have contributed to the improved status of American women since the colonial period.

2. Evaluate the motives and effects of US policy toward Native Americans.

3. Discuss the changing situation of the LGBT community and the causes for change.

4. Give a critical review of the aspects of African Americans' struggle for equality that you find distinctive from that of other minority groups.

5. Compare and contrast early and recent Asian American immigrants and the treatment they have received in the US.

6. Describe the make-up of America's Latino population and discuss the kinds of discrimination it has faced.

Further reading

Acuña, R. (1988) *Occupied America: A History of Chicanos*, New York: Harper & Row.

Berry M.F. and Blassingame, J.W. (1982) *Long Memory: The Black Experience in America*, Oxford: Oxford University Press.

Cordova, C.B. and del Pinal, J. (1996) *Hispanics-Latinos: Diverse People in a Multicultural Society*, Washington, DC: National Association of Hispanic Publications.

Franklin, J.H. and Moss, A.A. (1987) *From Slavery to Freedom: A History of Negro Americans*, New York: Alfred A. Knopf.

Hurtado, A.L. and Iverson, P. (eds) (1994) *Major Problems in American Indian History*, Lexington, MA: D.C. Heath.

Jonas, G. (2007) *Freedom's Sword: The NAACP and the Struggle against Racism in America, 1909–1969*, New York: Routledge.

McWilliams, C. (1990) *North from Mexico: The Spanish-Speaking People of the United States*, Westport, CT: Greenwood.

Norton, M.B. and Alexander, R.M. (1996) *Major Problems in American Women's History*, Lexington, MA: D.C. Heath.

Oswalt, W.O. and Neeley, S. (1996) *This Land Was Theirs: A Study of North American Indians*, Mountain View, CA: Mayfield.

Ruiz, V.L. and DuBois, E.C. (eds) (1994) *Unequal Sisters: A Multicultural Reader in US Women's History*, London: Routledge.

Takaki, R. (1998) *Strangers from a Different Shore: A History of Asian Americans*, 2nd edn, Boston, MA: Little, Brown.

Wolitski, R.J., Stall, R. and Valdiserri, R.O. (eds) (2008) *Unequal Opportunity: Health Disparities Affecting Gay and Bisexual Men in the United States*, New York: Oxford University Press.

Websites

www.gallup.com

www.washingtonpost.com

www.census.gov

www.census.gov/newsroom

www.policymic.com/articles/5208/on-international-womens-day-2012-gender-inequality-in-american-business-still-a-problem

www.thedailybeast.com/newsweek/2012/04/09/a-needed-revolution-rape-and-u-s-justice.html

www.apa.org/pi/lgbt/resources/history.aspx

www.aclu.org/lgbt-rights

www.gallup.com/poll/158066/special-report-adults-identify-lgbt.aspx

www.pewhispanic.org/2012/02/21/statistical-portrait-of-hispanics-in-the-united-states-2010

www.census.gov/cps (cps = current population surveys)

www.census.gov/aian

www.census.gov/population/hispanic

Chapter 5

Religious cultures

- Religious history
- Contemporary US religion
- Church, state and politics
- Religion and education
- Attitudes to religion
- *Exercises*
- *Further reading*
- *Websites*

This chapter addresses the role of religion in US society. It examines religious history and the diversity of contemporary denominations; considers the relationship between religion, the state and education; and assesses attitudes towards religion and spiritual experience.

Many Western countries have experienced modern declines in religious observance and increased secularization (non-sacred concerns). These changes have been attributed to the effects of industrialization, consumerism, materialism, individualism and expanded education. Although Americans have historically been very religious, albeit with periods of irreligion, there has arguably been a recent decrease in religious belief and practice.

However, the extent of US religiosity is difficult to assess since the US Census Bureau does not ask questions on religious identity. It published a *Statistical Abstract of the United States, 2010*, which gathered evidence of adult belief from sources, such as the American Religious Identification Survey 2008–9, church rolls and opinion polls. The Bureau reported that 80 percent of adult Americans regarded themselves as religious in one form or another, which was a higher figure than most other nations.

But while an AP/IPSOS survey in 2005 reported that 86 percent of respondents felt that religion was important to them, a 2005 poll by the Anti-Defamation League (ADL) found that 64 percent of respondents believed that religion was under attack and 53 percent felt that it was losing its influence in American life. Other polls have noted that although a majority of people say they are very interested in spiritual matters, they think that beliefs are increasingly treated as arbitrary and unimportant.

Formal membership of, or identification with, denominations is not always translated into active observance, and religious commitment varies across the US. Polls have long reported that 36–40 percent of Americans have gone to a religious service in the last week before the poll was taken, and 60 percent say that they attend on a weekly or monthly basis. Southerners appear to be the most observant, followed by Midwesterners, Easterners and Westerners. Religious observation may sometimes be more socially directed than devout. Spirituality may also exist outside formal denominational identity and suggests a growing disillusionment with organized or institutional religion and a striving for more personally valid forms of self-definition.

Nevertheless religion, in whatever form, does play a role in the US. It is illustrated in the large variety of religious groups that reflect personal, communal and ethnic identities for citizens; in its influence on national institutions and morality; and in the country's history.

Religious history

Contemporary US religious life and practices derive from Native American beliefs, colonial history and the waves of later immigrants into the country.

This historical development is characterized by certain features. First, there is a distinctive religious diversity or pluralism (many different faiths) in the US. Second, religious activity with evangelical (conversion or salvation-based) and fundamentalist characteristics (strict maintenance of traditional orthodox beliefs) has been important at various times. Third, these factors have often created conflict within faiths, between different religions and in the larger society. Fourth, there has been an emphasis on the social aspects of religion and the provision of social welfare by the churches. Fifth, religion has been closely linked to a belief in democracy and freedom. Sixth, religious identities and membership of specific churches have often been connected to social class and ethnicity. Seventh, there is a constitutional emphasis on separating religion from the state.

Throughout American history, all or some of these features have been reflected in periodic religious movements (awakenings or revivals, which have varied in intensity and scope), religious activism, missionary work, utopian ideals and an interest in ecumenism (cooperation between different faiths). There has also been religious discrimination and intolerance, periods when American religiosity has been very low and increasing secularism.

The colonial period

Colonial settlement resulted in many religious denominations. Some colonists practiced faiths that were often based on different types of established European Christianity. But dissenters from such traditions wished to create communities where they could practice their own religions without persecution and create an ideal "city upon a hill." Religion on these levels was central to, and influenced, people's daily and commercial lives.

Most early colonists were Christian Protestants whose faiths influenced future US society. There were, however, conflicts between denominations. For example, in the early seventeenth century, Virginia's population largely comprised members of the established Anglican Church of England. This Church taxed dissenters who settled in the colony. Quakers were banned and Baptist ministers were arrested. However, French Huguenots, German Protestants and Scots-Irish Presbyterians were allowed their own congregations.

Meanwhile, two groups of settlers arrived in New England and were differ-ent from the Virginia Anglicans. A first group (Pilgrims) came to Plymouth,

Massachusetts, in 1620 from England and Holland to found their own church. They were separatists who had left the Church of England because they disapproved of its doctrines and because they had suffered persecution. A second, larger group (Puritans) arrived in Massachusetts Bay in 1630 and wanted to purify the Church of England.

Neither group was religiously tolerant. They expelled Church of England members and restricted membership of their congregations to people who had personally experienced conversion. They believed that God had chosen or predestined specific individuals to achieve salvation. Hard work was a means of pleasing God, and any resulting prosperity was a sign that He regarded them favorably. It is argued that this so-called Puritan (Protestant) work ethic is a conditioning factor in a general American ambition to succeed materially in life.

Religious diversity was most obvious in the middle colonies. These were settled by Protestant groups such as Welsh and Dutch Calvinists, Scottish Presbyterians, Swedish and German Lutherans, Baptists and English Quakers. Protestants and Roman Catholics established themselves in Maryland (formed originally as a haven for Catholics), with religious toleration for all Christians. Puritan pressure during the English Civil War resulted in toleration for Roman Catholics becoming limited and it ended in 1692.

The first Catholics to arrive in America in the sixteenth century, outside the original 13 colonies, were missionaries from Spain, Portugal and France. They established churches and missions in the South and West of the country in present-day Texas, California, Florida and New Mexico.

A few European Jewish traders also settled in the English colonies, despite an official ban on Jewish immigration. Newport, Rhode Island, became the main colonial center of Jewish life, with other groups in New York, Charleston and Philadelphia.

Most of the 13 colonies had an official established church (and a link between church and state) from colonial times until the War for Independence. The Anglican Church served Virginia, Maryland, the Carolinas, Georgia and parts of New York, and the Congregational Church (Pilgrims/Puritans) was established in New England. Other groups, such as the Presbyterians, Lutherans and Baptists, did not become the established church in any colony.

The eighteenth century

There was a change of emphasis in the eighteenth century. Although some (if by no means all) early colonists had been motivated by religious beliefs, the majority of immigrants now travelled to the US for material advancement, free land or commercial adventure. There was a decline in religious influence and observation, and it is estimated that in 1750 only 17 percent of the population formally belonged to a religious group. However, many people might still have retained nominal adherence to a traditional homeland faith.

Immigrants continued to arrive in the eighteenth century, often with distinct religious identifications such as Scots-Irish Presbyterians from the north of Ireland. Some of these settled in New York and New England, where they shifted the Congregational Church towards Presbyterianism. Others went to New Jersey, Pennsylvania and western Virginia. German Lutherans continued to immigrate and Jews arrived from Germany and Poland, but the main emphasis was still on Protestant Christian denominations.

Two events affected colonial communities in the eighteenth century and produced more active religiosity, at least for a time: first, the Great Awakening (religious revival) and second, the American War for Independence. The Great Awakening affected the colonies in the 1730s and 1740s and was the forerunner of modern evangelical activities. It was an emotional reaction to the formalistic, unappealing nature of most religious practices. It began in Massachusetts among the Congregationalists and spread along the East Coast from Maine to Georgia and along the Western frontier to include Presbyterians, Methodists and Baptists.

Revivalist (evangelical) preachers tried to convert people to their faiths by stressing the need for repentance, rebirth and a personal experience of salvation. The Great Awakening created friction, and churches were split as ministers and congregations either supported the revivalists or opposed their emotionalism and conversion practices. The radicalism of the Great Awakening influenced revolutionary sentiment and the coming War for Independence.

The War for Independence from Britain was a time of conflict for American religion with divided loyalties among the churches. Scots-Irish Presbyterians, Lutherans, Baptists and Congregationalists were mainly on the American side of the struggle, while the Methodists remained neutral. Some Anglicans supported the British and others the American cause, as did Catholics in Pennsylvania and Maryland. Pacifist religious bodies, such as the Moravians, Quakers and Mennonites, were often persecuted during the war because of their beliefs.

The Methodist and Baptist churches recovered quickly after the war, but the Anglican Church lost much prestige and influence due to its ties with England. Attempts to retrieve its position failed and the creation of a new American Protestant Episcopal Church in its place proved to be necessary. This was an important step to a more clearly American church.

However, despite the Great Awakening and the War for Independence, religiosity at the end of the eighteenth century was weak and most Americans were not active church members. The Great Awakening did not have a lasting or deep effect, the Episcopal Church was largely inactive and other religious groups became austere and intellectual or departed from their original religious doctrines. Protestant Christianity appeared to be declining with the abolition of most established churches after the War for Independence.

PLATE 5.1 St. John's Episcopal Church, Washington, DC, was built by Benjamin Latrobe, who was also the architect for the Capitol and the White House. It is known as "the church of the Presidents," where every president since James Madison has worshiped.
(John Aikins/Corbis)

The nineteenth century

Religious groups recovered in the nineteenth century as further revivals occurred, the population expanded westwards, immigration increased, missionary activities grew and the churches involved themselves in social concerns as a result of industrialization and economic growth. However, the Civil War (1861–5) was a testing time for American religion.

A second Great Awakening came at the beginning of the century on the East Coast and spread westwards along the frontier. It sometimes led to superficial emotionalism and divisions within the churches, but it also increased the number of evangelical groups, such as Baptists, Presbyterians and Methodists. This growth influenced future religious development and the creation of modern evangelical and fundamentalist movements. A further influence, if restricted largely to literary intellectuals, was Transcendentalism, which stressed the individual and nature as a reaction to traditional Puritanism.

Religious groups were increasingly subject to conflict within themselves and with other churches, especially between 1830 and 1860. This resulted in theological quarrels, division of churches and the formation of many sects. For example, attempts to unite the Congregationalists and Presbyterians ended in separation. There was tension between the High (East Coast) and Low (frontier) Church wings of the Episcopal Church. Splits occurred among the Lutherans, but the arrival of conservative German immigrants after 1830 prevented the liberal wing from dominating the church. Norwegian and Swedish Lutheran immigrants from 1840 also supported the conservative wing.

New religious movements or sects, with very different beliefs, were formed as a reaction to traditional faiths in the nineteenth century, such as Spiritualism, Millerism (Seventh-Day Adventism), Mormonism (Church of Latter Day Saints), Perfectionism and Shakerism. Other religious groups, often with a strong social emphasis, were also established from the 1850s.

Meanwhile, the Roman Catholic Church was greatly strengthened by Irish, French and German immigration from 1830 and by immigrants from eastern and southern Europe (such as Italy) later in the century. The church, after earlier internal conflict, was eventually controlled by its hierarchy of bishops. It proved attractive to the new immigrants, and Irish settlers in particular were to influence the church in future years. Catholic newcomers suffered considerable prejudice and hostility from the dominant Protestant groups.

Indeed, some of the more extreme Protestant groups attempted to oppose the influence of Roman Catholic immigration and to maintain strict Puritan traditions. For example, the Woman's Christian Temperance Union (1874) tried to stop the use of alcohol and campaigned to maintain the Puritan Sabbath.

Between 1840 and 1880 the Jewish population expanded from 15,000 to 225,000 because of repression and persecution in Germany and central Europe. Some Jews were Orthodox, but many became members of the new Reform movement. This adapted traditional practices to modern conditions and helped Jews to assimilate more easily to American life. Jews experienced anti-Semitism and discrimination in society, particularly from Protestants.

Despite religious tensions and the emergence of new sects, a more liberal spirit developed during the nineteenth century. Churches became involved in education and created schools and colleges with religious identifications. From 1820 further immigration promoted new outlooks and activities among the churches. Influential inner-city missions were formed on the East Coast that addressed the new problems (poverty and unemployment) of a wealthier and bigger population. It is argued that these mission movements and their activism, rather than the two Great Awakenings, saved American Christianity and increased religiosity.

Slavery and the Civil War were divisive threats to religion. The anti-slavery position was based on biblical, humanitarian and democratic impulses, but there were conflicting interpretations of slavery from both anti- and pro-slavery camps. Some churches, like the Episcopal Church, tried to be neutral, while others were divided. Post-war America experienced religious uncertainty and inaction as churches and society tried to recover from the effects of the war and the abolition of slavery morally and practically.

After 1880 US wealth increased substantially, due to industrialization and a booming economy. Divisions grew between rich and poor, and there was much social misery and inequality. There were conflicts between employees and employers, leading to strikes, unemployment and industrial unrest. The churches responded to these problems. Some emphasized social and moral commitment, supported the workers and provided for their social and economic needs, and many clergy played an active role in the community. This social concern is still a feature of some contemporary religious groups in the US.

The twentieth century

Religious variety and activity in the US increased at the end of the nineteenth century and during the twentieth century as large numbers of immigrants arrived from central, eastern and southern Europe, Latin America and Asia.

This influx strengthened the Roman Catholic Church, but the new arrivals also included eastern religions, such as Hinduism, Sikhism and Islam, as well as considerable numbers of Jewish immigrants fleeing persecution in Europe. Eastern Orthodox churches were also established by Greek, Russian, Armenian and Syrian immigrants. Such groups concentrated in the bigger cities and some retained their own languages in religious and daily life. This produced tight-knit communities with strong ethnic identities, but it also distanced them from many Americans. The result was often intolerance (based upon ignorance and old colonial dominance) directed against the new arrivals.

It is argued that a diversity of religions led to competing pressures in US life in the twentieth century between pluralism (separatism) and ecumenism (closer relations between faiths), social action and spiritual renewal, and secularism and religious growth.

Religious pluralism can indicate vitality and toleration of different religions, but it may also be divisive as denominations quarrel with each other. The dominant Protestant majority in early US history promoted basic national characteristics and institutions, but it often treated Roman Catholic, Jewish and other faiths with suspicion and hostility. This situation slowly changed in the early twentieth century and considerably since the 1950s, due to immigration, population growth in ethnic communities, improved social attitudes and a decrease in the Protestant majority. Three major faiths (Protestant, Catholic and Jewish) then shared American religious life with many other churches, groups and sects.

The pluralistic and somewhat divisive nature of US religion has been offset by ecumenical movements among different faiths, which have become more tolerant and cooperative. Traditional churches divided by historical disputes, such as Congregationalists, Lutherans, Presbyterians and Methodists, became closer. Cooperation has occurred at local and national levels between Protestants, Catholics, Jews and Orthodox groups with the creation of ecumenical organizations. For example, the Anti-Defamation League (1913) and the National Conference of Christians and Jews (1928) reduced anti-Semitic tension in the early twentieth century. There was also a greater assimilation of immigrants into the larger society as homeland languages declined and "national" churches and synods merged. Internationally, American Protestants helped to found the World Council of Churches in 1948, and ecumenism was treated positively by the Second Vatican Council (1962–5), which encouraged Catholics to be more open to other religions and modern developments.

By the 1970s, ecumenism declined. There was a concern that individual faiths might become weaker through cooperation and an increasing conservatism caused divisions in some church groups. Nevertheless, Protestants, Catholics and Jews have become less divisive, and anti-Catholicism and anti-Semitism are not as virulent or as widespread as they once were. Catholics and Jews have achieved greater status and recognition in American life, and religions such as Islam, Buddhism and Hinduism have been generally accepted. The emphasis has turned to coexistence among many faiths, rather than ecumenism. However, suspicion still exists between a majority of Americans toward Mormonism and Islam.

There are also areas of tension that are reflected in opposed views of social action and spiritual renewal. Social action stresses religion's public role and follows American traditions of liberal theology and social commitment. Some churches have campaigned for social change, provided welfare services and have debated social problems and moral concerns such as starvation, racial inequality, poverty, refugees, the wars in Vietnam, Iraq and Afghanistan, industrial relations, abortion, same-sex relationships and educational issues. This liberal social position has often necessitated new theological interpretations of belief and practice.

Some evangelical and fundamentalist groups within Protestantism emphasize spiritual renewal and reflect a desire among many Americans for more personal religious commitment and simple faith. Such movements are founded on a close reading and literal interpretation of the Bible, although they do vary in their practices and beliefs. Generally, they are traditional and orthodox in a strict maintenance of their values, stress the importance of personal salvation, are suspicious of social action and oppose liberalizing trends. Their emphasis on fundamental beliefs and fellowship has led them to reject not only evolutionary theories (Darwinism) in favor of creationism (the literal Bible story), but also new radical interpretations of the Bible and what they consider to be corrupt forms of modern life. Protestant churches in the twentieth century, and especially since the 1960s, consequently experienced battles between liberals, modernists, evangelicals and fundamentalists.

Some fundamentalists left their churches to form new groups where they could practice their beliefs. Other people have joined evangelical churches. These groups are connected to earlier traditions of revivalism with their espousal of the Christian gospel, conversion, emotional experiences and personal salvation through admission of one's sins. Evangelicals and fundamentalists have become a powerful social and political force in recent decades, have attracted media and popular attention and have grown strongly. Nevertheless, some of these churches have collapsed because of limited support, fraud or scandals.

The terms "evangelical," "conservative," "the Christian Right," and "fundamentalist" tend to be used interchangeably and somewhat loosely. "Fundamentalist" can be applied to Protestant groups with absolutist, "authoritarian," orthodox beliefs, which are based on the Bible as the authoritative word of God. "Evangelical" can be applied to Christian denominations with very varied titles, but which may be based on the doctrine of salvation and converting people to their beliefs in a "born-again" experience or personal relationship with Christ. Evangelicalism emphasizes the role of scriptural authority, but can include modernist interpretations of biblical authority. Both groups may have a conservative message that is based on moral values, the role of the family and education. They provide certainties for many Americans and stress individual responsibility and commitment.

Evangelical ministers and fundamentalist movements often use television and radio to spread their message and have become very skillful in their use of the media. They own or control some 1,300 radio and television stations. The preachers can become popular celebrities, their media performances attract large audiences and advertising revenues, and religious broadcasting has become very profitable. After a fall in popularity and influence in the late 1980s, the evangelical churches recovered in the mid-1990s and now have a significant voice on the political right.

Spiritual renewal has also led people to join a wide variety of sects, cults and churches. Common to them all is an attempt to create a sense of belonging through close emotional fellowship. The more extreme groups, such as the

Moonies and some guru-led organizations, have aroused hostility among many Americans. Their techniques of recruitment, alleged brainwashing of members and religious fanaticism are heavily criticized.

Some Americans, in the search for personal spiritual growth, ethnic identity and answers to modern problems, have joined or converted to eastern religions such as Islam, Hinduism and Buddhism, and founded the African American Nation of Islam. Others seek religious or spiritual satisfaction in a wide range of alternative beliefs such as the occult, Native American religions, astrology and witchcraft.

It is argued that the emergence of so many religious and pseudo-religious groups and the possible diffusion of national identity in this amorphous situation have led concerned Americans to embrace a "civil religion" centered on US political traditions. It is a mixture of religion, morality and nationalism that emphasizes symbols, emblems and traditions, such as the national motto ("In God We Trust") and the pledge of allegiance to the flag ("one nation, under God"). "Civil religion" supposedly overarches the varieties of belief, although the Christian emphasis is evident, and gives the US a moral character and sacred mission. Although this may be a source of national integration, it can also be divisive, and its contemporary influence, while formerly evident in the public school system, is debatable.

There was also an increased secularism in twentieth-century US life that conflicted with religious growth. Personal decisions are made without recourse to religious teachings or interpretations. Secularism has particularly affected education. Some private schools and colleges had previously been created by churches as a way of promoting religious belief, but in the twentieth century public schools were increasingly secularized by state authorities. A more relaxed and informal American society, with increased leisure and entertainment opportunities, has also contributed to the growth of secularization.

However, more Americans were involved with religious groups and activities in the mid-twentieth century. This coincided with greater interest in religion after the Second World War. Since then, there has been decline in some churches and growth in others.

Contemporary US religion

US religion underwent changes after the post-war revival. The influence and membership of mainstream Protestant and other traditional denominations declined in the liberal social climate of the 1960s and 1970s. But increasing pluralism led to new religious groups such as fundamentalist and evangelical churches (which attracted large numbers of members), sects, cults and eastern religions, such as Islam, Hinduism and Buddhism.

Despite these changes, the large majority of religious Americans today are still within the Judeo-Christian tradition and US religion consists of three main faiths

PLATE 5.2 The Hazrat I Abubaker Afghan Mosque, Flushing, Queens, New York. Northern and Southern Afghanis worship in the building, but there are tensions between the two groups. The site has also witnessed anti-Taleban demonstrations, as here.
(Michael Setboun/ Photononstop/Corbis)

in terms of their history, numbers and influence: Protestantism, Catholicism and Judaism.

When respondents to polls and surveys say they belong to specific US denominations, some of them may be nominal or preferential rather than active adherents and others may not always be accurate in their replies. Religious organizations can differ in their counting methods and statistics should be regarded as approximate. Polls report movements in US religiosity as people change religions. Many belong to a different tradition than their birth identity, others reject organized religion and some embrace different forms of spirituality.

A Pew Trends in Religious Affiliation survey, 2007–12, reported that 73 percent of adults self-defined themselves as Christian, of whom 48 percent were Protestant (the lowest figure in US history), with white evangelicals at 19 percent, white mainline adherents at 15 percent, blacks at 8 percent and other Protestant groups at 6 percent. Roman Catholics counted for 22 percent (a decrease from 2008), while 2 percent were Mormon and 1 percent was Orthodox. Other faiths, such as Jews, Buddhists, Muslims and Hindus, counted for 6 percent. Unaffiliated respondents were 19.6 percent (the highest figure recorded historically) and consisted of atheists, agnostics, secularists and "nothing in particular."

Yet the poll nevertheless showed that some 80 percent of respondents still identified with a religious faith or sensibility; the same percentage said that religion was "very" or "somewhat" important in their lives; but 25 percent reported that they rarely attended religious services. The poll characterized the US as a "competitive religious marketplace," and the nation was said to be highly religious with different churches competing for new members. It was argued that any presumed decline in religious belief was slow and gradual.

The above percentages may be shown numerically by using data from the *Statistical Abstract of the United States, 2010*. The *Abstract* was poll-based and gave self-defined religious identifications of the *adult* population, of whom 173 million were Christians.

Protestants

Protestantism is the largest and most diverse of the US faiths. Although a majority of adult Americans identified themselves as Protestants, they were divided into many churches and sects, with conservative, mainstream and liberal outlooks. There is no one denomination for all Protestants. Each church is independent, supports itself financially, has its own ministers, constructs its own buildings and follows its own beliefs and practices.

For example, the Presbyterian (4.7 million members), Lutheran (8.7 million), Episcopalian (2.4 million), Reformed churches (206,000) and small Congregational churches (736,000) represent mainstream Protestantism from early US history. The memberships of the Baptist churches (36.1 million) and Methodists/Wesleyan (11.4 million) are now considered part of this mainstream Protestant grouping. The largest, mainly white, denomination was the Southern Baptist Convention (17.1 million), while the largest African American denomination was the National Baptist Convention (5 million).

Protestantism is divided between such mainstream churches and fundamentalist or evangelical churches, often with conservative beliefs. Mainstream churches have different emphases. The traditional ones tend to have somewhat liberal theological and social attitudes, are composed largely of middle- or upper-class people and have formal worship and service patterns. Churches, like the Southern and National Baptists, may consist of lower-income groups and encourage emotional responses to religion, such as "born-again" conversions.

While some traditional mainstream churches have lost members since the 1970s, African American, evangelical and fundamentalist Protestant churches, such as the Seventh-Day Adventists (938,000), the Church of the Nazarene (358,000), the Assemblies of God (810,000), Evangelical/Born Again (2.2 million) and Jehovah's Witness (1.9 million), have increased their membership. They offer absolutist moral instruction and traditional values and appeal to those who want moral direction and religious certainty. The mainstream churches have retreated somewhat from their earlier liberalism in order to attract members, although the American Episcopalian Church is in conflict with members of the worldwide Anglican Communion because of its consecration of an openly gay bishop and its liberal stance.

Roman Catholics

Although there was large Catholic immigration into the US in the nineteenth and twentieth centuries, the country was still mainly Protestant in religion and national attitudes.

The Roman Catholic Church is the second largest religion after Protestantism, but the biggest in terms of a single denomination. It has about 19,000 churches and 57.2 million self-defined adult adherents. Its membership (practicing or not) has stabilized in recent years because of Latino population growth and southeast Asian immigration from 1990 to 2008.

Catholicism was historically confined to ethnic groups such as the Irish, Polish, Italians and Germans in the big cities and was initially largely working class. This urban concentration enabled Catholics to achieve considerable political power at the local, if not the national, level. After the Second World War, Catholics greatly improved their educational standards, income and class status, and many affluent Catholics moved to the suburbs. The church built more churches and schools for its growing population, although parochial schools have now declined in number and influence.

The movement of Catholics from tightly knit urban communities to the suburbs has arguably meant a decline in Catholic identity. Catholics are now

PLATE 5.3 Taking communion in St. Martin of Tours Roman Catholic Church, St. Martinville, Louisiana.
(Philip Gould/Corbis)

more willing, after years of discrimination against them, to mix with non-Catholics. Hostility towards them has largely disappeared, illustrated by the election of Catholic John F. Kennedy as President in 1960. American Catholics are also influential in international campaigns and domestic social projects and tend to be more ecumenically minded today than they have been in the past.

Religious and social change has caused internal tensions within the community. Members are not as active in church activities as they were, and attendance at weekly mass has declined. The church is divided between liberals and conservatives with opposed opinions on birth control, abortion, the celibacy of priests, gay and lesbian relationships and the question of women priests. These concerns have clashed with conservative Vatican views. A serious development in recent years has been evidence of Catholic priests sexually abusing young people and the alleged cover-up of such behavior by the Catholic leadership. This has provoked horrified criticism within the church and by outsiders and a resulting lack of trust. Court cases and large compensation claims have sometimes resulted.

The Jewish community

Jews historically have settled mainly on the East Coast and in the big cities. After immigration, their religious practices changed somewhat and now range from traditional Orthodox to moderate Conservative and liberal Reform groups. Most groups have been concerned to preserve their Jewish heritage and traditions.

As the Jewish population grew, they established Hebrew schools and contributed to Jewish charities. The creation of the state of Israel in 1948 was an additional focus for Jewish identity. Although anti-Semitism increased in the early twentieth century, this has now been reduced because of changing social attitudes, ecumenism and sympathy for Jewish suffering in the Second World War. Jews have assimilated into American society and are more accepted than they once were. They have also become more liberal and secularized with increased intermarriage (nearly a third) between Jews and non-Jews, leading to fears about the collapse of the religious community. There are 2.7 million adult religious Jews divided into the Reform, Conservative and Orthodox traditions. But 1.1 million ethnic or cultural Jews are secular or non-religious or have become members of a faith other than Judaism.

Other religious groups

There are other significant US religious groups (amounting to 8.8 million adults) in addition to the three main faiths, such as Buddhism (1.2 million), Hinduism (582,000), Islam (1.4 million) and Sikhism (78,000). It is argued that Islam today is a fourth major faith in the US that, combined with other Asian religions, has a growing representative importance. Examples of other religions are Native American (186,000), Wiccan (342,000), Pagan (340,000) and Spiritualist (426,000).

Unaffiliated

The 2010 *Abstract* reported that 1.6 million adult respondents described themselves as atheist, 2 million as agnostic and 30.4 million as having no religion, while 11.9 million people did not answer. These unaffiliated respondents (Americans who did not identify themselves with any organized religion) increased from 14.3 million in 1990 to 34.2 million in 2008. The American Religious Identification Survey (2008–9) argued that the challenge to Christianity in the US does not come from other religions, but rather from a rejection of all forms of organized religion.

Church, state and politics

Church and state in the US are supposedly separate. The First Amendment of the Bill of Rights (1791) states that "Congress shall make no law respecting an establishment of religion, or prohibiting the free exercise thereof." This forbids state-supported religion, the creation of a state church and the promotion of religion. It also protects individuals' right to practice their own faiths. The First Amendment applies only to the federal government, not to the states. However, the Fourteenth Amendment (1868) has been interpreted to mean that the states must also protect and guarantee the rights of religion.

Religion, or the lack of it, is a private matter. Respondents to a Brookings Institution poll in September 2011 supported the principles of religious freedom, religious tolerance and strict separation of church and state. Of respondents, 88 percent agreed that the US was founded on the idea of religious freedom for all, including unpopular religious groups. And 95 percent accepted that all religious books should be treated with respect even if individuals did not share their religious beliefs. However, respondents were divided over whether Islam is incompatible with US national standards (47 percent agreed and 48 percent disagreed), while 54 percent agreed that Muslims are an important part of US religious life (43 percent disagreed).

Opinions differ in other areas. A CNN/*USA Today*/Gallup poll in 2003 found that 54 percent of respondents thought that the promoting of a religion or religious views by the government or in schools always harms the rights of those people who do not belong to that religion or support those views. But a *Newsweek* poll in 2002 reported that 54 percent of respondents felt that the government should not avoid promoting religion. An Anti-Defamation League (ADL) poll in 2005 found that many respondents supported a more direct role for religion in public life, such as organized school prayers, the teaching of creationism, allowing religious symbols such as the Ten Commandments to be displayed in public buildings and continuing the use of "one nation, under God" in the Pledge of Allegiance to the flag.

These findings suggest that Americans are divided on the question of religion in public life and that strict church–state separation is being questioned. Some people think that religion is under attack and others believe that the church–state barrier should be abolished. More dogmatic critics would like to Christianize America, and reject the nation's inclusive image. However, an AP/IPSOS survey in 2005 found that 61 percent of respondents were against attempts by religious leaders to influence government decisions and public policy.

A *Newsweek* poll in April 2009 reported that 33 percent of Americans thought that religion had played too big a role in US politics under George W. Bush's presidency, while 25 percent said it had too little influence. In the first Obama administration, 26 percent thought that religion was too influential, while 31 percent said that faith did not have enough weight in the political system. In the 2008 election campaign, 51 percent of respondents said their religion could have an impact on their personal politics. And 46 percent thought their faith was less likely to affect their vote on a candidate or an issue.

There were established churches before the War for Independence and Massachusetts had an official church into the 1830s, but eventually all churches were separated from the state. There are now no church taxes; the churches are not supposed to receive any direct state or federal support; there are no legal or official religious holidays; and no political party is formally affiliated to a specific denomination. Any attempt to introduce religious influence or role in these areas would, strictly speaking, be regarded as violating the Constitution.

Religious groups are therefore independent organizations and self-supporting. They depend upon their members' financial contributions for their existence and payment of expenses. Americans' donations to their churches are generous, with some 45 percent of all charitable donations going to religion. Fundamentalist and evangelical churches attract the greatest amounts. Local religious buildings and their congregations are the strengths and centers of US religion. They also provide social, cultural and community activities, supply relief aid for the poor and needy and engage in missionary work domestically and overseas.

But, as society has become more complex and government more pervasive, church and state have interfered with each other. States have historically restricted freedom of religion by prohibiting Catholics and Jews from voting or holding public office. Courts have also had to rule on special working practices for minority religions, such as Mormons and Seventh-Day Adventists. In these cases, the Supreme Court and Congress have often invalidated limitations by permitting exceptions to the general rule. The Supreme Court has also restricted adherents' free practice of religion if their behavior is against the public interest. The George W. Bush administration arguably weakened the church/state ban by its espousal of faith-based social services and federal funding of religious groups. The division between church and state depends largely upon fine interpretations, and Congress and the Supreme Court have reached decisions that appear to contradict the First Amendment.

Although religion is supposed to be a private matter, public and private lives are not inseparable. Given the prevalence and diversity of denominations in American life, it is inevitable that religion and its moral concerns should influence public and political debates on issues such as abortion, the death penalty, same-sex marriage and armed conflicts. For example, Pew research polls in 2003 found that although 53 percent of respondents were against gay marriage (with 38 percent in favor), this marked a decreased opposition from 65 percent in 1996. A Gallup poll in 2006 reported that Americans had become more liberal on abortion. Regarding abortion, 55 percent supported it under certain circumstances, 24 percent felt that it is legal in any circumstance and 20 percent believed that it was illegal in all cases.

A religious (or "civil religion") sensibility is reflected in national symbols and emblems such as the US seal, the currency and the Pledge of Allegiance to the American flag. US Presidents often belong to a religious group, politicians frequently refer to God and the Bible in their speeches, and many presidential campaign speeches in the 2012 election ended with "God bless America." US Presidents swear the inaugural oath of office on the Bible, sessions of Congress commence with prayers and both Houses of Congress have chaplains.

However, formal religion arguably has little direct influence in national political matters and institutions, or has not as yet reached the stage where it could seriously do so. Politicians are conscious of the constitutional position and its restrictions upon government action, as well as the restraints of religious tolerance. Nevertheless, personal beliefs and values may affect the way in which individuals react to political issues, how they vote in elections and which parties and candidates they support.

A source of national debate about religion and politics has revolved around the role of evangelical groups and their leaders. Many of them are very visible, actively propagate their beliefs and attempt to influence public opinion, social institutions and political processes. They do not restrict themselves to moral and religious matters, but campaign on political issues such as anti-abortion legislation and prayers in public schools. The evangelical right, sometimes known as "the moral majority" or the "Christian coalition/right" because of its absolutism and stress upon alleged American values, has supported conservative politicians in election campaigns, and some of its leaders have also attempted to gain political office.

The role of religion in politics and social issues is a divisive matter. A Pew Research Center poll in 2004 found that 51 percent of respondents thought that churches should be able to express political and social views, while 44 percent did not. Sixty five percent considered that churches should not favor any one candidate in a political election over another, while 25 percent thought they should. Yet a CNN/*USA Today*/Gallup poll in 2003 showed that 90 percent of respondents approved of the words "In God We Trust" on US coins. The Supreme Court has not ruled that these words and "one nation, under God" are unconstitutional.

Religion and education

Administrative and financial organization of public schools is generally carried out by local districts, and school boards composed of elected citizens oversee the schools in their area. They influence school policy and often what is to be taught. It is at this level that battles between fundamentalists and modernizers over the school curriculum have been fought. Education is supposed to be neutral. The constitutional separation of church from state means that public schools can teach about religion, but cannot promote it or endorse a particular religion. Any attempt to do so would be regarded as an infringement of the "establishment clause" of the First Amendment. This clause has often been tested in court cases dealing with religious holidays; religious dress; documents such as the Ten Commandments; the Pledge of Allegiance; school prayers; and the teaching of creationism and evolution. Schools and the courts have tried to balance separation with religious freedom. For example, in 1963 the Supreme Court ruled that religion may be taught in the public school curriculum as long as it is objective instruction about religion rather than promotion. Public schools may teach courses in the history of religion, comparative religion and the role of religion in US history.

After the colonial period when schools were often run by different denominations, most public schools supported a historically dominant Protestant Christianity by means of school prayers, religious instruction and activities, or denominational identity. But fear of Catholic growth in the nineteenth century led some states to ban schools from obtaining public funding for religious purposes and public schools were slowly secularized.

The Pledge of Allegiance and school prayers have been central to education debates. The Supreme Court has frequently ruled since 1942 that students cannot be compelled to recite the pledge, or be punished for refusing. In March 2010, the US Court of Appeals for the Ninth Circuit upheld the words "one nation, under God" arguing that they were of a "ceremonial and patriotic nature" and not promotion or establishment of religion. Use of the pledge in the school day varies, with some half of the states committed to it. However, some critics argue that this practice effectively indoctrinates schoolchildren with "civil religion."

In 1962, the Supreme Court in *Engel* v. *Vitale* removed elements of school religion. It ruled that laws requiring the reciting of the Lord's Prayer, Bible verses or prayers in public schools were unconstitutional because they violated the principle of separation between church and state by promoting religion. In 1984 the US Senate rejected two constitutional amendments that would have permitted prayers in public schools. Such decisions have thus banned prayers in public schools and the division of church and state remains, although varieties of government funding for school religious groups have evolved.

An important issue is whether or not religious organizations may use government money, grants and school vouchers, to subsidize religious schooling. In June 2002, the Supreme Court ruled in *Zelman* v. *Simmons-Harris* that

Cleveland, Ohio's voucher program did not promote the establishment of religion because the decision to use voucher funds to attend a religious school was at the personal discretion of the family to affect their children's education and was not dictated by the state. The question of whether private schools (church-supported or not) should receive public money is vigorously debated and the private sector generally receives no funding from federal or state governments. Although rising costs resulted in Congress granting Roman Catholic parochial schools free lunches, transportation, textbooks and health and social services in 1965, the Supreme Court has struck down most other forms of aid. Two 1985 decisions prohibited public school teachers from teaching courses in private religious schools with public funds.

However, the 2001 Supreme Court decision in *Good News Club* v. *Milford Central School* ruled that publicly funded schools must allow religious groups to use their facilities for religious activities during non-school hours if they provide the same use to other non-school organizations. Court rulings have also allowed state-university property to be used by students for religious purposes as long as that property can also be used by others for other purposes. But, in 1992 the Supreme Court banned clergy from offering prayers at graduation ceremonies in public schools. These decisions aim at distinguishing between state recognition of religion by the participation of officials at public ceremonies and the participation of students in voluntary religious activities on state property.

A 2003 *USA Today*/Gallup/CNN poll reported that 78 percent of respondents supported the reciting of a non-denominational prayer in public school. An Anti-Defamation League (ADL) poll in 2005 found that 47 percent of respondents believed that public school students should be able to express religious beliefs/group prayers during the school day, while 44 percent thought that public schools should only allow a moment of silence for individual prayer. Sixty nine percent of fundamentalist/evangelical Christians believed that group prayer is appropriate, while 25 percent supported individual prayer only.

On the other hand, parents send their children to religious or alternative schools because they feel that public schools do not reflect their values and want their children to attend faith schools. Private schools are run by churches or religious groups at both elementary and high school levels, such as Catholic, Jewish and Islamic schools. Such schools often provide an academic education with a religious orientation and atmosphere. The secular public school curriculum, the controversy over evolution and creationism, variable quality in schools and devout parents' disillusionment with the public school system has arguably contributed to home school teaching and other alternatives.

Some private schools, particularly those founded in the 1970s and 1980s, have no religious identification and little if any federal grants. It is argued that while religious people should be able to choose their own schools, public tax money should not support them. It is felt that public schools have established a system that teaches students of many faiths and cultures and enables them to live with differences without the promotion of religion.

Attitudes to religion

Historically, American attitudes to religion and religious belief have been generally positive, although there have been declines in recent years and more varied individual responses. A Gallup poll in December 2010 showed that 54 percent of respondents felt that religion was very important in their lives and 26 percent thought it fairly important. Therefore, 80 percent considered that religion was personally significant for them, irrespective of whether or not they were members of a denomination. But 70 percent also felt that religion is losing its influence in America and only 25 percent thought that it was increasing its impact.

It is argued that Americans were more religious in the 1940s and 1950s although they appear to be as individually religious now as they had been in the late 1970s and 1980s. This distinction between declining formal church or synagogue membership and personal belief is reflected in the current 61 percent of Americans who reported being a church or synagogue member to Gallup, which is among the lowest measurements since the 1930s.

Significant changes in religiosity have occurred in recent years. Although polls had traditionally shown that most respondents believed that religion could answer all or most problems, a *Newsweek* poll in April 2009 found that a historic low of only 48 percent thought that faith would now answer all or most of the country's difficulties. There seemed to be a view that religion was old-fashioned, and changing perceptions about the religious and social composition of the US were also noted in the poll. Since the 2009 inauguration of Barack Obama, 62 percent of respondents considered the US to be a Christian nation, compared with 69 and 71 percent during the George W. Bush administrations. Respondents showed a movement to more liberal positions on social issues. Only 25 percent said that school boards should be able to fire homosexual teachers, down from 51 percent in 1987. Those who claimed to have "old-fashioned values about family and marriage" had decreased to 74 percent.

Nevertheless, the poll found that Americans' personal beliefs have not changed much in the last 20 years. Nine in ten Americans have faith in a superior spiritual being or creator and 78 percent said prayer was an important part of daily life. Forty eight percent described themselves as both "religious and spiritual;" 30 percent said they were "spiritual but not religious;" and 9 percent said they were neither religious nor spiritual.

However, a Gallup poll in July 2012, found that only 44 percent of respondents had a great deal or quite a lot of confidence in "the church or organized religion," which was a low point from 68 percent in 1975 and illustrates a long-time decline in Americans' confidence in institutional religion since the

1970s. Confidence fell in the mid-to late 1980s as a possible reaction to scandals involving evangelist television preachers. It was then affected by charges of child sex abuse by Catholic priests and cover-ups by the church across the US. These findings reflected a general negativity towards other social institutions, such as banks, television news and public schools. Nevertheless, the church and organized religion still ranked fourth in the Gallup poll of 16 institutions. Fifty six percent of Protestants expressed a great deal or quite a lot of confidence in organized religion, compared with 46 percent of Catholics. This decline in confidence does not necessarily indicate a large decrease in Americans' personal attachment to religion or its importance in their lives.

The varied personal beliefs of Americans include expressions of traditional faith, such as God, miracles, heaven, angels, the soul, the devil and examples of Christian dogma; a sense of spirituality outside organized religion; and some support for alternative belief systems (see Table 5.1). Although such findings were relatively high and consistent in Harris surveys in 2005 and 2007, the 2009 Harris and other polls have shown a decline in most of the items from high earlier levels. According to the poll, there were also big differences between the beliefs

TABLE 5.1   American personal beliefs, 2009

	Believe (%)	Don't believe (%)	Undecided (%)
God	82	9	2
Miracles	76	13	12
Heaven	75	13	12
Jesus is God (or Son of God)	73	16	11
Angels	72	15	12
Survival of soul after death	71	10	19
Resurrection of Jesus	70	17	13
Hell	61	24	16
Virgin birth (of Jesus to Mary)	61	22	17
The devil	60	7	13
Darwin's theory of evolution	45	32	22
Ghosts	42	38	20
Creationism	40	30	30
Unidentified flying objects (UFOs)	32	39	29
Astrology	26	52	22
Witches	23	59	17
Reincarnation and rebirth	20	53	28

Source: The Harris Poll, December 2009.

of Catholics, Protestants, Born Again Christians and Jews. Many people were nominal adherents to a faith without subscribing to all its beliefs and other unaffiliated individuals might believe in elements from several faiths. Large minorities of adults also accept ghosts, UFOs, astrology, witches and reincarnation, although these show declining support and more "undecided" respondents from previous years and other polls.

Evolution and creationism continue to be debated in relation to religion and education. Although results differ somewhat between polls, respondents to a Gallup 2001 poll doubted scientific evolution (without God) as the explanation for the origin of human beings. Biblical creationism was accepted by 45 percent, 37 percent believed in God-guided evolution and 12 percent accepted evolution without the guidance of God. By the time of a 2006 CBS poll, 55 percent of respondents supported the creationist view that God created humans in their present form; 27 percent accepted theistic evolution that humans evolved, but God guided the process; and 13 percent agreed with naturalistic evolution that God did not guide the process. Asked in a 2005 Anti-Defamation League (ADL) poll whether Darwin or the Bible is the more likely explanation for the origins of human life on earth, 57 percent of respondents cited the Bible while 31 percent chose Darwin. Support for biblical creationism had apparently increased while that for theistic evolution decreased.

However, a Gallup poll in 2007 found that the number of people who believed that the Bible is the actual Word of God decreased to 31 percent (1991–2007) from 38 percent (1976–84.) The Harris Poll, November 2009 (see table 5.1) found that 45 percent of American adults believed in Darwin's theory of evolution, 32 per cent did not believe and 22 percent were undecided. On the other hand, 40 percent of respondents believed in creationism, 30 percent did not and 30 percent were undecided. In effect, more people in Table 5.1 believe in miracles, heaven, angels, hell and the devil than in either evolution or creationism.

In terms of education, the 2001 Gallup poll reported that 68 percent supported teaching creationism together with evolution in public schools; 40 percent favored teaching only creationism; but this was opposed by 55 percent. By 2005, an ADL poll found that 56 percent of respondents favored and 39 percent opposed the teaching of creationism alongside evolution in public schools "as equally valid explanations for the origins of human life." Among fundamentalist/evangelical/charismatic Christians, 70 percent favored teaching creationism, while 28 percent were opposed.

The 2001 Gallup poll reported that the use of school property after teaching hours for student religious meetings was favored by 72 percent (26 per cent opposed); 80 percent believed that students should be allowed to recite a spoken prayer at school graduations; 66 percent thought spoken prayer should be allowed in the classroom (opposed by 34 percent); and 62 percent felt that religion had too little presence in public schools.

There are consistent threads running through US opinion polls that comment upon the larger changes above. Many respondents think that religion plays too small a role in most people's lives today. Others do not think that the ethical and moral standards of Americans are as high as they should be; that morals are one of the top problems facing the country; and that the country's moral and cultural values have changed for the worse since the 1960s because the US has become too permissive and/or liberal.

Exercises

Explain and examine the significance of the following names and terms:

secularization	Protestantism	evangelicalism
civil religion	pluralism	school prayers
Puritans	fundamentalism	Congregationalists
Episcopal	Church social action	sectarianism
ecumenism	Great Awakenings	denomination
creationism	evolution	Fourteenth Amendment
Quakers	dissenters	Awakenings/revivals
sect/cult	established church	Darwin
creationism	permissive	graduation
"civil religion"	Mormons	Pledge of Allegiance

Write short essays on the following questions:

1. How is the diversity of contemporary denominations reflected in, and due to, American religious history?

2. Describe and examine the ways in which American religion has been characterized by division and conflict.

3. Analyze the growth and present position of one of America's main faiths: Protestantism, Catholicism or Judaism.

4. Examine the public opinion poll findings in the text and evaluate whether they are contradictory or significant illustrations of US religious life.

Further reading

Abrams, E. (1997) *Faith or Fear: How Jews can survive in a Christian America*, New York: Free Press.

Ahlstrom, S. (1972) *A Religious History of the American People*, New Haven, CT: Yale University Press.

Buck, C. (2009) *Religious Myths and Visions of America: How Minority Faiths Redefined America's World Role*, Westport, CT: Praeger Publishers.

Dionne, E.J., Elshtain, J.B. and Drogosz, K.M. (2004) *One Electorate Under God? A Dialogue on Religion and American Politics*, Washington, DC: Brookings Institution Press.

Eck, D. (2002) *A New Religious America: The World's Most Religiously Diverse Nation*, New York: HarperOne.

Fowler, R.B., Hertzke, A.D., Olson, L.R. and den Dulk, K.R. (eds) (2004) *Religion and Politics in America*, Boulder, CO: Westview Press.

Goldstein, N. and Brown-Foster, W. (2007) *Religion and the State*, New York: Infobase Publishing.

Haddad, R.T. and Lummis, A.T. (1987) *Islamic Values in the United States*, Oxford: Oxford University Press.

Jocks, C. (2001) *Native American Religions*, London: Routledge.

Lambert, F. (2010) *Religion in American Politics: A Short History*, Princeton, NJ: Princeton University Press.

Melton, J.G. (2009) *Encyclopedia of American Religions*, Gale: Gale Directory Library.

Putnam, R.D. and Campbell, D.E. (2010) *American Grace: How Religion Divides and Unites Us*, New York: Simon & Schuster.

Queen, E.L., Prothero, S.R. and Shattuck, G.H. (eds) (2009) *Encyclopedia of American Religious History*, New York: Facts on File.

Witte, J. (2000) *Religion and the American Constitutional Experiment: Essential Rights and Liberties*, Boulder, CO: Westview Press.

The World Almanac and Book of Facts (annual) New York, NY: World Almanac Books.

Wright, J.W. (ed.) (annual) *The New York Times Almanac*, New York: Penguin Books.

Wuthnow, R. (1988) *The Restructuring of American Religion*, Princeton, NJ: Princeton University Press.

Websites

www.has.vcu.edu/wrs
www.dallasnews.com/religion

Chapter 6

Political institutions
The federal government

Stable political institutions have been particularly important in a nation of immigrants. Many commentators feel that loyalty to the basic structures and principles of government has acted as the cement that has held together so large and diverse a nation. Today, the US holds several records for political stability and longevity. Arguably the oldest functioning democracy, the country also has the world's oldest written constitution and political party (the Democratic Party). Much has changed in American government and politics since the nation declared its independence in 1776. The Constitution of 1787 has endured not least because it has proven amenable to changing interpretations and open enough to assimilate important extra-constitutional elements. Even so, political institutions in the US have been, and continue to be, the subject of heated debate. As Barack Obama began his second term, sharpened partisan polarization and divided government with a president of one party and majorities of the other major party in one or both houses of congress led to political deadlock and a decline in the public's confidence in government.

Historical origins

The English authorities allowed the American colonists to evolve political institutions (governors, assemblies and courts) with little outside interference. Partially based on local control and the consent of the inhabitants, these traditions of self-government later inspired the independence movement, formed the foundation for the constitutions of the independent states after 1776 and served as the model for the federal government erected through the Constitution of 1787.

At first most Americans opposed a strong central government, which they identified with British oppression. The first US constitution, the Articles of Confederation (1781–8), established a loose league of independent states under a very weak central government. With no executive or judicial branch, the national government consisted only of a one-house legislature that lacked financial, diplomatic and military power. Much like the United Nations, the confederation had to ask the member states for everything, from military forces to money for operating expenses.

Soon chaos in the nation's economy and international relations made members of the merchant classes support stronger central government. These "federalists" argued for the adoption of the new constitution drafted in Philadelphia in 1787.

The anti-federalists, who pictured the country's future as largely agricultural, opposed the new constitution because it endangered the sovereignty of the states and lacked a list of protections for individuals. Only when agreement was reached that ten amendments to satisfy these objections (later called the Bill of Rights) would be added was the constitution ratified. Thus, the new framework of national government reflected ideas from both sides of the debate.

This constitution returned to the colonial tradition of a government with three branches (the legislative, executive and judicial). Unlike revolutionary-era state governments, however, it did not make the legislature paramount. Instead, it provided for branches that had to cooperate to perform the functions of government. It also changed the nature of the union. The loose confederacy became a federation whose national government had powers that remedied the weaknesses of the Articles. Federal law became supreme in the areas covered by those powers. But the states' territorial integrity and their sovereignty in all other areas were guaranteed.

Three compromises secured the states' approval for the new government. The first balanced the representation of small and large states in Congress. In the House of Representatives the number of seats per state was made proportional to population to please the states with large populations. In the Senate every state was given two seats, regardless of population, to please the small states. The second compromise patched over conflicts between the North and South regarding slavery. Once representation in one chamber of Congress was made dependent on population, the issue was how to count the large number of slaves in the South, who were not citizens and who were legally property rather than people. In the North, the states had abolished slavery or contained very few slaves. The compromise stated that three-fifths of the slaves would count for representation in the House, but that the importing of slaves could be outlawed by 1808. In the early years of the nation this compromise gave the slave states additional power in the House of Representatives and the Electoral College that chose the president. The drafters also compromised on economic disagreements by permitting Congress to tax imports but not exports, which simultaneously kept the prices of Southern agricultural exports low and opened the door for tariffs to protect Northern manufacturers from cheap imported goods. Critics, then and since, have pointed out that two of these compromises tacitly approved slavery by giving it advantages in the framework of the federal government. (See the Appendix for the three compromises in Article I of the Constitution.)

The constitutional framework

Four-fifths of the original text of the Constitution remains unchanged, and only 17 amendments have been added after the Bill of Rights. Yet its thought and language have remained flexible enough to be interpreted differently by

PLATE 6.1 The Capitol, Washington, DC.
(Wes Thompson/Corbis)

PLATE 6.2 The first cabinet of the US in 1789: President George Washington, Thomas Jefferson, Alexander Hamilton, Henry Knox and Edmond Randolph.
(Time Life Pictures)

succeeding generations. The changes in US constitutionalism have been significant but few. They have come through amendments and judicial review rather than revolutionary upheavals. The enduring principles in the Constitution are republicanism, federalism, the separation of powers and the system of checks and balances.

A republican form of government

Republicanism is the belief in a government without any classes of people privileged by birth (thus excluding a royal family and an aristocracy) or by occupational class (prohibiting, for example, a privileged class of clergy). The Constitution of 1787 specifically prohibits inherited titles and an established national religion in the US. Article IV, Section 4 of the document, moreover, guarantees each state in the union a republican form of government.

Federalism

The Constitution lays the foundation for federalism through the concepts of "reserved" and "delegated" powers in the Tenth Amendment. It reserves to the states or people those powers not specified or reasonably inferred as federal from the wording in the Constitution. American federalism is a political system in which the governing power (sovereignty) is shared between the national government and the states. The states delegated some powers to the national government in 1787 but reserved most powers to themselves. The powers of both are limited by the rights reserved for the people in the Preamble of the Constitution and the Bill of Rights. The preamble stresses popular sovereignty (the idea that "the people" are the power behind government). The people's representatives created the government and can alter or totally replace it.

The US has a hierarchy of law. The federal Constitution is the country's supreme law. Acts of Congress signed by the president as well as state and local laws must conform to it. State and local laws must in addition conform to federal statutes and the state constitution. This legal hierarchy led the federal Supreme Court to assume the role of final interpreter of the US Constitution through "judicial review." Connecting state and national law, the court decides what government activity is permissible on any level under the Constitution. The US Constitution limits the court's work and thus judicial review to "cases and controversies." This means the court cannot interpret the constitutionality of a law unless someone brings legal charges against that law to a lower court and appeals the case to the US Supreme Court.

The Constitution's broad language has allowed the Supreme Court to expand federal power into areas originally left to the states. Congress, for example, has extended its activities through clauses giving it broad power to regulate commerce, provide for the general welfare and create all laws that are "necessary and

Across the nation today the Democratic Party label tends to represent a moderate-to-liberal political orientation. During the same period, the Republican Party has become more uniformly conservative as its moderate-to-liberal wing in the Northeast, Upper Midwest and Pacific Northwest has shrunk and lost influence to conservative activists. The ideological center of the Republican Party supports a small federal government, states rights, minimal regulation of business, low taxes and private solutions to poverty and social problems. Since the "Reagan revolution" in the 1980s, party allegiance to these policies has become more pronounced as its center shifts to the right.

After they win the party's nomination, presidential candidates usually move toward the center of the party and the electorate in order to assemble a coalition that can ensure victory. This has been particularly evident since 1996 as partisan polarization increased. In 1996, presidential candidate Bob Dole seemed moderate compared to most delegates at the Republican convention, but in 2000 and again in 2004 George W. Bush moved further right than many delegates. In 2008 and 2012 the situation was reversed when John McCain and then Mitt Romney seemed moderate compared to the center and right wing of the party, even though they took more rightist positions during the caucus-primary campaign in an effort to keep in touch with the "party base" and the Tea Party Movement from 2010 onwards. Sarah Palin, although she also called herself a maverick in 2008, was widely seen as chosen to secure the loyalty of these more conservative parts of the party base. Four years later vice-presidential candidate Paul Ryan assertively proposed right-of-center conservative positions that sharp spending cuts were the best way to deal with the economic crisis because that would reduce the budget deficit and national debt.

Democrats are more in favor of government management of the economy, a public social safety net and unions. Bill Clinton, who moved the party to the political center in the 1990s, had a party majority behind his moderate democrat label but nearly alienated his party's liberal wing in 1996. Barack Obama and the party leadership in both houses of Congress achieved a long-term goal of liberal Democratic politics when they passed the Affordable Health Care for America Act in 2009. For 35 years, opinion between the parties has also divided over a number of social issues. More Democrats have favored civil rights and affirmative action programs for minorities, gun control and abortion rights. More Republicans have favored reducing government spending and balancing the federal budget, but President Clinton adopted both of these positions and milder forms of Republican stances on welfare reform, taxes and small government. By the late 1990s both parties seemed further to the right, but in the next two presidential elections, differing views on these issues marked the party platforms and split the voters into almost equal camps.

Al Gore edged the Democratic Party back towards its historic base, and in 2004 John Kerry attempted to balance traditional Democratic positions on domestic issues while charting an equally tough but "smarter" course in the wars in Iraq and Afghanistan and the global war on terror. Meanwhile, George W. Bush appealed to and mobilized the conservative wing of the Republican Party with increasing success. John McCain was less successful at getting out the conservative Republican vote. Obama's campaign rhetoric, agenda in his first term, and second-term appointments, however, showed a determination to put competence and pragmatic problem-solving before partisan bickering and deadlock. Clear popular and electoral-college majorities presented him with support as he took office on January 20, 2013. That seemed to help him win sufficient Republican votes in the out-going Congress to keep from falling off the "fiscal cliff" by avoiding the passage of a package of drastic tax and spending cuts. Republican votes also allowed for temporarily raising the nation's debt ceiling to pay the government's current financial obligations. These bipartisan victories gave some hope that the period of inflexible partisan deadlock might be easing.

A range of economic and social indicators also showed differences between the parties in 2012. Democrats had, on average, lower incomes, less education and less prestigious occupations. They were also pronouncedly more often female, Jewish, urban and members of racial minority groups. Until the 1980s, most white Catholic ethnics were also Democrats, but now they more often split their allegiance, in 2008 and 2012 more in favor of the Democrats than in the last several elections. Under National Chairperson Howard Dean, between 2004 and the next election the Democrats successfully carried out a grassroots registration drive in every state, no matter how it had voted in previous elections, and by 2008 it was the majority party nationwide. The Republicans' appeal, on the other hand, has seemed to some critics somewhat more regional, too exclusively male and "white," and in need of fresh leadership by the end of 2012.

Party organization

The federal system results in parties that organize and function on three distinct levels. State and local party organizations vary a great deal. They are affiliated with, but not controlled by, the national parties, which usually do not interfere in their activities except to offer funds or services. The parties have organizing committees on every level with the Republican and Democratic national committees and their chairs at the top. Some critics say cooperation between the party levels is growing stronger. Others note an advantage in the current separated levels. The state and local parties are active on a continuous basis, while the national organizations, until recently, have lain dormant between presidential elections. The party that loses presidential elections (as the Democrats did most of the time between 1968 and 1988) can sustain its strength in Congress and state governments. Both parties seem weak compared with European parties. Nearly all candidates label themselves as Democrat or Republican, but the party does not control their election campaigns or the policies they advocate.

PLATE 6.3 President Barack Obama and Republican presidential nominee Mitt Romney exchange views about the country's foreign policy during the third presidential debate which was held at Lynn University in Boca Raton, Florida in October 2012.
(Keystone USA-ZUMA/Rex Features)

Independent candidates and "third" parties

Independent candidates and minor or splinter parties (so-called "third" parties) have a long history in America. They seldom win federal elections because of election rules and the public's loyalty to one of the major parties, which about half the voters inherit from their parents. Independents' victories nearly always occur in state or local contests in which exceptional circumstances play a larger role.

There are several types of third parties. In national elections, independents such as Ralph Nader (in 2000 and 2004) and some third parties attract votes from people who are dissatisfied with the major parties and the government in general. Other third parties, such as the Socialist and Libertarian parties, represent ideologies that have only small followings in the US. Others are single-issue organizations, such as the Prohibition, Women's, Right to Life and "Green" Parties. The most important third parties have been those that result from splits in the major parties. One of these was the "Bull Moose" Progressive Party formed from the Republican Party's liberal wing by Theodore Roosevelt. It won more than 27 percent of the vote in the presidential election of 1912, which helped put Democrat Woodrow Wilson in office. In the 1990s and 2000s third parties perhaps also decided who became president. The impact of third parties, however, is most evident in the adoption of their policy suggestions, such as primary elections, direct election of senators, women's suffrage, income tax and a balanced budget by the major parties. Republican Ron Paul in 2012 called himself a Libertarian and boasted of a platform fitting that ideological stance. Still, he pragmatically chose to run as Republican, which allowed him to participate in party debates and be taken seriously by a broader office.

The legislative branch

In addition to the staffs of individual members and congressional committees, Congress draws expertise from its own library, research service, and accounting, budget and technology-assessment offices.

During the crisis decades of the Cold War, the president seemed more important than Congress because of the executive's capacity for quick and decisive action. But since the 1970s, Congress has attempted, with limited success, to reassert authority over the nation's legislative agenda, military involvements and international commerce. A very powerful institution, it is no longer the dominant branch of the federal government, as the founders intended. Its main functions are law-making (mostly dealing with the president's legislative agenda), forming structures and programs to implement policy, overseeing the resulting bureaucracy, raising and allocating government funds and advising the president on foreign affairs and appointments.

Differences between the chambers

While the chambers of Congress are in theory equally powerful, there are several significant differences in their membership, organization and practices. As originally intended, the House continues to respond more quickly than the Senate to the electorate's mood. Elections every two years in smaller geographical units allow representatives to more closely reflect the current views of local voters than do senators, who serve six-year terms and represent whole states. The large majority of both chambers has always consisted of middle-aged white men, many of whom are usually lawyers. After the 2012 elections, for example, only 20 senators were women, and that was a record high.

The House contains much the more diverse membership. For example, when the new Congress (the 113th) took office in 2013, it included record numbers of women and members of minority groups: 61 women, 42 African Americans, 28 Latinos, 10 Asian Americans and three openly gay members, while the Senate had 20 women, three Latinos, one Asian American, one African American and one openly gay member. In 2007 the House chose Californian Nancy Pelosi as its first woman speaker. Since the mid-1990s the number of women and minority group

PLATE 6.4 Speaker of the House of Representatives, Democrat Nancy Pelosi, who represents the 8th district of California—much of San Francisco and vicinity—strikes a comic pose with her successor, Republican John Boehner, who represents the 8th district of Ohio, which includes rural and suburban areas between Cincinnati and Dayton in the state's southwest corner. With smiles they pretend to struggle for control of the gavel of the House, which is used to open its sessions. (*Shaun Thew/epa/Corbis*)

members in Congress have continued to rise, although their representation remains far below their portion of the nation's population

There are constitutional differences between the chambers as well. To qualify for a seat in the Senate, a person must be 30 years old, a citizen for nine years and a resident of the state where elected. Representatives must be 25, seven years a citizen and (by custom) a resident of their district. Financial bills must begin in the House, although the Senate usually amends them. Treaties and presidential appointments must be approved by the Senate. Size, however, is the constitutional difference that has the most important effect on the chambers.

Because of its much greater size, the House must regulate its business carefully. The Speaker of the House and the Rules Committee are given considerable power to schedule the work of the chamber, limit debate and restrict amendments to a bill from the floor. The speaker also influences the assignment of members and bills to committees, decides which bills are brought up for a vote and has total power over who speaks during debate. The speaker is chosen by the majority party and in turn chooses his party's members on the Rules Committee. The majority party also elects a majority leader as the speaker's next in command and a whip to help round up votes. The other party selects a minority leader and whip.

The smaller Senate has much more relaxed procedures and no officer with power comparable to those of the speaker. Bills can be considered in any order and at any time a majority of the chamber wishes. There are majority and minority leaders, and both parties use the whip system to get out the vote. The Constitution appoints the vice-president presiding officer of the Senate and requires the senators to elect a president *pro tempore* to chair the chamber in the vice-president's absence. Traditionally the vice-president is often absent from the chamber and attends mostly for ceremonial occasions. In the unusual situation when there is a tie vote, the Constitution gives the vice-president the power to break the deadlock. The George W. Bush presidency, however, interpreted the meaning of presiding over the Senate differently. It decided that Vice-President Richard Cheney should lead the chamber's business on a regular basis, and because the parties had equal numbers of seats during Bush's terms, Cheney exercised his right to break ties more often than most vice-presidents.

Most members usually find the position of president *pro tempore* of the Senate so powerless that it is turned over to a junior senator. The real leader of the chamber is customarily the majority leader, but even he has no formal power to limit debate or amendments. Members can therefore engage in a filibuster (an attempt to defeat a bill by talking until its supporters withdraw it so that other business can be finished). Only if 60 members of the chamber vote for closure, which limits speeches to one hour, can a filibuster be stopped. In practice filibusters seldom occur. When they do, it signals an issue (or presidential appointment) considered so important that senators are unable to compromise, and therefore filibusters receive considerable notice. Amendments to a bill during

Senate debates can be irrelevant to its subject or purpose. Some of these "riders" are attached in an attempt to ensure the bill's defeat. Others are added to secure the passage of proposals that would have great difficulty in winning a majority if forwarded separately.

Congressional organization

Members of Congress organize themselves in several ways. The most important of these is by party. Members divide along party lines on between two-fifths and two-thirds of the votes that take place in Congress. Special party groups pick the officers of each chamber and decide which committees members will work on. Each party gets a number of committee members equal to the percentage of seats it won in the last elections. The majority party wins the leadership positions and the most committee staffing.

Members also act on the basis of other loyalties. In the House, state delegations are important, especially since the members from states with large populations represent big, potentially unified voting blocks on some issues. Congress has well over 100 caucuses (interest groups formed to lobby other members) that allow members to gather in groups that are increasingly important rivals to the parties as the source of policy proposals. There are conservative, moderate and liberal caucuses for each party, as well as caucuses formed to promote regional, economic, ethnic, racial and women's issues that cross both party and chamber divisions. Three decades ago Congress had only four caucuses. Today some commentators claim they cause the fragmentation of Congressional planning.

Powers and functions of Congress

The Constitution grants Congress "all legislative powers" in the federal government. Only Congress can make laws. The president, interest groups and private citizens may want laws passed by Congress, but only if they can convince a member of *each* chamber to introduce their proposals is there a chance that these will become federal law.

Law-making is only the best known of the legislative branch's duties. Members are truly representatives, so much of their work involves "casework" (handling pressure groups' and voters' complaints and requests). The national legislature alone can make the federal budget. No federal funds can be raised, allocated or spent without its direction. Congress also has the constitutional authority to regulate foreign and inter-state commerce. Only it has the power to raise, finance and regulate military forces and to declare war. The legislative branch has great power over the other arms of the national government. It created all the federal courts below the Supreme Court, can (and has) changed the number of Supreme Court justices and decides which cases the federal courts can hear by defining jurisdictions. Congress, not the president, established the departments and the executive bureaucracy.

The committee system

Congress does most of its work in committees in which members gain the expertise and power to make their mark on public policy. The volume and complexity of legislation introduced each year became so huge that committees became an indispensable tool for the division of labor. The committee system assigns members to specific legislative work, the supervision of executive departments and agencies, hearings on public issues and (in Senate committees) on presidential appointments.

Members strive for assignments on committees of the greatest concern to their states or congressional districts. As government became involved in wider areas of life, the two dozen or so standing (permanent) committees in each chamber have spawned many subcommittees. Thus, for example, one is not surprised to see a House member from Mississippi as the chairman of the agricultural subcommittee dealing with cotton. The most senior member of the majority party traditionally becomes chair of a committee and through this position exercises control over its power to "kill" or promote a proposal. Since the early 1970s, however, subcommittees have multiplied in number and have won greater independence, and the chair has been chosen by secret ballot, which has not always resulted in election by seniority.

How a bill becomes an Act of Congress

The steps in the law-making process are similar in both chambers. Bills can be introduced in one chamber first or in both simultaneously. After that, the bill is referred to a committee, which usually refers it to a subcommittee. There members air their views, gather reports from experts and lobbyists and hold hearings to get opinions on the proposal. The next step is a "mark-up session" during which the subcommittee agrees on changes in the bill. It is then returned to the committee for another mark-up session before it goes to the whole chamber for debate and a vote on passage.

Most bills "die" in committee or subcommittee because they were introduced only to publicize a member's willingness to "do something" about an issue or because they are too flawed or controversial for passage. If a bill passes both chambers, amendments added in one or both houses may result in different texts. Then a conference committee with members from both chambers produces a compromise text. If it passes final voting in the House and Senate, the compromise bill is sent to the president, who may sign or veto it.

Congressional elections

Elections for Congress take place in two different subdivisions of the nation: congressional districts, each of which chooses one member of the House of Representatives, and states, each of which selects two members of the Senate. Congressional elections take place every two years, when all members of the House of Representatives and one-third of the Senate face re-election.

Redistricting (reapportionment of congressional seats)

The House expanded as new states entered the union and their populations grew. But in 1929 its size was fixed at 435 (with three additional non-voting delegates from the District of Columbia). Since then the seats are divided among the states according to their population by a process called reapportionment (reassignment of the number of House seats to each state) after every ten-year federal census. The Constitution guarantees each state a minimum of one representative. The number any state has above this minimum depends on how large its population is compared to that of the other states. Since the size of the House is constant, states with declining or slowly growing populations lose seats, and those with more rapidly growing populations gain seats. From 1950 to 2010, the political power of the Northeastern and Great Lakes states in the House declined while that of parts of the South, Southwest and Pacific coast rose. At the last redistricting, for example, New York and Ohio lost two seats, Florida gained two, and Texas added four.

The 1962 Supreme Court ruling in *Baker* v. *Carr* required redistricting (the redrawing of the geographical lines between districts) to follow the one-person-one-vote principle by creating congressional districts with equal populations. In 2012 most districts contained about 710,000 people, a number adjusted up after the 2010 census. Amendments to the federal Voting Rights Act in the 1980s required that a state's plan for redrawn district lines must make it likely that minority-group members would be elected to the House in numbers equivalent to the group's portion of the population of the state, but court challenges to the constitutionality of "minority majority" districts reduced their number greatly. The protests to that were few, however, because by the 1990s record numbers of minorities were getting elected to Congress.

Today, the use of sophisticated statistical computer models makes it possible for the majority in state legislatures to design a legal redistricting plan that satisfies virtually any political priorities it has. In the redistricting based on the 2010 census, on the one hand, in six states (Maryland, Pennsylvania, Georgia, Florida, Michigan and Texas) the legislature created "safe" districts for the majority party that effectively eliminated competition from the other major party. On the other hand, another six states (New Jersey, Arizona, California, Idaho, Washington and Hawaii) chose a bi- or non-partisan commission as a way to protect candidates from both parties.

Elections for one-member districts in a non-parliamentary system

The two-member constituencies for the Senate are a major exception to the principle of single-member election districts in the US. Even these, however, function as one-member districts because only one of a state's senators is elected in any election year. One key to understanding the nature of Congress lies in remembering that the US does not have a parliamentary form of government. In a parliament, the prime minister is usually the leader of the majority party in the legislature after a general election. Members of a parliament keep in line with party policies because voting independently can cause the fall of the government. In that kind of system, members owe their seats to political parties, and voters choose between parties rather than individual candidates. Voting independently in office can lead to de-selection by the party at the next election.

Congress does not choose the chief executive. Its members can vote without fear that the government will fall if they do not support their party. This means that they can give their first allegiance to their state or congressional district, rather than to their party or to the chief executive. Members of Congress owe their seats to elections in which their personalities and individual positions on issues matter more than party labels. The parties cannot control who enters congressional elections or directs these campaigns. Most candidates organize their own campaign staff and cover the cost of running for office through their own fundraising. The party is but one of several sources of support.

To run for a seat in Congress, a person must usually win a primary election first. Two or more candidates from the same party compete in a primary for the right to represent the party in the general election campaign. They may put themselves forward or be recruited by the party. State laws require people to document the seriousness of their bid for the party label by collecting a certain number of signatures supporting their candidacy before their names are put on the primary ballot. Victory in a primary is often achieved with a plurality rather than a majority of the votes because the field of candidates is frequently between three and five. In some states, a run-off primary is held between the two front-runners when no candidate wins a majority. In the general election there are usually two candidates, a Democrat and a Republican, although independent or third party candidates sometimes run.

Being a member of Congress has become a career. Between 1946 and 2012 more than 90 percent of House members and about 75 percent of senators won re-election. Most observers agree that incumbents (sitting members) have advantages over challengers. They use their office for media attention, their names and faces are consequently better known, and they can take credit for helping to pass government programs that benefit the state or district. In 2012 opinion polls showed that voter dissatisfaction with Congress was much greater than it was with President Obama. Still, incumbent members of Congress won re-election at only slightly lower rates. So strong is the reputation and gratitude members of Congress earn for their case work for constituents at home.

The Democrats had majorities in both houses of Congress for almost the entire time from 1954 to 1994, losing control only of the Senate between 1980 and 1986. The advantages of incumbency helped the party stay in power so long, but backfired in 1994–6 as voters made Democrats the target of their discontent with government. The mid-term elections (those between presidential election years) usually result in losses for the majority party, and in 1994 cost the Democrats control of both chambers. The Republicans won majorities in both houses for the first time in 40 years then and, on taking office, made a major shift in the leadership, committee composition and staffing of Congress. They kept a majority in both houses and, except for a short period early in George W. Bush's first term, they consolidated their control over Congress after 2000, gaining increasing majorities in the 2002 and 2004 elections. The partisan tide turned at that point, however. The Democrats won majorities in both houses in 2006 and strengthened them considerably two years later, giving Obama the majorities he needed for health reform early in his first term.

The pendulum swung again in favor of the Republicans at the 2010 mid-term elections, in part because of the surge of the rightist Tea Party movement, which successfully targeted vulnerable Democrats and moderate Republicans. The Republicans dominated the House of Representatives under Speaker John Boehner of Ohio and slowed down or stalled the president's agenda, while a slim Democratic majority in the Senate tempered House action. In the 2012 House elections Democrats gained eight seats. Republicans maintained a majority but lost the same number, leaving them with 234 seats to the Democrats' 201. In the senatorial elections, the Democrats, who had many more seats at risk, increased their majority by two seats to 53. Congress was still divided in 2013, but many candidates favored by the Tea Party did not do well and the president's party improved its position marginally.

The executive branch

Some 2.7 million civilians and 1.4 million active-duty military employees work in this largest branch of the federal government. The degree of control the president has over the 15 departments, 90 independent agencies, four branches of the military and numerable government corporations in the federal bureaucracy depends on the rules set up by Congress. More than 99 percent of civilian federal bureaucrats, for example, are hired through competitive examinations required by the Civil Service Act, rather than by presidential appointment. The president nominates the highest officials in the executive branch: the secretaries and assistant secretaries who lead the departments, the chief administrators of agencies and commissions and the ranking officers of American embassies. These appointments must be approved by the Senate. Only the roughly 2,000 high-level positions in the Executive Office of the President (EOP) are filled without congressional approval.

The Executive Office of the President

The main components of the EOP that operate outside the White House are the Council of Economic Advisers, the National Security Council, the Office of Management and Budget and the Central Intelligence Agency (CIA). Inside the White House are the first lady's staff and the president's own staff, which includes his personal advisers (some of whom are carried over from his election staff), his press secretary, congressional liaison officer and chief of staff. The structure and operation of the EOP and the upper levels of the executive branch vary, depending on the style and character of the president. For instance, the cabinet, although it is composed of department secretaries and other key officials, has played a smaller role in the policy development of most recent administrations.

Qualifications for and powers of the presidency

The president's powers and qualifications reflect the constitutional clauses intended to prevent the development of presidential government while providing for strong national leadership. The president must be a natural-born citizen, at least 35 years old, and have been a resident of the US for at least 14 years. He is more independent of the legislature than the chief executives of most democratic governments because he is elected separately from Congress and cannot be removed from office by a vote of no-confidence.

The price of his independence is having no guarantee of majorities in the Houses of Congress, the difficulties of lobbying for support in an institution of which he is not a member and the limits put on his powers by the system of checks and balances. But the chief executive is the only official elected by voters in all the states, and on that basis, the president can claim to be the sole politician who rises above the self-seeking goals of party politics in the national interest.

Presidential duties are stated in the Constitution, delegated by Congress or are the result of circumstances. The most important extra-constitutional duties are acting as chief of state and party leader. The president became the nation's ceremonial head of state by default, because the Constitution provides a republican form of government with no office for that purpose. He became the national leader of his party as parties developed into the organizers of the nation's political life and the presidency became increasingly powerful. The president's popularity with voters can often affect the success of his party's candidates for other offices.

The office's constitutional powers are the result of interpreting rather vague phrases in that document. The president is the administrative head of the nation,

PLATE 6.5 Barack Obama takes the oath of office for his second term in January 2013 with his family and notables in both parties on the platform looking on.
(Rex Features)

for example, because the Constitution states that "the executive power shall be vested in a President." What that and other constitutional phrases mean in practice has evolved from the claims that presidents have made without provoking Congress or the courts to effectively oppose them. As one political scientist has famously put it, in a system of checks and balances with branches sharing powers, the president's power is not to command but to *persuade*—to convince other political actors that what the president wants is what they want. The vague constitutional powers give the chief executive great leeway but not nearly so many or so specific powers as those enumerated for Congress in the Constitution.

As chief administrator, the president is required to see that the laws written by Congress are carried out. This is understood to mean managing the bureaucracy and enforcing existing policies, but interpreted broadly it has, among other things, enabled presidents to break a strike or send troops to integrate a public school. A long series of presidents have thus been able to read current conditions, the Constitution or both as justification for a generous expansion of executive powers at the expense of the traditional balance among the three federal branches.

George W. Bush, for example, attempted to persuade politicians and the public that his view of the "unitary executive" reflected the intent of the drafters of the Constitution and was essential after the terrorist attacks of September 11, 2001. With this theory of presidential power he asserted that the executive branch should not be subject to the usual critical oversight (inspection) of congressional committees; that the president and his high-level appointees should be able to hire and fire government officials without senatorial interference; and that his administration's redefinition of the Geneva Conventions, the international understanding of "torture," and civil rights at home should not be questioned by the federal courts. As long as the nation felt acutely threatened by the 9/11 attacks, the administration's popularity with the general public remained high and criticism of the "unitary" executive remained relatively muted. Facing a severe international economic crisis, two ongoing wars, and serious domestic problems with high immigration as well as the nation's educational and health services, Barack Obama has found the temptation to expand presidential powers difficult to resist and, for example, signed a reauthorization of the USA Patriot Act.

Chief law-maker

The president's role as legislative leader developed in part from constitutional clauses requiring him to inform Congress about the "state of the nation" and to suggest the "measures" he considers "necessary or expedient." Another clause allows him to convene a special session of Congress if he deems it necessary. However, the president did not usually set the legislative agenda until the twentieth century.

In 1921 Congress weakened its monopoly on the "power of the purse" by the Budget and Accounting Act, which delegated to the president the power to screen the budget proposals of executive-branch departments and agencies. As a result, the White House routinely sets policy priorities by proposing how much money shall be given to government programs. But not until the Great Depression of the 1930s did the president become heavily involved in drafting a coordinated "package" of bills for congressional action. The New Deal proposals of Franklin D. Roosevelt marked a new era in presidential legislative activity, but then the president sent bills to Congress and let it decide what to do with them. Today, presidents follow their progress through Congress closely and use legislative aides to lobby hard for their passage. Obama received criticism for not guiding his health reform proposals more closely.

A president who is an effective legislative initiator and lobbyist has less need of his veto power to stop the passage of bills. Vetoes can take place in two ways: with a veto message giving presidential objections or by no action being taken within ten days of the adjournment of Congress on bills that come to the White House (the so-called pocket veto). The president's veto power is limited. Congress may override it with two-thirds majorities, and only from 1995 to 1997 did the executive have a line-item veto on financial bills to annul just objectionable parts of legislation. Thus members of Congress can press unwanted proposals on the president as "riders" to bills the executive wants passed.

In part to counter such tactics by members of Congress, presidents since Ronald Reagan in the 1980s have made expanded use of the "signing statement," a legal opinion from the president included with the text of the new law that bears the chief executive's signature. Clinton found somewhat less need for these statements, but George W. Bush's extensive reliance on them in controversial situations, especially with regard to the treatment of military prisoners and financing for defense, resulted in mounting opposition. The signing statement defines how the executive intends to implement the law. It identifies provisions that the president finds unclear, politically unacceptable or unconstitutional and so announces that these may not be carried out. Bush defended his position by explicitly referring to the unitary executive branch that required these powers to carry out its constitutional duties. On the other hand, opponents of his way of using the signing statement say that it restores the president's line-item veto. It allows the executive to replace Congress as the branch that interprets a law's intent and to replace the Supreme Court as the judge of constitutionality. Obama has not raised controversy by his use of signing statements.

The president and foreign policy

The Constitution names the president as commander-in-chief, making him the highest ranking officer in the armed services, but gives Congress the power to declare war. The founders' attempt to give the legislature control over the executive's military power proved so limited that in 1973 Congress passed the War Powers Act to restrain the president by requiring congressional approval for deployment of American troops abroad within specified time limits. Presidents have unanimously called the Act unconstitutional and have followed its notification procedure only when it suited them. Since the Second World War most wars the US has engaged in have never been declared. Congress has instead passed resolutions giving the chief executive nearly carte blanche to conduct these "armed conflicts" as he sees fit.

The president's military power is one of several factors that strengthen his position as foreign policy leader. This is the arena where the executive branch has most clearly developed its dominance. Presidents have learned to circumvent the constitutional clauses that require approval by two-thirds of the Senate for ratification of a treaty and a simple majority for confirmation of diplomatic appointments. The national security adviser, who owes his position solely to the president's choice, has become most presidents' main adviser in formulating foreign policy. And decisions are most often carried out through executive agreements, which do not have to be approved by the Senate.

The president has at his disposal four major organizations to support his conduct of foreign affairs: the Departments of State and Defense, the CIA and the National Security Council. Faced with these facts, Congress continues to assert its role in foreign policy but recognizes presidential leadership. In addition, since 2002 the chief executive has a new permanent division of the executive branch, the Department of Homeland Security (DHS), to assist him in mobilizing and disciplining the public for national defense during the global war on terrorism, an open-ended period of national crisis that some commentators have christened the "second cold war" (see Chapter 8).

Presidential elections: money, caucuses and primaries

Electing the president is a long, complicated and costly affair that is getting longer. After conferring with political advisers, individuals hold press conferences 18 months or more before the election to announce that they are running for president. Several serious candidates from each party commonly propose themselves. Over the following months these candidates "test the water" to see if support for their candidacy in different parts of the nation is warm enough to raise the $100 million or more necessary to pay for the upcoming primary-caucus campaign. Most would-be candidates drop out of the contest during this demanding "invisible primary," which seemed to strongly favor those with support among the nation's most wealthy until 2004, when Democrat Howard Dean raised more than sufficient funds through small donations made over the internet. In the winter and spring of 2008 the Obama campaign succeeded in becoming a popular internet movement supported by millions of activists who communicated through blogs, Facebook and film clips and messages on YouTube. Multitudes of small donors contributed and volunteered their grassroots efforts through Obama's website, and his campaign employed Google to maximize the effectiveness of its use of the internet. The resulting effort was arguably broader based, better financed and more likely to set precedents for the future than any campaign in recent memory. The pre-primary started earlier and was more visible than ever before in the 2012 election. "Wannabe" Republican candidates lined up against Obama for an unprecedented number of debates among themselves in the fall before the election year. They and Obama all used social media but none so effectively as the president himself.

Since the election-campaign finance reforms of the 1970s, candidates can win matching public funds to pay for this part of the election campaign on the condition that they accept a spending cap and that they demonstrate that they have broad-based citizen support by getting many small donations in 20 different states. Even though the spending cap was about $50 million for the nomination campaign in 2004, both candidates refused public funding so they could spend more. Four years later Obama pledged to spend within the cap of public funding ($42 million) but changed his mind as his internet funding initiatives caught fire.

Eventually the vast coverage and financial support he gained that way demonstrated the broad public approval his candidacy had won and allowed him to outspend the opposition by a margin of $4 and $5 to one. See the section on campaign financing below.

From January to June of the presidential election year the states conduct the process of narrowing the field of candidates to one from each party through two electoral procedures, caucuses or primaries. Both procedures are indirect: party voters choose delegates to the party's national convention and give these delegates the authority to make its official nomination of a candidate. Most states use presidential primaries to narrow the field of candidates, but 15 held party meetings called presidential caucuses in 2004. Because they result in the choice of roughly 80 percent of convention delegates, presidential primaries attract much more attention than the caucuses. Many are closed, that is, they are elections in which only registered members of the party holding the primary can vote. Thus one state can have two presidential primaries, a closed primary for each of the major parties. Some are open primaries, voters from either party can participate, and a few are semi-open, allowing both independents and voters from one party to vote. The costs and level of support needed across a country the size of the US lead most would-be party nominees to withdraw from the race relatively early in the primary-caucus season.

In the past several elections, through so-called "front-loading," growing numbers of states have moved their primaries to dates earlier in the season in their eagerness to gain more of the candidates' and media attention. As a result, the winner of the Democratic Party's nomination in 2004, John Kerry, was clear at the beginning of March, months before he was officially chosen by his party's convention in July. In 2012 Mitt Romney faced a more difficult primary-caucus competition, even though he had lived in Iowa for four years to prepare and was hugely well funded for the most front-loaded series of contests yet. Serious divisions in his party and its doubt that he personified its ideological core were the main cases of his problems. Rick Santorum and Ron Paul, the competitors for the nomination who won the second and third most number of delegates at the convention, took positions to Romney's right, Santorum on social issues and Paul on economic policy. As in 2008 Iowa held the first caucus on January 3, and despite his long residence there, Romney lost to Santorum. In New Hampshire, the first state with a primary, he regained his promise as the Republican who could defeat Obama by winning handily. In the rapid succession primaries through Super Tuesday on March 6 Romney won most states but Santorum captured five states and Newt Gingrich, another candidate to Romney's right, won two. It was late April before Romney could feel that he was not only the front-runner but also the presumptive nominee.

Campaign financing

The government provides some financing for party conventions and full public funding for the post-convention campaigns of each major party's nominees up to a spending cap ($85 million for each candidate in 2008), if they opt for government funding. Because he raised and spent far in excess of that limit, Obama did not accept public money in 2008. McCain found the government caps far too low in the most expensive presidential campaign in history, in which the two leading candidates together spent more than an estimated $1.5 billion. Central provisions of the Bipartisan Campaign Reform Act (BCRA) of 2002 established rules to control the ways public or private money can be used during the election process. Most important, the Act banned the use of "soft money" raised in a party's name and limited funding by independent political action committees (PACs), because these sources of money no longer mostly paid for grassroots political participation but instead funded "issue ads" in the print and broadcast media close to election day that attack the opponent's position while seeming to educate the public. The rapid changes in technology and soaring costs by 2008 already convinced many that campaign finance reform was again needed.

In January 2010 the Supreme Court ruled on several provisions of the BCRA in a 5–4 decision (*Citizens United* v. *the FEC*). The court held that corporations have the same First Amendment rights to freedom of expression as individuals, also regarding contributions to campaign communications, including advertisements and films. Their contributions to "political speech," like anyone else's are essential in a democracy, and so should not be limited. In effect, this eliminated BCRA's limits on campaign spending. While the court upheld the Act's disclosure provisions, it led to greatly increased spending by so-called super PACs, which still have to be independent of any candidate but now can attack an opposing candidate directly and are no longer subject to limits on the source of money or on how much is raised or spent.

During the 2012 Republican primary-caucus season, super PACs spent more than the candidates' own campaigns. Five super PACs produced and broadcast campaign material in favor of Mitt Romney. Obama attracted less financial support in his second bid for the Oval Office, but also received somewhat late help from several super PACs, although they were not all as well endowed. The disclosure rules under BCRA have shown that all but a very small amount of super PAC money came from wealthy individuals, not corporations. Again some argued that wealth might make the difference for one of the candidates. The result, however, showed that plentiful campaign financing does not guarantee public support, and that a variety of other actors may prove decisive for electoral victory.

Media politics: the conventions, ads and presidential debates

During the "primary season" the media keep a running count of the delegates pledged to each candidate and track the front-runners' progress towards a majority of delegate votes at the party conventions in July and August. As a result, in recent decades each party's choice has been clear before the convention. The party "in the White House" has re-nominated the incumbent (the person in the office), and a single "out party" candidate has accumulated a delegate majority at his convention by the end of the primaries and caucuses. Still, the proportional representation from primaries that the Democrats and some states now require sends more divided blocks of delegates to the conventions. Caucuses and primaries bind delegates only on the first roll-call vote of the states. If no candidate wins a majority, delegates are free to switch loyalties on later votes, and the final choice of the convention, theoretically at least, could be unexpected. In practice there have been no such surprises at recent conventions.

If present trends continue, the interest in the convention will lie elsewhere. Because the convention is televised, both parties present a "packaged media show" of unity designed to demonstrate that the internal disagreements of the primary season are forgotten. Most national party meetings between the early 1990s and 2012 have been the well-orchestrated media events that are typical of today's party conventions, with factions such as Jesse Jackson's Rainbow Coalition and Republican John McCain's supporters accepting subordinate roles. In 2012 Mitt Romney moved to the right on several issues and told the party faithful at the convention what they wanted to hear.

Presidential candidates announced their vice-presidential "running mates" weeks in advance in recent decades, denying television viewers that convention suspense. In 2008 and 2012 Obama chose Joe Biden, an experienced elder senator, who "balanced the ticket." Romney waited until close to the Republican convention before choosing Paul Ryan, a much younger man to his political right with budgetary policies that Tea Party movement supporters applauded. Today the party conventions offer competing media presentations of the parties and their candidates. The key question is which of these mass appeals is the more successful at convincing the voting public to identify with its candidate and view of the country's choices.

The parties and their candidates eventually face each other in the post-convention campaign that runs from late August until the voters go to the polls at the beginning of November. Candidates still crisscross the country to make themselves and their stands on the issues known, but now stay in a city only long enough to arrange for the media to take them into the public's living rooms. More than in earlier phases of the campaign, hugely expensive short television "spots" are used by the major parties, candidates and super PACs, as much to portray the faults of their opponents (negative campaigning) as to put themselves in the best possible light. Because of the high cost of television campaigning, candidates also depend on getting free coverage by making the evening news with their regular campaign activities.

Since the *Citizens United* decision, television advertisements sponsored and funded by independent partisan groups have played an especially visible (some would say decisive) role in the media battles of presidential elections. In 1988, a turning point in this trend, Republican partisans used a television ad featuring a close-up of Willie Horton, an African American convict in Massachusetts (who had committed a violent crime while on a weekend furlough from prison) to label Democratic candidate Michael Dukakis "soft" on crime, even though, as governor of the state, Dukakis had opposed the furlough plan. In a similar fashion, groups outside candidates' and parties' official organizations have since then looked for and given media coverage to scandalous behavior allegedly involving opponents. In 2004 both Republicans and Democrats attempted to gain electoral advantage by attacking the military record of the opposing candidate. The "Swift-boat Veterans for Truth" who impugned Kerry's service in the Vietnam War continued their television attacks long after Republican Senator John McCain and then President Bush decried the ads and defended John Kerry's record. In 2008 Hillary Clinton's famous telephone-in-the-night ad raised questions about Obama's experience to deal with foreign policy, and Republican ads and websites warned about his associations with political radicals during the general election campaign. In 2012 super PACs questioned Obama's birthplace, his having an un-American ideology, and his "Obamacare," which allegedly would destroy the country's economy.

In the closing months of the campaign, public debates that are televised live nationwide offer the candidates the best chance to exploit the mass media audience for a campaign boost. In recent years, there have been three presidential debates and one vice-presidential debate. Since the first televised debate in 1960, when Senator John F. Kennedy bested Vice-President Richard Nixon in visual appearance and style, the debates have seemed to favor the challenger over the incumbent. A larger audience watches the debates than any other single event in the campaign, and a large segment of voters say the debates are likely to influence their choice. Both candidates are wary of making mistakes in front of this enormous audience and so eagerly prepare to meet any question with a well-informed answer. Yet, more often than not, the debates are an unreliable predictor of who will be elected. In 2004 opinion surveys indicated that the public viewed Kerry as the winner of all the debates, but Bush won re-election; in 2012 the media and polls declared Obama loser of the first debate but by small margins the winner of the other two in a race seemingly so close that the debates gave no sure sign. A combination of other factors, such as the economic situation, the public's division over key issues and the candidates' performance in un-televised campaign activities, are often decisive.

Election day

On election day the television networks display huge maps of the country to track two different tallies of the results. One is the "popular vote" (a count of how many voters across the country have supported the candidates). At first these figures are estimates compiled by polling organizations who ask people how they voted as they exit the polling stations. By late evening, the count for eastern states may be official. But because of the difference in time zones, the popular vote in the Pacific West will not be known until very late.

The popular vote, however, does not determine who wins. Not only are the candidates chosen in an indirect fashion through the primaries, but the final election is also decided indirectly. In accordance with rules in the Constitution, the popular vote is not counted nationally, but by state. The second tally on election-day television screens is the electoral-college vote. Each state has a number of votes in the college equal to its members in Congress (two senators plus its number of representatives in the House). The District of Columbia has three votes, making a total of 538 "electors" in the college. After the ten-year census, the number of electors per state is adjusted to reflect the changing size of their populations and so, congressional delegations (see Figure 6.1). The members of the electoral college travel to their respective state capitals in mid-December and cast the ballots which officially decide the election when they are counted in the Senate in January. The media make the electoral result clear long before then because, except for the electors from Maine and Nebraska, members of the college are pledged to vote together for the winning candidate in each state. The Supreme Court has determined that states cannot *require* electors to vote for that candidate, but few electors have not. The plurality system has its most dramatic effect in the electoral-college vote.

The candidate who wins a state (even with a minority of its popular vote) receives *all* the votes in the college. The system is supposed to reward "small states" which get three electoral votes no matter how small their population. Today, however, most people are concentrated in a dozen or so "big states" and only a few of these are "competitive" (divided in their support for the candidates). Thus most time and money in the campaign is spent in states like Florida and Ohio to win large blocks of highly contested electoral-college votes. On the other hand, when an election is exceptionally close, as in 2000, even the three electoral votes of the smallest states could be decisive.

In such a system, most voters are unwilling to "waste" their votes on third-party candidates, who almost never win whole states and votes in the college. Still, the 2000 election showed how the small number of votes that third-party candidates win *within* states can determine the outcome of the entire national contest. In ten states (a total of 105 electors in the college) the race was so close that the winner's margin of success was less than the vote taken by Nader's Green Party, Buchanan's reform ticket or these minor parties together.

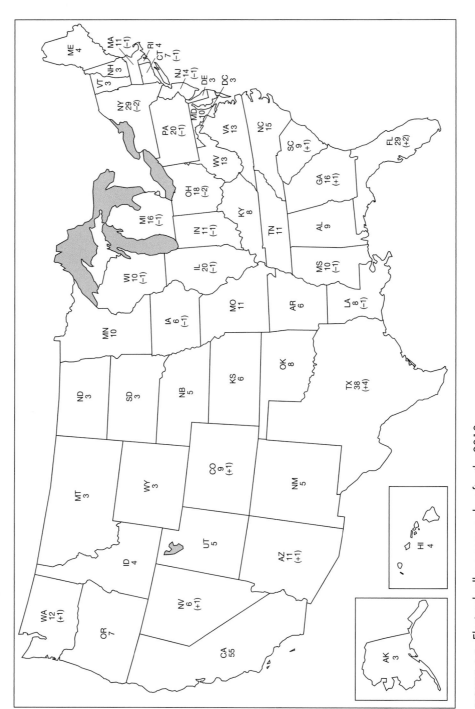

FIGURE 6.1 Electoral-college geography after the 2010 census.

Note: Changes in states' electoral votes because of the 2010 census are shown in parenthesis.

TABLE 6.1 US presidential elections, 1932–2012

Year	Candidates	Parties	% of popular vote	electoral college vote
1932	*Franklin D. Roosevelt*	*Democratic*	*57.4*	*472*
	Herbert C. Hoover	Republican	39.7	59
1936	*Franklin D. Roosevelt*	*Democratic*	*60.8*	*523*
	Alfred M. Landon	Republican	36.5	8
1940	*Franklin D. Roosevelt*	*Democratic*	*54.8*	*449*
	Wendell L. Wilkie	Republican	44.8	82
1944	*Franklin D. Roosevelt*	*Democratic*	*53.5*	*432*
	Thomas E. Dewey	Republican	46.0	99
1948	*Harry S. Truman*	*Democratic*	*49.6*	*303*
	Thomas E. Dewey	Republican	45.1	189
1952	*Dwight D. Eisenhower*	*Republican*	*55.1*	*442*
	Adlai E. Stevenson	Democratic	44.4	89
1956	*Dwight D. Eisenhower*	*Republican*	*57.6*	*457*
	Adlai E. Stevenson	Democratic	42.1	73
1960	*John F. Kennedy*	*Democratic*	*49.7*	*303*
	Richard M. Nixon	Republican	49.5	219
1964	*Lyndon B. Johnson*	*Democratic*	*61.1*	*486*
	Barry M. Goldwater	Republican	38.5	52
1968	*Richard M. Nixon*	*Republican*	*43.3*	*301*
	Hubert H. Humphrey	Democratic	42.7	191
	George C. Wallace	Independent	13.5	46
1972	*Richard M. Nixon*	*Republican*	*60.7*	*520*
	George S. McGovern	Democratic	37.5	17
1976	*Jimmy Carter*	*Democratic*	*50.1*	*297*
	Gerald R. Ford	Republican	48.0	240
1980	*Ronald Reagan*	*Republican*	*50.8*	*489*
	Jimmy Carter	Democratic	41.0	49
1984	*Ronald Reagan*	*Republican*	*58.8*	*525*
	Walter Mondale	Democratic	40.6	13
1988	*George H.W. Bush*	*Republican*	*53.4*	*426*
	Michael Dukakis	Democratic	45.6	111
1992	*Bill Clinton*	*Democratic*	*43.0*	*370*
	George H.W. Bush	Republican	38.0	168
1996	*Bill Clinton*	*Democratic*	*49.4*	*379*
	Bob Dole	Republican	41.0	159
2000	*George W. Bush*	*Republican*	*47.9*	*271*
	Albert Gore, Jr.	Democratic	48.4	266
2004	*George W. Bush*	*Republican*	*51.0*	*286*
	John Kerry	Democratic	48.0	249
2008	*Barack Obama*	*Democratic*	*53.0*	*365*
	John McCain	Republican	46.0	173
2012	*Barack Obama*	*Democratic*	*51.0*	*332*
	Mitt Romney	Republican	47.0	206

Note: Victors in italics.

In 2000 the election was closest in Florida, where George W. Bush won by 0.01 percent of the vote. Victory was clear only after court challenges over election recounts in Florida counties ended with the US Supreme Court decision that these recounts did not apply uniform standards to all votes and so were unconstitutional. The state's election arrangements became globally infamous because of the differences exposed in the voting machines and counting procedures, which not only decided the election result (by a margin of 537 votes!) but undercounted or wrongly counted the votes of the elderly and minorities. In 2004 Ohio was the state that, by a thin popular vote margin, provided Bush with the margin of victory in the electoral college to become president. Bush's victory was clearer, in these decisive "swing" states and in the nation as a whole. In 2008 and 2012, despite some close state contests, Obama's electoral college triumph was overwhelmingly clear, and the historically usual pattern of electoral college results returned.

Reform the system?

Two larger realities were exposed in 2000: first, Americans had divided with a fine evenness between the views represented by the major candidates and, second, the presidential election system, in theory and practice, had undemocratic elements. There has long been debate about whether election of the president through the electoral college should be continued, but no concerted effort for change has emerged. Critics remind the public that a close election can be thrown into the House of Representatives to be decided by an undemocratic one vote per state ballot there, as the Constitution requires, if no candidate wins a majority in the electoral college. (Only because of the unprecedented Supreme Court decision was this avoided in 2000.) A candidate can win the popular vote but lose in the college, political scientists note, as occurred three times in the 1800s and again in 2000, when Gore won half a million more votes but lost in the election. Supporters of the status quo note that, in the American federal system, the college properly gives weight to states and also produces a clearer result. (Those effects were also evident in 2000, but hardly in a satisfying way.)

The flaws in the *practice* of the system seemed as least as grave in 2000. Former President Jimmy Carter, who had inspected and critiqued elections in many parts of the world, reported a 5 percent error rate in Florida, one that fell below international election commission standards. Since the results were nearly as close in nine or more other states and similar variations in machinery and counting appeared in these places, the need for reform of these arrangements across the nation seemed clear. In 2002 Congress passed the Help America Vote Act (HAVA) that required each state to submit a plan for uniform voting procedures and standards and that provided federal funds for implementing changes.

Although that reform was still incomplete, the 2004 election revealed a fairer, more smoothly operating system. By 2008, at least to the Democrats, the most problematic phase of the presidential election process seemed to be the caucus-primary season rather than the electoral college, and they discussed proposals for three or four regional primaries to give more states a relatively equal chance to attract the candidates' attention. In 2008 and 2012 inequalities in the voting systems in some states, such as Florida and Ohio, still appeared when voters in poorer city districts had to wait for hours to cast their ballots.

The judicial branch

The only court specifically mentioned in the Constitution is the US Supreme Court. However, Congress has established lesser federal courts in a three-tier system, as well as courts for tax, customs, patent and military law. District courts have original jurisdiction in most federal cases. Only about one-sixth of the decisions of these courts are appealed to the next tier, the US courts of appeals.

Most of the US Supreme Court's work consists of hearing cases from US courts of appeals or state supreme courts. These cases raise federal questions (controversies arising under the Constitution, federal law or treaties). In addition it has original jurisdiction in cases that involve a state or officials of the federal government. The number of petitions reaching the court has risen rapidly since 1945 when the total was only 1,460 to around 10,000 in 2012. Presently, in a year the court gives around 100 of these cases plenary review with attorneys' oral arguments. It then writes a formal written decision in 80–90 of these cases. It decides how to deal with another 50–60 cases per year without plenary review. The decisions of lower federal courts become final in cases it refuses to hear, which means those judges also exercise judicial review, although usually that means following earlier decisions set by the US Supreme Court.

The Constitution creates a separate judicial branch with a single Supreme Court that has an unspecified number of justices with terms of office dependent only on their "good behavior." In practice, the number of justices has varied between five and ten, according to the will of Congress, but in recent history has been eight, plus a chief justice. Terms of office have, by tradition, been for life or until voluntary retirement. As no justice has ever been impeached, life terms have given justices an impressive degree of independence. Of the 144 men and four women nominated to the Court, about four in five have been confirmed by the Senate. In 1987 Robert Bork became the last presidential nominee to be rejected.

Judicial review

Today, the fame and influence of the Supreme Court result from its power of judicial review, the right to decide in cases determining whether congressional, presidential and states' acts are in accordance with the Constitution and to declare them void if it deems they are not (see "The constitutional framework" earlier in this chapter). The court claimed the right of judicial review by stages and won gradual acceptance for its practice between 1796 and 1865. In the first year the court asserted its right to invalidate state laws that it considered unconstitutional. In *Marbury* v. *Madison* (1803), it claimed the power to invalidate an unconstitutional federal law. Later decisions extended judicial review to cover executive acts. The court's review power maintains the supremacy of federal law and a uniform interpretation of the Constitution from state to state. As a practical fact, only the Union victory in the Civil War established the supremacy of federal law, the US Constitution and the Supreme Court as their interpreter.

Once that pattern of authority was accepted, Supreme Court decisions became a powerful force shaping public policy because they became precedents that all other state and federal courts followed in similar cases. But there remain two views on how the court should exercise the power of judicial review. One, called judicial restraint, holds that the justices should limit their review to applying the rules explicitly stated or clearly implied in the Constitution or Acts of Congress. If cases raise questions not clearly answered by existing law, the court should leave those questions for the elected politicians to decide. The other view, termed judicial activism, maintains that justices ought to let the general intent or principles underlying the text of the Constitution and federal statutes be their guide in applying often vague legal language to a changing society. In the activist view, the court should not hesitate to intervene in political questions to protect the Constitution and prevent infringements on individual rights.

In the course of US history, there have been cycles of judicial activism and restraint. The activist period before the Civil War was followed by a cycle of restraint that lasted until 1937. During these years the court generally held that the government's right to regulate the economy was not clearly implied in the Constitution. Instead it asserted that private business and property were protected from federal regulation by the Fourteenth Amendment, even though the Amendment was originally intended to guarantee the rights of former slaves.

In the 1890s the court handed down a series of decisions that legalized racial segregation and the disenfranchisement of African Americans in the South by ruling that the regulation of public facilities and elections exceeded the constitutional powers of the national government. In the 1930s the court invalidated so many of the economic programs in Franklin D. Roosevelt's New Deal that he proposed "packing" the court with more amenable justices until one member of the court provided a majority for the president by adopting new views in 1937. A new period of judicial activism began in that year, extending to the end of the 1980s, during which the court rarely invalidated economic legislation but overturned dozens of laws that it believed infringed individuals' rights. It reversed its earlier stand on segregation in the *Brown* decision (1954) and went on to protect the rights of the criminally accused, minority voting rights, affirmative action

PLATE 6.6 The US Supreme Court in session.
(*Priscilla Coleman*)

programs to increase educational opportunities for racial minorities, abortion rights and the right to unrestricted political expression, even if that means burning the American flag.

Republicans Ronald Reagan and George H.W. Bush appointed five justices who they hoped would move the court into another period of judicial restraint. Once on the bench, however, justices have frequently surprised and disappointed their sponsors. Moderately liberal President Clinton appointed a second woman, Ruth Bader Ginsburg, whose views generally do not coincide with those of the alleged conservatives. In 2003, the supposed "conservative" court declared unconstitutional a state law that prohibited consensual sex among adult homosexuals in *Lawrence and Garner* v. *Texas*. In his second term, however, President Bush tipped the balanced in the conservative justices' direction with his appointment of Samuel A. Alito and Chief Justice John G. Roberts. Since then a number of narrow 5–4 decisions have allowed considerably more government limitation of access to the courts, abortion rights and affirmative action programs, and the court is showing a willingness to reconsider earlier decisions in voting rights and segregation cases. During Obama's first term he appointed two liberal women justices, Sonia Sotomayor (2009) and Elena Kagan (2010), both of whom argued for the constitutionality of his Affordable Care for Americans health reform legislation when it came before the court.

Some commentators criticize a system in which an appointed judicial body can overrule the democratically elected branches of government. Others point out that in more than 200 years the court has invalidated only around 120 sections of federal law but nearly ten times as many provisions of state law. These rulings, it must be remembered, were all in response to disagreements between specific parties and limited to the particular points of law raised by those parties. Nevertheless, the court's judicial review can be overridden, since Congress and the president (and state governments) can revise their acts and constitutional amendments can be passed.

Attitudes to branches of the federal government

The Supreme Court's decisions relieve the other branches of taking positions on politically sensitive questions. The court has reversed itself when older decisions no longer seem valid and, according to a study covering its rulings from the mid-1930s to the mid-1980s, it was in line with public opinion at least as often as the other branches. Evidence from Gallup, Roper and Pew Center opinion surveys from the mid-1980s through to 2012 showed that the American public trusted only the military, organized religion, the police and banks more than the court. In those years, people in the US had more confidence in the court than the president, and two to three times more confidence in it than in Congress. In the 2008 poll, however, confidence in the court sank somewhat, and the public expressed less positive attitudes to it than to small businesses, the public schools and the medical system—in addition to the institutions mentioned above.

This suggests that the question of whether judicial review by the Supreme Court is a democratic process is more complicated than it at first appears. Though the justices are not elected, they are responsive to and receive support from popular opinion. It is notable that public confidence in the court did not fall in the polls soon after its controversial decision that resolved the disputed presidential election of 2000. Public attitudes to the president are less stable than those regarding the Supreme Court. Whether the chief executive deserves it or not, the public lays the blame or credit for the nation's current situation and how it is handled at his door. As President Harry Truman famously said, "The buck stops here," referring to his desk. Thus, Clinton got credit for the economic boom of the 1990s and George W. Bush was blamed for the market crash and economic downturn at the end of his second term. On the other hand, the public always unites behind the president in times of military crisis. Its confidence in the president during the Gulf War in 1991, and after the terrorist attacks on the World Trade Center and the Pentagon in 2001, was much higher than it was for the Supreme Court or Congress.

The public had little confidence in Congress in the 1990s, when the institution had support from only a quarter or fifth of the people polled, and by 2012 the Gallup poll showed the worst ever rating for the legislature (11 percent), the lowest support given any institution among the 16 major ones included in the poll since 1973. Unlike President Bush, Congress won no boost for its response to the 9/11 attacks or the joint resolution in favor of his war on terror. By tradition, and especially since 1945, the public expects the president to conduct foreign policy and Congress to handle the allocation of financial resources. The faltering economy from 2008 through 2012 and the deadlock between the Republican-dominated House of Representatives and President Obama over the nation's budget may partially explain the decline in esteem for the national legislature. Some commentators note the irony that the branch the founders of the US government intended to be the most democratic (Congress) is the one least popular with the public, while others say the public treats it precisely as the founders intended by reacting most critically to the part of government they require to be most responsive to people's needs and changing attitudes.

Exercises

Explain and examine the following names and terms:

Articles of Confederation	"third" parties	incumbents
popular sovereignty	Speaker of the House	presidential appointments
"reserved" powers	majority leader	presidential veto
filibuster	presidential caucuses	"necessary and proper" clause
the separation of powers	"unitary executive"	electoral college
winner-takes-all system	reapportionment	original jurisdiction
a two-party region	judicial review	primary and caucus elections
Citizens United	presidential debates	divided government

Write short essays on the following questions:

1. How are the principles of federalism and limited government protected by the Constitution of 1787 and its amendments?

2. Compare and contrast the chambers of Congress, giving particular attention to the effects of their different size, membership and terms of office.

3. Discuss the powers of the president and contrast his position with that of a prime minister in a parliamentary government.

4. Describe American parties and elections and discuss the causes and effects of their most distinctive elements.

5. Critically discuss the stages in the presidential election system, defending in a balanced fashion how democratic you think the process is.

6. What are some of the arguments for and against the Supreme Court's power of judicial review?

Further reading

Barone, M. and Ujifusa, G. (annual) *The Almanac of American Politics*, Washington, DC: National Journal.

Ceaser, J.W. and Busch, A. (2001) *The Perfect Tie: The True Story of the 2000 Presidential Election*, Lanham, MD: Rowman & Littlefield.

Fisher, L. (1995) *Presidential War Power*, Lawrence, KS: University Press of Kansas.

Freeman, J. (2002) *A Room at a Time: How Women Entered Party Politics*, Lanham, MD: Rowman & Littlefield.

Hudson, William E. (2012) *American Democracy in Peril: Eight Challenges to America's Future*, Washington, DC: Congressional Quarterly Press.

Lowi, T.J. and Ginsberg, B. (2004) *American Government: Freedom and Power*, 8th edn, New York: W.W. Norton.

Websites

www.justice.gov
www.congress.org/congressorg/home
www.whitehouse.gov
www.supremecourt.gov
http://elections.nytimes.com/2012/results/president
http://www.opensecrets.org/pacs/superpacs.php
http://thomas.loc.gov
http://fpc.state.gov
www.politics1.com
www.oyez.org/cases/2000-2009/2008/2008_08_205
http://c-span.org
www.latimes.com
www.washingtonpost.com/wp-dyn/politics

Chapter 7

Political institutions
State and local government

Both advocates and critics of the European Union have compared it to a "United States of Europe." Europeans are presently grappling with dilemmas of constitutionality and government structure similar to those weighed by the drafters of the Constitution of 1787. The vastly different historical situation of European nations today makes comparison dubious. Nonetheless, political leaders in both times and places have considered the similar issues of how much power should be centralized and how much left to national ("state" in the US) or local government.

The answers the founding fathers gave to these and related questions defined the particular brand of federalism originally established in the US. But such issues are not decided once and for all. They are part of an ongoing debate about the nature and purposes of government. The answers given at different times provide a map of the evolving character of American federalism and state and local government in the US.

The place of state government in American federalism

One whole article of the Constitution is devoted to the states. Article IV recognizes the limited sovereignty of the states by denying the federal authorities the power to alter the boundaries of existing states without their permission. The federal capital, Washington, could be founded only because the states of Maryland and Virginia agreed to give up some of their territory to create the District of Columbia. Constitutional procedures for the admission of new states on an equal footing (having "full faith and credit") with the original 13 and a clause guaranteeing them a republican form of government recognize *states* as the main building blocks of the American system. The importance of the states is also woven into other provisions of the Constitution, such as the rule that membership in both chambers of Congress and the election of the president are determined by state. In addition, amendments to the US Constitution can only be made with the approval of three-quarters of the states. The above protections and privileges alone go a long way towards explaining the movements for statehood in Puerto Rico and the District of Columbia.

At the time, it was thought that the Constitution provided for an appropriate division of powers between the national authorities, the states and the people. As one of the founding fathers, James Madison, explained, "the great and aggregate interests" were "referred to the national, and the local and particular to state governments." Thus some powers are prohibited the states by the Constitution. They can neither coin money, nor conduct their own foreign policy, keep their own military services, make war or set their own customs duties.

All these were recognized as "delegated powers," aggregate interests that had to be exclusively the national government's to prevent conflicts among the states and between them and the federal government. In addition, the Constitution specifically gives the national authorities the responsibility for protecting the states from foreign invasion and internal rebellion. To protect the rights of the people from both levels of government, clauses such as the right to a jury trial were included in the main document and many more rights were secured through the Bill of Rights.

A considerable list of powers remained that were "reserved," considered to be local and particular interests inappropriate for the federal government. To the states were reserved the establishment of local governments and protecting public safety and morals, which came to mean providing police, fire and sanitation departments, among other institutions. States also took responsibility for furnishing educational and health facilities as well as for levying taxes and borrowing to fund all these activities.

States wrote their own codes of civil and criminal law. The maintenance of internal transportation networks, issuing of licenses for activities within the state (marriage licenses and certification for the professions, for example), and incorporation of businesses were taken to be parts of their regulation of state commerce. Not least, state legislatures determined voting qualifications and conducted elections for all levels of government. Moreover, the Tenth Amendment, which reserves to the states or people those powers not granted the federal government, was then thought to be an important constitutional guarantee of the states' sovereignty.

Some government activities were commonly understood to be *concurrent powers*, ones shared by the states and national authorities, because the Constitution does not designate one level of government as primarily responsible. These functions included law-making, establishing courts, taxing, borrowing and providing for the general welfare. A basic principle of federalism is that two levels of government exercise authority and powers over the same territory. That apparent overlapping has not usually been problematic because the national government applies these powers to relations between the states, while each state exercises them only within its borders.

The growth of federal power

Over time, however, the existence of concurrent powers and disputes concerning them have worked to the advantage of the federal authorities. Despite the kind of federalism the Constitution defines, power has shifted dramatically from the states to the federal government for those and several other reasons. Briefly put, historical circumstances and practical politics have determined the balance of power between the states and the nation more than has constitutional theory.

Not only the defeat of states' rights advocates in the Civil War but also a series of historical crises (such as the world wars, the Depression, the problems of urbanization and industrialization, the Cold War, common standards in education nationally and, today, the war on terrorism) have proved to be beyond the capacities of the states and so have strengthened the national government. In these crises, whether they were domestic or international, the then accepted limits of national power were also judged too confining for the solution of the problems at hand. Therefore, at these times, the federal government has interpreted its constitutional powers quite broadly, and the states (and usually the federal courts) have accepted the transfer of power to the national authorities.

A number of changes that increased national power resulted from constitutional amendments. For example, until after the Civil War, the Bill of Rights was assumed to apply only to relations between citizens and the national government. But two general phrases in the Fourteenth Amendment (1868) require *states* to offer citizens "due process of law" and "equal protection of the laws." The US Supreme Court has interpreted these phrases to mean that states too must meet the standards set in the Bill of Rights. The court has therefore upheld federal civil rights legislation as well as the demands of individuals for protection from state actions. Other amendments have limited states' power over tax revenues, voting rights and elections.

Most of the growth in federal power, however, has come through law-making and political pressure. Congress has used the so-called "elastic clause" of the Constitution to set precedents for federal legislation in almost every area of life. That clause gives Congress the right to make any laws that are "necessary and proper" to carry out its other powers. Frequently the president has lobbied Congress to invoke this and other broad constitutional phrases because the public expects the chief executive to lead the nation out of troubled times. Both these federal branches have cited their concurrent power of promoting the "general welfare" as a reason for encroaching on state authority.

Federal laws have often included grants-in-aid (funding earmarked for specific purposes) as a means of persuading states to give the national government a say in their internal affairs. Grants-in-aid hold out the possibility of gaining resources to solve pressing problems, but usually require states to accept federal regulations determining how the money will be used. Many grants are offered as "matching funds," which means a state receives no more support from Washington for a project than it contributes itself. Just such an arrangement was used for the No Child Left Behind Act education reform in 2001, the Help America Vote Act election reform in 2002, and the Affordable Health Act of 2009.

The promise of funding operates as a powerful incentive. The threat to *deny* funds is as powerful a pressure for getting states to give up their own standards for federal standards. Simply by choosing to fund some kinds of activities and not others, the federal government has often been able to set states' policy agenda. The combined effects of concurrent powers, national crises, constitutional amendments, Supreme Court decisions, congressional legislation and grants-in-aid have been a strong trend toward centralized government over the past two centuries.

The evolution of state government and federalism in the US

The foundation for the expansion of federal powers was laid between 1803 and 1865, when the Supreme Court established its power of judicial review and the tradition of broadly interpreting the federal government's constitutional powers. Even so, both the national and the state governments exercised their powers in a small way for most of the nineteenth century. Until the 1930s the main way the federal government affected most citizens was through its help in promoting the economy by developing the frontier. Its armies fought Native Americans and forced them farther west. It gave new states federal land for schools and joined states and private entrepreneurs to build roads and canals. From the 1860s on, Congress wrote legislation providing free or cheap land on the frontier for settlers homesteading in the wilderness and companies engaged in building trans-continental railroads.

Dual federalism

When the federal government attempted to legislate in the areas of public health, safety and order in the 1800s, the Supreme Court ruled that these were *solely* the concern of the states. Likewise it decided that the regulation of business was purely a matter for the states. On the whole, the court acted in accordance with the theory known as "dual federalism." The court asserted that state and federal governments have clearly separated spheres in which each is sovereign. It interpreted the Constitution narrowly, limiting government activity on any level to explicitly granted powers. Thus, it commonly approved neither federal nor state laws regulating industry and labor. Strongly influenced by laissez-faire economic theory, from the 1880s through to the 1920s the court refused to accept laws to regulate child labor, minimum wages and working hours, safety or working conditions.

At the start of the Great Depression, the states were still the sole provider of most services understood to be reserved to them by the drafters of the Constitution. Washington, DC, did not regulate citizens' behavior and provided them with very few services beyond the post office. The combination of the economic crisis, Franklin D. Roosevelt's New Deal legislation and the court's advocacy of a new theory of federalism transformed the governmental landscape by 1939.

Cooperative federalism

By the late 1930s the national authorities' regulation of the economy and creation of a social security safety net ushered in the era of "cooperative federalism." The court interpreted the Tenth Amendment and elastic clause broadly. It viewed the division of powers between state and federal governments as less distinct and less important than the ways they might work together. Many of the most vital activities of the authorities were now assumed to be among the concurrent powers of government. Sweeping expansions of both state and federal powers resulted from the change in the court's philosophy, but Washington's share of all money spent on domestic needs nearly tripled while the states' expenditures on these problems remained the same.

Grants-in-aid programs began with the New Deal laws and grew rapidly in number for almost 40 years. In the 1950s such grants resulted in heavy federal involvement in secondary and higher education as part of the effort to compete with the Soviet Union's technological progress. They also supplied states with funds for the massive interstate highway system built at the time. In the 1960s grants helped pay for efforts to enforce civil and voting rights legislation as well as the ambitious goals of Lyndon B. Johnson's Great Society and War on Poverty programs. Johnson aimed at nothing less than the realization of equal opportunity and a better quality of life for all Americans.

Grants-in-aid mushroomed in kind, number and expense. The federal government became active in local law enforcement, low-rent housing projects, urban mass-transit, health services and job training. It *shared* responsibility for virtually all the services that had been exclusively the functions of the states. For the first time, moreover, it encouraged applications for aid directly from local governments and private community groups, frequently bypassing the state authorities in its decisions on financing.

"New federalism"

By the early 1970s, a counterreaction set in. State and local governments complained of over-regulation, wasteful bureaucratic red tape and the tendency of the national government to legislate "unfunded mandates" (laws that place new duties on the states without supplying sufficient or any funding). Conservatives in both parties called for a return to dual federalism, and many said that President Nixon's proposals in 1972 amounted to just that, although he called them "new federalism." His revenue-sharing cut most strings attached to federal grants so that the lower levels of government could gain more power in setting priorities and standards. Combining many grant programs into large block grants for sectors such as health or education services aimed to accomplish the same purposes. New federalism had little success in stopping the shift of power from the states to the national government. Members of Congress were unwilling to give up taking credit for and exercising control over the distribution of federal money to their districts or states. Revenue-sharing was ended in 1986, and most grant programs returned to their former pattern even earlier.

President Reagan promised to revive new federalism, but the main effect of his administration was to reverse the trend of increasing federal aid to state and local government. Such aid dropped by 25 percent in the early 1980s, and to date has grown only slightly, in spite of the federal budget surpluses of the 1990s (which turned into many trillions in red ink by 2009). Federal grant programs grew in the 1990s and the following decade, but state and local governments had to bear more of the cost of new programs. In exchange, congressional leaders and all presidents since Nixon have agreed to set fewer binding federal regulations on grant programs. In practice, those promises have often not been kept and unfunded mandates have multiplied.

American devolution and deregulation

During the past decade or so the federal government has left the solution of growing numbers of national problems to the states through an American form of devolution. Such decentralization of policymaking inevitably means that inequalities among the states grow, because cuts in federal grants hurt poor states most. During the 1990s boom, the wealthier states made up for the loss of federal funds through increased state incomes, while the poorer states cut services and hovered near bankruptcy. In the next decade rich and poor states alike cut services to the bone as they made the drastic reductions required to satisfy the balanced-budget clauses of their constitutions in worsening economic conditions.

Most political commentators interpreted the Republican triumph in the 1994 mid-term elections as a sign that the national mood favored the devolution of power and responsibility away from the national government. In 1996 federal aid for needy families was devolved to the states with Democratic President Clinton's approval. From then to 2000, Clinton agreed with Congress on the removal or relaxation of federal regulation of telecommunications, agriculture, civil rights, pollution prevention, environmental protection, and stock and investment markets. In the same years Supreme Court decisions disallowed Acts of Congress that would have enforced national regulations through clauses permitting citizens to sue the government. Instead, either the states regulated private institutions dealing with these areas of life or they were allowed to regulate themselves.

The rebirth of big federal government

During his first term, George W. Bush, a self-proclaimed "compassionate conservative," met some conventional expectations of conservatives in the debate over federalism but not others. By 2005 he had pressed through two large tax-reduction packages and promised wholesale tax reform in his second term. Thus he apparently aimed both to reduce the size of the national government by starving it of funds and to free the public (especially those with capital) of the burden of federal taxation. On the other hand, some called him America's first "big-government conservative" because he intruded into policy areas traditionally belonging to the states, especially education, and enlarged federal spending by some 29 percent (triple its rate of growth rate during the 1990s).

President Bush also implemented a very ambitious and costly agenda for national standards in the public schools (the No Child Left Behind Act), faith-based federal social services, sex education programs from the national Department of Education promoting abstinence and a Medicare prescription-drug plan for the elderly. He pursued these goals simultaneously with initiatives in foreign policy and national security that required the funding of a military build-up, astronomic costs of long land wars in Afghanistan and Iraq and the much higher costs and number of federal regulations of homeland security arrangements since the attacks of September 11, 2001 (9/11). Then in late 2008 the greatest economic crisis struck the nation since the stock market crash of 1929.

In the attempt to prevent a decline into another long depression, by the end of Obama's first term of office the federal government had bought the nation's largest insurer to save it from bankruptcy, rescued leading financial institutions to prevent the collapse of the banking industry, lent some billions to bail out the failing automakers in Detroit, spent billions on stimulus packages, and launched expensive universal health care for the first time in the nation's history. In all these actions the national government bought or invested in private businesses and negotiated long-term involvement in the private sector. A combination of the domestic ambitions of the Bush and Obama presidencies, their foreign policy and the economic crisis produced a situation in which the imbalance between federal and state power was arguably as great as in the 1930s or even greater. Partisan disagreement and public concern focused increasingly on growing public spending and debt in the 2012 elections and inter-branch negotiations over tax and spending limits in 2013.

The structure of state government

As the fundamental principles of all American governments were first developed by the original states, it is hardly surprising that the structure of state and federal governments are similar. Each of the 50 states has a written constitution. Each also has a separation of powers among three branches that share power through a system of checks and balances.

All of the state legislatures, except Nebraska's, have the same format as Congress with two houses, usually called the state senate and state assembly. State legislatures also work through committees and pass laws through a process very like that used in Congress. Like the president, the chief executive of a state, the governor, enjoys the powers of administration, appointment and veto. The structure of a state judiciary is also broadly parallel to the federal court system. In most states there is a state supreme court and under it appeals courts and (parallel to the US district courts) county or municipal courts.

There are, however, some important differences in the structure of state governments. State constitutions are typically several times longer than the US Constitution because they contain many more detailed provisions and much more specific language. Instead of reserving whatever powers are left undefined to a lower level of government or the people, the drafters of state constitutions attempt to be as explicit as possible. Such detailed documents less easily adapt themselves to broad interpretation and consequently are much more frequently amended. New York state's constitution has been amended more than 200 times in the past century, for example, while only 27 amendments have been added to the US Constitution since 1787. Most states have written entirely new constitutions or extensively rewritten their old ones not once but several times.

The branches of government also have distinctive elements at the state level. Most state legislators are part-time law-makers. They often divide their time between the legislature and a law practice or business in their home districts. State legislators have fixed terms of office like members of Congress, but they do not choose to run for re-election as often. Instead, they go back to full-time work in their current private jobs or use their government experience to enter a new line of work. Thus, well over a third of all members in state legislatures are newcomers at any time and as many are relatively inexperienced.

State legislators' interest in careers in government is low for several reasons. Compared to what they can earn in the private sector, the annual salary is low. Traveling between the capital and the member's district as well as maintaining an office in both places requires considerable time and expense. Sitting in the state legislature does not bring much prestige, even though it disrupts family life and leads to the forced neglect of members' other part-time profession or business. Some experts on American government argue that the states should change to full-time, professional, well-paid legislatures. But tradition and the enormous cost of converting to full-time law-makers make the present situation likely to persist. The traditional view is that having part-time legislators is an advantage. Their businesses or jobs in local districts keep them concerned about the well-being of the community they represent. As one political scientist explained, "Part-time legislators really have something at home, unlike congressmen who don't have anything to come home for except trying to get votes."

In practice, the debate may be moot, however, because the federal government's increasing withdrawal from grants-in-aid programs has forced state governments to assume more responsibility. The increased workload of state law-makers has already produced a strong movement towards full-time legislatures in the more populous states.

There are also important differences between a governor's situation and that of the president. On the one hand, most governors have two powers the president lacks. They usually have more complete control over the state budget. Most also have the line-item veto, which allows them to accept some parts of a bill passed by the legislature while vetoing other parts. On the other hand, in many states the governor's power is weaker than the president's in four important ways. First, many are not free to make as many appointments as the president does. More state officials are elected than at the federal level of government.

Second, many states have a tradition of electing several of a governor's department heads. For example, the state treasurer, attorney general and commissioner of education are often elected. These other state executives are popularly considered part of the governor's "team" at election time. But each must get elected separately and that makes them more independent of the governor. Many times, these department heads do not even belong to the governor's party. State parties often seem less important to voters than selecting a team of state executives that represent a range of different races, ethnic groups, economic interests, and policy alternatives.

Third, governors have less control over suggestions for new laws. Starting early in the twentieth century, many states developed two procedures for taking suggestions for new laws (or changes in old laws) directly to the voters, bypassing the governor and usually the legislature. The "initiative" allows citizens to call for a vote on a state law or constitutional amendment, either in the legislature or by the public at the next election. Those proposing the initiative must petition the state for this vote by collecting signatures from somewhere between 5 to 10 percent of the state's registered voters. A little under half of the states currently permit some form of voter initiative.

The referendum, a direct vote of the public on an issue, may be the result of a successful initiative, a requirement for amending the state constitution, or an item put on the ballot by the state legislature. Known as "propositions," referenda are allowed in half the states. Referenda on constitutional changes are required in all but one state.

It is politically dangerous for governors to oppose procedures that make state government more democratic by giving ordinary voters a say in state law-making, even though some propositions may have harmful effects. Thus state executives have found it difficult to speak out against proposals similar to Proposition 13, passed in California in 1978, which so reduce taxes that state and local governments must cut back on basic services. In the 1970s the use of referenda grew rapidly and in the 1980s numbered nearly 250 in every congressional election year, leading some critics to doubt whether the public could be informed enough to vote intelligently on so many issues. In the 1990s the trend continued and politicians made little protest, even though the most common and successful proposal put limits on the number of terms they could run for office. By 2000, however, term limits had been found unconstitutional for federal offices, and the tide of propositions at election time had started to abate somewhat. In the course of the following decade there were still many different issues voters had a chance to decide, but among the most controversial were proposals to permit or ban same-sex marriage and the legalization of marijuana for medical purposes.

The fourth important way governors have lost power is through special district governments, authorities designed to deal with a specific problem that crosses governmental boundaries. Some special districts have become so powerful that they are popularly called regional governments. Most special districts have been established since the First World War. Some have been suggested by federal authorities but, like all forms of local government, special districts are created by the states.

State legislatures do not aim to weaken the governor's position by founding special districts; rather, legislatures simply recognize that growing problems, such as air pollution, land and water shortages, refuse disposal and regional traffic jams, cannot be efficiently handled within one legal jurisdiction. Several states and often many local governments share the responsibility for dealing with these problems. Coordination between so many separate authorities becomes difficult if not impossible. Many of America's big cities are merely the centers of much larger metropolitan areas that include many suburbs, several satellite cites and even "pockets" of rural territory. Most special districts have been established in just these areas, where the need for coordinated public services is greatest.

Special districts are governed by official representatives from the various local and state governments in the area where regional problems exist. But special districts also have their own staffs and budgets. Usually both are funded mostly by grants from the federal government and are therefore outside the governor's control. Presidents Ronald Reagan and George H.W. Bush said they intended to reduce the role and importance of special districts. But although the number of special districts reached nearly 30,000 by the beginning of the 1990s, neither they nor later presidents have taken any significant action in the matter, because the problems the districts are set up to solve have only become more serious. Thus, it is instead likely that special districts will gradually take more planning initiative from state governors and state governments generally.

The judiciary branch of state government is different from the federal judiciary in two important ways. First, many state and local judges are elected, rather than appointed, to terms of office that vary from four to 15 years. In many states, even the state supreme court justices are elected. Generally, the election of judges is meant to make the judicial branch more responsive to changes in public opinion. It is also meant to make the removal of unpopular or incompetent judges easier. Of course, as a result of their election, state and local judges are more frequently accused of being swayed by political pressures. Once on the bench, judges are required by law to be impartial. Therefore, it is not considered unusual that both major parties will endorse the same person for judge, if that candidate is known as a fair and competent jurist.

Second, the state supreme court cannot be sure of handing down the final decision in the most important cases that come to it. Of course, that is because

PLATE 7.1   Florida's Supreme Court Justices in 2000.
(Corbis)

the federal Constitution takes precedence over all other law, and the US Supreme Court, therefore, has the power to review the constitutionality of both federal and state laws. The importance of this fact became abundantly clear in 2000, when the US Supreme Court reversed the decision of the supreme court of Florida to allow manual recounts of the presidential election in the state, and thus determined the outcome of the presidential election as a whole.

Local government

The 50 states are divided into some 83,000 units of local government. In addition to the special districts, there are counties, towns, cities, boroughs and school districts. The states create these (and other) kinds of local governments and determine their powers. No local government in the US has sovereignty (power in its own right). Units of local government are not even mentioned in the federal Constitution. They exist because they have been created by the states as instruments, tools to help the state carry out its responsibilities. Some local governments have been established by state constitutions while others came into being through acts of state legislatures. Special districts often result from agreements among two or more states.

Local governments vary tremendously across the country, because each state has developed its own system of local authority. Most states are divided into counties, although in Louisiana the parallel unit of government is called a "parish" and in Alaska a "borough." Counties also vary greatly in population, size and function. Still, most counties share several general responsibilities. They are usually the main units of government in rural areas. Counties rarely have any law-making power, but instead act as agents of the state. They serve as administrative units that carry out some state-wide programs in local areas, such as keeping records and issuing different kinds of licenses.

All the powers of local government are really powers of the state. The state just delegates the work of providing local facilities and services to smaller units of government. Thus the states often set general standards and guidelines, but ask counties to carry out the functions that are delegated. Typically, these functions include providing local transportation systems, schools, fire and police protection, water and sanitation systems and medical programs and buildings. Counties also collect the local property taxes to pay for these services.

County government usually consists of a board of somewhere between three and 12 members, a county court and the chief officers of county departments. Board members, or commissioners as they are often called in more populous counties, are elected and serve on a part-time basis. Their powers usually include deciding how local taxes should be raised and spent for county programs, as well as the authority to establish zoning codes that regulate the purpose for which land may be used.

The boards have no influence over the county court, but their power of the purse and zoning gives them significant control over local department heads. The county superintendent of schools, for example, must have the board's support to raise more money for local schools or to have a site for a new school approved. Other administrative officers commonly found in a county include the county sheriff, the medical examiner or coroner, commissioner of health, the recorder or registrar of property deeds and the clerk (who issues licenses and keeps population records). Because they carry out state law on a daily basis, all these officers of county government usually determine what the law means in practice for most residents.

In built-up, heavily populated areas, the states have usually created substitutes for county government. In urban areas, most tasks that used to be performed by counties have been taken over by municipal governments: cities, towns, villages, boroughs or special districts. The meaning of these common terms varies widely, according to the legal definitions established by each state. For example, "city" usually indicates an urban unit of local government with a population of at least several tens of thousands. Most states define smaller built-up areas as villages, towns or boroughs. There are, however, many exceptions to this rule of thumb. In Kansas, a "city" may have a population of only 200 people. In Illinois, the suburban "village" of Oak Park has a population of more than 50,000. The term "town" also has various meanings in different parts of the country. In New England, much of the land had been divided into towns *before* state governments were established. Counties were only later mapped out and never became as important as towns in providing the main services of local government in the New England states.

The confusion of terms is not made easier by the US Census Bureau, which has developed its own vocabulary for analyzing units of population. Documents from the federal government often discuss "metropolitan statistical areas" (MSAs) and "consolidated metropolitan statistical areas" (CMSAs). These terms are very useful for mapping the population concentrations that cross the boundaries of state and local governments. They have often helped demonstrate the need for special districts, but they have no legal status as units of government. Most states have granted urban units of government some form of home rule, a legal status amounting to limited local autonomy. This gives them a degree of legislative power to establish local law and usually a municipal charter that functions as a kind of local constitution. Ordinarily this charter of incorporation cannot be altered without the approval of local residents. However, if there is disagreement with the state over the limits of the powers granted in the charter, state and federal courts almost always interpret the municipal government's powers narrowly.

The structure of municipal governments varies widely. In most a mayor is the chief executive, and the mayor decides policy together with a city council. The amount of power allowed the office under the city charter may make the mayor merely a figurehead or the primary decision-maker in local affairs. Since the early 1900s, a large number of cities have experimented with or adopted "city-manager

PLATE 7.2 A street sign outside Los Angeles' City Hall shows its sister cities.
(Seth Joel/Corbis)

government," in which the city council is the chief political organ of government and a professional administrator, the city manager, carries out its decisions.

The council writes local laws, called "ordinances," in the policy areas granted it by the state charter. The mayor may or may not have the veto power over such council legislation. As in counties, a range of officials carry out local policy in specific sectors of local government activity. The mayor or city manager usually prepares an annual budget proposal based of these officials' requests for money and available sources of income, and submits it to the council for approval.

Until recently, the financing of both county and municipal government came primarily from real estate taxes, but by 1990 property taxes supplied only about a third of funding. Another third came from state governments, and a tenth came from the federal government. Both state and federal financing was generally tied to grants-in-aid programs that gave these other authorities an important role in local decision-making and often aimed to alleviate the effects of local poverty or socio-economic inequality. The remainder of local funding generally came from a variety of fees and charges. To make ends meet and launch new programs, large cities have increasingly raised additional revenue through sales and income taxes.

The meanings and powers of local governments vary so much for three main reasons. First, local authorities developed in several different historical periods. Second, these governments reflect the effects of local conditions, such as climate, natural resources and the various population groups that have settled there over time, bringing with them a variety of traditions for handling local affairs. Third and most important, each state is free to give local governments whatever powers and functions it chooses.

To citizens, the state's definition of local government is very significant. In practice, local governments are delegated the job of providing most of the vital services citizens expect today. And the territory of local governments often overlaps. Towns, villages and cities often have authority inside parts of a county. Therefore, citizens must learn which local government is responsible for each necessary service. Otherwise, it becomes impossible to apply for the local services state law gives people a right to expect. A citizen cannot even complain effectively about problems with the water supply, refuse removal, school system and so on without knowing what unit of local government to contact.

There are arguments for and against the great number, variety and over-lapping authority of governments in the US. Some observers maintain that the situation is quite democratic in that it gives many citizens opportunities to participate in government and to affect the making of policy. Critics, however, note that voter participation is highest in national elections and lowest in local elections. Some suggest that US voters participate less in *all* elections than people in other developed countries because there are more opportunities for participation than the public has the capacity to focus on.

Another disadvantage often cited is that the complex sharing of powers and functions by all levels of government has become too difficult to disentangle for

FIGURE 7.1 Local governments and cities in the Great Lakes region.

many people, so that they have great difficulties securing the very services that government is instituted to offer. The same complexity makes individuals turn to organized lobbies that have the time and resources to influence policy. Thus, instead of bringing government to the people, some pundits complain, the current situation encourages the growth and power of special-interest groups.

Benefits of multiple governments are emphasized by other commentators. Some believe state and local governments with significant powers allow the nation to experiment with alternate solutions to problems on a small scale. That is why the states have long been termed "50 laboratories for democracy." In recent years both states and cities have pioneered new plans for public education, health service management, pollution control and welfare reform, to name just a few examples. Many if not most governmental reforms since late in the twentieth century have been tested out at lower levels of government before being adopted nationally.

Other observers insist that only such varied and overlapping governments can respond to the sharply contrasting conditions that exist in a country as diverse as the US. Smaller units of government can respond more quickly and appropriately to such differences. But local solutions are bound to generate inequality as well, in this view of the situation, and that is why the federal government must step in to protect minority rights and to even out economic disparities.

Exercises

Explain and examine the significance of the following terms:

delegated powers	dual federalism	propositions
concurrent powers	cooperative federalism	special districts
elastic clause	new federalism	ordinances
grants-in-aid	state constitutions	local governments
full faith and credit	devolution	unfunded mandates

Write short essays on the following questions:

1. Discuss the reasons for and the effects of the changes in American federalism since 1787.

2. Compare and contrast the structure of the state and federal governments.

3. Give a critical evaluation of the use of the initiative and referendum in state government.

4. What are some arguments for and against the election of judges?

5. In your opinion, does the variety of overlapping governments in the US represent a factor for increased democracy?

Further reading

Book of the States (biennially published) Lexington, KY: Council of State Governments.

Bowman, A.O. and Kearny, R. (1986) *The Resurgence of the States*, Englewood Cliffs, NJ: Prentice-Hall.

Census of Governments (published every fifth year) Washington, DC: US Government Printing Office.

Dye, T.R. (1990) *American Federalism: Competition Among Governments*, Lexington, MA: Lexington Books.

State of the States (annually published) Washington, DC: PEW Center on the States.

Websites

www.stateline.org/live
www.access.wa.gov
www.state.ny.us
www.state.tx.us
www.state.ne.us
www.state.me.us

Chapter 8

Foreign policy

A nation apart? American attitudes to world affairs

On the one hand, the foreign policy of the US is like that of all nations: it has been a mixture of self-interest and an attempt to act according to commonly held ideals. On the other hand, a factor that makes America's (and all nations') foreign policy distinctive is the size and strength of each relative to other nations at critical times in its history. In the beginning of its history the US, then a weak and inconsequential actor on the world stage, emphasized what the American political scientist Joseph S. Nye terms "soft power" (attracting support by example, ideals and diplomacy) to the near exclusion of other means of handling international affairs. Today, the nation is the world's only superpower and, in the view of some commentators, it too seldom uses soft power, especially since the terrorist attacks of September 11, 2001, and relies too frequently or hastily instead on "hard power" (achieving support and goals through economic sanctions and military threats or force). The Obama administration, intent on concluding the wars in Iraq and Afghanistan, has tried to redress the balance with a greater willingness to talk and negotiate through what he and Secretary of State Hillary Clinton call "smart power."

For the US, the nation's vulnerability in relation to the European nations involved in the settlement of North America was decisive in its foreign relations until 1900 or, some argue, 1945. Only from the twentieth century on have other nations significantly challenged the Euro-centered character of American foreign relations. This situation, of course, also results from Europe's leadership in world affairs generally during much of American history and the predominance of Europeans among immigrants to the US until recently.

Its history of settlement and immigration is another major influence on the character of US foreign policy. European colonists and later immigrants have usually had mixed feelings toward their homelands. They emigrated to escape aspects of their home societies but simultaneously harbored deep attachments to the old country. Consequently, immigration has produced both isolationism and internationalism in American foreign policy, as Americans expressed their wish to avoid or cultivate contacts with former homelands. Immigrants brought with them their homeland's history of international relations and often lobbied the American government to fight the old country's enemies and help its friends. Longer-settled Americans have periodically doubted the loyalty of recent immigrants. The US has a history of perceiving threats to internal security from foreign agitators that has caused repression at home and strained its relations abroad.

Before Europeans founded lasting settlements on the East Coast, "promotional literature" written by European explorers established the idea that "America" would evolve a new and better phase of civilization. Uncorrupted by the past, America would offer people a chance to start over and do better. From the earliest colonists, migrants to America have wanted to prove this "promise of America" true to justify their decision to emigrate. Thus grew up the faith in American exceptionalism. This is the belief (rhetorical or sincere) that America's foreign affairs, unlike those of other nations, are not self-interested but are based on a mission to offer the world a better form of society characterized by the ideals of "the American creed:" the US version of a republican form of government, economic and political freedom, egalitarian social relations and democracy.

When he spoke of a "city upon a hill" that "the eyes of all people are upon" in 1630, the Puritan leader John Winthrop had in mind a religiously reformed community that would be a model for change in England. But later American leaders from George Washington to Barack Obama who have echoed Winthrop's words or sentiment were confirming Americans' sense that they had a unique mission to set an example for the rest of the world, to export American freedom and democracy and so conduct a foreign policy unlike that of any other nation. Whether real or imagined, American exceptionalism has had palpable effects on the history of US foreign relations.

In reality, the basic concerns that greatly influence the foreign relations of other nations have also played major roles in the formulation of American policy. Of necessity, the US too has protected what it saw as its vital interests: economic success at home and abroad, access to important natural resources, support for its ideological views, respect for its military power and assistance in times of crisis. In practice, the US has often seemed as concerned with *realpolitik* as other nations, in spite of both sincere and rhetorical devotion to ideals like those described above.

A third factor, the nation's geographical position, has also made its foreign relations unique. If one looks at the globe as Americans do, with the US in the center, two "facts" that have colored much of US foreign policy history seem clear. First, broad oceans separate the Americas from the other continents. Second, most of the world's population and farmland, and *all* of the other great powers, are located in Europe and Asia.

For more than 300 years the relative physical isolation created by the oceans encouraged those migrating to North America to believe they were leaving behind whatever they disliked in their home societies. Here was the basis for US isolationism, the belief that Americans could withdraw from involvement with the rest of the world and focus on domestic (internal) affairs. As the country expanded across the continent, its great size offered another excuse for believing the US "was world enough" for its inhabitants. Successive transportation, communication and weaponry revolutions, as well as the internationalization of the economy eventually made isolationism founded on geographical separation an indefensible foreign policy position. However, traditional attitudes continue to influence the views of many Americans.

Paradoxically, geographical separation has also contributed to a tradition of national insecurity. Looking outward and seeing the great powers of Europe and Asia on all sides, Americans have periodically felt surrounded. That anxiety resulted in a determination to create national security in the North American quarter of the globe. The US has sought to be a quarter-sphere hegemon (the only great power on the continent), worked to drive European powers out, and striven to control the land, sea, air and, finally, the outer space approaches to North America.

The *felt* need for continental security has been regularly advanced as a justification for territorial expansion through war, purchase or negotiation. The people who first bore the brunt of this preoccupation with security were the Native Americans. Success in driving them westward fuelled Americans' ambitions and sense that they had a destiny to "civilize" the continent.

Security was also the rationale for a ring of far-flung military bases and, later, of radar stations beyond the country's borders. The US, it should be remembered, entered both world wars primarily because of threats to its control of the continental sea approaches. In the 1980s President Reagan's strategic defense initiative (SDI) sought to extend this 200-year-old principle of quarter-sphere security to the space approaches to the US. He envisioned using high-tech weaponry placed in space to shoot down missiles armed with nuclear warheads that might be sent to attack the US. At first, supporters of the SDI viewed the likely attacker as the USSR, but with the end of the Cold War, so-called "rogue nations" who ignored international law and supported terrorism appeared to be the most serious threat.

In the 1990s and early twenty-first century, therefore, American presidents continued to support research and development for a "national missile shield" against such threats. Shortly after taking office, George W. Bush announced a vastly bigger shield and offered America's allies protection behind it. Just months later terrorists used American passenger jets as fuel-laden bombs to destroy the Twin Towers of the World Trade Center in Manhattan and one side of the Pentagon in Washington, DC. Not since 1812 had a foreign force attacked the North American mainland, killed thousands "at home" and wrecked symbols of US military and economic power.

The sudden vulnerability felt by the public seemed to make a mockery of the long search for security at the root of US foreign policy. Many asked why the FBI and CIA had not uncovered the terrorists' plans. But their representatives and foreign policy specialists in Congress, it appeared, had been warning of such "low tech" terrorism for years. The Twin Towers had been attacked with a car bomb some years earlier. In the immediate aftermath, some commentators reckoned that the tragedy proved that a missile shield could not make the nation safe, but the president and public polls showed increased determination to regain the

PLATE 8.1 On the morning of September 11, 2001, terrorists piloted United Airlines Flight 175, its crew and passengers into the World Trade Center in New York City. The World Trade Center south tower (L) burst into flames after being struck by Flight 175. The north tower burns following an earlier attack by a hijacked airliner on the same morning.
(Sean Adair/Reuters/Corbis)

nation's former sense of safety by all possible means, including SDI, whatever the cost. As the "War on Terror" grew into wars in Afghanistan and Iraq and security measures that limited civil liberties and privacy at home, a small but growing number of voices asked what in the history of America's relations in the world had contributed to the catastrophic events of 9/11, and weighed alternative foreign policy futures. Still, many interpreted Bush's 2004 election victory as a mandate to stay the course in the prosecution of the multifaceted War on Terror he forwarded. Four years later, the sitting president's foreign policy was very unpopular, several Democratic candidates vying to replace him said the nation needed to restore its global soft power, and the victory went to Obama, the only competitive aspirant for the office who had opposed the Iraq war before the election. He, however, promised to prosecute the war in Afghanistan with greater vigor even as the nation withdrew from Iraq and more frequently used diplomacy and multilateral cooperation in pursuing its global goals.

From neutrality to isolationism, 1776–1830

The first period in the history of American foreign affairs covers the years from 1776 until around 1830. During this time, it can be argued, US policy toward other countries (especially the European powers) resembled that of the newly established Third World nations in the twentieth century. Like those nations, the US tried to steer clear of alliances with great powers and instead strove to keep its neutrality in foreign affairs and to act unilaterally. Fear of becoming a pawn of British or French schemes for expanded international power was the mainspring of American policy in this period.

Around 1800, the US was a political and economic midget. It was hemmed in by British colonies to the north, French Louisiana in the west and, in the south, by the rich and powerful Spanish Empire that included Florida and today's Southwest. During the colonial period, every war between the European powers had its American phase, and the new nation could not afford to have that pattern continue if it was to stabilize its political institutions and economy. Thus the US for many years stayed aloof from the Napoleonic Wars and refused to become involved in the French Revolution, even though the French had been an indispensable ally in the War of Independence with Britain.

After serving as the nation's first president, George Washington stated the existing policy in general terms in his so-called Farewell Address (1796). Its main principle consisted of avoiding political and military alliances while cultivating trading relations with other countries. President Washington also advised the nation to remember its uniqueness and resulting need for unilateral action. When the US strayed from these principles by entering the Napoleonic Wars on the side of France in 1812, the results were disastrous. British forces burned Washington, DC, the US won not a single important victory, and the cost was enormous. After that object lesson, the core ideas of the Address remained a pillar of American foreign policy until after the Second World War.

The Alien and Sedition Acts (1798) were more evidence of the American fear of becoming a pawn of European powers. These laws were directed against foreign subversives who might undermine the nation from within. Fear of French sympathizers inspired the Acts, which allowed the president and courts to fine, imprison or deport any foreigner who seemed a danger to national security. The Acts were an early sign of deep insecurities about the loyalties of newcomers in a nation of immigrants.

The foreign policy statement from the early period that contributed most to the development of later policy was the Monroe Doctrine. Between 1800 and the 1820s, many Spanish colonies in Central and South America rebelled and declared their independence. The US wanted to recognize these new nations but feared conflict with Spain and the possibility that Britain or France would intervene and return them to Spanish control. America was too weak to prevent European interference in Latin America, but it formally expressed its opposition to outside meddling in their affairs through the Monroe Doctrine.

The Monroe Doctrine can be reduced to three basic principles. The first (called non-colonization) is that the US opposed any new colonies in the Americas. The second (non-intervention) demanded that the European powers remain uninvolved in the affairs of New World nations. In return for Europe's compliance with these rules, the US would observe a third principle (non-interference) that amounted to accepting the presence of the remaining European colonies in the Americas and keeping aloof from European affairs. The US could not enforce any of these principles until around 1900, when it had constructed a powerful navy. Until then, the British navy prevented other European nations from violating the Doctrine and opened Latin America for British economic influence.

The Monroe Doctrine transformed American neutrality into isolationism and combined it with the country's sense of having a special mission in the world. The Americas were declared the US's exclusive sphere of interest. European-style kingdoms and Old World politics were to have no place in the hemisphere, so that only the US's brand of republican government would influence Latin America. In short, the Doctrine expressed the mixture of idealism and ideological domination that was to become typical of US relations with Latin America.

From expansionism to imperialism, 1783–1914

The second period of American foreign policy overlaps with the first but extends into the early years of the twentieth century. During this time, the US was preoccupied with developments that Americans often viewed as internal affairs: the settlement of a frontier that constantly moved further west, the struggle over whether slavery should be extended into new states or abolished, and the effort to construct transportation systems to bind the continent together and ease the exploitation of its resources. Because all these processes consisted of, or were related to, territorial expansion, they were also central to the conduct of foreign affairs.

Early in the nineteenth century, the US roughly tripled its territory through treaty and purchase. Agreements with Britain added the land between the Appalachians and the Mississippi River, the northern section of Maine and parts of Minnesota and the Dakotas. America bought Florida from Spain, and France offered the US the land from the Mississippi to the Rocky Mountains in the Louisiana Purchase. Most Americans viewed these as legal and unaggressive ways to consolidate US territory and minimize the dangers of European interference. It was assumed that the European powers could legally transfer hegemony over the Native Americans with the right to their homelands. In reality, much of American foreign policy to about 1900 consisted of war and treaty negotiations with these native peoples.

Such enormous increases in the country's size inspired the growth of an intense national pride. The feats of frontier settlers evolved into myth and a set of idealized character traits. The farther west people and institutions were, the more truly American they appeared in the popular mind. Some advocates of expansion emphasized that only a nation spanning the continent could effectively isolate itself from external threats. Others told themselves that they were extending the benefits of democracy to less advanced peoples. Most Americans and European immigrants felt certain that they developed the land and made it bear fruit more than the Native Americans did, and simultaneously gave little or no attention to the destruction of the natural environment that this development brought. Forthrightly racist expansionists said the "red and brown" peoples were inferior and therefore had to be confined, conquered or at least dominated.

By the 1840s, the idea of America's expansion to the Pacific was being popularized as the nation's Manifest Destiny (its apparently inevitable, divinely determined fate). Since it was obviously meant to be, that expansion was also right, argued the expansionists. "Oregon fever" sent thousands trekking across the plains and mountains. Facing threats of armed conflict, Britain gave up its claims to the present Pacific Northwest and parts of the mountain states in border negotiations. Americans were more militantly aggressive toward Mexico. American settlers seized power in Texas and asked that the area be annexed to the US. When the Texas border with Mexico was disputed in 1846, the US offered to buy the territory in question but took the first excuse to take it by war after Mexico refused to sell. Expansion in the Southwest aroused strong opposition, especially in New England, where many argued against acquiring Texas (a slave-owning republic) and against endangering the lives of US troops to make more territory available for slavery. So Texans waited ten years for annexation, and the Mexican War was the source of violent congressional debate. In 1848, however, the treaty at its end added the Southwest, California and most of the southern mountain states to US territory.

In the decades after the Civil War, expansionists gained support from several sources. Businessmen and farmers demanded the opening of new markets abroad to prevent overproduction causing economic depressions at home. Military strategists pointed out that a strong navy and overseas bases were necessary to keep these markets open and protect US shipping. Religious leaders fused the ideas of Manifest Destiny and the "white man's burden" to support overseas missions and the "civilizing" of foreign peoples. Nationalists, now using the language of Social Darwinism, claimed Americans were surely the fittest to survive in the international competition for territory and influence. When the federal government declared the Western frontier closed in 1890, some people feared that Americans would lose their strength and endurance if they did not find frontiers abroad. In a famous trend-setting essay the University of Wisconsin historian Frederick Jackson Turner posited that the frontier represented the essentially "American" and had been responsible for the Americanizing of the country's immigrants.

Buoyed up on this wave of public opinion, US foreign policy became territorially and economically imperialist around the turn of the century. That is to say, America used hard power to impose its control on overseas peoples, both formally (through colonization, annexation and military occupation) and informally (through military threats, economic domination and political subversion). In 1898 the US declared war on Spain as an imperialist power that was stifling Cuban freedom. Having won that "splendid little war" (as the American secretary of state called it), the US acquired economic control over Cuba and the right to intervene in its affairs. It also acquired (as colonies) Puerto Rico, Guam Island and the Philippine Islands, where Filipino nationalists fought a bloody war for independence from the US.

American trade expanded rapidly, especially in Asia and Latin America. Hawaii, Samoa and Wake Island were annexed and served as suitable bases for further economic expansion eastward. In an effort to protect its growing trade in China, the US contributed troops to an alliance of European powers that put down a Chinese rebellion. It also announced the "Open Door Policy," which demanded equal access to Chinese markets to counter the Europeans' claim to exclusive trade rights in China. In Latin America, President Theodore Roosevelt instigated and ensured the success of a Panamanian revolt against Colombia in 1903 in order to secure the right to build and control the Panama Canal. A year later he announced the revision of the Monroe Doctrine known as the Roosevelt Corollary. According to the corollary, the US was justified in intervening in the internal affairs of Latin American nations if their politics or economies became unstable. The European powers, however, were again warned that America would not passively permit their intervention in the western hemisphere. Between 1900 and 1917, the US intervened in six different Latin American countries through presidential action.

Critics known as the "anti-imperialists" actively opposed overseas expansion. As a result of their efforts, for example, Cuba was not annexed and the Philippines were promised their freedom as early as 1916 (although the promise was not kept until 1934). Some anti-imperialists claimed that unilateral executive action sending US military forces abroad for intervention or colonization upset the balance of power in foreign policy between the president and Congress by increasing his importance as commander-in-chief. Other opponents of imperialism stressed that America could gain access to foreign markets without oppressing other peoples. Prominent leaders of the Progressive Movement protested that America ought to clean up its political corruption and inequalities at home instead of exhausting its energies abroad. Both traditionalists and the Progressives also asked Americans to remember their historic commitment to self-determination in the Declaration of Independence.

Isolationism and internationalism, 1914–45

For nearly three years the US maintained the fiction that the First World War was a European conflict that did not concern America. That was the neutral pose that President Woodrow Wilson held because it reflected the traditional isolationist views of the US electorate. But neutrality was impossible to preserve for three reasons. Wilson, along with many other US politicians, felt strong sympathies for the Allies. The majority of Americans shared his belief in loyalty to Anglo-American traditions, despite vocal German American and Irish American minorities opposed to an alliance with Britain. Finally, the US economy depended on trade with the warring nations, who each tried to prevent goods from reaching its enemy.

Most Americans had taken sides but were still reluctant to commit their fortunes and lives to intervention. Both Wilson and the public needed to believe they were entering the war for high moral reasons rather than the country's economic interests. Some two months before the US declared war, Wilson provided that rationale through a new vision of collective security in his famous Fourteen Points, which appealed to the tradition of the American mission to create a new world order.

The essential elements of the Fourteen Points can be reduced to three major categories. The first was all nations' right to self-determination. National boundaries were to be redrawn after the war so that every "people" could freely determine whether it wished to be an independent country. The principle of self-determination amounted to a plan for popular referenda on ethnic nationhood in Europe with no formula for determining how this would be implemented. The second category was a general set of principles for governing international conduct after the war. These were meant to prevent a return to the traditional European balance-of-power strategies that Wilson believed had caused the war. Among the main principles included were free trade, freedom of the seas, global disarmament and the outlawing of secret alliances. Making efforts for these ideals, but especially for the remaining points, would implement Wilson's proposal for *collective security*, a League of Nations that would put self-determination and the other principles into effect and defend them. The key provision here was the public commitment of each League member to defend the principles and each other by diplomatic and military means, when necessary. Except for the League, most of the points were cornerstones of the US's traditional rhetoric if not of its practical policy.

The Fourteen Points constituted Wilson's public justification for participating in the war, and were but one set of conditions meant to limit US involvement. American troops remained separate from the Allied armies and fought under American commanders. Wilson called the US an "associate" rather than an ally to emphasize that it was in an emergency coalition, not a lasting alliance (and therefore remained true to the injunction against such alliances in Washington's Farewell Address).

When it finally came, American participation in the war was decisive but very limited. Significant numbers of American troops fought in Europe only during the last eight months of the war. About 110,000 US soldiers died in that time, compared to the 900,000 British, 1.4 million French and almost 2 million German troops that died in four years.

The conditions on American aid to the Allied war effort, combined with the Allies' very different experience with a long and destructive conflict, made the US position seem morally arrogant. Although America claimed to be materially disinterested, its call for freedom of the seas and free trade would benefit the US most since its industrial plant was booming and its fleet the least damaged. The Allies wanted revenge and to make Germany pay for war damages. They rejected all the Fourteen Points but the League.

The US Senate failed to ratify the treaty Wilson brought home from the Paris peace conference. Many senators rejected the idea of the League because they were unwilling to bind the US to membership in a permanent international alliance that could limit US sovereignty. The foreign-policymakers who took over after Wilson were not isolationists. Rather, they wanted to design safeguards for peace that would not limit America's traditional freedom to act unilaterally in world affairs. In 1921, the US negotiated separate treaties with the defeated central powers. The League was formed but, without US participation, it never became an effective international force.

During the rest of the 1920s US foreign policy centered on eliminating obstacles to American trade. International peace and stability were essential largely so that, once established, US trade would remain free of interference. Many Americans also believed free trade fostered peace by making nations more open and familiar with each other. However, the US and European nations failed to agree on a plan to revive European economies by cancelling or easing their war debts to America, and in 1930 Congress passed the protectionist Smoot–Hawley Tariff, which effectively closed the US market to most European goods.

In the same years, the country advocated peace through disarmament and called for arms reduction and the destruction of some 2 million tons of navy ships. It reaffirmed and extended the Open Door Policy. Finally, it initiated the Kellogg–Briand Pact in 1928 under which 62 nations signed a pledge not to use war as an instrument of national policy. Critics called this pact, and others the US entered at the time, a "paper peace" since it depended on voluntary compliance alone.

In the 1930s, however, this limited internationalism was replaced by isolationism. As the German war machine marched into land after land and the rest of Europe rearmed, American voters made it clear that their last wish was to be dragged into another Old World war. More than four-fifths of the people surveyed in a Gallup poll in March of 1941 were opposed to US intervention. At about that time, President Franklin D. Roosevelt had won congressional approval for the Lend-Lease Act, a disguised giveaway plan he invented because domestic opposition to open aid to the Allies was massive. Under Lend-Lease, the president could sell, but also let the Allies borrow or lease, war material, on the promise that it would be returned after the war.

The Japanese surprise attack on Pearl Harbor on December 7, 1941 accomplished overnight what Roosevelt could not in years of effort: it united the American people in a fervent commitment to war. In a few days Congress had declared war on all the Axis powers and announced its support of the Allies. Almost as quickly, Roosevelt constructed a vision of a new world order for the post-war period. Determined to succeed where Wilson had failed, Roosevelt called the Allies the "United Nations" almost from the start. He also ensured that American troops were integrated with those of Britain and France. Joint command and cooperation, he decided, would prevent complaints about American arrogance.

Roosevelt expressed his vision for world order after the war in his so-called Four Freedoms and proposal for the United Nations (UN). Cleansed of advantages to US business the Four Freedoms were essentially the rights contained in the American Bill of Rights (freedom of religion, speech and expression) or broad extensions of those, such as freedom from want and fear, that amount to a version of the American dream. The UN was to help make the Four Freedoms realities.

PLATE 8.2 A physically weakened US President Franklin D. Roosevelt sits between British Prime Minister Winston Churchill (L) and Soviet leader Josef Stalin (R) at the Yalta Conference in February 1945.

(Rex Features)

A number of the UN's features were intended to make it a more effective organization than the League had been. Unlike its predecessor, the UN can take preventative action, ask members to contribute troops to an international "peace-keeping" force, and act against aggressors (whether or not they are members) without approval from all its members. The UN charter's weaknesses, for example, in dealing with civil wars (within nations), human rights globally, and genocide would become progressively clear over time.

At the Yalta Conference in February 1945, Roosevelt won Stalin's and Churchill's support for the UN. On other important issues, the results of the conference were much less clear. Roosevelt could not convince the other leaders to give up the concept of spheres of influence in Europe. He thought, however, that they had agreed to the establishment of democratic governments under no other nation's direct control in eastern Europe. All three leaders agreed that post-war Germany should not become a military power again quickly, but they could not resolve their differences on how to prevent that from happening. They therefore had to put off specific plans for dealing with post-war Germany.

The Cold War era, 1946–92

As Soviet forces set up pro-communist governments in eastern Europe in the weeks after the Yalta Conference, Roosevelt discovered how differently he and Stalin interpreted its results. Before he could establish a policy to deal with the new situation, Roosevelt died of a sudden heart attack. In August 1945, President Truman ordered the dropping of atomic bombs on Hiroshima and Nagasaki. He justified the mass slaughter of civilians by saying the attack would save many more lives (both American and Japanese) because it would bring the war to a rapid close without an invasion of the Japanese home islands. The chain of events dividing the globe into the opposing blocks of the Cold War was under way. A year later, Churchill said an "iron curtain" existed between Soviet-controlled eastern Europe and western Europe with its American ally.

As the former allies struggled to influence the governments emerging on the borders of the Soviet Union after the war, American policymakers became convinced that the Soviets were intent on establishing communist regimes around the world. In 1947 President Truman announced what became known as the Truman Doctrine in a speech to Congress during which he asked for funds to fight communist aggression in Turkey and Greece. According to the Doctrine, the US had to follow a policy of *containment* to prevent communist expansion anywhere in the world. The Soviet ideology, inherently a threat to the US and to democratic institutions, was being spread through internal subversion as well as outside pressure. In a "domino effect," as it was called, one nation after another would fall to Soviet domination unless the US led the "free world" by actively intervening to prevent it. Thus the stage was set for direct American involvement in internal conflicts and wars, not only in Latin America (where the Roosevelt Corollary justified intervention) but also around the world. Containment became the cornerstone of American foreign policy throughout the Cold War. Pursuing containment protected and expanded US interests abroad and its implementation contributed to the formulation of other foreign policy initiatives.

In the late 1940s the US took steps to meet the communist threat and in the process revolutionized its foreign policy. It kept its military forces near wartime levels, extending mandatory military service into peacetime and continuing its military build-up. When the Soviets rejected international inspection plans to enforce a ban on nuclear weapons, the US reacted by expanding atomic research and giving nuclear weapons a central place in its arsenal. The National Security Act of 1947 reorganized the federal government to meet Cold War threats by centralizing control over all branches of the military in a new Department of Defense (the "Pentagon") and creating the National Security Council (NSC) and the Central Intelligence Agency (CIA).

In a sense, the Act put the country in a state of permanent military readiness by transferring enlarged powers over defense to the president and by making it

PLATE 8.3 A dramatic atomic mushroom cloud, this one from a US military detonation in the country's isolated southwestern desert testing grounds after World War II, became an image seared into the minds of people all over the world after the nuclear attacks on Nagasaki and Hiroshima, Japan.
(Stocktrek/Corbis)

easier for him to take aggressive action internationally without a declaration of war. By 1950 a NSC report known as NSC-68 defined the US stance: more than ever, America had an important mission in the world; on the US lay the responsibility to lead the free world. To that end, the nation had to quadruple its military budget so that it could take the initiative in containing communism.

Meanwhile, Secretary of State Marshall became convinced that the US ought to fund the economic revival of Europe. The motives for the so-called Marshall Plan were mixed. In general the hope was to learn from the mistakes of US policy after the First World War. Humanitarian concerns and ethnic ties played important roles in building congressional and public support of the plan. Economic concerns also inspired approval. Assisting Europe could absorb surpluses that threatened to cause an economic recession in the US, and a revitalized Europe would provide markets for American goods. Finally, it was believed that prosperous economies would strengthen European resistance to communism and thus contribute to the goal of containment. Approximately $15 billion were spent on this program while it was in effect from 1948 to 1951.

The vision of one world united through the Four Freedoms faded and was replaced by the sense that the world consisted of two warring camps threatening each other with nuclear destruction. Therefore, the United States reversed its historic refusal to form permanent military alliances. The first of these, the Organization of American States (OAS), was founded in 1948, and was followed by the North Atlantic Treaty Organization (NATO) in 1949 and similar mutual defense pacts that eventually covered the globe. Commitment to internationalism had irreversibly replaced the country's traditional isolationism.

When Soviet troops entered Hungary in 1956 and crushed the revolt against Soviet domination, Hungarian Americans protested strongly. President Eisenhower announced that the United States would not intervene in their homeland because the Truman Doctrine did not extend to nations within the Warsaw Pact (the eastern European–Soviet alliance organized as a counterforce to NATO). In 1968 when the Soviet Union and Warsaw Pact nations put down a popular revolt in Czechoslovakia, the US followed the same policy of non-involvement.

In the early 1950s, the fear of communism set the stage for Senator Joseph McCarthy's hunt for Americans that were involved in "un-American activities" as spies or tools of the Soviets. In a general sense "McCarthyism" was nothing new, although his blatant accusations against government officials as well as Hollywood stars through charges of guilt by association with suspected members of leftist organizations were unprecedented. Fear of communist influence and Bolshevik immigrants appeared in the "Red Scare" of the 1920s and was part of the old distrust of the foreign that stretched, in some form, all the way back to the Alien and Sedition Acts. McCarthy and his supporters did not create the wave of anti-communist hysteria. They merely exploited the public anxieties built up by the Cold War and the threat of nuclear destruction.

These anxieties led to historic changes in the position of the military in American society. Before the arms race during the Cold War the US had always greatly reduced the size of its military arsenal and standing forces after a major war. From the early 1950s onward that no longer happened. Instead, the economic, governmental, and military organizations involved with weapons (raw material producers, manufacturers of weapon systems, executive agencies, congressional committees and branches of the military) have expanded and developed into a mutually supportive network. As early as January 1961, Dwight D. Eisenhower warned of the dangers this could pose for a democracy in his farewell address saying, "In the councils of government, we must guard against the acquisition of unwarranted influence, whether sought or unsought, by the military–industrial complex." Today, economic prosperity in widely scattered parts of the country depends on the complex. Lobbyists, bureaucrats, generals and members of Congress have stakes in its further development. With the Cold War replaced by the War on Terror, in the early 2000s critics have continued to analyze what some call the militarization of America and decry its consequences.

The CIA's covert involvement in the Bay of Pigs affair and the Cuban Missile Crisis raised Cold War tensions to new heights. Ironically, the superpowers' nuclear arsenals made mutual assured destruction (MAD) the basis for deterrence and the best chance of avoiding war. However, after the missile crisis, relations between the two superpowers began to improve. Developments furthering this trend included the Nuclear Test Ban Treaty of 1963 and the decision that neither superpower would intervene in the Israeli–Arab war. In the 1970s, President Nixon initiated the policy known as détente (peaceful coexistence) and the gradual reduction of nuclear arsenals that later presidents continued. Despite unstable periods in the superpowers' relationship in the decades to come, a similar understanding was reached during the Gulf War almost 30 years later in 1991, when both countries condemned the Iraqi occupation of Kuwait in the United Nations and joined in contributing forces to drive President Saddam Hussein's troops back into Iraq.

In Asia, the United States committed itself to containing communism in Korea, Vietnam, Cambodia and Laos. The Vietnam War, the first the US had lost since the War of 1812, produced massive anti-war protests at home and widespread anti-American demonstrations abroad. The conduct of the war demoralized the younger generation at home as well as US combat troops. The cost of the war drained funds from President Johnson's programs to deal with domestic poverty and inequality. The frustrations of trying to win a "limited war" led President Nixon to authorize the secret bombing of Laos and Cambodia without congressional approval.

The Vietnam War became a traumatic experience to the American people, and has therefore colored later involvement in other countries. During the Gulf and Afghanistan wars, the US chose to act in a multinational coalition after securing approval from the UN, even though Americans constituted the largest group of participants. Low-intensity warfare and short engagements executed with precision through technological weaponry, it was hoped, could replace the prolonged military engagement and high casualty levels of the Korean and Vietnam wars. The loss of American lives has declined in recent US wars, but what is life-saving technology for the superpower has led to escalating death rates for civilians in areas of military conflict and has not led to brief conflicts in civil and guerilla wars.

An important turning point in US foreign relations came when President Nixon opened talks with the leaders of mainland China, taking advantage of a split between China and the Soviet Union, and thus reduced the apparent threat of communism. In the following years American policy was less concerned with military control and, especially during the Carter presidency, more emphasis was put on supporting human rights in other countries. This angered the Soviets, as stories of dissidents confined in psychiatric "hospitals" became well known through the work of Aleksandr Solzhenitsyn. In the later 1970s the relationship between the two powers grew tenser as a result.

The US–Soviet relationship went through several pendulum swings. American policy toward Latin America, for example, varied with the temperature of the Cold War. Still, the commitment to containment has generally led to US support for right-wing regimes in America's "backyard," where apparent stability has often seemed more vital than human rights. In that frame of mind, covert American operations helped unseat the democratically elected Salvador Allende during the Nixon administration, and in the 1980s the Reagan administration refused to stop giving the right-wing Contra rebels aid in their guerrilla war against the Sandinista government of Nicaragua when Congress cut off funding for the Contras. The Iran–Contras scandal revealed that Oliver North and others among Reagan's officials had secretly sold weapons to Iran and used the profits to aid the Contras, in direct contradiction of congressional policy and the administration's public statements. For some commentators, the lesson seemed to be that the Cold War produced an "imperial presidency" that undermined both the balance of power between the branches of government and the Constitution.

After proclaiming strong opposition to the communists' "evil empire" and carrying out a massive military build-up, President Reagan pursued peaceful coexistence. On the Asian scene, he extended the détente policy of previous presidents when he signed a series of agreements with the People's Republic of China in 1984. He accepted friendly overtures from the general secretary of the Communist Party in the USSR, Mikhail Gorbachev, which led to disarmament treaties in his second term and agreements on increasing trade and cultural relations under President George H.W. Bush.

In November 1989 the symbol of a divided Europe, the Berlin Wall, was torn down by cheering crowds from both sides, and the following summer East and West Germany were reunited by a treaty signed by the four allies from the Second World War. In 1992, due to internal ethnic conflicts and economic strains, the

Soviet Union split into a loose federation of republics, and in the following years both some of its subordinate parts and nations in the Warsaw Pact declared their independence.

The sole superpower in the post-Cold War era

In the twenty-four years since 1989, some main contours of the post-Cold War world and America's place in it became apparent. The elimination of the Iron Curtain and lowered nuclear tension caused jubilation and optimistic attempts to fashion a better future across Europe, central Asia, and the US. European leaders moved quickly to include ten of the recently independent eastern European countries in the European Union (EU) by 2004 and two more by 2007. These countries thus grew less dependent on America for trade and military needs.

Many former Eastern Bloc nations exhibited strong support for US foreign policy views, partly perhaps in gratitude for America's long record of opposing their Soviet oppressors. Several of these nations indicated a wish to become members of NATO and some (most notably Poland) did, which reaffirmed their ties to the US even as that organization struggled to redefine its purpose and took on military duties outside the territory covered by the alliance. On the one hand, NATO took responsibility for winning the campaign against Osama bin Laden's terrorists and the Taliban in Afghanistan and, on the other, Georgia's wish to join the organization led to loud saber-rattling from Russia.

In the first decade of the twenty-first century US relations with Europe were sometimes tense. When the continent's nations divided sharply over the approach to war with Iraq, most former Eastern Bloc countries were prominent in their agreement with the US position and later sent considerable numbers of troops and equipment as part of George W. Bush's "coalition of the willing." US Secretary of Defense Donald Rumsfeld famously contrasted this "new" Europe with the "old" one that asked that UN inspectors be allowed more time to search for weapons of mass destruction (WMD) in Iraq and questioned the need to depose Saddam Hussein. Between 2002–3 and 2008 friction between the US and many of its traditional allies in Europe and elsewhere grew. Explanations for this frequently focused on the policies of the Bush administration: its tendency to act unilaterally or covertly, its insistence on preventive war in Iraq, and its imprisonment and brutal interrogation of "enemy combatants" there, at the Guantanamo base and elsewhere (in violation of the Geneva Conventions) in the War on Terror.

Military conflicts and political unrest continued within the Russian federation and in newly independent neighboring nations. The US wanted to aid these nations with their reconstruction, just as the Marshall Plan had helped war-torn western Europe but, under Presidents Bill Clinton and George H.W. Bush, debated on how to do so without interfering too much in their internal affairs or provoking Russia. The initial attempt to do this came through the loose co-operation of the Partnership for Peace, but the US largely left the handling of these problems to Russia. A more constructive result of the end of superpower rivalry appeared in US–Russian agreement during the Gulf War of 1991 that drove Saddam Hussein's invaders out of Kuwait.

By the end of the first Iraq war the world generally viewed the US as the sole superpower, and during much of the 1990s the USSR's economy, military and empire continued to implode. From then on, however, through wrenching economic adjustments, conflicts, and agreements internally and with neighboring states, a new Russian federation emerged that asserted itself on the world stage and flexed economic power through its gas and petroleum resources. Although President George W. Bush and Prime Minister (former president) Vladimir Putin functioned amiably together through personal diplomacy at the start of the 2000s, the US–Russian relationship remains uneasy. Russia dislikes the eastern expansion of NATO and is convinced that the plans to place advanced radar-satellite installations for a missile shield in the Czech Republic and Poland, announced as a protection for the US, Russia, and European allies alike against "rogue" states in the Middle East or central Asia, is actually further evidence of American expansionism. In 2012 it was not clear that Obama's efforts had succeeded in laying a stronger foundation of trust between the two nations, although superficially at least relations seemed more amiable.

In his first term, centrist Democrat President Bill Clinton made strengthening the domestic economy by increasing free trade his primary foreign policy goal. By 1995 both the North American Free Trade Agreement (NAFTA), between Canada, Mexico and the US, and the Uruguay General Agreement on Tariffs and Trade (GATT) had been ratified by the Senate. During the second Bush presidency trade negotiations proved more difficult as the interests of unions at home, developing nations abroad and the concerns of the world's environmentalists about pollution and global warming complicated the process. The Obama administration has supported free trade and increased exports energetically.

George H.W. Bush and Clinton also attempted to define America's role in dealing with a major after-effect of the Cold War: the increasing disorder in Asia, Africa and Central America that involved former "client states" of the super-powers. As the sole remaining superpower, the US faced mounting pressure at home and abroad to act in these crises, but American policymakers in the 1990s were at first reluctant to be on call as the world's police officer. In the hope that neighboring countries would step in (the Europeans in the former Yugoslavia and other African nations in that continent's many "trouble spots"), the US delayed too long in acting during Clinton's time in office, according to some critics. Then America initiated a series of multilateral strategic interventions in humanitarian crises (in Bosnia, Somalia and Haiti) and diplomatic efforts to bring peace in longstanding conflicts (in Northern Ireland, North Korea and Palestine).

The results of what some critics called the "new interventionism" were mixed. American participation seemed effective in ending "ethnic cleansing" in the Balkan conflict, for example, but the mission to feed starving civilians in Somalia changed into ill-executed efforts at "nation-building" that ended in the death and post-mortem humiliation of US soldiers followed by American withdrawal. Commentators debated over how often and how forcibly the superpower should act, those abroad generally wanting international leadership from America but expecting it to come in concert (most often through the UN) and in agreement with their policy aims. A prominent group of critics at home, supported by the Clinton administration, took this same view, but there was heated disagreement (most prominently from the so-called neo-conservatives) about how much the US should allow its foreign policy to be influenced by the agendas of other nations and international organizations. A consensus appeared only about regret at America's not having intervened to end the genocide in Rwanda. While in Africa ex-President Clinton called that his administration's worst error, and in 2003 George W. Bush was prompt in asking for international action to stop the slaughter in Sudan's civil war. Later he traveled to Africa and allocated large resources to fighting the AIDS epidemic there.

After taking office in 2001, George W. Bush formed a team of foreign policy officials and advisers that included both moderates, such as Secretary of State Colin Powell, reported "pragmatists," such as National Security Adviser Condoleezza Rice, and leaders often associated with neo-conservative views, such as Vice-President Dick Cheney, Secretary of Defense Donald Rumsfeld and his chief assistant, Paul Wolfowitz. On the one hand, neo-conservative-policy commentators urged a new foreign policy realism. That approach dictated that the US should review its international commitments, acting energetically to achieve key objectives and withdraw, while rejecting or scaling down involvements that did not serve the country's interests. Early in his first term, Bush's administration was involved with such a review, and its findings resulted in withdrawal from the Anti-Ballistic Missile Treaty and the Kyoto Protocol on global warming, rejection of the International Criminal Court, and disengagement from diplomatic efforts in Korea and the Middle East. In agreement with neo-conservative advisers, Bush also embarked on a major modernization and expansion of the country's military capabilities.

Until the terrorist attacks of 9/11, the Bush regime repudiated the Clinton administration's policies and criticized its willingness to engage US troops abroad. But from that day, other parts of the neo-conservative agenda marked the administration's handling of US foreign policy. The president announced a global war on terrorism, and within weeks the US military was engaged in pursuing Osama bin Laden, eliminating the al-Qaeda terrorist-training camps in Afghanistan, and replacing the Taliban regime that had sheltered them. The US took note of its unchallenged status as the sole superpower and acted accordingly. It adopted a strongly interventionist stance to change the world according to

American ideals and interests, rather than merely to manage the world's crises as a kind of global police officer. It used military force to bring regime change where it judged such action necessary.

In an age of global terrorism, President Bush announced, the US could no longer wait for threats to materialize. Instead it had to use its intelligence-gathering capacities to discover threats and then strike enemies first, abroad, before they could attack the American homeland. The US would take "pre-emptive action," attacking an enemy as it prepared to strike, and "preventative action," attacking even without evidence of an imminent enemy strike.

As early as the 1980s, neo-conservatives had identified "rogue states" as the dispensers of terrorism and, therefore, as the prime candidates for US-led change. Bush identified some of these nations as an "axis of evil" stretching from North Korea through Iran to Iraq. His administration convinced Congress of the imminent threat of Iraq's plans to use WMD (weapons of mass destruction) and of its connections with al-Qaeda. Despite entrenched opposition, both at home and in the UN Security Council, the US and its allies invaded and occupied that nation in early 2003. Although the president declared victory in major military operations in less than three months, the war wore on and American casualties rose as the "coalition of the willing" attempted to restore public order and put in place a stable democratic government.

Practicing the neo-conservative principle that the US should institute American-style democracy and market capitalism in the Middle East proved much more difficult than toppling Saddam Hussein's dictatorship. The president's "mission accomplished" media event on an aircraft carrier in May 2003 looked increasingly hollow as the war continued. By 2007 the internal debate in American military circles about the lack of progress in the war leaned toward replacing the doctrine formulated by General Powell (that the US should use high technology and overwhelming force to make wars short and American casualties low) with the Petraeus Doctrine. The new view emphasized that after 2000 armed conflicts would be protracted and continuous, and the US military's role more complex, involving less frequent use of force and more negotiation and empowerment of local allies in "stability operations." Critics doubted that any orthodoxy of approach could suit the variety of international conflicts and noted that the new willingness of Sunni insurgents to cooperate with American occupiers might matter more than the US military's new approach. The only point no one doubted was these Sunnis' willingness to accept US dollars as they "joined" the counter-insurgency in Iraq.

Meeting the challenge of continued global terrorism, much of it arising from radical Islamic groups, the war on terrorism could be credited with the destruction of many terrorist groups abroad and with preventing additional attacks on home soil. Its successes became controversial, however, due to the high financial burdens and serious limitations on individuals' civil liberties that resulted from the implementation of the administration's chief anti-terrorism law, the USA Patriot

Act. At election time in late 2004, a majority of the American public, while critical of some aspects of the war in Iraq and of efforts to counter terrorism, felt the Bush leadership deserved a second term to follow through on its foreign policy goals. Shortly afterwards, the president announced plans to retain the more conservative members of his foreign policy team and to promote Condoleezza Rice to Secretary of State, after Colin Powell resigned his post. By the next election, however, regardless of the Petraeus Doctrine, the president's and the war's popularity had sunk so low that Republicans did not want the chief executive at their campaign events. The winning candidate was the senator with the most consistent record of opposing the war in Iraq.

On assuming office, President Obama demonstrated his desire to make a fresh start that he hoped would open new opportunities for multilateral talks whose only predetermined position was America's willingness to work out agreements on the basis of shared interests. This was the basis for his speech to the Islamic nations of the world at Cairo University, the reopening of talks with North Korea, and trips to Europe. The contrast of his stance and global polls showing rapidly improving attitudes to US foreign policy were a factor in encouraging Norway's Nobel Peace Prize committee to award the new president the prize, they said, to urge him to fulfill his promise. But although his administration's rhetoric and actions brought less open hostility, the roots of the problems involving relations with countries such as North Korea, Iran, the nations experiencing uprisings to overthrow dictatorships during the "Arab Spring," and non-state actors such as the Islamic terrorist cells in desert northwest Africa remained intractable. The complex dynamics of motives and historical memories of American policies going back through the decades of the Cold War and beyond were not to be solved by verbal demonstrations of good will—or even the avoidance of hostile action—in a president's first term. For some opponents, the Obama administration's use of robot drone planes and the successful military action to kill Osama bin Laden in Pakistan only proved that the US was still willing to violate another country's sovereign territory to achieve its goals.

The foreign policy establishment debate

The governmental structures of the US are yet another factor that make American foreign affairs distinctive. The Constitution's system of checks and balances requires the executive and legislative branches to share responsibility for the nation's relations with other countries. The nature of these branches, moreover, has resulted in opportunities for other institutions and groups to develop ways of influencing foreign policy decision-making. As a result, the official and unofficial groups that play a part in the foreign policy establishment are many and varied. There are several competing centers of power whose importance changes over time and according to the situation.

PLATE 8.4 In April 2003 images of the arrival of US marines in downtown Baghdad near the monument to Saddam Hussein's leadership focused the world's attention on America's "coalition of the willing" that joined the George W. Bush administration's war to bring regime change in Iraq. Soon the most sent image from the same Baghdad square showed Hussein's statue being pulled down by people in the streets.
(Sipa Press/Rex Features)

During the nation's history, the balance of power between the two branches over foreign policy has shifted. Congress was the dominant partner for most of the nineteenth century, except for the Civil War years. The consensus of opinion is that the shift toward executive power during the 1900s resulted from the near constant international crises involving the US. The president grew increasingly dominant until failures of executive policy involved with the Vietnam War provoked both congressional attempts to correct the balance between the branches and greater presidential caution in making foreign commitments. As a result of the success of the Reagan presidency's initiatives and the 9/11 crisis, however, a high degree of executive dominance in foreign policy has returned.

The president has several powers that make him the single most important figure in US foreign policy today. Each of these, however, is shared with other groups. He is the commander-in-chief but, with few exceptions, the president has been a civilian with very limited military experience. He therefore depends on the advice of the leaders of the armed forces and other experts in international relations to meet his responsibility for national security. Even if the president is convinced that the vital interests or territory of the US is seriously threatened, he cannot declare war. Only Congress can do that and, since the Second World War, it has been especially reluctant to do so. Consequently, presidents have increasingly successfully committed the nation to military action in other ways when they have perceived crises involving national security. The common pattern of events in recent decades is that the president commits US military personnel or otherwise responds to an attack on American interests or citizens, and soon after informs Congress, asking for a joint resolution of support from both of its houses if the "military conflict" is likely to be of longer duration.

As the chief executive, one of the president's primary duties is to carry out foreign policy, but the Constitution requires the approval of both houses of Congress for the governmental expenditures that all foreign policy initiatives depend on. Not only must the president win majorities for his policies, therefore, but he can also expect military leaders and bureaucrats to lobby Congress in favor of competing programs. Further, congressional involvement does not stop there. The legislature often exercises its investigatory power to evaluate whether money is being spent as Acts of Congress stipulated and stops funding or repeals those Acts if it is dissatisfied.

The more specific foreign policy powers of the president are also limited, but chief executives have been released from the most important checks on these powers. No other official can nominate people to ambassadorial and other high-level positions in the American foreign service, but all such appointments must be approved by a majority in the Senate. Congress itself removed this limit in 1939, with the creation of the Executive Office of the President (EOP), which allows presidents to rely on White House advisers, who do not need Senate approval. The EOP's National Security Council eclipsed the Departments of State and Defense as the center of policymaking in foreign relations by the mid-1960s, and diminished congressional influence in foreign policy. The president alone can negotiate treaties with other governments, but all treaties must be ratified by an extraordinary majority (two-thirds) in the Senate. Approval from so many senators has often seemed doubtful, especially since the First World War, however, and so presidents have increasingly depended on more informal executive agreements, which do not require Senate approval.

Two important foreign policy roles of the president, acting as both chief diplomat and ceremonial head of state, have grown greatly in importance since the beginning of high-speed air travel, electronic communication and supersonic weaponry. The possibility for extensive personal diplomacy between world leaders and the media attention it commands have made the president the visible maker of foreign policy more than ever before. During the Cold War with the threat of nuclear destruction in minutes and, since 2001, the possibility of a catastrophic terrorist attack, the greater speed of executive action is a convincing argument for presidential control of foreign affairs.

The organization of the congressional and executive institutions in the foreign policy establishment creates opportunities for many interest groups to exercise influence. Each chamber of Congress has a permanent committee that specializes in foreign policy with subcommittees to deal with all the major regions of the world and important international issues. Both chambers have, in addition, several other committees (with their subcommittees) that are involved in foreign policy decisions, such as the armed services, energy, commerce and intelligence committees.

The State Department and Department of Defense are, like Congress, organized into groups of specialists that focus on particular issues of international affairs or areas of the world. These groups formulate policy suggestions that they send through bureaucratic channels to the secretary of state or the secretary of defense, who forward them to the EOP and Congress. Although the president usually decides on major policy concerns, department bureaucrats manage the daily implementation of policy. They can also hold investigative hearings. For these reasons, the full range of pressure groups and members of Congress try to catch the ear of influential officials in the State Department and Department of Defense.

There has long been debate about the foreign policy establishment. According to some critics, deliberation and lobbying in roughly parallel structures in Congress and the departments produce wasteful redundancy, lost information and unnecessary confusion over policy alternatives. These observers emphasize that the foreign policy establishment has yet another component, the personal advisers and agencies in the EOP. The president's national security adviser, the National Security Agency (NSA), the joint chiefs of staff of the military and the Central Intelligence Agency (CIA) and other intelligence agencies often evolve a third set of priorities and policies. Is it any wonder that over the half century of the Cold War some 45 separate national security and intelligence-gathering units grew up? This situation was partly to blame for the intelligence failures leading to the 9/11 terrorist attacks. One of the chief governmental changes in the wake of the tragedies consolidated many of those programs into a single new structure, the Department of Homeland Security (DHS), in 2002.

Exercises

Explain and examine the significance of the following names and terms:

isolationism	exceptionalism	Washington's Farewell Address
soft power	hard power	Alien and Sedition Acts
Monroe Doctrine	expansionism	Roosevelt Corollary
manifest destiny	imperialism	"smart power"

anti-imperialists	Fourteen Points	limited internationalism
Four Freedoms	Yalta Conference	Truman Doctrine
Marshall Plan	McCarthyism	National Security Act
Vietnam War	détente	Gulf War
9/11	Iran–Contras scandal	post-Cold War era
hegemony	USA Patriot Act	Department of Homeland Security
Iraq War	Petraeus Doctrine	Islamic terrorist cells

Write short essays on the following questions:

1. Critically evaluate the degree to which US foreign policy is (or has been) distinct from that of other nations.

2. Summarize what you think are the important historical trends and turning points in the evolution of America's relations with the rest of the world.

3. Critically evaluate the significant changes in US foreign policy from 1945 to 1989. Evaluate the most important changes from 1989 to the present.

4. Describe the institutional structures in America's foreign policy establishment and critically discuss how well they serve as a basis for the formulation of the nation's foreign policy.

Further reading

Dobson, A.P. and Marsh, S. (2006) *American Foreign Policy Since 1945*, 2nd edn, London: Routledge.

Haass, R.N. (2009) *War of Necessity, War of Choice: A Memoir of Two Iraq Wars*, New York: Simon & Schuster.

Johnson, L.K. (2007) *Seven Sins of American Foreign Policy*, London: Longman.

Kennedy, P.M. (1987) *The Rise and Fall of the Great Powers: Economic Change and Military Conflict from 1500 to 2000*, New York: Random House.

Lipset, S.M. (1996) *American Exceptionalism: A Double-Edged Sword*, New York: W.W. Norton.

Magstadt, T.M. (2004) *An Empire if You Can Keep It: Power and Principle in American Foreign Policy*, Washington, DC: Congressional Quarterly Press.

Merrill, D. and Paterson, T.G. (2009) *Major Problems in American Foreign Relations, Vol. II: Since 1914*, Boston, MA: Houghton Mifflin.

Nye, J.S., Jr. (2004) *Soft Power: The Means to Success in World Politics*, New York: Public Affairs.

Paterson, T.G. (1995) *Major Problems in American Foreign Relations, Vol. I*, 4th edn, Boston, MA: Houghton Mifflin.

Websites

www.whitehouse.gov/issues/foreign-policy
www.foreignaffairs.com
www.cfr.org/publication
http://thomas.loc.gov
www.carnegieendowment.org
www.latimes.com
www.washingtonpost.com
www.cnn.com
www.nytimes.com
www.theatlantic.com/doc/200810/petraeus-doctrine/2
http://news.bbc.co.uk/2/hi/americas/6249565.stm

Chapter 9

The legal system

- Legal history
- The sources of US law
- The court system
- Federal and state court proceedings
- The legal profession
- Crime and punishment
- Attitudes to the legal system
- *Exercises*
- *Further reading*
- *Websites*

This chapter examines the historical development of the US legal system; describes the court system, and federal and state court proceedings; considers the role of the legal profession; comments upon crime and punishment; and concludes with attitudes to the legal system.

The legal system consists for practical purposes of judges and lawyers who service the state and federal law apparatus of independent courts. These are concerned with two main types of law (civil law and criminal law). The individual cases that are dealt with by the courts and other institutions are accordingly classified as either civil or criminal.

Civil law involves non-criminal claims for compensation (often financial) by individuals (or groups) who have allegedly suffered loss or damage through the acts of others. Domestic actions (divorce, children and custody), automobile accidents and personal injury cases are the largest civil actions. Other examples are corporate matters and libel. Civil law has a service role and tries to secure social harmony by settling disputes between individuals or organizations. This is achieved preferably by settlement during the course of litigation and negotiations. If no settlement is agreed, the case goes to a full trial.

Criminal law involves the trial and punishment of persons who have committed crimes against society, such as theft, assault or murder. State, local and federal authorities prosecute groups or individuals in an attempt to establish guilt, which may result in a fine, imprisonment or (in some serious cases) execution. This is the control aspect of the legal system and the criminal law protects society by punishing those who have broken social codes embodied in the law. The trial and any punishment are also supposed to act as deterrents to potential offenders, although the effectiveness of deterrence is hotly debated.

The legal system plays a central role on public and private levels of American society, to a greater extent perhaps than in other countries. The law is regarded very much as part of daily life and not as a remote abstraction. Legal issues and court decisions are matters of widespread interest, concern and comment. They are also closely intertwined with the nation's political, social and economic life. Americans make active use of their legal system and are a litigious people. They are willing to take legal actions, are accustomed to seeking redress from the courts and had 728,200 lawyers in 2010 to assist them with their cases.

There are several reasons for this cultural behavior. First, active participation in the legal process derives from a colonial and frontier tradition of individualism in which Americans defended their own interests and rights. However, legal actions can also result from group causes or class actions. The War for Independence, for example, began with collective legal complaints by some (if not all) colonists against British rule and showed that law (if formulated correctly) could potentially protect individuals and communities against oppression by government and other authorities. However, there can also be a tension between individualistic and group values in US society.

Second, public and private life is influenced by a constitutionalism which stems from the Declaration of Independence (1776), the US Constitution (1787) and the Bill of Rights (1789). These documents try to create a framework for the good society and acceptable social behavior. They guarantee civil rights and freedoms for citizens and stipulate a separation of powers between an independent judiciary and the executive and legislative branches of government. Americans' expectations of social and political justice depend, ideally, on the safeguards in these documents, irrespective of whether they are actually achieved in all cases.

Third, such constitutional features are founded on a tradition of legalism (the belief that conflicts can be legally and fairly resolved at individual and national levels), which also stems from colonial times. Civil disputes between citizens, institutions and groups, as well as criminal cases have to be legally decided by the federal and state court systems.

Issues of justice and rights are therefore a basic concern for Americans. They expect action from the criminal law, and go to the courts for satisfaction if they feel that their civil rights have been infringed by federal or state governments, doctors, hospitals, airlines, neighbors, employers, the educational system, manufacturers or companies. But, although an American "legal rights culture" has grown, this does not mean that all such cases succeed.

A very large number of civil and criminal cases are handled annually by the courts. Most are determined at state and local (rather than federal) levels. Americans have a constitutional right to have their cases quickly determined in a public trial by an impartial judge or jury (a selected number of citizens who decide the facts in many court cases).

However, despite a concern with legal justice and claims that US society is humane and moral, justice, fair treatment and appropriate outcomes are not always achieved. The ideal may not be matched by the reality, raising questions about the quality of the legal system. The crucial question is one of access to civil and criminal courts, and some individuals may not succeed. Access often depends upon the nature of a case, wealth, social class and the level of court involved.

It is argued that the criminal and civil systems and some police forces must be reformed; that the disadvantaged and poor do not receive satisfaction despite legal aid (federal or state help to those who cannot afford legal fees); that the legal system is biased towards the powerful and the wealthy; that high legal costs are an obstacle to litigants seeking help; and that the legal system is not living up to its founding ideals.

The law can also be brought into disrepute by dubious or inadequate conduct and defense procedures by trial lawyers in criminal and civil cases; by prosecution incompetence; by plea bargaining, which allows an accused person to avoid the heaviest criminal and civil penalties; by contingency fees, which specify high percentage payments to lawyers for successful results; by juries which may be biased on racial, social or political grounds; by tampering with or fabrication of evidence; by suspect police procedures and conduct; by lawyers who are accused of driving up costs; and by allegedly partial judges. The question of victims' rights and compensation has become a contentious issue as has the behavior of trial lawyers, particularly those who act for the defense in "celebrity" cases.

Legal history

The legal system is founded on customs brought to the US by European colonists. Many elements were English, such as the common law (judge-made law), parliamentary/royal statutes and judges. These were later adapted to American features such as the US Constitution, the relationship between state and federal government, and judicial review (the power of superior courts to invalidate laws and actions that violate federal and state constitutions).

When the British colonized parts of North America in the seventeenth century, the English common law, statute law and judges were adopted by some colonies. But other British and European settlers had left their homelands to avoid oppressive institutions and to create a better society. They rejected the common law and created a code system of simple rules, which started in the Massachusetts Bay Colony in 1634.

However, as life stabilized in the colonies and as the population grew, such codes were insufficient to govern a more complex society. English legal structures became acceptable. Significantly, colonists in pre-independence America protested that the British Crown had denied them their traditional common-law rights and the Declaration of Independence (1776) contained legal grievances based upon these rights.

After the War for Independence, the 13 original states adopted the common law as the basis for their legal systems. But, since some states contained non-British settlers such as the Dutch, Germans and Swedes, the common law had to accommodate other legal customs. This process was repeated when the US incorporated territories such as California (1850). Each state interpreted and developed the common law in individual ways. But it was not adopted when the US purchased Louisiana (1803), which had its own French law.

The War for Independence involved discussions about the independent role of state governments. Federal government developed later and led to a division of authority between state and federal institutions. This process means that most laws today operate at the state and local level. The 50 states have their own legal systems, create their own laws in their own legislatures and have their own police forces and law courts. All (except Louisiana) apply their version of the common law, and most lawyers are qualified to practice in only one state.

Although anti-British feeling after independence led to criticism of the common law, lawyers and judges, this was reduced by new political factors. In 1787, delegates from the 13 states at the Constitutional Convention in Philadelphia framed a Constitution for the US, which became law in 1789. This stipulated that, while states remained sovereign in many areas, a new federal union of the states was also sovereign in its own sphere of competence.

Article III of the Constitution created a third branch of government, the independent federal judiciary: "The judicial power of the United States shall be vested in one Supreme Court and in such inferior courts as the Congress may from time to time ordain and establish." The founders of the US considered the judiciary to be the weakest branch of government, restricted to applying the Constitution and the laws. But it later developed a central importance, particularly the Supreme Court in Washington, DC.

The Judiciary Act (1789) created new federal courts with two roles. They interpret the meaning of laws and administrative acts (statutory construction) and examine laws and administrative action by national or state authorities in the light of the US Constitution (judicial review). This latter function was initially

PLATE 9.1 The sitting Associate Justices and one Chief Justice of the US Supreme Court, Washington, DC, 2010. Top row (left to right): Sonia Sotomayor, Stephen G. Breyer, Samuel. A. Alito and Elena Kagan. Bottom row (left to right): Clarence Thomas, Antonin Scalia, Chief Justice John G. Roberts, Anthony Kennedy and Ruth Bader Ginsburg.
(Rex Features)

contested by states' rights activists. But it was finally conceded and was an important factor in establishing a united nation.

These developments resulted in a legal organization for the whole country, and authority was divided between state and federal courts. The states had their own courts, common law, constitutions, statutes and jurisdiction over state law. But if a state court decision violated federal laws or involved a federal question, the US Supreme Court could ultimately review and overturn it. Some federal and state matters may thus proceed from local courts to the Supreme Court, and federal laws and the Constitution have (in theory) a uniform application throughout the country.

The independent judiciary was gradually strengthened. It is regarded as an essential safeguard against potential abuse by the executive and legislative branches and fits into the US system of separation of powers and checks and balances. By 2012, some 3,679 federal judges had been formally appointed by the president, subject to approval by the Senate. They serve until retirement and can only be removed for gross misconduct. All other judges at various levels are appointed by methods peculiar to individual states or are elected by voters.

A further factor increased the standing of the judiciary and courts. The Constitution contained few rights for individual citizens. Consequently, a Bill of Rights in the form of ten amendments was voted by Congress in 1789 and ratified by the states in 1791. But these rights only applied at the federal level until the 1920s. The Bill of Rights protects citizens against imprisonment without just cause, excessive fines or other oppression. However, the courts still have to interpret the Bill and amendments in individual court cases.

Two other developments have strengthened the place of law in US society. First, Congress (given limited power by the Constitution) later regulated American life through inter-state commerce Acts. The authority to "regulate commerce among the several States" (the commerce clause) and to create laws "necessary and proper" to carry out its powers enables Congress to pass social and economic legislation for the whole country. These laws may be examined by federal courts, although traditionally they have not interfered overmuch.

Second, law has become complex due to increases in federal and state legislation. This means that business people, consumers and other individuals are now more concerned with and directly affected by the law. They are very cautious about their legal transactions, contracts and court appearances and frequently need the assistance of professional lawyers.

Courts and judges in the US, but especially at the federal level, make policy to varying degrees as they interpret and apply the law. It is argued that the courts are therefore political and legislative institutions, and the judiciary is part of these processes. But judges do not make law or policy in the explicit way that politicians do. They function indirectly in the process of resolving disputes brought to their courts.

The sources of US law

The two most important sources of contemporary US law are the common (judge-made or case) law and statutory law.

Versions of the English common law were accepted in all American states (except Louisiana) and much state law is now common law. It is administered and interpreted by the courts and is found in court decisions of judges, who generally decide matters by adopting principles of law and decisions (precedents) from previous similar cases.

However, the authority of precedent declined in the late nineteenth and early twentieth centuries. American judges now decide cases in terms of existing law (with an element of precedent) and a sense of justice, so that the decision is fair and reasonable in the light of contemporary conditions (described as American Realism). Generally, they follow the precedents unless there are good reasons for ignoring them.

Statutory law consists of laws that have been passed by state or federal legislatures. This legislation is now very important. It expanded from the nineteenth century as state and federal government intruded increasingly into everyday affairs. The meaning and application of legislation is interpreted and determined by the courts. Many social, economic and family matters are provided for by state statutes and are handled by state courts. At federal level, statutory law is virtually the only type of law and includes the Constitution, treaties, Acts of Congress, presidential proclamations, executive orders and rules of federal departments.

The court system

The courts (see Figure 9.1) play a central and influential role in US society. They directly affect the daily lives of citizens and their decisions are widely debated. Social and personal struggles are reflected in civil and criminal court battles, and courts attract positive and negative criticism.

US courts operate at federal and state/local levels and have their own areas of authority or jurisdiction. State and local courts handle most of the legal work and are the most immediate for Americans. The federal courts account for some 2 percent of cases tried annually. But the existence of separate court systems can make litigation complicated.

Parties in a case may, in certain circumstances, appeal a court decision to a higher court. An appeal is an examination of procedures and legal principles on which the decision was based in the previous trial, and may include any new admissible evidence.

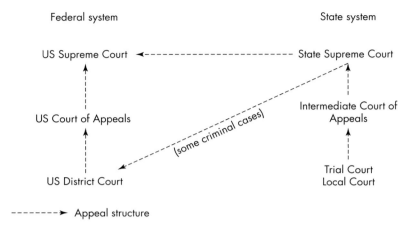

FIGURE 9.1 The main US courts.

The federal court system

Federal courts deal with cases that arise under the Constitution, federal law and disputes involving the federal government. They also hear matters concerning governments or citizens of different states and thus play a part in state law. If a case in the highest state court of appeal involves a federal question, it can be appealed to the US Supreme Court. The three levels of courts in the federal system are, in ascending order of appeal:

1. US district courts
2. US courts of appeal ("circuit courts")
3. The Supreme Court in Washington, DC

A case involving federal jurisdiction is heard first in a district court. An appeal may (rarely) be made to a US court of appeal and, in the last resort, to the US Supreme Court.

Most federal cases are settled in the district courts. There are 94 of these courts in the US (with states having at least one court) organized into 12 regional circuits. They are trial courts in which a judge (sometimes with a jury) decides cases on evidence presented.

District courts have jurisdiction to hear most categories of federal cases, including both civil and criminal matters. They try breaches of federal criminal law, such as bank robbery, drug-dealing, kidnapping, mail fraud, inter-state crime, currency fraud and assassination. Much of the work of the district courts, however, is in areas of civil law, such as taxation, civil rights, administrative regulations, disputes between states, bankruptcy and special cases dealing with international trade, customs and claims against the US. Their caseload has increased since the mid-1960s in civil matters, due to more federal legislation.

At the next federal level, there are 12 general appeals courts and each court belongs to a regional circuit of three to nine states (except for the one court that serves only the District of Columbia). These courts (with from three to five judges examining a case) mainly hear appeals from decisions of the district courts and federal administrative agencies within the relevant circuits. Most of their decisions are final and set a precedent for future similar cases. It is argued that these are the most important judicial-policymakers in the US. They are not, however, the ultimate authority because their decisions can be overturned by the US Supreme Court. There is also an additional US court of appeals for the Federal Circuit, which specializes in patents, federal employment law and international trade.

The US Supreme Court in Washington, DC is the apex of the federal court system. It comprises a chief justice and eight associate justices, assisted by law clerks. It has jurisdiction in national and federal matters. But its main role is that of an appeal court, and it hears cases from lower federal and state courts. These appeals usually involve constitutional issues, questions of federal law and conflicts between two or more of the states.

The court has authority to review any executive and legislative action or law passed by a level of government (if challenged in a court case) and can declare it unconstitutional after judging its compatibility with the Constitution. Although not given power of judicial review by the Constitution, the Supreme Court developed such jurisdiction from the Judiciary Act (1789). It enables the court to profoundly influence many aspects of American life.

Its decisions have given protection and rights to African Americans and other minorities, produced influential decisions on education and religion and affected the death penalty, gun law and abortion issues. However, it has ruled that a relatively small number of federal laws have been unconstitutional, compared to the greater invalidation of state and local laws. Supreme Court decisions can be overturned by the court itself, a constitutional amendment or by Congress introducing legislation to override a decision of the court.

The Supreme Court rules on about 100 cases each year out of some 7,000 submitted to it, and decides itself whether or not it will hear particular cases. It usually accepts cases that involve a constitutional principle, an important question of federal law or a conflict between state and federal law. It does not have the power to make laws. However, since its authority is independent of the other branches of government and it interprets the Constitution, its decisions often have a legislative, policymaking (and arguably political) force.

In general the court plays a conservative role, following legal tradition and precedent. But it has had periods of controversial "liberal activism" and been criticized for exceeding its job of interpreting statutory law and the Constitution; usurping the prerogatives of Congress; obstructing the popular will; and preventing the passing of economic and social legislation. It has chosen to rule on high-profile cases and declined to act in other matters that might have seemed appropriate for review. Nevertheless, its caseload has expanded due to new legislation in civil rights and federal regulations. This has increased its "political" profile.

The state and local court system

State and local courts constitute a large, complicated and individualistic system. They have a wider jurisdiction than federal courts and much heavier workloads. They determine the guilt or innocence of persons accused of violating state criminal laws and decide civil disputes. Most criminal and civil cases, such as assaults, theft (larceny), murder (homicide), and divorce and property disputes are settled within the state system.

The Constitution stipulates that the states have areas of authority (or sovereignty) outside the federal system. They have their own criminal and civil legal systems, laws, prisons, police forces, courts and associations of lawyers. Court systems and laws are similar in most states. But there are differences, such as the number of courts, court structures and names, procedure, the appointment or election of judges and some variation in laws and punishment for crimes. The states guard their independence and are self-contained legal units whose courts deliver judgments from which there is often no further appeal. But jurisdiction can be shared between federal and state bodies if an issue or appeal has federal implications.

PLATE 9.2 Columbia County Courthouse (1887), Dayton, Washington State, is the oldest working courthouse in Washington's 39 counties.
(Nik Wheeler/Corbis)

PLATE 9.3 Scene in a local court, presided over by a judge.
(Priscilla Coleman)

Local courts are the lowest state courts and have limited jurisdiction. They hear minor civil and criminal cases (misdemeanors) that often cannot be appealed and mostly do not need a jury to decide the issue. Their names vary according to locality and the nature of the case. They may be known as police courts, town or city courts or justice of the peace courts.

Trial courts are the next highest and handle criminal matters (except misdemeanors), which will usually be heard before a judge and jury, and some civil cases. They may consist of the following in different states:

- district, county or municipal courts, which decide civil and criminal cases,
- juvenile or family courts, which hear domestic, juvenile and delinquency cases,
- probate courts, which rule on wills and hear claims against estates, and
- criminal courts, which determine criminal cases.

About three-quarters of the states have intermediate appeal courts that hear appeals from lower courts. But the highest court is the state supreme court, which hears civil and criminal appeals from inferior state courts and can employ judicial review. Federal and constitutional matters may be appealed from this court to the US Supreme Court and some criminal cases can be appealed to the federal district courts.

Federal and state court proceedings

American legal proceedings in both criminal and civil cases are based on due process (basic legal rights, accepted procedures, formal trial and correct information) and the adversary system. The latter enables competing parties to present their views to an impartial third party, under procedural rules that allow the evidence to be given in a fair and orderly manner. A trial under the adversary process is designed to determine the facts under the appropriate law and to resolve cases by producing a judgment. It is the impartial third party (judge or jury) who decides the case based on the evidence presented to the court.

The legal language and emphasis on correct procedure in court are supposed to safeguard the rights of citizens and to ensure equal protection under the law. In practice, most civil disputes and some criminal cases are not resolved through court trials and many legal problems do not result in lawsuits. Lawyers may try to avoid civil and (some) criminal contests in court by arranging settlements during the course of negotiation and litigation or by other devices, such as plea bargaining (guilty plea to a lesser crime and punishment.)

Criminal proceedings

A range of rights and protections for citizens in criminal cases is provided by amendments to the Bill of Rights and by later judicial decisions (see Figure 9.2).

These stipulate that individuals shall not be deprived of life, liberty or property without due process of law and should be given a speedy and public trial, usually by jury, in the location of the alleged crime. Accused persons can question witnesses and compel most witnesses to appear on their behalf. They have the right to a lawyer for their defense (at public expense if necessary), the right to remain silent and a right against self-incrimination.

There is protection against excessive bail (payment to secure freedom prior to trial); the police cannot force a confession from a suspect by duress or threats and may not hold persons for more than two days without charging them with a criminal offence. Long imprisonment in isolation prior to trial is illegal and a confession obtained by the police in these circumstances is unacceptable to a court. It is argued, however, that such safeguards are not always observed by the criminal justice system and individuals' rights may be abused.

Trial by jury is a basic tradition in America and is guaranteed in indictable (serious) criminal cases. It may also be employed in other criminal trials. A defendant charged with a criminal offence may have been previously indicted by

Pre-trial procedure

1. Arrest of suspect by police (*Miranda* v. *Arizona*, 1966; rights must be read to suspect).
2. Custody (suspect may be held for up to 48 hours without formal charge).
3. Initial appearance of suspect before a judge. Judge determines whether there is sufficient evidence of a crime (probable cause) to charge the defendant, who is informed of the charge details and his/her legal rights. If no charge is preferred, the defendant is released. If defendant is charged, the judge will set bail (the amount of money or conditions to release defendant from custody until trial) and determine legal representation.
4. Arraignment. Defendant appears in court for the reading of the indictment/information/charge. Their rights are explained and they enter a plea. On a not-guilty plea, a trial date is set. On a guilty plea, a date is set for sentencing.
5. Plea bargaining. Both sides come to an agreement on the charges without a full trial (for example, plead guilty to a lesser offence).
6. Discovery. If a case is set for trial, prosecution and defense disclose their witnesses and prosecution must generally produce all evidence against the defendant to the defense.

Trial procedure in court

1. Trial held before a judge, who presides, and a jury, which decides the facts of the case.
2. Selection of (usually) 12 jurors to form the jury.
3. Opening statements firstly by the state (prosecution) followed by the defense.
4. Presentation of evidence and examination of witnesses by the prosecution. At close, the defense may seek a motion to dismiss the action. If unsuccessful, the defense presents its evidence. At close, rebuttal evidence may be called by the prosecution.
5. Objections to the nature of the questioning may be made by either side. Questioning may consist of examination, cross-examination and additional questioning.
6. After all the evidence has been presented, there are final motions in the absence of the jury for a directed verdict from the judge. If this fails, the jury returns to listen to closing arguments first by the defense and then by the prosecution.
7. These are followed by the judge's instructions to the jury, the jury deliberation and the jury decision (verdict). Motions after verdict may be submitted (for example, for a new trial). If unsuccessful, the judge then enters a judgment on this decision and sets a date for sentencing.

Source: adapted from ABA, *Law and the Courts: A Handbook of Courtroom Procedures.*

FIGURE 9.2 Outline of procedure in criminal cases.

a grand jury or sometimes by a process of information at state level. The trial jury consists of between six and 12 ordinary citizens (depending on the level of the court), who make a decision based on the facts before them in court. A unanimous decision is needed in federal criminal cases and in most criminal cases in all states (although majority verdicts may sometimes be allowed).

After trial, the Seventh Amendment guarantees that the accepted facts on which a trial was based cannot be re-examined in appeal to a higher court and the appeal must be based on other grounds, such as new evidence. The Eighth Amendment provides protection for the guilty from cruel and unusual punishment (see the death penalty debate below).

District attorneys conduct criminal prosecutions under these rules at the local (county or city) levels. At the federal level, prosecuting attorneys from the Department of Justice and the offices of the attorney general and solicitor general represent the government in initiating and trying criminal cases and suggest cases to the courts.

It is estimated that some 94 percent of criminal cases in the US are settled by a plea bargain, rather than by a jury trial. This system allows courts to cut the length and number of trials and enables defendants to reduce the severity of charges against them. But it also disadvantages those who cannot afford skilled lawyers to argue a case.

Civil proceedings

Civil cases in federal and state courts are divided into categories. The majority deal with matters such as accident and personal injury claims. The plaintiff serves documents on the defendant and, unless the case is settled out of court by negotiation, it goes to trial before a judge and, sometimes, a jury. In more expensive cases, a jury trial must be held. A majority (rather than a unanimous) jury decision is permitted in civil cases in some states. A current concern is the amount of punitive damages being awarded in some cases by the civil courts.

The legal profession

Hostility was shown towards judges after independence because of anti-British feeling, and in the nineteenth century attempts were made to democratize and de-professionalize the legal system. It has been argued that some judges have been too political or have bowed to pressure and others have been accused of incompetence and corruption. But generally US judges are now given respect. However, lawyers (such as corporate, divorce and "celebrity" trial lawyers) can be treated with suspicion or antagonism. Defense and prosecution trial lawyers have attracted negative comments for their alleged manipulation of evidence, the media and the jury. They might argue that they are doing their best for their clients.

The judiciary

Federal judges are nominated by the president, confirmed by the Senate and appointed for life. Selection often reflects political and legal considerations. They hold office during good behavior and can be removed only by impeachment (trial by Senate for gross misconduct). This process has been rarely used and never successfully against a Supreme Court justice.

State and local judges may now be appointed, selected or elected (by the people) depending on the practices of individual states. They may also be investigated by state commissions, which may recommend their disciplining or removal.

The judiciary has a range of functions and duties. It enforces the legitimate laws and regulations of the legislative and executive branches of government, but it also protects citizens against arbitrary acts by either executive or legislature. Judicial review gives the judiciary a crucial authority, and judges' freedom from control by the other branches of government means that they are theoretically "above politics." This enables the courts and the judges to follow relatively independent courses of action within the law.

The authority of judges is generally supported by the public. The justices of the Supreme Court, for example, can be very influential (if not always trusted) and their decisions affect ordinary people's lives. Judges may, however, vary in their political inclinations from "liberal" to "conservative," and this may be reflected in their decisions.

Lawyers

Americans have tended to distrust lawyers, although they do often need their services. This antagonism today might be due to their courtroom behavior in some cases, to the perception that they drive up legal costs or to the large number of lawyers in society. In addition to their legal roles, their numbers make them very visible in business, politics and public life and the American Bar Association (ABA) reported that there were 1,225,452 licensed lawyers in 2011. The employment of lawyers is expected to grow by 10 percent between 2010 and 2020. However, it is argued that competition for a declining number of legal jobs is intense because more students graduate from the law schools each year.

Members of the legal profession, known as "attorneys-at-law," "counselors" or simply "lawyers," exercise broad functions in the law, although many now specialize in one particular area of expertise. They act as advocates (presenting criminal and civil cases in court) and advisers (giving legal assistance such as the drafting of contracts, trusts, wills and settlements). They advise and represent individuals, businesses or government agencies.

Most lawyers today will have obtained a law degree from the law school of a university, usually after a four-year bachelor's degree in another subject. The value of the three-year law degree varies with the status of the school, although the best (such as Harvard and Yale) are world-famous and of high quality. The degree gives the lawyer a general grounding in American law through academic lectures and practical casework. But lawyers also have to know the law of the state in which they will practice and must pass the state bar examination.

Lawyers work for federal, local and state government or in industry and commerce, but the majority are in private or corporate legal offices and cater for individual and corporate clients. Some work on their own account (48 percent) and serve a range of clients. However, most lawyers practice in firms. Some 15 percent work in small firms with 2–5 lawyers, consisting of office attorneys and trial lawyers, who perform different functions. The remainder work in bigger firms, which have many lawyers and may have offices worldwide. The three categories of lawyers in big firms are senior partners and junior partners, who receive a share of the profits, and associates, who are paid a fixed salary.

The lawyer's income is frequently a high one in the medium-to-large firms and is, on average, one of the highest in the country, with a median annual wage of $112,760 in 2010. Top students of the best law schools are normally able to join a prestigious law firm at a good salary and may quickly proceed to a partnership.

The financing of a law firm, in addition to ordinary commercial fees, may include other features. The contingency fee (payment upon results in personal injury cases) can be charged at rates which may reach over 50 percent of the damages awarded. But *pro-bono* legal help without fees may be provided for those who cannot afford to pay for legal services, and firms may participate in state and federal legal aid programs for the poor. The provision of legal aid is an important and expensive federal program, particularly since fees for legal services are generally very high. The public also seem to think that lawyers are overly concerned with money and that they drive up costs and their fees.

Lawyers have organized themselves at national and state levels into bar associations, which supervise the profession, protect professional interests and discipline their members. The American Bar Association (ABA) was created nationally in 1878. Most states require that lawyers must be members of the state bar association, which is affiliated to the ABA, in order to practice law in a state.

The ABA is regarded as a conservative organization and is often criticized. But its lobbying has improved the status of lawyers. It has fought for improvements in the law, legal education and the legal system. It also serves as a source of legal information to the public. The expert opinion and special status of the ABA are influential in the nomination of judges and in proposing changes in criminal and civil law.

Crime and punishment

Crime

Popular images, official statistics and personal experience surveys have traditionally suggested that the US has a high crime rate in real terms and in comparison with other countries. Much of this is associated with professional crime organizations, street gangs, drug-dealing and usage, and low-level offences. But crime is spread unevenly across the country and among victims, and international comparisons indicate that US crime statistics are not exceptional in all cases and rates for some crimes are lower than in other countries.

It is argued that crime rates in the US have declined since the mid-1990s. But there are different methodologies for measuring crime and two contrasting sets of figures appeared in September and October 2012. Federal Bureau of Investigation (FBI) statistics of serious, aggravated crime reported to the police showed that in 2011 there was an estimated total of 1,203,564 violent crimes. Robbery had decreased by 4 percent, aggravated assault by 3.9 percent, rape by 2.5 percent and murder and non-negligent manslaughter by 0.7 percent. There was an estimated total of 9,063,173 property crimes. Motor vehicle theft had declined by 3.3 percent and larceny-theft offences by 0.7 percent, but there had been an increase of 0.9 percent in burglaries. Overall, FBI figures showed that the number of violent crimes had decreased by 3.9 percent and property crime declined by 0.5 percent.

However, the Bureau of Justice Statistics released in October 2012 showed that the rate of violent crime among victims aged 12 or older had in fact increased by 17 percent in 2011 from 2010. This figure derived from a 22 percent increase in both aggravated and simple assaults, many of which are not reported to law enforcement agencies. It is based on the National Crime Survey, which attempts to correct non-reporting by collecting data from households and individuals to obtain a complete record of crime. Despite the disparity, it was argued that the overall crime rate still remained significantly lower than 20 years before.

The majority of persistent offences are property crimes and a smaller proportion is violent crime against individuals. It is estimated that firearms are used in three-quarters of all these cases (particularly murder). The FBI reported that the US murder rate in 2011 was 14,612—a decline of 0.7 percent from 2010. But this murder rate is high among industrialized nations, with the South accounting for 43.6 percent, the West for 21 percent, the Midwest for 20.6 percent and the Northeast for 14.8 percent of total murders in 2011.

The incidence of crime is much higher in some cities, certain city areas and regions (rather than rural locations); many offences are still unreported; and only 20 percent of reported crimes are solved and their perpetrators convicted. It is estimated that 60 percent of all crimes are committed by 5 percent of the population and the majority of these persons have a criminal record. The South accounted for 41.3 percent of violent crimes, the West for 22.9 percent, the Midwest for 19.5 percent and the Northeast for 16.2 percent in 2011.

Young people aged between 15 and 19 are statistically the most criminally inclined age group. However, their numbers have declined as increased jobs, prosperity and "zero tolerance" police policies in the 1990s reduced the crime statistics. In some urban areas, murder is the main cause of death among non-white males between the ages of 24 and 45 and non-whites have a higher victimization rate than whites. African Americans (12 percent of the population) dispro-portionately account for 35 percent of arrests for drug possession, 55 percent of convictions and 74 percent of prison sentences. The number of crimes, criminals and victims may increase with rising unemployment and recession.

The reasons for crime are notoriously arguable and varied. Some critics maintain that the police and courts are too lenient in their treatment of criminal suspects and sentencing patterns, while the police criticize the courts and defense lawyers. Others blame slums, social deprivation, poverty, bad schools, lack of opportunities and role models, unemployment, lack of discipline, unstable or dysfunctional families, inadequate or non-existent parenting skills, drugs, organized crime, teenage gangs and the availability of guns and other weapons.

Law enforcement

In 2009, city, county, state, college, university and Native American agencies employed some 1,021,456 full-time law enforcement officers. About 69.2 percent were sworn and armed with arrest powers and publicly funded. State law is implemented by the police and detectives in the cities and by sheriffs or marshals and constables (deputies) in rural areas. Federal crimes are the responsibility of the Federal Bureau of Investigation (FBI), which also provides technical assistance to state and local law enforcement agencies. However, there is sometimes tension over jurisdiction between the FBI and local or state authorities.

Crime prevention is a difficult job for law enforcement officials and the courts. Public demands for stronger punishment for criminals and increased rights and compensation for crime victims and their families create pressure and are expensive. Overcrowded prisons, accessibility of guns, uncertain civil rights and arguments about the death penalty influence the crime debate. Courts and law enforcement officers thus have difficulties in coping with the legitimate needs and demands of society and the rights of suspects.

Rights of criminal suspects

The Constitution ideally guarantees equal justice under the law for all citizens and the individual's right to freedom and security. Constitutional amendments and court decisions also protect the rights of criminal suspects.

The Fourth Amendment protects citizens against unreasonable search and seizure. It is generally illegal for the police to search people's homes, persons or papers unless they have a warrant. The Supreme Court has created exceptions so that the police can in some circumstances search and act without a warrant. However, incriminating evidence that results from an illegal police search is controversially excluded from a criminal trial.

Another rule established by the Supreme Court in *Miranda* v. *Arizona* (1966) extended the protection of criminal suspects. The police must read suspects their legal rights on arrest and under custody. These include the right to remain silent, to have an attorney present during questioning, and to consult a lawyer before making a statement. If the police proceed incorrectly, any evidence obtained from questioning cannot be used in court. This may mean that persons who could be guilty go free because of a technicality.

Many protections for criminal suspects stem from liberal Supreme Court decisions in the 1960s. Conservatives campaign for the reversal of these rulings and other provisions that arguably overprotect suspects. They maintain that such rules hinder law enforcement and the protection of society, and shift the balance of doubt towards suspects. Liberals argue that any reduction in the rights of criminal suspects may affect innocent people and leaves too much power and control in the hands of the police and the criminal justice system.

The death penalty

Capital punishment is hotly debated in the US. In 1972, the Supreme Court ruled in *Furman* v. *Georgia* that the death penalty for convicted murderers was "cruel and unusual punishment" (Eighth Amendment) and unconstitutional. This decision was reversed in 1976 in *Gregg* v. *Georgia*, which ruled that the death penalty was not unconstitutional if it is applied in a fair and impartial manner. Critics argue that the court decided the case in a narrow legal sense and ignored the ethical implications of the "cruel and unusual" clause. For them, the death penalty illustrates the gap between law and justice in American society; that it is unconstitutional as a cruel and unusual punishment; and does not serve as a deterrent.

As of 2012, 33 states, the federal government and the US military retain the death penalty. Given the uncertain state of the law and opposition to capital punishment, the number of executions fluctuated after 1976. Department of Justice statistics showed that 1,312 convicted murderers were executed in the US between 1976 and 2012. Of these, according to the Death Penalty Information Center, 740 (56 percent) were white, 452 (35 percent) were black, 101 (7 percent) were Latino, 24 (2 percent) were other races/ethnic groups and 12 were female. Texas carried out the most executions at 489 (37 percent).

In 2007–8, the Supreme Court effectively imposed a moratorium on the death penalty by agreeing to hear a challenge against the most common method of applying capital punishment, that of lethal injection by a triple mixture of drugs. This development delayed executions by halting injection, which was allegedly subject to weaknesses and risks and therefore a cruel, unusual and unconstitutional punishment. Meanwhile, the concern about executing the wrong person had led to more complex and expensive appeals, and the number of executions in 2007 declined to 42.

On April 16, 2008, the Supreme Court rejected lethal injection appeals from Kentucky, Alabama and Texas, and thus allowed states to again proceed with executions. The court decided that the execution method had to present a "substantial" or "objectively intolerable" risk of serious harm for it to constitute cruel and unusual punishment.

The death penalty has been supported in recent years. A Pew Research Center survey in November 2011 reported that 34 percent of respondents favored and 28 percent strongly favored the punishment for convicted murderers, 7 percent did not know/refused to answer, with 20 percent opposed and 11 percent strongly opposed. It seems that two-thirds of Americans support the death penalty and three-quarters believe that it is either used with the right frequency or not used often enough. Other surveys in 2011 showed that majorities in most social groups

PLATE 9.4 Prisoner on death row facing execution in a gas chamber, 1989, San Quentin State Prison, California. The prisoner is held in a special wing of a prison prior to execution, in some cases for many years, awaiting the results of appeals against conviction and sentence. *(Sipa/Rex Features)*

favored capital punishment. However, fewer Democrats than Republicans, and fewer women than men supported the death penalty

A majority of Americans agree that although an innocent person might have been executed, they still defend the death penalty. However, support for the death penalty can vary, depending on the alternatives and the circumstances of individual cases. For example, support declines to about half of the population when Americans are given the opportunity to choose the alternative of life imprisonment with no possibility of parole. On the other hand, in instances of terrible crimes, support can rise to 80 percent.

A Gallup poll in October 2011 found that 52 percent of respondents thought that the death penalty was applied fairly; 41 percent unfairly; and 6 percent had no opinion. Thirty two percent felt that it acts as a deterrent to murder; 64 percent did not; and 4 percent had no opinion. A Gallup poll in May 2012 reported that 58 percent of respondents found the death penalty morally acceptable; 34 percent thought it morally wrong; and 6 percent considered that it depended on the situation.

Prisons

The US has a higher percentage of its population behind bars than any other country and spends billions of dollars a year on its prisons. However, according to the US Bureau of Justice statistics (BJS), there were 1,612,395 adult prisoners in US federal and state prisons at the end of 2010. This was a decrease of 5,575 (0.3 percent) from 2009, marked the first reduction since 1972 and amounted to one in 200 US residents. Of the total, federal prisoners increased by 0.8 percent (1,653), inmates under state authority declined by 0.5 percent (7,228), and prison releases (708,677) outnumbered admissions (703,798) for the first time since 1977. Other prisoners are kept in locally operated jails, which hold persons awaiting trial or sentencing, as well as those sentenced to one year or less. Florida, Louisiana, California, Texas and Illinois have recently had the most prisoners in their facilities.

American administrations, in response to public concern about crime, have followed tough policies in the last 25 years and favored the following:

- the death penalty,
- putting more police on the streets,
- building more prisons,
- allowing some prisons to be run by private firms,
- stressing punishment above rehabilitation,
- reducing parole,
- giving longer and tougher sentences for serious crimes and
- imposing immediate custodial sentences on criminals who repeat serious crimes ("three strikes and you're out").

The arguable decrease in recent overall crime figures has been partly attributed to these factors, as well as to a relatively healthy economy until 2007–8, demographic changes (with an ageing population and declining numbers of 15- to 19-year-olds), community policing and zero toleration of crime. The US government says that its tactics of tough and effective policies to tackle crime are working.

But critics say that such policies have directed the US penal system away from rehabilitation, storing up problems for the future. Prison policies are challenged by reformers advocating improved welfare systems, better education and drug-treatment programs, with prevention, rather than punishment and detention, being the aims. Many prisons tend to be old and do not serve as positive examples of rehabilitation. The Commission on Safety and Abuse in America's Prisons (CSAAP) heard testimony in 2006 on the violence, abuse and over-crowding in US prisons and argued that the US public is ignorant of this situation. The CSAAP believes that prisons must accept public accountability; recommends increased use of direct supervision of inmates; and seeks tighter regulations over the use of weapons such as pepper spray and stun guns. It sees prison as a place of opportunity that can have a positive impact on inmates and prepares them to return to their communities as productive citizens.

Gun control

The Second Amendment states that "A well regulated Militia, being necessary to the security of a free State, the right of the people to keep and bear arms, shall not be infringed." Does this mean that all Americans may own guns, or only those who serve in a militia?

The Supreme Court had never definitively interpreted the Second Amendment, but in June 2008 it heard an appeal in *District of Columbia* v. *Heller*. This concerned a decision by the US Court of Appeals (District of Columbia Circuit), which decided that a handgun ban by Washington, DC was an unconstitutional infringement of the Second Amendment.

The Supreme Court ruled by a majority of 5–4 that the ban on the private possession of handguns in Washington, DC was unconstitutional. It said that the Constitution "protects an individual right to possess a firearm unconnected with service in a militia, and to use that arm for traditionally lawful purposes, such as self-defense within the home." The National Rifle Association (NRA) then filed legal challenges to overturn handgun bans in San Francisco and Chicago. However, the court's ruling also stated that the right was not unlimited. "It is not a right to keep and carry any weapon whatsoever in any manner whatsoever and for whatever purpose." Arguably the Constitution gives authorities the means to combat gun abuse and to regulate gun use. The issue therefore is how far the right to possess guns can be regulated.

The possession of guns is debated by those who wish to control or ban them and by those who regard gun ownership as an individual right. It is difficult to pass gun control legislation, despite the fact that handguns are used in murders, rapes, robberies and assaults; and there have been mass killings in recent years, including attacks in schools (such as Newtown, Connecticut, in 2012 when 20 children and six teachers were killed), universities, cinemas and shopping centers. A Gallup poll in February 2008 found that 34 percent of the US adult population owns a gun, amounting to some 283 million privately owned firearms.

The National Rifle Association (NRA) and lobbies against gun control (militia groups and hunters) vigorously oppose restrictions on the sale and use of firearms as a violation of the Constitution. After Newtown, the NRA argued that there should be armed guards in all schools, although some public opinion wanted a ban on the sale of automatic weapons.

Gun control laws were passed by Congress in 1993 and 1994, influenced by the Brady Campaign to Prevent Gun Violence. These included:

- the imposition of a five-day waiting period for the purchase of handguns to allow checks into the buyer's background,
- registration of all handguns,
- a ban on the sale of semi-automatic assault weapons and machine guns until 2004,
- stronger penalties for gun offences and
- tighter licensing rules for gun-dealers.

However, these laws were not excessively stringent, were for trial periods, could be circumvented, could be variously applied in different states and did not seriously challenge the "right-to-guns" culture. The US has few gun laws that are applicable to the whole country, but many different gun regulations in individual states. In 2007 there was a 73 percent increase in concealed-handgun permit applications in Virginia. Gun-rights activists believed that this was a result of earlier bloodshed at Virginia Tech University. The Supreme Court's ruling on the right to bear arms could enable states to impose limits on carrying concealed weapons, regulate the sale of guns and stop some categories from owning them. But it is likely that there will be more challenges and litigation on the issue of gun control.

Recent polls indicate that positions on gun ownership and regulation have remained largely unchanged, despite mass shootings. A Pew Research Center poll in July 2012 found that 46 percent of respondents felt that the most important aspect of the firearms debate was the protection of the right of Americans to own guns; while 47 percent thought that the most important issue was to control gun ownership. It was felt that mass shootings were isolated acts of troubled individuals (67 percent) rather than reflecting problems in US society (24 percent.) However, a CNN/ORC International poll in August 2012 reported that while 13 percent of respondents said that there should be no restrictions on owning guns, 76 percent thought that there should be some restrictions. Ninety-six percent of respondents favored background checks on gun purchasers

(4 percent opposed); 57 percent favored and 42 percent opposed a ban on the manufacture, sale and possession of semi-automatic assault guns; 60 percent favored and 40 percent opposed a ban on the sale and possession of high-capacity ammunition clips; 91 percent favored and 8 percent opposed preventing convicted felons or people with mental health problems from owning guns; 76 percent favored and 23 percent opposed gun owners being required to register their guns with local government; and 10 percent approved and 89 percent opposed preventing all Americans from owning guns.

The Obama administration may develop tough policies towards gun owner-ship after Newtown, such as the re-introduction of a ban on assault weapons; a national gun ownership register that tracks the purchase and sale of guns; universal background checks on buyers' convictions and mental health checks; and penalties for carrying weapons near schools.

Self-defense

The issue of gun control is connected to self-defense and fears about crime. Historically, people's right to defend themselves, their families and their property against crime has been a basic (and often necessary) tradition in American life. Although there was little change in the number of Americans who actually reported that they had been crime victims in the last 20 years, crime victimization did increase in 2011 according to the Bureau of Justice Statistics, 2012. These figures were based on the National Crime Victimization Survey (NCVS) which is a self-reporting agency and collects information from crime victims. In 2011, the rate of violent victimization increased by 17 percent to 22.5 victimizations per 1,000 persons age 12 or older. But the actual difference between 2010 and 2011 (3.3 victimizations) was below the average annual change over the past 20 years (4.3 victimizations).

Despite the apparent decline in the crime figures over time, there is still a lack of public confidence in the ability of the courts and legislators to cope with crime or to adequately and effectively protect individual citizens. People consequently feel that they must safeguard themselves in the face of people determined to commit criminal acts. Security has become a priority for many individuals, who devise ways (such as Neighborhood Watch schemes) to protect themselves and their homes from attacks, violence and burglaries. They also tend to avoid certain areas because of crime concerns.

Attitudes to the legal system

A Gallup poll in June 2012 prior to the presidential election campaign did not prioritize crime before the economy as one of the most important problems facing the US. This was a change from the 1980s and early 1990s when organized crime, violence, gangs, assaults and drug-usage had consistently appeared as leading concerns in polls and crime figures were high.

Nevertheless, although fear of crime is considered to be greater than its actuality, many Americans believe that crime and violence might directly affect their own lives and feel threatened. A Gallup poll in March 2012 reported that respondents were worried about crime and violence a great deal (42 percent) or a fair amount (31 percent).

FBI statistics have suggested that crime in the US has declined since the 1990s, but 69 percent of respondents to a Gallup poll in October 2011 felt that there was more crime in the US than a year previously, and 48 percent thought there was more crime in their local areas. Seventeen percent thought that the problem of crime was extremely serious, 37 percent as very serious and 40 percent as moderately serious.

There are opposing attitudes about crime and how to deal with it. A Gallup poll in January 2012 found that 50 percent of respondents were very/somewhat satisfied with official policies to reduce or control crime, but 45 percent were very/somewhat dissatisfied. Many Americans wish for tough responses to crime but others want to fight it through better education and job training.

Sixty-two percent of respondents to a General Social Survey in March 2010 said that the courts did not deal "harshly enough with criminals," while 18 percent thought that their response was "about right," and 13 percent said that it was too harsh. Sixty-three percent felt that crime could be combated by having more job and community programs for young people, longer jail sentences for those convicted of violent crimes (49 percent), restrictions on the amount of violence shown on television and films (48 percent), more police on the streets (46 percent) and stricter gun control laws (41 percent).

Historically, US legal institutions have not attracted great support. A Gallup poll in June 2012 reported that 26 percent of respondents had a great deal of confidence in the police and 30 percent had quite a lot. The figures for the Supreme Court were respectively 15 percent and 22 percent. Those for the criminal justice system were 11 percent and 18 percent. A Gallup poll in March 2011 found that 34 percent of respondents thought that the courts, legal system and judges collectively had too much power and 49 percent that they had about the right amount. A Harris poll in May 2011 reported that 11 percent of respondents had confidence in law firms, 49 percent had some confidence and 33 percent hardly any.

Attitudes to the legal system vary according to negative publicity about police matters and high-profile cases, and the opposed views of liberals and conservatives. Conservatives are strong on law and order, feel that the rights of criminal suspects and defendants should be restricted, favor strong criminal penalties, harsh punishment and the death penalty, and seek to overturn liberal legislation. Liberals tend to be suspicious of the police and law-enforcement agencies, are against what they see as tough criminal legislation and penalties, and favor extended civil rights for individuals.

Some critics argue that Americans often have variable attitudes to crime and violence, which create a self-perpetuating image of the US as a crime-ridden, lawless and violent society. Many professionals and academics seem to agree that America's fundamental problem is the cult of violence itself and feel that one way to reduce this is to restrict access to guns. Others argue that the American media concentrates on the portrayal of violence, which is then copied and replicated by individuals and groups in society.

Exercises

Explain and examine the significance of the following names and terms:

legalism	precedent	impeachment
common law	jurisdiction	civil law
judicial review	constitutionalism	US district courts
legal aid	plea-bargaining	state supreme court
statutory law	ABA	adversary system
judiciary	Bill of Rights	contingency fees
Miranda v. Arizona	rights culture	pro bono
litigation	commerce clause	jury
Supreme Court	NRA	militia
criminal law	prosecutor	appeal

Write short essays on the following questions:

1. Why is law such an important part of American life?

2. Critically discuss the historical evolution of American law and the legal system.

3. Examine the arguments for and against the death penalty and gun control.

4. Attempt to explain attitudes to crime in the US by analyzing the polls in the text.

5. What is the role of the US Supreme Court?

Further reading

Abadinsky, H. (1995) *Law and Justice: An Introduction to the American Legal System*, Chicago, IL: Nelson-Hall.

American Bar Association (latest edition) *Law and the Courts: A Handbook of Courtroom Procedures*, Chicago, IL: ABA Press.

Apple, J.G. and Deyling, R.P. (1995) *A Primer on the Civil-Law System*, Washington, DC: Federal Judicial Center.

Bedau, H. (ed.) (2003) *Debating the Death Penalty: Should America Have Capital Punishment? The Experts on Both Sides Make Their Best Case*, Oxford: Oxford University Press.

Biskupic, J. and Witt, E. (1997) *Guide to the US Supreme Court*, Washington, DC: Congressional Quarterly Press.

Carp, R.A. and Stidham, R. (1998) *Judicial Process in America*, Washington, DC: Congressional Quarterly Press.

Fine, T.M. (1997) *American Legal Systems: A Resource and Reference Guide*, Cincinnati, OH: Anderson.

Friedman, L.M. (1986) *A History of American Law*, Safety Harbor, FL: Touchstone Books.

Friedman, L.M. (2004) *Law in America: A Short History*, New York: Random House, Modern Library Chronicles.

Hall, K.L., Finkelman, P. and Ely, J.W. (2010) *American Legal History: Cases and Materials*, Oxford: Oxford University Press.

Stumpf, H.P. and Culver, J.H. (1992) *The Politics of State Courts*, New York: Longman Press.

Tushnet, M.V. (1999) *Taking the Constitution Away from the Courts*, Princeton, NJ: Princeton University Press.

Websites

www.usa.gov

Bureau of Justice Statistics: http://bjs.ojp.usdoj.gov

Collected polls on crime: www.pollingreport.com/crime.htm

Crime: www.fbi.gov

Death penalty: www.deathpenaltyinfo.org

www.clarkprosecutor.org/html/death/usexecute.htm

http://publicreligion.org/research/2011

Gallup: www.gallup.com

Gun control: CNN/ORC POLL 7, August 7–8, 2012, http://politicalticker.blogs.cnn.com/2012/08/09/cnnorc-poll-august-7-8-guns

National Crime Survey: http://bjs.gov

Roper Center Public Opinion Archives: www.ropercenter.uconn.edu

The economy

This chapter describes US economic history, economic theories and social class; evaluates the contemporary economy; and analyzes attitudes to the economic system.

Historically, the US economy has been characterized by technological change, and periods of recession, adaptation and steady (often rapid) growth. Agriculture was the main economic activity from colonial times to the mid-nineteenth century. It then quickly became more mechanized and efficient and used fewer workers. Industrial and manufacturing output also increased greatly from the nineteenth century. Such growth led to the US becoming the world's richest country and the leading industrial nation by the early twentieth century.

Between 1945 and 1970, the US achieved a large degree of self-sufficiency and an economic dominance, which resulted in American influence over the world economy. Since the 1970s, major changes have been the growth of service industries; a decline in traditional manufacturing industry; a relative weakening in the US position as other countries became more competitive; instability in trade; and fluctuating budget deficits and dollar values. Globalization (interdependence of world trade and business) affected the US economy as it adapted to the changing international order. The US was no longer the only important economic engine in the global economy and faced competition from Japan, China, India, other Asian Rim countries and the European Union (EU).

Following a recession in the early 1990s, the economy grew strongly with increased output, low inflation and a drop in unemployment. But it slowed again in 2000–1 and, although improving by 2004, it experienced a credit (loans) and banking crisis, financial market turmoil, a collapsing housing sector, a budget deficit, rising unemployment and recession in 2007–9. The US economy in 2012 was still suffering from unemployment, spending cuts and a lack of investment and job creation. It affected public confidence and was the main issue in the 2012 presidential election campaign. By the end of that year, however, there was some improvement in growth, inflation, jobs and the housing market.

Economic history

US economic expansion from the nineteenth century can be explained by the country's size, substantial natural resources, commercial structures, population growth, the characteristics of the people, and the basic ideological principles that support economic activity.

Prior to the colonial period, the indigenous Native American inhabitants of North America had varied economies, ranging from nomadic food-gathering, fishing and hunting to settled agricultural communities. A similar basic economy was adopted by colonial Americans, who later developed sophisticated agricultural systems based on small farms.

British settlers in the seventeenth century were often employed by British companies that were granted trading charters by the English Crown, such as the Virginia Company that established Jamestown in 1607. The colonies provided Britain with raw materials but were not supposed to compete in manufacturing exports with the mother country. This relationship collapsed when Britain tried to impose taxation and more trade restrictions. After the War for Independence (1775–83), the US developed its economic markets. A greater variety of goods was produced by the eighteenth century as Americans expanded agriculture, farmed the prairies, increased their commercial interests and exported more products.

A belief in possibilities and personal advancement encouraged pragmatism, hard work and individual initiative in the people. These qualities have been linked to religion (the Protestant work ethic) and the pioneer spirit of early settlers, whose survival lay in their own ingenuity and efforts. Many, if not all, Americans today continue these values: retrain if unemployment occurs, create new jobs or businesses and move to fresh opportunities.

The US in 1800 was still an agricultural society. Some 95 percent of the people lived in rural areas and the economy was based largely on self-sufficiency. But nineteenth-century growth combined significant agricultural advances with expanding industrial and manufacturing bases. These were aided by government financial support and protectionism as well as by a transport revolution that established railway, canal and road infrastructures.

Agricultural productivity increased as small farmers made use of the transportation system, specialized in selected crops or animals, sold their products to a wider internal market and developed their export potential. But this growth led to overproduction and reduced prices. By the start of the twentieth century farmers were having difficulties.

Economic progress in the nineteenth century was also affected by the Civil War (1861–5) when 23 states of the industrializing North were opposed by 11 Southern agricultural states on the issues of slavery and secession. A Northern victory led to an emphasis on the nation's industrial base, with great advances in the production of basic manufactured goods.

Between the Civil War and the First World War (1914–18), the US rapidly industrialized and became a more urban and suburban country. Expansion was based on natural resources, iron production, and steam and electrical power. It was later helped by technical advances and inventions such as the internal combustion engine, the telegraph and telephone, radio, typewriters, assembly-line production and interchangeable-parts technology. Economies of scale in production and distribution led to the growth of large manufacturing units, and the export of manufactured goods became more important than raw materials.

Economic activity was largely free from restrictions. Business operated for profit in a "market economy" that determined the need for and price of goods, and conditioned the activity of independent buyers and sellers. Few restrictions (such as government intervention) were placed on business, and people were largely able to pursue their own economic interests. But this led to an unregulated capitalism as big business and the profit motive became central features of American life. Industrial progress was accompanied by slumps, unemployment and harsh working and living conditions for the expanding population (including African Americans from the South and European immigrants between 1890 and 1910).

The growing economy resulted in the development of new products and the creation of corporations (large business companies) in most economic sectors. These based their production and competition policies on marketing, advertising, advanced technology, cheap products, rationalization of the work process, efficient management organization and good service. The growth of corporations enabled the US to export many types of manufactured items abroad and consumer goods were spread throughout the domestic American market.

Larger corporations were formed through mergers and takeovers, leading to giant trusts and monopolies, which controlled competition. Trusts were associated

PLATE 10.1 Aerial view of Microsoft's main corporate campus, Redmond, Washington State, 2005.
(Dan Lamont/Corbis)

with owners such as Rockefeller in oil and Carnegie in steel, whose economic and political power influenced the whole economy. It was increasingly felt that government should regulate the trusts and monopolies, which were seen as anti-competitive.

Some anti-trust legislation (the 1890 Sherman Anti-Trust Act) had already been passed. But the trusts still controlled many large areas of production. President Theodore Roosevelt (1901–9) tried to regulate them by preventing restrictive deals between companies on products, prices, output levels and market shares; by limiting mergers that minimized competition; and by improving employment conditions (such as an eight-hour working day). President Woodrow Wilson (1913–21) also attempted to regulate commercial markets. He passed a new anti-trust law, reduced protective tariffs against foreign competition and introduced reforms in agricultural and labor areas.

However, large corporations still had power and the 1920s ("the Roaring Twenties") created instability and hardship for many people. Low taxes led to a rise in living standards, but too much money circulated in the economy and the consumption of services and goods increased. There was overproduction by factories and farms; overprotection of business against foreign competition through tariff barriers; and financial speculation. The economy collapsed in October 1929 with the Wall Street Crash on the stock market. This marked the beginning of the worst economic depression in US history (the Great Depression).

Demands were made for more government regulation of business activity and for help to those who were suffering socially and economically. President Franklin D. Roosevelt (1933–45) argued that the Depression was due to faults in the capitalist structure, tried to remedy the situation with his New Deal and was the first president to substantially intervene in the economy. New regulatory powers over the stock market were initiated by a Securities and Exchange Commission (SEC) and other commissions supervised public utilities such as electricity. The unemployed were given jobs in public-works projects and financial help was granted to farmers who were suffering badly. A Social Security Act (1935) was the first major federal legislation to provide security against unemployment, job-related accidents and old age. These measures aimed to stabilize the economy, regulate commercial institutions, create internal demand for American products and prevent social and economic hardship.

The New Deal did not solve all the problems. Consequently, governments since the 1930s have intervened to varying degrees in the economy by legislation, by using regulatory powers to influence commercial life or by controlled purchases from the private marketplace. But US governments are not generally opposed to business and have themselves invested in private sectors such as research, aerospace, development and defense. They aided economic growth in the nine-teenth century; protected US industry, farmers and manufacturers against foreign competition; used public money to encourage private business; and gave land to private interests to develop transport systems. The economy grew and competed successfully with European countries. Despite their supposed embrace of free trade, US governments still protect the national economy internationally by granting subsidies and using measures such as tariff barriers, while also experiencing problems themselves in entering some overseas markets because of foreign trade restrictions.

The 1944 Bretton Woods Conference was an attempt at international cooperation, economic liberalization and free trade after the experiences of the two world wars and the Great Depression. It was held in New Hampshire and tried to create a system of monetary management among the world's major industrial states, which was intended to stabilize economies, currencies and relations between countries. It established the International Monetary Fund (IMF) and the International Bank for Reconstruction and Development (now part of the World Bank). The Bretton Woods system was relatively effective until the early 1970s but then declined because of inherent weaknesses and the role of dominant currencies, such as the American dollar. However, the IMF and World Bank continue to function.

The US economy grew after the Second World War (1939–45) and by the 1950s had achieved global dominance. Large corporations, such as Exxon Mobil, Walmart, General Motors, Chevron, ConocoPhillips, General Electric, Ford Motor, IBM, Hewlett-Packard, Bank of America Corp, Citigroup, AT&T, Verizon Communications and JP Morgan Chase, continue to influence American business in 2013. Some are multinational organizations owned by financial groups (rather than individuals) with diversified interests and plants worldwide, but there are many smaller companies and businesses (three-quarters of the corporate market) that create most jobs and can be very successful and influential.

Since the mid-twentieth century the US economy has experienced periods of high inflation, high unemployment, large trade gaps, government budget deficits, international competition and recessionary forces. However, it grew from 1994 with low inflation, low unemployment, stable prices, budget surpluses, job creation and a vibrant stock market, before suffering a slowdown in the early 2000s. It recovered somewhat by 2004, but there were still weaknesses in job creation, unemployment, stock market volatility, inadequate exports, excessive imports and variable Gross Domestic Product (GDP) growth. These underlying weaknesses were subjected to very high energy and oil prices, and a sub-prime property crisis in 2007, which led to financial market and banking disarray, recession in 2008 and public dissatisfaction with the management of the economy.

The US faces change and challenge in the twenty-first century because of economic cycles, recession, international competition, political uncertainty and technological advances in computing, telecommunications and finance. It has to meet the risks and advantages of globalization, the growing economic strength of western Europe and strong competitive economies in China, India, Japan and Latin America.

American economic liberalism: theory and practice

The founders of the US stressed economic freedom. They were influenced by philosophers such as Adam Smith and argued that consumers and producers should pursue their own self-interest and profit-making in a free enterprise economy. The market (not central government) decides what should be produced and what prices should be charged for goods based on supply and demand. Greater competition and trade would result, society would benefit, the economy could produce what was needed, consumers could buy articles at competitive prices and market forces would control the production and efficient distribution of goods.

Many areas of the economy, such as industry, business, airlines, telephone systems, energy supplies and railways, are therefore in private rather than public ownership and US governments have historically been confined to a regulatory role in the economy. Since the 1930s they have employed anti-monopoly and deregulation measures (removal of restrictions to create freer markets) to promote competition in services and prices. They have broken up airlines, railroads, trucking companies, telephone and telegraph systems, utilities and postal services. But an attempt by the Justice Department to split Microsoft into two parts because of alleged monopolistic behavior was dismissed in 2001 by the US Court of Appeals.

Governments (particularly Democratic) and official bodies now intervene more actively in business. They exert influence through monetary and fiscal policy such as interest rate changes by the Federal Reserve System; through subsidies and controls on prices; and as purchasers of goods and equipment, especially in the defense and aerospace industries. Regulation also includes safety standards for manufactured products; labor, welfare and equal-employment reform; environmental protection; training schemes; and pro-union legislative improvements in working conditions (such as increases in the federal minimum wage with the last rise in 2009 to $7.25 an hour). Federal restrictions may curb freedom of operation for employers (and states) and show the more intrusive role of contemporary government. However, there is some room for maneuver and in the case of the national minimum wage, for example, states have freedom to specify an amount above or below the federal rate and payment for specific jobs that may vary within and among states.

Economic restrictions are fiercely debated. Conservatives and corporations argue that there is too much regulation, bureaucracy, interference and taxation. Liberals generally support an interventionist role in economic matters. Americans have a distrust of "big government," disagree about the appropriate role of government in the economy and are skeptical about the ability of government to solve many economic and social problems. But they also dislike the near-monopolistic nature of some "big business," which may dominate consumer choice and give bad service and products. A Gallup poll in June 2012 found that only 9 percent of respondents had a great deal of confidence in big business, 12 percent had quite a lot and 40 percent had some. On the other hand, 30 percent of respondents had a great deal of confidence in small business, 33 percent had quite a lot and 29 percent had some.

The US also has a big public sector involving, among other features, state and federal government, the police, fire protection, public education, public health, parks, roads and social security benefits. Free enterprise values are not necessarily associated with these areas and the US does not have an absolute "free market" system. Although Americans may generally support free enterprise, individual initiative and the ability of a competitive market to deliver goods, services and resources nationwide, not all individuals can pursue economic success because of their differing circumstances and the influence of factors such as corporate power. A belief in individualism does not imply automatic success, although it is generally felt that achievement and material prosperity may result from personal hard work. Debates have therefore been concerned largely with how much government regulation and unrestricted corporate power there should be in the economic system, and whether programs in both public and private sectors actually work efficiently and deliver beneficial results.

US attitudes were tested in 2008. An economic recession followed a credit squeeze, consumer debt and the collapse of banks, insurance houses and the housing market. Many people opposed the $700 billion government rescue of the private financial sector and the free enterprise system and demanded an evaluation of their operations. Debates continued about how many austerity spending cuts and tax increases were necessary to rectify the economy.

Corporate behavior can seriously affect the economy, such as insider dealing on the stock exchange and the collapse of corporations, such as Enron (2001). It can also result in government takeover of banks (Bear Stearns), the nationalization of insurance/mortgage houses (Freddie Mac and Fannie Mae) and the collapse of Lehman Brothers in 2008. Historically, the American people have been very skeptical of the stock market, banks and insurance houses and the Wall Street Crash of 1929 casts a long shadow. The 2012 Gallup poll above found that only 9 percent of respondents had a great deal of confidence in banks, 12 percent had quite a lot and 42 percent had some.

A 2008 study by the American Human Development Index concluded that the US economic system has deep weaknesses in providing opportunity and choices to all Americans to advance themselves. Despite a belief in unrestricted free enterprise as the best way to help Americans out of poverty, the report said that this system does little to lessen inequalities.

Social class and economic inequality

Although the US is often portrayed as a classless and egalitarian society, there have always been social and economic inequalities between Americans. These formed a class model divided into working, middle and upper classes based on jobs, income, capital and birth. Nineteenth-century industrialization increased the class and wealth gaps between industrialists, manufacturers, financiers and landowners on the one hand and workers on the other. It was argued that class divisions were a natural result of the freedom of competition.

In the twentieth century, workers were increasingly placed either in the white-collar service sector or the industrial blue-collar sector. It was felt that these groups fell outside European notions of the "working class" and should more appropriately be seen as "lower middle class." However, many Americans still saw themselves as "workers."

A mass-consumption society, a reduced manufacturing base and a rise in living standards led to a decline in blue-collar workers, an increase in service-sector white-collar employees and a growth in professional and executive grades. Class distinctions became less rigid, middle-class values were influential and many Americans considered themselves as middle class in terms of income, lifestyle and aspiration. But a minority developed outside these groups, described as an unemployable and alienated under-class, which is often dependent upon state and voluntary sector benefits.

A Pew Research Center poll in September 2012 reported that respondents had arguably reevaluated their positions in the traditional class system, i.e. upper class, upper-middle class, middle class, lower-middle class or lower class. The survey used "lower class" to include those who were historically placed in the lower or lower-middle class and "upper class" for those who identified themselves as upper or upper-middle class. Respondents who considered themselves to be lower class had increased from 25 percent of the adult population in 2008 to about 32 percent in 2012. More Democrats than Republicans placed themselves in the lower class. These changes reflected corresponding overall decreases in the middle and upper classes (see Table 10.1).

TABLE 10.1 Self-defined class in the US, 2012

Class	% 2012	% 2008
Lower	32	25
Middle class	49	53
Upper	17	21

Source: adapted from the Pew Research Center, September 10, 2012.

The US is a very wealthy country and provides most of its people with one of the world's highest standards of living. According to the US Bureau of the Census, annual median family income of all races was $61,355 in 2007 (half of families received above this figure and half received less). But median income for African American and Latino families fell behind those of white and Asian workers, resulting in the formers' relative income inequality. Per capita disparities also occur in white and Asian male and female earnings and in per capita incomes for male and female African Americans and Latinos.

It is estimated that some 1 percent of US households own 30.4 percent of the nation's wealth, compared with 36.8 percent for the next highest 9 percent and 32.8 percent for the remaining 90 percent. The gap between rich and poor in the US is considerable. This inequality of income and wealth was seen in 2007 when 37.3 million Americans (12.5 per cent of the population) lived below the poverty lines of $21,947 for a family of four and $10,952 for a single person. These people included 24.5 percent African Americans, 10.2 percent Asians, 21.5 percent Latinos and 10.5 percent whites.

Economic inequality is due to actual increase in relative poverty; low wages for female workers; low income for some ethnic groups and the unskilled/semi-skilled; an under-class; the decline of trade unions; and low tax rates for the wealthy. Tax cuts (which benefit the affluent more than the poor), reduced welfare payments and an economic downturn may result in a society even more divided between the very rich and the very poor. Tax and austerity cuts were hotly debated topics in the 2012 presidential election campaign.

The contemporary economy

Taxation and federal budgets

Most of the US government's income (used for public spending) comes from income tax paid by individuals and social security contributions paid by firms and workers. Corporate taxes (by companies on profits) and excise duties are a relatively small part of total federal receipts.

Americans pay federal income tax and also property tax, sales tax and state income tax, in addition to medical and dental costs. Tax increases to pay for government spending arouse opposition, especially from the middle class and the rich, and may determine election results. But tax cuts can significantly reduce the provision of public services.

The median family with an income of $61,355 in 2007 paid about 25 percent of income in various taxes. Those with higher incomes pay proportionally more taxes. The amount of tax people pay depends on tax cuts, on tax breaks, on their ability to cope with complex tax forms and on their claims for a range of deductions, such as interest on home mortgages (loans to buy property) and medical expenses.

High government borrowing and spending in the 1980s and early 1990s resulted in large federal budget deficits (the gap between government income and expenditure). Budget deficits are seen as a sign of whether a government is out of control. Attempts to cut the deficit succeeded in the late 1990s and led to budget surpluses. But surpluses began to fall in 2001. The deficit (public debt) grew again from the early 2000s to the recession years of 2008–9, and had risen to –$1,296 trillion in 2011, or 8.7 percent of GDP.

Features of the contemporary economy

The US is the world's biggest economic power in terms of its Gross Domestic Product (GDP). This comprises the goods, services, capital and income that the country produces and in 2011 was an estimated $15.29 trillion with per capita GDP of $49,000. An estimated 1.2 percent of GDP was derived from forestry, agriculture and fishing; 19.2 percent from industry and manufacturing; and 79.6 percent from service industries.

The GDP shows that the US has a diversified economy. Its wealth reflects large natural resources (coal, oil, natural gas, copper, lead, phosphates, uranium, bauxite, iron, timber and hydroelectricity), agricultural output, industrial production and service-sector income. The US produces 25 percent of the world's agricultural products and manufactured goods (such as machinery, automotive components and vehicles, aircraft, chemicals and high-technology hardware). Traditional manufacturing industries (such as automobiles) have had setbacks and agriculture is under threat, but service sectors have expanded.

The US is the world's biggest importer and exporter. This fact and the size of its economy mean that the US is a crucial factor in global trade and business. But the US economy does not dominate as it did after the Second World War because of its recurrent weaknesses and because the economies of other competing countries have grown strongly.

Internationally, the US balance of trade with other countries has been in deficit (importing more goods than it has exported) since 1980. In 2009, for example, exports amounted to $1,056,043 million while imports were $1,559,625 million. These imports are in traditionally strong American sectors such as automobiles, petroleum, food and drink, machinery, iron and steel and consumer goods such as television sets, cameras and computers. The sectors have suffered because of strong and cheaper foreign competition. However, the deficit is helped to some extent by invisible exports such as financial services.

Globalization and weaknesses in its internal economy have undercut US advantages and forced it to become more interdependent with the economies of other countries and to reduce its protectionism. American investment capital and assets are an important element in the Canadian, Latin American, European and Asian economies. But there is also considerable foreign investment and asset-holding in the US domestic economy.

US governments and corporations aim at a cooperative and stable international trading environment. In 2011, America's main export partners were Canada (19 percent), Mexico (13.3 percent), China (7 percent) and Japan (4.5 percent), while it imported primarily from China (18.4 percent), Canada (14.2 percent), Mexico (11.7 percent), Japan (5.8 percent) and Germany (4.4 percent). The US finalized the GATT (General Agreement on Tariffs and Trade) talks in 1994, which aimed to promote freer and less protectionist world trade. However, conflicts continue between free trade and protectionism. US attempts to balance world trading blocs culminated in the North American Free Trade Agreement (NAFTA) in 1994 with Canada and Mexico. This was enlarged to 34 countries in 2001, including Latin America, and covers 800 million people. Another free trade agreement between the US and Costa Rica, the Dominican Republic, El Salvador, Guatemala, Honduras and Nicaragua (Central American Free Trade Agreement, CAFTA) was formed in 2006–9. The US is trying to stabilize its relationships with the European Union, China, India, Japan and other Pacific countries, to improve the economies of Third World countries and to increase trade enforcement. It is also pledged to complete the Trans-Pacific Partnership with Pacific Rim nations and is trying to finalize a free trade agreement with the EU.

The US economy experienced difficulties from the 1970s until the early 1990s due partly to international factors (such as competition) and partly to domestic conditions and recession. US prices and costs (particularly in manufacturing) did not equal those of other competing countries, growth rates varied considerably, inflation (increase in the average level of consumer prices) fluctuated and unemployment grew. It was argued that the poor performance of the US economy was due to an emphasis on traditional manufacturing industry. The country had not adapted adequately to a "post-industrial age," in which high-technology and service industries were a dominant part of GDP, or to a globalized economy.

Critics maintained that the US needed to modernize its factories, improve its products, reduce costs and prices, invest in services, high-technology industries and specialist training, and should promote industrial policies through government action. But Republicans wanted lower taxes and less regulation of the economy. As in most countries, the relationship of industry and manufacturing to the service sector was also problematic.

The economy recovered and grew from 1994 under the Clinton presidency and careful economic management by the Federal Reserve. Industry was restructured and productivity increased with reductions in the workforce, new technology, freer trade and tougher corporate management. Stable interest rates encouraged companies to invest and eased loan burdens. Unemployment and inflation fell. Smaller companies survived and 10 million new jobs were created. Prices and wages stabilized, productivity and growth improved, the dollar was strong and many people prospered in the mid- to late-1990s. However, much of

TABLE 10.2 US annual inflation rate, 2002–12 (CPI)

Year	%	Year	%
2002	1.6	2008	3.8
2003	2.3	2009	−0.4
2004	2.7	2010	1.6
2005	3.4	2011	3.2
2006	3.2	2012 (Oct)	2.2
2007	2.8		

Source: adapted from US Bureau of Labor Statistics, 2012.

the growth was in the service sector, which has many low-paid, unskilled or semi-skilled and part-time jobs.

The early twenty-first century saw another slowdown with growth and manufacturing weak and unemployment and inflation increasing. Consumer confidence slumped and the Federal Reserve in 2000–1 reduced interest rates to rectify the downturn. Moderate recovery took place in 2002 with the GDP growth rate rising to 2.4 percent, although the stock market declined sharply. In 2003, growth in output and productivity, the recovery of the stock market and GDP growth at 3.1 percent were promising signs. But in early 2004 job creation remained weak, jobs had been lost, interest rates rose and strong economic expansion was in doubt. Unemployment slowly continued to decline through 2004, although growth fluctuated and inflation grew to 2.7 percent. Long-term problems included inadequate investment in the economic infrastructure, trade and budget deficits and the stagnation or decline of family and individual incomes in the lower economic groups. Economic problems in 2004 were high oil prices, a weak dollar, uncertainty on the stock exchange and rising interest rates.

Difficulties continued with weak exports, low consumer spending and reduced factory output. The economy shrank and unemployment increased from 7.3 percent in 2008. A sub-prime credit crisis forced the government to rescue the private financial markets with public money. The Federal Reserve cut interest rates to 1 percent in October 2008 in an attempt to stimulate credit, promote economic growth and counter the threat of deflation (where falling prices conflict with low or no consumer spending). By 2012, the economy was still weak, although some positive signs were detected in growth, employment and the housing market. It was argued that economic recovery needed a balanced budget package of increased taxes on the rich and spending cuts to be agreed by the Obama administration and political parties in Congress. Otherwise, a so-called "fiscal cliff" would generate US and global recession. In the event, an increased tax rate for richer Americans was agreed, but substantial economic problems remained in the short term.

The workforce

The workforce (labor force) of 140 million (2009) is divided by occupation into managerial, professional and technical, sales and office, other services, manufacturing, extraction, transportation and crafts, and farming, forestry and fishing. It has mobility and flexibility, but not all workers gained from economic growth in the 1990s. The growth of technology has, for some critics, led to a "two-tier" labor market in which those at the bottom lack the professional, educational and technical skills of those at the top. The former, who may not be union members, do not receive pay rises, health insurance coverage and other benefits comparable to the latter. Since 1975, most gains in household income have gone to the top 20 percent of households. Less-skilled male workers have experienced weak wage growth, job insecurity, unemployment and falling living standards. Unemployment was high from 2002 and particularly so during the economic difficulties of 2007–12.

The economic status of women as employees and employers has improved. More women (59.5 percent of the workforce in 2008) work than in the 1960s. While the proportion of men with jobs has fallen, that of working women has risen. Male average earnings have fallen while those of women have grown. However, although women's wages gained on men's for the first time in the 1980s, women's earnings are still about 73 percent of men's ($810 median weekly earnings for men and $672 for women in 2010). Those women in part-time or unskilled work have the lowest financial rewards, but have suffered less than unskilled men because low-skilled men and women have different jobs.

Labor statistics show that about 14 percent of employed women work in managerial, administrative and executive positions, 18 percent in a professional specialty, 40 percent in technical, sales and administrative support, 17.4 percent in service occupations, 2.1 percent in production, craft and repair, 7.1 percent as operators and laborers and 1.1 percent in farming, forestry and fishing. Some

TABLE 10.3 US unemployment rate (percentage of workforce), 2002–12

Year	%	Year	%
2002	6.0	2008	7.3
2003	5.7	2009	9.9
2004	5.4	2010	9.4
2005	4.9	2011	8.5
2006	4.4	2012 (Oct)	7.9
2007	5.0		

Source: adapted from US Bureau of Labor Statistics, 2012.

occupations are comprised of more than 90 percent female workers, such as dental hygienists, preschool and kindergarten teachers, hairdressers, administrative assistants and secretaries, speech-language pathologists and licensed practical and vocational nurses.

Well-educated women have received the highest rewards and the earnings of the top 5 percent of working women have risen. The biggest gains have been for well-educated, high-income women (particularly those married to high-income husbands) who continue working after marriage. However, fewer wives of lower-skilled men have joined the workforce and the wages of lower-skilled working wives have risen more slowly than those of better-educated women. Family income has thus risen at the top levels and fallen at the bottom.

There has also been an increase in women business-owners. Their businesses are a growing and influential part of the corporate economy and are often entrepreneurial, small, home-operated and in the service or retail sector. Such firms can suffer from adverse economic conditions and a downturn. But women-owned businesses in the manufacturing and construction sectors are growing and more women are attending business schools.

Industry and manufacturing

Historically, manufacturing and industrial production has been a crucial factor in the US economy. Today, the sector is a leading global power, technologically advanced, very diversified and had 19.2 percent of US GDP in 2011. Important areas are the manufacture of heavy transport and automotive equipment (vehicles, aircraft and aerospace components), non-electrical goods, electrical machinery, food products, chemicals, steel, consumer goods, mining, lumber/timber, oil, telecommunications, electronics and high-technology hardware.

The traditional industrial and manufacturing heartland of the US is the Midwest region of the Great Lakes, southern Michigan, northern Ohio and Pennsylvania around Pittsburgh. Growth and production here has fluctuated, declined in some "rust bowl" areas or switched to high-technology industry, and other industrial regions have grown in the Northeast, Northwest and Southwest (California). These specialize in high-technology and computer manufactures. Other fast-growing industrial regions are the Southeast and Texas, where steel, chemical and high-technology industries have developed.

The industrial and manufacturing base is represented by corporations, such as General Motors (Detroit) and Ford (Michigan) in vehicles, Exxon (New York) in oil-refining, IBM (International Business Machines, New York) in computers, General Electric (Connecticut) in electronics and Boeing (Seattle) in aerospace and defense. However, the automobile industry had serious problems in 2008, with giants such as General Motors, Ford and Chrysler facing the prospect of bankruptcy and requiring government bailouts.

PLATE 10.2 Boeing 757 jet aircraft production line at the Renton, Washington State factory near Seattle, 1991.
(Matthew McVay/Corbis)

Industrial and manufacturing production growth rates fluctuated in the 2000s (-1.7 percent in 2007), but the US is still the world's second largest producer of industrial goods. In 2007, 13.7 million Americans were employed in manufacturing and together with others in mining, construction and chemicals made up 22.6 percent of the workforce (reduced to 20.3 percent in 2009). But, under recessionary forces, the number of blue-collar workers and industrial plants continues to decline.

Service industries

Service industries have grown faster than other sectors since the 1950s and are now the leading economic sector, with 79.6 percent of GDP in 2011 despite recession. This process is echoed in other industrialized countries and has encouraged debates about "post-industrial" societies as the manufacturing sector has contracted out services such as transportation, marketing, accounting and communications, which were previously performed in-house.

The service industries vary in size from small firms to large corporations. They have developed nationwide, but particularly in the Northeast. They include government services, business and health, banking, finance consultancy, computer and data processing, hotels, restaurants, leisure activities, trade, personal services (including child day-care) and communications. However, although more people are now employed in the service sector, many of them are in unskilled or semi-skilled and part-time positions and some aspects of the sector tend to be manager-intensive rather than labor-intensive.

It is argued that the service sector is financed by and dependent upon the consumer wealth and profits generated by technical advances in agriculture and manufacturing. The open question is whether the service sector can sustain itself and grow at a time when the industrial sector may decline, or whether complementary and balancing sectors will develop. However, many service companies are forecast to be the fastest-growing industries in the near future and most managed to survive the recession in 2008–9.

Agriculture, forestry and fisheries

Although US agriculture, forestry and fisheries have a large productivity, they contributed only some 1.2 percent to the GDP in 2011 and formed 0.6 percent of the labor force, down from 0.7 percent in 2009.

Agriculture

About 47 percent of the US land area is farmland and is devoted to crops and livestock. The Midwest is an important agricultural region in the country, with corn (maize) and wheat as its main crops and large-scale livestock and dairy farming in the upper Midwest states.

The South is a center of traditional crops, such as tobacco (the Southeast and Kentucky), corn and cotton (the South and Southwest). Its economy has now diversified and grown, so that Texas and Florida are the US's main providers of cattle, sheep, cotton and rice. The West is important for cattle and wheat-farming in the Great Plains, fruit and vineyards in the Pacific states and livestock herds in the Southwestern and Rocky Mountain states.

The US is one of the world's largest food producers and exporters (corn, wheat, soybeans and cotton) and is largely self-sufficient in farm produce, although there are some imports. In 2008 only 3.3 million people lived on the 2.2 million farms (less than 1 percent of the total population). Small subsistence farms have decreased, farm sizes have increased (agribusinesses) and labor has been reduced as competition, mechanization, technological advances and specialized farms have increased. High productivity has also resulted in occasional surpluses and reduced prices.

Agricultural exports declined in the 1980s as other world markets expanded. Farmers had difficulties because of import restrictions by foreign countries and high dollar values. But free-trade GATT and World Trade Organization (WTO) agreements on reduced tariff barriers have helped to stabilize the world position of American agriculture. However, global tariffs and protectionism still continue and more work needs to be done to liberalize world trade.

Forestry

Forests cover 33.1 percent of the US, mostly in the West but also in the South and the North. About 80 percent of the forests comprise softwoods and 20 percent hardwoods; two-thirds produce wood items and timber commercially. Some 70 percent of forests are privately owned, the federal government owns 20 percent and state or local government supervises the rest. In recent years, the environmental aspect of forestry has grown, with an emphasis on ecosystem management and increased recreational and wildlife uses of the public forests.

Fisheries

The US ranked fourth in 2007 after China, Peru and Indonesia among world fishing nations in terms of fish catches. Fishing fleets operate from ports on the Atlantic, the Pacific, the Gulf of Mexico and the Great Lakes. Alaska is the leading state and Louisiana has a large catch (chiefly shellfish), as do Texas and California. Massachusetts and Maine, important fishing centers since the colonial era, are major players in the fisheries industry. Their traditional fishing grounds (shared with the Atlantic provinces of Canada) are in danger of depletion.

Environmental issues

The federal Energy Information Administration (EIA) publishes independent environmental statistics and analysis, and the regional Energy Protection Agency (EPA) protects health and the environment by preparing and enforcing regulations based on laws passed by Congress. Public concerns about the environment are influenced by the US economy, political ideologies and the policies of politicians and business. Vehicle, industrial and domestic burning of fossil fuels (such as coal and oil) resulted in the US becoming the world's largest producer of carbon dioxide emissions. Air pollution and acid rain are widespread, and water pollution results from the run-off of agricultural pesticides and fertilizers, and from industrial waste. There are limited natural fresh-water resources in much of the western part of the country and desertification has occurred. Farmers have suffered from dust bowl conditions in recent years due to drought, rising temperatures and over-use of the land. Storms, hurricanes and heat waves have increased fears about climate change and global warming.

Despite signing, but not ratifying, the Kyoto Climate Change Protocol 1997–2005, critics argued that the US had not demonstrated a willingness to tackle domestic and international environmental concerns. Nevertheless, in 2012 carbon dioxide emissions in the US were at their lowest level for 20 years and the country led the world in reducing emissions over the previous six years from their peak in 2007. Arguably these improvements were partly due to a US switch to heating by natural gas, which emits less carbon, and partly to a retreat from coal usage. Hydraulic fracturing ("fracking") has accessed shale gas and oil locked in underground rocks and delivered reduced gas prices. Renewable energy resources, such as wind turbines, biofuels and solar panels also contributed to reduced emissions. But the burning of fossil fuels continues and contributes to global warming, and it is unclear how long the improvement and recoverable supplies will last as energy consumption increases. The Doha 2012 UN Climate Change Conference did not follow up the Kyoto Protocol by considering what concrete practical global action was needed.

There are contrasting environmental views in the US. A Harris poll in 2005 found that 74 percent of respondents felt that environmental improvements must be made despite the cost to the economy. Although others agreed that the environment was getting worse, there were disagreements about its precise state and what remedial action could or should be taken. A 2008 Pew Research Center study found that belief in the existence of global warming had decreased and a Gallup poll in 2010 also showed increased skepticism. Respondents were less worried about global warming, less convinced that it was happening, and thought that scientists were uncertain about its existence.

However, in an apparent change of attitude, the fall 2011 National Survey of American Opinion on Climate Change reported that the number of believers in global warming had reached the highest level since 2009. Some 62 percent of respondents thought that there was significant evidence of average temperature rises, while 26 percent did not.

A GfK Roper Consulting Green Gauge survey in 2011 examined public attitudes on climate change and tried to assess individual behavior. It found that increased environmental knowledge meant that fewer Americans believed that they could individually make a big difference, but that 46 percent thought that they could contribute a small personal effort. Three in four respondents thought businesses should be environmentally friendly in their production processes despite economic problems. The survey argued that behavior change and green adaptation are possible in areas where they make practical and financial sense.

In immediate terms, 58 percent of respondents sorted their garbage; 29 percent bought products made from or packaged in recycled materials; and 18 percent reduced automobile usage by using mass transport. Some 33 percent were optimistic and 18 percent were pessimistic about the environmental future. However, although 48 percent of respondents thought that concern for the environment was somewhat important, an increasing number thought that economic security should be put before environmental protection.

Financial and industrial institutions

American economic development was not accompanied by the creation of national financial institutions. Governments avoided centralizing the economic system until the twentieth century, and most financial and industrial institutions operated as private and local concerns.

Corporations and entrepreneurs

The corporations of the nineteenth and early twentieth centuries, which were owned by individuals such as Henry Ford (automobiles), John D. Rockefeller (oil) and Andrew Carnegie (steel), and smaller corporations under personal or family proprietors, have decreased in numbers. Many businesses today are owned by financial conglomerates or multinational companies, which invest in company shares for profit.

The actual running of the businesses is often done by professional accountants, executives or managers who may own only a small percentage of the corporation's stock or shares. The rise of an American executive and managerial culture was aided by the creation of business management schools, which may be separate institutions or sometimes attached to universities, and which initiated degrees such as the Master of Business Administration (MBA) and taught business techniques to their students.

Big corporations such as Exxon, Walmart, General Motors, Ford Motor, General Electric, Citigroup, IBM and AT&T now dominate American business and influence consumer patterns. Smaller corporations may be taken over by larger ones and large corporations expand through mergers in the pursuit of markets and profits.

Small companies account for three-quarters of the corporate system and are an important part of the business world. They generate more new jobs than larger corporations, tend to be created by entrepreneurs or are family concerns and are often associated with the service sector. Some succeed and some fail, such as the dot.com businesses in the 1990s.

The ethos of American business attracts people who want to succeed and are prepared to work hard to achieve material success, careers and status, although some Americans are not sympathetic to this culture. Workers and businesspeople had problems in the early 1990s under the pressures of domestic and international recession. Although the financial and business markets improved with the upturn in the economy from 1994, they experienced difficulties in 2000–4 and more seriously with the sub-prime credit crisis in 2008. Banks and financial institutions suffered and there was large unemployment. Prominent among those affected was Citigroup, once the biggest and most powerful company and bank in the world. It suffered huge losses in the global financial crisis of 2008; was rescued in a stimulus package by the US government; and now ranks twentieth globally.

Wall Street

"Wall Street" is the financial center of the US, and is situated in lower and mid-town Manhattan, in New York City. It comprises business institutions, such as stockbrokers and financial companies (for example, Merrill Lynch, which was sold to Bank of America in 2008 as a result of sub-prime write-downs), banks, insurance corporations, commodity exchanges (that deal in coffee, cotton, metal or corn) and the New York Stock Exchange (NYSE). These institutions deal with huge sums of money and control and invest much of Americans' capital. Corporate America's performance in 2000–8 left much to be desired, and there was evidence of fraudulent behavior, dubious accounting practices, insider dealing, greed and incompetence. A public complaint after the financial markets had been saved by a government bailout in 2008 was that the banks were not eager to start lending again, particularly to small businesses that needed help. A Harris poll in February 2010 reported that only 8 percent of respondents had a great deal of confidence in Wall Street.

Large corporations are dependent for their financing and prosperity upon stock exchanges on which stocks and shares in selected businesses are bought and sold. This system, as well as raising investment money, is an important indicator

PLATE 10.3 Traders work on the floor of the New York Stock Exchange, 2011, where stocks and bonds are bought and sold.
(Keystone USA-ZUMA/Rex Features)

of businesses' financial standing. New York City's two stock exchanges (the NYSE and the American Stock Exchange) handle the majority of stock sales and purchases in the US. The computerized NASDAQ deals with hi-tech shares but does not have a trading floor like the NYSE on Wall Street. The performance of the stock market has varied considerably in the 2000s and has been increasingly influenced by international factors, such as rising oil prices.

The NYSE (founded by the Buttonwood Agreement in 1792) comprises about 1,300 members who trade in stocks and bonds either for themselves or as agents for clients. It is a market for the buying and selling of these instruments that are listed on the exchange's trading register and are sold to the highest bidder, and whose value can fluctuate. A company must have a specified amount of stock and a minimum turnover of trade before it can be listed on the NYSE.

The NYSE is internationally known for its Dow Jones Industrial Average. This is a list that contains the prices of stocks and bonds in selected industrial and commercial companies on the exchange. It is adjusted throughout the working day and its movements are shown in points. The Dow Jones is influential and international financiers, investors and governments see it as an accurate indicator of the US's economic health.

The banking system

Americans have long been suspicious of banks and market traders. The 1929 Wall Street Crash, when banks collapsed and clients lost money, still affects people, and fears revive when the stock market performs badly as in 1987, in 2001 after the 9/11 terrorist attacks on New York and in 2008 with the credit crisis. A Gallup poll in June 2012 found that 9 percent of respondents had a great deal of confidence in the banks and 12 percent had quite a lot.

US law is supposed to regulate the banking system and curb any excessive growth of individual banks. There are about 8,600 different commercial banks in the US, which provide personal and corporate financial services for clients. Some banks are incorporated (or licensed) under national charter and are known as National Banks. Others are regulated under state charters. The banking system has been increasingly deregulated to allow other financial competitors, and banks have moved into new (and riskier) areas such as securities trading, currency-dealing and insurance. There are also many non-bank institutions, such as personal credit groups and savings-and-loans associations.

It is argued that the banking system is not as closely regulated at federal and state level as it should be, particularly at a time when financial institutions are expanding and when fraud and bank collapses still regularly occur. Some critics argue for more accountability and increased control and regulation over American financial markets. Others want to preserve an unrestricted market and the free enterprise economic system.

optimism. For example, a 1995 *Time*/CNN poll found that 86 percent of respondents agreed with the statement "People have to realize that they can only count on their own skills and abilities if they're going to win in this world."

Exercises

Explain and examine the significance of the following names and terms:

AFL–CIO	Wall Street	entrepreneurs
Federal Reserve	NYSE	New Deal
Dow Jones Industrial Average	anti-trust laws	corporations
recession	inflation	monopoly
service industries	NAFTA	trade balance
budget deficit	GDP	deregulation
Rockefeller	NASDAQ	Roaring Twenties
blue-collar workers	Bretton Woods	raw materials
"fiscal cliff"	the Great Depression	globalization
free trade	tariffs	Adam Smith

Write short essays on the following questions:

1. What is meant by the American "free enterprise" economic system? Examine its advantages and disadvantages.

2. Comment critically on the present state of the US economy.

3. What do the opinion polls in this chapter tell us about people's attitudes to the economic system?

4. What are the strengths and weaknesses of the US trade-union movement?

Further reading

Brenner, R. (2002) *The Boom and the Bubble: The US Economy Today*, London: Verso.

Chandler, A.D. Jr. (1993) *The Visible Hand: The Managerial Revolution in American Business*, Cambridge, MA: Belknap Press of Harvard University Press.

Dethloff, H.C. (1997) *The United States and the Global Economy Since 1945*, New York: Harcourt Brace.

GfK Roper Consulting Green Gauge US Survey/ Johnson, S.C. (2011) *The Environment: Public Attitudes and Individual Behavior – A Twenty-Year Evolution*.

Gordon, J.S. (2005) *Empire of Wealth: The Epic History of American Economic Power*, New York: Harper Perennial.

Heilbroner, R. and Singer, A. (1999) *The Economic Transformation of America: 1600 to the Present*, New York: Harcourt Brace.

Krugman, P. (2004) *The Great Unravelling: From Boom to Bust in Three Scandalous Years*, London: Penguin.

Lind, M. (2012) *Land of Promise: An Economic History of the United States*, New York: Harper.

Stiglitz, J. (2002) *Globalization and its Discontents*, New York: Norton.

Websites

AFL–CIO: www.aflcio.org
Class and social trends: www.pewsocialtrends.org
Economic statistics, income and poverty: www.census.gov
Environment: www.brookings.edu/papers/2012/02/climate-change-rabe-borick
Institute for Policy Studies – Reports: www.ips-dc.org
New York Stock Exchange: www.nyse.com
US Bureau of Labor Statistics: www.bls.gov
US Bureau of Economic Analysis (BEA): www.bea.gov
US Federal Reserve: www.federalreserve.gov
US Department of Labor: www.dol.gov
US Government's Official Web Portal: www.usa.gov
US Department of State (US Economy): infousa.state.gov
US Government Printing Office: www.access.gpo.gov/su_docs/budget/index.html
infousa.state.gov/economy/econ_trade.html

Chapter 11

Social services

- Social services history
- The organization of contemporary social services
- Public social services
- The needy and the poverty line
- Voluntary services
- Healthcare
- Housing
- Attitudes to social services
- *Exercises*
- *Further reading*
- *Websites*

This chapter examines the history of social services in the US, their structural organization and the facilities that are provided for individuals and groups by the public, private and voluntary sectors. They include healthcare, retirement pensions, unemployment payments, housing needs, disability allowances and "welfare" aid.

The public sector supplies state and federal benefits and aid to individuals and their families on both contributory and non-contributory bases. Private sector businesses, such as hospitals, deliver services to people who pay for them out of their own capital or from insurance policies paid for by premiums. The voluntary non-profit sector and charities are additional to the public and private frameworks; are funded mainly from personal and corporate donations; and provide aid to those in need, mostly without payment.

The availability and nature of US social services has changed under the influence of historical events and the attitudes of people and politicians. They are also conditioned by experiences with the actual workings of social institutions and the demands of social life.

Americans have traditionally seen themselves as self-reliant and independent. Social provision has been a personal matter and the responsibility of individuals or families rather than state or federal institutions. People are still expected to look after themselves or buy services from a private-enterprise market, which is theoretically supposed to satisfy demand.

But, since the 1930s, there has been a greater awareness that some people (and not only the poor) are sometimes unable to provide for themselves because of economic and social circumstances. Reformers have felt that the delivery of social help should be a national responsibility. The scope of many services has consequently changed and been extended to new areas of social security, welfare assistance, insurance, healthcare and housing needs.

Such provisions have not created a welfare state similar to models in some European nations, which often have a centrally organized, comprehensive and universally accessible social services apparatus financed by general taxation and workers' national insurance contributions. Critics have long argued that while the percentage of the Gross Domestic Product (GDP) devoted to private and public social and health programs in the US is one of the largest in the world, the actual system is patchy, expensive and unequal.

The social services have grown since the 1930s and are now diverse and complex. It is argued by some that a universal system would be more rational, responsive to need and cover all citizens. Others oppose such proposals on traditional grounds of self-reliance, private markets and questions of funding. Spending on public and welfare services has increased since the 1960s and the country does help some of its most needy inhabitants, such as people with disabilities, children, the sick, war veterans, the unemployed and pensioners. Nevertheless, Americans generally still expect other individuals to provide for themselves. Government policies in 1996 restricted existing welfare programs, suggesting that the US was moving away from European models and towards more privatized services. But renewed calls for improvement resulted in major legislation in 2010 for a reformed healthcare system.

Social services history

Four hundred years ago, the US was primarily a scattered rural society in which most Americans worked in farming and there were few large urban centers. Until the 1930s, there were no widespread public services for the population. The large majority had to be self-reliant in providing for their own social, health, employment and housing needs.

Free market economic theories and images of the independent farmer and sturdy frontiersman conditioned American mythologies. But early pioneers could be cooperative and provided collective support and protection, as did many Native American communities. Such contrasting images illustrate the tension in US life between individualism and communalism. They also affect how Americans respond to debates about provision of social services today.

Industrialization and urbanization increased in the late eighteenth and nineteenth centuries, bringing wealth to many people but misery to others. Social assistance was still largely private and individualistic or sometimes provided by voluntary charities, such as the aid given by ethnic and religious groups to their members. However, a small amount of help was also supplied by state and local governments. This mixture of services was conditioned by the tradition of self-reliance. There was (and still is) a distinction made in the US between the "deserving" poor who could be helped to better themselves through aid and the "undeserving" poor who were allegedly unwilling to work and improve their own conditions.

Most Americans did not approve of central government organizing too many of society's affairs and jealously protected their independence. Politicians avoided intervention in, and government spending on, social help. Consequently, no adequate national system of public social services developed in the late nineteenth and early twentieth centuries.

The existing system of self-reliance, fragmented aid and laissez-faire social philosophy (letting things take their own course) could not cope with the economic collapse, large-scale unemployment and poverty caused by the 1930s Great Depression, which followed the 1929 stock market crash. The resources of private, public and voluntary organizations proved insufficient in the 1930s when an estimated 40 percent of the population lived in relative poverty.

The situation improved with President Franklin D. Roosevelt's New Deal in the mid-1930s. Roosevelt wanted to rectify faults in the economy and to provide social protection. Many contemporary government aid programs stem from his policies, which recognized federal responsibility for the poor and needy. Regulatory agencies were created. Social Security legislation in 1935 established pension and unemployment benefits for workers, which depended on the contributions paid by employees during their working lives. The Wagner Act protected labor rights to collective bargaining and the Fair Labor Standards Act introduced a minimum wage and restricted working hours. The Works Progress Administration provided jobs in public sector programs for the unemployed and tried to improve the social and economic problems of African and Native Americans.

However, these programs were not comprehensive and were directed towards people who were willing to work. Publicly-financed non-contributory welfare

PLATE 11.1 Men waiting outside gangster Al Capone's soup kitchen for the needy, Chicago, November 13, 1930, which distributed free food to the unemployed during the Great Depression.
(Bettmann/Corbis)

was unpopular in 1930s America, and there was antagonism towards those who would not help themselves. But new federal welfare programs, Aid to Families with Dependent Children (AFDC) and General Assistance (GA), did help the needy, families, children and people with disabilities.

After the 1930s, reformers argued for increased social services. Federal and state governments became more involved in planning social policies. Government thinking changed as publicly-funded programs expanded after the Second World War. Groups agitated for more assistance. War veterans, for example, were given federal medical, educational and housing benefits (the "GI Bill of Rights"). A new culture of "entitlement" or "rights" to public services became apparent. There was also a feeling in some quarters that the US should be able to care for more of its citizens, particularly those who were in need.

Although the federal government gradually became more concerned with providing public social services, this expansion was piecemeal and a response to need and popular pressure, rather than a commitment to a consistent national policy. Nevertheless, social programs were developing and covered greater numbers of people.

From the 1960s to the 1980s, more federal and state money was spent on public social services. Medicare (1965) provided healthcare for the over-65s, Medicaid (1965) organized health services for the poor under-65s and a food-stamp program gave coupons (electronic debit cards since 2004) to the needy for the purchase of food in specified shops. New government departments, such as the US Department of Housing and Urban Development, Department of Transportation and Corporation for Public Broadcasting supervised social developments.

President Lyndon B. Johnson (1963–9) introduced programs in his "War on Poverty" and "Great Society" campaigns, which were intended to alleviate need and suffering. He introduced initiatives (such as preschool "Head Start" classes for children of low-income families, funding for school districts and grants to enable poor students to enter college) that attacked poverty and unemployment through education, job training and regional development. However, such policies did not create an American welfare state. They were intended as opportunities for people who were prepared to work and better themselves.

Nevertheless, the reforms formed a basis for future public social services, and agencies and departments were established to implement the new programs. In this expansive climate, some of the poor and needy increasingly came to regard non-contributory welfare and healthcare as a right and the number of claimants grew.

Spending on public social services increased through the 1970s and 1980s and there was a move away from defense and military expenditure. But presidents after Johnson differed in their attitudes to social service and welfare schemes. It also became more difficult to persuade Congress to allocate public money to such provision. Economic problems by 1980, such as rising inflation, curtailed new social legislation.

Republican President Reagan (1981–9) tried to reduce the cost of public programs. He wanted Americans to be responsible for their own lives through self-help and to depend less on government aid. However, the cost of Social Security and welfare schemes to the federal budget increased. Public social programs grew relatively quickly, but Republican administrations have not been keen to raise income taxes to pay for them.

The George H.W. Bush administration (1989–93) attempted to reduce public spending, but was forced to meet increased demand by tax rises. The Clinton administration (1993–2001) tried to introduce universal healthcare in 1993, financed by individual and corporate contributions, which would improve the delivery of health services by controlling costs. This reform collapsed due to opposition from the public and business. Instead, there were demands from a Republican Congress for greater curbs on social services spending.

In 1996, Clinton changed US welfare policy by cutting public spending on AFDC. Some saw this as an unraveling of New Deal programs, returning the US to semi-privatized social services and negatively affecting large numbers of people, such as families and children. Others argued that the welfare reforms moved the US positively from a system of debilitating non-contributory benefit entitlement to one of personal responsibility.

Welfare aid was devolved from federal authorities to the individual states in 1996–7. There are now different programs (Temporary Assistance for Needy Families, TANF) and scales of help. Federal grants have been directed by the states to training schemes and many people have moved from welfare into jobs, education and training. But economic downturns and rising unemployment can create problems for individuals and families.

Opinion polls during the George W. Bush (2001–9) administrations suggested conflicting attitudes to social services. The public (if not business) seemed to favor universal healthcare financed out of increased taxation but were lukewarm on attempts to ease the cost of drugs for pensioners. Bush advocated a partial privatization of Social Security and welfare programs to offset the costs of the system, which was initially welcomed and later opposed. His proposal to channel federal funds in order to deliver social welfare was controversial because it gave state money directly to religious bodies. More workers are also needed to cover federal pension costs for the growing number of pensioners, and critics warned that it might be necessary to raise taxes or lower pensions progressively to prevent the collapse of Social Security, Medicare and Medicaid by 2041.

There was opposition when the Obama administration passed the Patient Protection and Affordable Care Act (PPACA) through Congress in 2010 (see below). The Act was intended to extend health insurance coverage to some 50 million uninsured Americans by 2014. It was a landmark reform of healthcare to equal the passing of Medicare and Medicaid. Most of its provisions were narrowly upheld by the US Supreme Court in 2012.

The organization of contemporary social services

Americans rely for their social protection on contributory and non-contributory federal and state programs (public sector); insurance-based services paid for by individuals or workplace groups (private sector); and help given by publicly-supported voluntary bodies to the needy. These sectors overlap and people may receive help from several of them at various times as they privately insure themselves by paying for healthcare and pension plans in addition to contributing to federal Social Security and employer–employee benefit packages. They also benefit from subsidies in education, home loans, tax breaks and (now) healthcare.

Social services in the public sector are large budget items for government, but the quality of some public services varies from state to state. This is partly because of "matching funds" policies (whereby states have to equal federal grants or groups compete in matching programs and finance within a state); the wealth of individual states; their prioritization of programs; states' cost of living and their need to produce balanced budgets.

Budget responsibilities for the main public-sector organization are allocated between Washington, DC and the states. At the federal level, public services are administered through government programs and different departments, such as the Department of Health and Human Services. Its creation as the Department of Health, Education and Welfare (HEW) in 1953 acknowledged national responsibility for, and the importance of, social services. This federal organization has a large number of departments and responsibilities.

The state and local levels implement and deliver their own and federal public social services. These are also often divided between separate bodies, although in some states there are umbrella agencies that combine health, welfare and other related programs.

Public social services

Public social services constitute a complex patchwork of provisions, but are generally divided into two parts. The first is the Social Security system, to which workers contribute during their working lives and through which benefits are earned. The second includes people who receive assistance based on need. This is awarded according to means or income ("means-testing"), but is not tied to contributions, and is generally known as "welfare."

Some citizens depend upon a welfare safety net based on public funds. Others debate its bureaucratic complexity, inefficiency, incompleteness, effects on the morals and initiative of welfare clients, abuse and cost. Public sector services (particularly in healthcare, Social Security and welfare) continue to be controversial issues in American politics.

Social Security benefits

Social Security is the largest social services program in the US. It is administered from Washington and in 2010 its payments to beneficiaries amounted to $670,872 million. But critics allege that it keeps only 40 percent of people over 65 out of economic difficulties.

Social Security originated in the 1935 Social Security Act. It is a social insurance program and covers one main area: the Old Age, Survivors, Disability and Health Insurance program (OASDHI). This is concerned with benefits, such as retirement, pensions, disability, healthcare, survivorship and death. Employees and employers each pay one half of the Social Security tax and the self-employed pay the whole of the tax during their working lives.

Workers (and their families) receive benefits based on these contributions. They include, for example, pensions on retirement at the age of 65 at an annual average of $11,232 in 2009 for a single worker on $20,000 earnings and average annual disability payments of $11,496 for a single worker at age 55 on $20,000 earnings in 2009.

Medical care for the elderly over 65 (Medicare) is usually grouped under Social Security. It was formed in 1965, covered much of the costs for the hospital medical treatment of 46 million elderly (over 65) and disabled people in 2009 and cost $430,093 million. Because of the incomplete coverage of Medicare, many elderly people cannot afford the full cost of some types of treatment, particularly the most expensive and long-term. They usually need additional private insurance or savings for the balance of medical fees. The 2010 PPACA legislation created a panel to study Medicare spending and attempts to find ways to reduce waste and fraud in the system.

Illness, accident and unemployment payments are also included under Social Security. The US Treasury holds a trust fund for Unemployment Compensation, which is organized by the Department of Labor with each state administering its own program. Most workers are covered; unemployment benefits generally last for up to 26 weeks; and the general compensation is between 50 and 70 percent of an average weekly pre-tax wage. In 2009, the average weekly benefit was $309.58.

Opinion polls have recently ranked Social Security as a prominent concern for respondents. A Harris poll in January 2007 found that Social Security is very important to the American public, with 88 percent saying they would support reform to ensure that the Social Security Fund had enough money to provide benefits for all Americans. However, a CBS News poll in October 2007 reported that 30 percent of respondents thought that Social Security was in crisis, in serious trouble (36 percent) or in some trouble (26 percent). A Harris poll in 2005 found that 58 percent of respondents were in favor of allowing an effective privatization of the program by allowing individual investments of Social Security taxes in the stocks or bond market. But, according to PollingReport.com, a number of other

PLATE 11.2 Protestors in favor of protecting and continuing Social Security campaign at the US Capitol, Washington, DC.
(Bettmann/Corbis)

polls in 2006 and 2005 disapproved of this idea, with majorities of between 60 and 62 percent. Fifty-one percent of respondents in a July 2005 CBS News/*New York Times* poll did not believe that the Social Security Fund will have the money to provide the expected benefits on retirement; 81 percent thought that it was the government's responsibility to provide a decent standard of living for the elderly; but 67 percent were opposed to raising the retirement age to preserve Social Security.

Social Security is problematic because more workers are needed to support a growing elderly population and because of the cost of the system. It has been estimated that the fund will be exhausted by 2041 and that pensions will be progressively reduced. The future of Medicare is more precarious and the program may be exhausted by 2020. Alternatives to collapse of both programs might be higher taxes or privatization. However, as part of the 2010 healthcare reforms, Medicare benefits for the old and disabled were increased in 2011 and drug companies were obliged to pay annual fees.

Since Social Security may not cover all the bills payable for old age, illness and unemployment, many Americans have to call upon additional private resources, such as savings, investments and insurance. Some employers and unions may also provide further insurance services for employees (retirement, unemployment, health and life insurance), sometimes based on employer/union and worker contributions.

Welfare programs

Public debate about poverty in the US led to federal legislation from the 1960s. This provided financial help, work, training and rehabilitation for the needy and poor, resources to house and feed the homeless and healthcare for the sick. Aid was dependent upon means-testing of individuals to prove lack of financial provision. The cost of these programs now amounts to some 6 percent of the federal budget.

Expenditure on welfare programs has been traditionally shared by federal, state and local governments. Generally, federal funds or grants are distributed (devolved) to the states, which should spend equal (or matching) amounts of money to the federal funds. There is no uniform system and each state organizes its own program. It defines, on the basis of a balanced budget, which families and individuals qualify for assistance in terms of needs.

Until 1996, the main federal welfare programs, or non-contributory aid to the needy, consisted of Medicaid, AFDC and food stamps. There are other programs under the GA scheme that provide income support, cash grants, housing aid, Supplemental Security Income (SSI) for the elderly poor, school meals and help with other basic necessities.

Medicaid is a direct federal health program, which started in 1965. It gives federal grants to states for the free health treatment of the poor and needy under 65, blind and disabled people and families with dependent children, who lack the money or insurance to pay for the service. Because of matching-fund policies, the scope of Medicaid varies among states with some providing more aid than others. In 2008 it catered for 60 million persons with families at a cost of $356.3 billion and covered some 41 percent of all births in the US and 40 percent of all nursing facility care. But it was argued that Medicaid covered only about 40 percent of the poor, the working poor were often outside the claims limits and it was estimated that 25 percent of the uninsured did not sign up for it. Under the PPACA 2010 the poorest Americans without insurance will be included in Medicaid (see healthcare below).

Aid to Families with Dependent Children (AFDC) was until 1996 a program of federal aid to the poor. Aid to families (including single parents) with children was based on need. Payments varied between states, with Southern states generally paying less than Northern ones. By 1996, AFDC supported 15 million persons, of whom two-thirds were children.

AFDC was abolished in 1996. Welfare responsibility passed to the states, which receive federal block grants to run their own programs, called Temporary

Assistance for Needy Families (TANF). The states determine eligibility and benefit levels. There is now a five-year lifetime limit on welfare benefits, which are not granted automatically, and most fit adults are required to work after two years on welfare. In 2009, TANF payments covered some 4.2 million recipients. The states with most TANF recipients in 2008 were California, Illinois, Michigan, New York and Ohio.

As part of TANF schemes, "Workfare" (work plus welfare) programs require that welfare recipients, such as single parents, should be prepared to work (often in public service jobs), take part in job training schemes or attend educational courses. Care facilities are sometimes provided for families with small children, but these are often inadequate. Such programs were intended to encourage recipients to move off welfare and into secure jobs.

The "food stamp" program derives from the 1964 Food Stamp Act. It provides food aid for eligible needy people and their families who have assets of less than $2,000 and who lack an adequate diet. Historically, recipients received coupons or stamps that were used to buy food in approved shops at an average rate of one-third of its normal price. Paper food stamps were a symbol of poverty in the US but were changed to Electronic Benefit Transfer (EBT) cards in 2004 and are limited to a period of three months unless the recipients are working. The Department of Agriculture annually defines an adequate low-cost diet and administers the federal-financed program through state governments.

In 2009, when housing foreclosures, job losses and rising prices were added to a credit squeeze, 34 million Americans relied on the food program to feed themselves and their families, an increase from 28 million in 2008. In March 2010, the program reached an all-time high of 40.2 million at a monthly cost of $6.3 billion. But price increases have reduced the value of the benefit, which has not increased relative to costs, and people are unable to purchase food as they did previously.

This welfare system provides some assistance for the needy, but people who are unemployed for long periods (and who have no resources) may receive little help from the government. Employment is therefore a crucial factor for most Americans and determines their ability to provide for themselves. The restructuring of AFDC means that after two years on welfare an individual must find a job. Hardship exemptions are available for the very poor who cannot find work when the benefit ends. But most people will be dependent on obtaining jobs, which tend to be low-paid. The successful employment rate among welfare recipients increased from 11 percent in 1996 to 32.5 percent in 2006, but it had dropped to 25.9 percent in 2008 when the credit crisis broke and unemployment was high.

According to the US Department of Health and Human Services in October 2012, 4.1 percent of the population was on "welfare" at a cost of $131.9 billion. Thirty-eight percent were white, 39.8 percent were black, 15.7 percent were Latino and 2.4 percent were Asian.

The needy and the poverty line

Welfare payments in the US have historically been made to people who do not have the resources to live at an appropriate minimum standard. Eligibility for many welfare programs is based on the "official poverty level," which is calculated annually by the Federal Social Security Administration. It determines earned income levels below which a household is classified as "poor," exclusive of non-cash benefits such as food cards. The weighted average poverty threshold for a family of four in 2009 was $21,947 and $10,952 for single people.

The number of people living in poverty fluctuates because of unemployment and the state of the economy. Figures from the US Bureau of the Census have reported that the percentage of those below the poverty line rose from 13 percent in 1980 to 13.5 percent in 1990 and then declined to 11.3 percent in 2000 before rising again with the sub-prime crisis in 2008 to a 15-year-high of 14.3 percent in 2009. This last figure amounted to 43.6 million Americans of whom 25.8 per cent were black, 12.5 per cent were Asian, 12.3 percent were white and 25.3 per cent were Latino. In 2009, the statistics also showed that 20.7 percent of children under 18 and 8.9 percent of people aged 65 and over were defined as poor, although the latter group had declined from 10.1 percent in 2005.

Poverty remains a reality for a sizeable minority of Americans who have low or no incomes. The poorest and most deprived people are concentrated in inner-city areas, but poverty is also a feature of rural regions. Poor households may consist of single parents with children, or people who may be pensioners, disabled or unemployed.

A tax aid designed to lift the working poor (with or without dependent children) above the poverty line is the earned-income tax credit (EITC) established in 1975. Instead of facing higher taxes as their incomes increase, low-earning individuals can claim EITC and qualify for a tax credit up to a maximum wage. This means that they receive lump-sum payments or refunds from the Internal Revenue Service (IRS). More people would be in poverty without this aid, but the working poor are still a vulnerable group.

Although fewer Americans are poor today than in the past, the poverty rate for 2009 of 43.6 million people was very considerable and the gap between rich and poor is arguably increasing. Critics maintain that the federal government should provide funds to eradicate poverty. Others feel that welfare programs are expensive and inefficient and do not give incentives to the poor to help themselves. It is argued that an "under-class" has developed that is dependent on welfare ("dependency culture") and includes disaffected people who have opted out of national life. The 1996 restriction of federal welfare may break the cycle of dependency, but its success assumes growth in the national economy and the creation of jobs.

Single-parent families

US Census figures showed that in 2009 there were 78.9 million family households in the US. Of these, 26.2 percent were families headed by a single person, with 19.4 million children under 18, up from 13 percent in 1970. The vast majority of single-parent families (22.8 percent) were headed by a mother only (divorced, widowed or never married) and 3.4 percent were headed by a father only. In ethnic terms, 21.1 percent of white children under 18 lived with a single parent, as did 53.6 percent of black children, 49 per cent of American Indian children, 16 per cent of Asian children and 27.4 percent of Latino children.

Single-parent families have often been associated with the needy, the poverty line, welfare programs and minority groups. But the 2000 census, for example, reported that there were 2 million single-father families (where 84 percent of fathers were employed) and 9.7 million single-mother families (where 72.9 percent of the mothers were employed). Some single-parent families have incomes above the official poverty level and their children receive only a minimum of welfare payments such as free school meals.

Voluntary services

Given the inability of federal and state governments to meet all the social requirements of the people, the existence of voluntary organizations that help those in need continues to be important. They are a complementary third sector to the private and public sectors.

A range of social services is organized by local and national bodies, which help the disadvantaged and campaign on their behalf. Historically, contributions (with tax breaks or relief) by Americans to such bodies are generous and 75 percent of households give money to them. Nationally, institutions such as the Rockefeller and Ford foundations and other smaller bodies perform important roles in funding care research and health and welfare programs.

On a grassroots level, voluntary organizations (such as charities and churches) and

PLATE 11.3 A Franciscan nun cuts a girl's hair at St. Raphael Social Service Center, Hamilton, Ohio, 1995.
(Steve Liss/Time & Life/Getty)

unpaid volunteers are crucial for people in local communities. They provide professional and non-professional aid; organize help for sick or elderly people; run hospitals, care centers, clinics, retirement homes and shelters for the homeless; and visit old, disabled and needy people. They give what is often much-needed assistance and comfort. An estimated 50 percent of Americans over 18 (particularly retired persons) do volunteer work.

Healthcare

The delivery of healthcare is structurally divided into private, public and voluntary sectors. But although the US is the world's highest per capita spender on healthcare, amounting in 2008 to an estimated 16.2 percent of its GDP ($2,338 billion or $7,681 per person), it is argued that this has not given better medical outcomes overall, some people are excluded and there is insufficient preventative care. The quality of medical provision is varied and complex. Available and adequate care depends upon wealth, gender, ethnicity, residence or location, and insurance coverage. Wealthy white males in affluent neighborhoods and some of the poor and elderly may be well covered by private and public facilities respectively. But many people under 65, those on average incomes, females, those from a non-white background and people who live in rural areas or inner-city locations may have difficulties in obtaining satisfactory healthcare. Healthcare has been traditionally led by the private sector, with many workers and their employers benefiting from health insurance policies that can facilitate speedier access to treatment and more advanced medical technologies. Those who historically could not afford insurance or capital payments were often restricted to emergency treatment or the use of Medicaid and Medicare.

In 2010, it was estimated that about 84 percent of Americans (and their families) had some type of private sector health insurance or support against the cost of health treatment. The remainder received public sector healthcare from state hospitals, government programs, such as Medicaid and the Social Security subscription-based Medicare, or voluntary non-profit hospitals. In 2009, 50.7 million people or 16.7 percent of the population (an increase of 12.3 million since 2000) had no health cover either because they could not afford it at a time when insurance costs and unemployment were rising or for other reasons, such as not signing up to Medicaid or because they were young people who saw little need for coverage. Higher numbers of people were without cover for shorter periods of time in any given year.

Changes were made to US healthcare by the Patient Protection and Affordable Care Act (PPACA) in March 2010. The Act survived constitutional challenges and was upheld in most of its provisions by the Supreme Court in 2012. It is intended to give a better healthcare system by requiring almost all US citizens and legal residents to buy insurance, to provide subsidies for those who cannot afford insurance, to give incentives for companies to provide health cover, to establish health insurance exchanges to expand coverage to more people, and to fine individuals, companies and insurers who do not comply with the Act. This health restructuring involves a mixture of regulation, subsidies and fines in order to improve care and delivery, control insurers, reduce medical costs and give value for money.

It is intended that these measures will reduce the total of 50 million uninsured people, provide health insurance for most Americans for the first time by 2019 and reduce the overall costs of healthcare by having most people pay into an insurance system. Some 32 million citizens will be required to take out insurance from 2014 when the system becomes operative. Uninsured workers earning up to $88,000 a year who do not have health insurance from their employers will receive federal subsidies (paid for out of national taxation) on a sliding scale to buy their own cover. Subsidies will decrease as incomes increase and families earning more than 400 percent of the poverty level would receive no subsidy.

The PPACA expands Medicaid coverage to the poorest individuals under the age of 65 whose annual income is up to 133 percent of the federal poverty level, which would add about 16 million people to its rolls. For example, a family of four earning less than $29,326 would be eligible for Medicaid. But this expansion of Medicaid is dependent upon state approval and states are not forced to participate in the program. It is argued that some 11 million uninsured poorest adults may not gain access to Medicaid if states rejected expansion nor would they qualify for exchange subsidies. But if states declined to cover their poorest adults, they would not lose their existing federal aid for Medicaid treatment of categories such as pregnant women and families with children. It is argued that such developments would limit the planned universal coverage of the legislation.

Those who do not comply with the Act will be fined and the Supreme Court ruled in 2012 that this "individual mandate" should be treated as a tax and therefore constitutional. Such annual fines start in 2014 at 1 percent of taxable annual income, and peak in 2016 at 2.5 percent of income. Individuals are exempt from the fine if the lowest-cost healthcare plan exceeds 8 percent of their income. Companies with more than 50 employees will also be fined $3,000 a year ("the employer mandate") for each full-time employee who lacks company coverage and who therefore requires a government subsidy to purchase health insurance. Companies with fewer than 50 employees will be exempt from these penalties.

Healthcare exchanges were also established and are intended to oversee the legislation and improve consumer choice by allowing people to compare health plans from insurers and chose the one that is best and cheapest for them.

Insurers must follow PPACA regulations if they wish to be listed with the healthcare exchanges, which would give them access to millions of additional customers. They will be required to cover all applicants and barred from denying individuals coverage because of preexisting medical conditions or gender and other restrictions, and from dropping covered individuals once they become sick, or for any reason apart from fraud. They are also required to offer coverage to children under 26 on their parents' policies. Insurers might have to spend up to 80 percent of customers' premiums on providing healthcare or on improving quality. The PPACA imposes a tax on healthcare plans costing more than $8,500 for individuals and $23,000 for families. This should encourage people to choose cheaper healthcare plans.

The Congressional Budget Office estimated that the PPACA will cost $940 billion over ten years but would also lower future budget deficits and Medicare spending. The full implementation of the PPACA mechanisms will take time and the success or failure of the Act will not be immediately known.

There was little Republican support for the reform bill and liberal Democrats argued that it involved too much consideration for insurers and needed a greater public service emphasis. It was maintained that the legislation will leave some 23 million people without insurance in 2019, one-third of whom could be undocumented immigrants. The funding apparatus for the uninsured seems weak for some critics. It is argued that the reforms will expand medical coverage at a heavy cost to taxpayers, who finance the subsidy scheme, and there are doubts that healthcare inflation will be restricted. The insurance industry may not be restrained by regulation, even though it will gain from an expansion of the private insurance market. However, since Medicaid and Medicare will continue as before, it is thought, despite some misgivings, that the PPACA will strengthen these programs by reform measures and by curbing costs and fraud.

State and local governments do provide a range of public health facilities for categories of people from the poor to war veterans and the armed forces. They operate or support hospitals, mental institutions, retirement homes and maternity and child-health services. Public facilities are also supplemented by non-profit voluntary organizations, universities and other bodies, which provide free healthcare for the local population. Public health services suffer from varying standards, inadequate coverage of the needy and differences in the amount of money spent on them.

The cost of employers' health plans increased in 2010, whether it was paid wholly by the business or shared with employees, and had become a problem. Employment-based health benefits are the most common form of health insurance in the US, followed by workers with individually purchased insurance coverage through their own employers. Due to the 2007–9 recession, the percentage of individuals in the first group fell from 62.4 percent in 2008 to 58.7 percent in 2010 and those in the second group fell from 54.2 percent in 2007 to 51.5 percent in 2010. The number of very different plans was confusing and expensive and other costs, such as wages, inflation and family coverage were also increasing. Many businesses said that they could not afford healthcare for their employees and much will depend upon the controls over insurers built into the PPACA.

Historically, single health insurance policies might not cover the costs of all possible eventualities and individuals might have to buy several policies in order to protect themselves adequately. They may still eventually have to pay out of capital or other resources for treatment that is not covered (or only partly covered) by insurance policies.

People's anxieties about illness are conditioned by high insurance premiums, which may be improved under the PPACA jurisdiction, and also by the cost of treatment, which (for serious or chronic illness) can be very expensive. There is some hostility towards the medical profession and drug companies whom the public often suspect of pushing up medical and drug costs. Doctors constitute an influential professional interest and lobbying group. Many of them and insurance companies have traditionally been opposed to "socialized" medicine in the US.

Private hospitals and clinics are generally well-equipped, efficient and run by a variety of commercial organizations. Many of those in the public sector, financed by state and federal funds, tend to lack resources and adequate funding. The US therefore has a range of high-quality medical facilities, but gaining access to them is a problem for many people.

The 16.2 percent of GDP derived from private, public and voluntary healthcare services in 2008 constitutes a major business sector and is larger than health spending in other countries. Much of it is derived from incomes of the medical profession (with primary care doctors having a median annual salary in

PLATE 11.4 A *National Geographic* documentary reported on US medical research into Twin Transfusion Syndrome (TTS), June 13, 2007. TTS is a disease of the placenta that affects identical twin pregnancies and results in the twins growing at different rates.
(Jodi Cobb/National Geographic Society/Corbis)

2010 of $202,392 and specialists earning $356,885), management or administrative costs and the expense of equipment and drugs.

Pharmaceutical companies spend billions of dollars on research and development of new drugs, medicines can be expensive and the profits on successful new drugs are consequently high. Hospitals and medical schools also spend substantial amounts on research because new techniques and discoveries will bring them prestige, patients and money, while also benefiting many people. The result for many consumers is ever improving quality and effectiveness of medical care, but more expensive treatment.

It is argued that, since medical services can vary, Americans are not receiving the full benefit of such expenditure. Compared with other countries, the US spends more on healthcare but helps fewer people. In 2001, the World Health Organization ranked the US at 37th out of 191 countries for the quality of its health performance. It found that the top 10 percent of Americans are the healthiest people in the world, a middle group receive a mediocre health deal, while the bottom 5–10 percent have bad services. The main reasons for such findings were the lack of universal health insurance and poor access to healthcare. A report from the Commonwealth Fund in 2010 ranked the performance of the US healthcare system last in a list of six other countries (Australia, Canada, Germany, the Netherlands, New Zealand and the United Kingdom). According to the report, the US spends twice as much as residents of other developed countries on healthcare, but performs badly on quality, efficiency, access to care, equity of the system and the ability of its citizens to lead long, healthy and productive lives. The US did not receive good value for its healthcare investment.

Recent developments have added to healthcare costs. In an expanding compensation culture, there have been more lawsuits by patients against doctors and hospitals because of alleged inadequate or wrong treatment. Trial lawyers can profit considerably by fighting personal-injury lawsuits on a contingency fee basis (no win, no fee), but the rise in such cases forces doctors to insure themselves against the risks of being sued. Medical care and vital decisions can be adversely influenced by these considerations. Drug companies also have to pay high compensation when medicines damage patients. Medicaid spending has had to cope with the high healthcare costs involved in treating patients with AIDS (acquired immune deficiency syndrome) and HIV (human immunodeficiency virus) and others with acute and chronic illnesses. Lawyers' fees, insurance policies and higher drug prices increase the overall cost of treatment, which passes to the patient or insurer, while both the public and private sectors have to spend more to alleviate serious illness. Healthcare coverage, for some critics, is the single biggest domestic crisis facing the US and threatens all but the wealthiest Americans.

These demands upon the healthcare system and its alleged limitations have resulted in the US falling in the world rankings for life expectancy from 11th to 42nd place in 20 years according to the US Census Bureau in 2007. This fall may be explained by expensive health insurance, Americans lacking health coverage, increased obesity (with one-third of US adults being obese according to the National Center for Health Statistics) and relative improvement in other countries' lifestyles. Despite US economic dominance, the decline reflects a disparity of wealth. In 2007, life expectancy for all races and both sexes was 77.9 with 75.4 for males and 80.4 for females. But there are unequal rates in the population. African Americans had a life expectancy of 73.6 years, five years shorter than white Americans; African American males had a life expectancy of 70 and females 76.8. The US also has a higher infant mortality rate than many other countries with 6.8 deaths for every 1,000 live births.

Nevertheless, deaths from serious diseases and illnesses, such as heart disease, cancer, strokes, respiratory problems and HIV, have declined. These trends are due to improved diets, increased exercise and greater health awareness in the population, as well as better medical care and equipment. A Gallup poll in June 2001 reported that, despite growing problems with obesity at all ages, 54 percent of respondents were very satisfied and 35 percent were somewhat satisfied with their personal health. However, deaths resulting from Alzheimer's disease, hypertension, kidney disease and Parkinson's disease have increased recently and some fear that a reversal in life expectancy will affect an increasing number of Americans.

Housing

Homes have traditionally been important for Americans and their families. They give a sense of material satisfaction and personal identification. This ideal of the intact nuclear family may have faded because of high divorce rates, single-parent households and single-occupier properties, but US housing patterns still tend to reflect traditional values.

Americans may move home many times and homeownership is associated with socio-economic mobility. A family will move frequently in the early years from apartments to houses and up the rungs of the housing ladder. There may be further transfers from urban locations to the suburbs in the same city, to new areas in the same state, or to different states.

Most Americans want to own their own homes, after renting in early adult years, and two-thirds prefer to live in suburban areas. Ownership and mobility are affected by poverty and unemployment. The housing market is consequently divided between the private sector for those who are able to buy or rent and the public sector mainly for those who require assistance in obtaining low-rent property.

According to the latest figures from the 2007 Census Bureau, there were 110.7 million occupied housing units in the US. Of these, 75.6 million (68.3 percent) were occupied by homeowners, with 64.5 percent being owner-occupied single-family houses, often of a detached type usually having front and back yards. Of the remaining units, 35 million (31.7 percent) were occupied by renters. Traditional houses were in the large majority and the median age of all housing structures was 34 years. They illustrate the huge growth of the housing industry during the 1970s and 1980s when 35.8 million units were built, and later in the 1990s and early 2000s. But homeownership rates have declined since 2006 to 67.4 percent in 2009 and the percentages dropped even more sharply after the crash of the housing market in 2008 with its many foreclosures. Other people live in apartments (rented or purchased) and the rest occupy a variety of housing units, such as fixed trailers or caravans in trailer parks.

Most private houses and apartments historically are reasonably priced, but they are also subject to price fluctuations and problems in the housing market. They are often of a good standard, with many amenities. Owners generally borrow money (a mortgage or loan) that is secured by the value of their house and income to pay for them. In 2009, the median one-family house cost $216,700 (a price reduction of 25.9 percent from 2008) and had an average monthly repayment on the mortgage of $1,514 in 2008, or about 30 percent of average family income.

PLATE 11.5 Harlem is historically a deprived, mainly Puerto Rican/African American area of New York with its own community identity. The "Spirit of East Harlem," commissioned by Hope Community Inc in 1978, was created by Hank Prussing (and others). The four-story mural features local residents engaging in everyday activities, but the neighborhood has since radically changed.
(Frederic Soltan/Corbis)

House prices rose faster than incomes in the 1980s and prevented many people from buying homes. The housing market then suffered from the economic recession of the early 1990s, after which prices and house-building increased again.

However, in 2007–8, the private housing market suffered seriously from the sub-prime or credit crisis and a resultant recession. Mortgages had been too easily given to individuals and lenders had over-extended themselves. The market collapsed when borrowers could not repay their mortgages and when there was insufficient credit available to maintain the system or to provide loans. People lost their property to foreclosures (3.9 million in 2009) or repossession and many house prices halved. The lack of credit fed into the banking and financial system and led to the collapse of major banks and loan facilities and the prosecution of bankers and financiers for fraudulent trading. The ensuing decline drove the American economy into recession in 2009. However, a Harris poll conducted for a Zillow Homeowner Confidence Survey surprisingly found in August 2008 that despite serious housing problems and the credit crunch, homeowners had high confidence in the value of their own homes.

Public sector housing in the US provides for the minority of Americans who are unable to buy property or afford private rented accommodation. The supply of social housing has been conditioned by the bias towards private provision. Individuals are expected to make their own housing arrangements, rather than assuming that these are a public responsibility.

The growth of urban slums and substandard housing in the nineteenth century resulted in social misery and threats to public health, and led to the creation in 1934 of the Federal Housing Administration. This body (now the Department of Housing and Urban Development) provided loans to organizations that built low-rent accommodation for low-income and needy people. Local and state governments also constructed public housing and implemented stricter building and planning codes, health protection and public sanitation regulations to deal with slum conditions.

Attempts to create more low-cost public housing with federal funds in the cities and other areas in the 1960s and 1970s were often opposed by property-owners and sometimes by state and local governments for political, economic, racial and religious reasons. Although racial and religious discrimination in renting such housing has been curtailed, it still exists. While many states and cities have imposed fair-housing laws, some low-income people and minority groups in urban centers live in barely habitable housing and entry to low-cost housing for those who are unemployed or on welfare can be restricted. Recently, there have been moves to exploit inner-city land and to replace inferior buildings with low-cost housing. Bad housing conditions are also experienced by people living in small towns and rural areas.

Despite economic growth in the late 1990s and early 2000s, housing problems for the poor worsened. There was a shortage of affordable apartments and 4 million families paid more than half their income in rent. Those spending more than 30 percent of their income on rent also increased between 2000 and 2005 due to stagnating wages for the unskilled, high property values and government's failure to supply enough subsidized housing. In 2008, President George W. Bush's National Housing Trust Fund provided communities with funds to build, rehabilitate and preserve housing for people on the lowest incomes.

Some 15 million households qualify for federal housing assistance, but only about 4.5 million families receive it. About one-third of these live in public housing projects, while the rest receive subsidies that allow them to live in private housing. In both cases, the tenants contribute 30 percent of their income towards the rent and the government provides the rest. But the public housing sector also suffered because of the 2008–9 economic recession.

The homeless

Although homelessness is mainly a temporary situation, homeless people are visible in many American communities. However, it is difficult to define who the homeless are and what can or should be done to help them. Action is restricted by a lack of reliable information on the causes of homelessness and the actual number of people living on the streets or in shelters.

Local, state and federal governments in the US have historically failed to provide sufficient low-cost rented accommodation for low-income groups and the federal government has reduced subsidies for such housing from the 1980s. The number of poor Americans fluctuated in the 1980s and 1990s and resulted in homeless people throughout the nation, particularly African Americans, men, families with children and veterans. Estimates of their numbers vary, with official figures from the Department of Housing and Urban Development in 2008 of 664,414. In 2007 the National Alliance to End Homelessness estimated that 600,000 families with 1.35 million children experienced homelessness each year and that the real total could be double that figure. It estimated that 23 percent were chronically homeless; 56 percent lived in shelters; one in three homeless children had a psychiatric disorder; and that nine out of ten homeless mothers had been victimized. But the amount of time that a person was homeless on average had been reduced and hunger had decreased. New York and California had the most homeless people in 2008, followed by Florida and Michigan.

Voluntary organizations, funded by private donations, attempt to help the homeless by providing shelter and food for limited periods. There are a large number of federal assistance schemes for the homeless controlled by a range of federal departments. Despite this federal funding, known as the McKinney program, states and cities finance most of the care for the homeless. They have recently successfully developed an initiative ("housing first") that places homeless persons in apartments of their own and has cut chronic homelessness.

Attitudes to social services

Social services in the US have recently been dominated by issues of healthcare. These have been debated in terms of competing economic and political interests, legal arguments, poverty and inequality in US society, polarized public opinion and the role of government.

Respondents to a Gallup poll in June 2012 reported that, of the most important non-economic problems facing the country, healthcare ranked second after dissatisfaction with the performance of government. Earlier, a *Financial Times*/Harris poll in July 2008 reported that 33 percent of Americans believed that the healthcare system "has so much wrong with it that we need to completely rebuild it" and 50 percent thought that "fundamental changes are needed to make it work better." More specifically, a Gallup poll in November 2007 reported that respondents thought the two most urgent health problems facing the country were access to the health system (30 percent) and its cost (26 percent). In terms of economic priorities, an ABC News/*Washington Post* poll in June 2008 reported that 66 percent of respondents felt that providing healthcare for all Americans (with raised taxes to pay for it) was more important than keeping taxes down (31 percent). From a financial point of view, earlier polls asked whether respondents could cover the cost of healthcare if their family suffered major illness: 40 percent said that they could cope easily, 44 percent with difficulty and 14 percent not at all. The lack of insurance for all was felt to be very serious.

Many people thought that the healthcare legislation in 2010 was controversial, complex and inadequately explained by the administration. It attracted both negative and positive responses. According to a Pew Research Center poll, which was completed before the passage of the PPACA in March 2010, 48 percent of respondents opposed the legislation, while 38 percent favored it. A Kaiser Family Foundation (KFF) poll at the same date showed 46 percent of respondents supported the bill and 42 percent opposed it. A Gallup poll in 2011, before the PPACA went to the Supreme Court on appeal, reported that 50 percent of respondents thought it was the responsibility of the federal government to make sure that all Americans have healthcare coverage and 46 percent did not. A later Gallup poll in February 2012, before the Supreme Court appeal, found that 66 percent of respondents felt that the requirement that every American must buy health insurance is unconstitutional and 20 percent thought that it was constitutional. Eighty-seven percent of Republicans considered it unconstitutional, with Independents at 65 percent and Democrats at 38 percent.

Other polls have reflected what Americans view as the strengths and weaknesses of the Act. They suggest uncertainty as to whether or not it will improve healthcare, increase access and restrict costs. Fifty-two percent of a skeptical electorate disapproved of the healthcare law in July 2012 after it had survived a legal challenge in the Supreme Court. However, a large majority of US medical students in a PLOS ONE research article in September 2011 recognized that healthcare reform was needed, supported the PPACA and thought that access to care would increase. But they had concerns about whether it would improve the quality of health provision or succeed in cost restriction, and felt that reforms had not gone far enough.

The PPACA in 2010 did not satisfy everyone, and it is argued that much needs to be resolved with further political struggles and economic problems. The difficulties of healthcare involve questions of how to raise money to pay for the services, how to face political intransigence and how to agree upon the models that will deliver the benefits. Previously, individuals and business were generally unwilling to pay higher taxes and contributions to support national schemes. More now seem willing to pay higher taxes for a better and reformed healthcare system, but there are inconsistent opinions about how this improvement should be implemented. Popular debate in the 2012 presidential campaign focused on the contexts of class, taxation, distribution of wealth, party affiliation, how to fund social services and healthcare, and who would benefit. A Pew Research Center survey in July 2012 found that 71 percent of respondents said that Romney's health policies were likely to benefit wealthy people; and 60 percent felt that Obama's policies would help the poor.

Americans are ambivalent about the role that government should play in helping the poor obtain social services. In April 2012, 71 percent of respondents (compared to 85 percent in 1994) to a Pew Research Center survey thought that many poor people are too dependent on government assistance programs and that the government cannot afford to do more for the poor than it is already doing. But 59 percent agreed that the government has a responsibility to care for those in need and provide all citizens with the basic necessities of life, with 59 percent agreeing that the government should guarantee every citizen enough to eat and a place to sleep (39 percent disagreed). A minority of 43 percent agreed that the government should help needy people even if it adds to the national debt/deficit. But a Pew survey in June 2012 reported that views on government assistance to the poor and the social services varied greatly between Republicans and Democrats. The percentage of Republicans supporting government responsibility to aid the poor fell in recent years to 25-year lows.

In terms of the tax burden that is required to pay for social services, Americans had mixed views on whether the poor and the middle class pay their fair share in taxes, but have clear opinions about the rich. In the July 2012 Pew Research Center survey, 58 percent of respondents said upper-income Americans pay too little in federal taxes. Thirty-seven percent thought that lower income people paid too much in taxes; 34 percent a fair share; and 20 percent too little. Forty-three percent agreed that the government should help needy people even if it means going deeper in debt, while 52 percent disagreed.

Exercises

Explain and examine the significance of the following names and terms:

welfare	AFDC/TANF	single-parent families
Medicaid	"Workfare"	War on Poverty
medical lawsuits	poverty level	unemployment compensation
OASDHI	EBT cards	GI Bill of Rights
Medicare	self-reliance	non-contributory benefits
New Deal	mortgage	social security
homeless	HEW	EITC
PPACA	subsidies	"individual mandate"

Write short essays on the following questions:

1. Critically discuss the provision for healthcare in the US and the effects of the PPACA.

2. Examine the division between public, private and voluntary provision for social services.

3. Explain what is meant by Social Security and discuss its present state.

4. Examine the results of public opinion polls in this chapter and assess the attitudes of Americans to social services.

Further reading

Alcock, P. and Craig, G. (2001) *International Social Policy: Welfare Systems in the Developed World*, London: Palgrave Macmillan.

DeNavas-Walt, C., Proctor, B. and Mills, R. (2004) *Income, Poverty, and Health Insurance Coverage in the United Sates, 2003*, Washington, DC: US Census Bureau.

Fields, J. (2004) "America's Families and Living Arrangements: 2003," US Census Bureau Reports, November.

Gilens, M. (1999) *Why Americans Hate Welfare*, Chicago, IL: University of Chicago Press.

Patterson, J.T. (1981) *America's Struggle Against Poverty, 1900–1980*, Cambridge, MA: Harvard University Press.

Peterson, P. (1999) *Gray Dawn: How the Coming Age Wave Will Transform America – And The World*, New York: Random House.

Putnam, R. (2000) *Bowling Alone: The Collapse and Revival of American Community*, New York: Simon & Schuster.

Skocpol, T. (1995) *Social Policy in the United States*, Princeton, NJ: Princeton University Press.

Stiglitz, J. (2003) *The Roaring Nineties: Seeds of Destruction*, New York, Norton.

Websites

Homelessness and links: womenshousing.org
Health: www.hhs.gov
Medicine: www.medicare.gov
Social Security: www.socialsecurity.gov
Social services: infousa.state.gov/government/govt_social.html

Chapter 12

Education

- American attitudes to education: high expectations
- American educational history
- Elementary and secondary schools
- Higher education
- Recent problems and policy debates
- *Exercises*
- *Further Reading*
- *Websites*

American attitudes to education: high expectations

Since the colonial period, Americans have expected a great deal from their educational institutions. Just teaching the usual subjects has rarely satisfied demands on the schools. Americans have also wanted learning to serve other social institutions, ideals and goals. Such expectations invite disappointment and controversy. Combined with the circumstances of the country's history, they have also led to a very distinctive educational system.

With its fusion of church and state, Puritan New England aimed at religious indoctrination, making even learning the alphabet a series of theological lessons, although maxims of "good sense" for getting on in the world also received attention. American optimism shines through in much later pedagogy. In the colonial South education was mostly reserved for a very small elite, planters' sons and the "finishing" of their daughters. The tradition of class and gender differences in education would also persist. The founding fathers hoped schooling would discover natural merit in citizens and nurture an elite to defend the republic from tyranny. People on the frontier dreamed education would be the "great leveler," a compensator for their alleged inferiority to coastal society and a guarantee of democratic equality.

Well into the twentieth century, schoolbooks fairly glowed with faith in the possibility of endless self-improvement for boys dedicated to American ideals. The schools taught girls to play a supportive role, African Americans to know their place, Native Americans to be civilized and immigrants to be American workers. Until recently, only a few private institutions and schools outside the mainstream provided correctives to this hierarchy. Since the mid-1950s, civil rights movements (starting with African Americans' demands for educational equality) have made schools a center of contention over which traditions and ideals, what order in society and what means of reaching those goals Americans should support.

At the beginning of the twenty-first century, Gallup polls gave a reasonably clear list of the traditional and newer attitudes and goals the public has regarding the nation's schools. As in the past, the public was not satisfied with public education. In surveys, more than half the public felt that private or church-related parochial schools were superior to the public school system, and would send their children to private schools if cost were not an issue. Thus support continued for President George W. Bush's approval of government vouchers to cover the cost of sending children to private schools if parents found local public schools inadequate, and President Obama supported school reforms that patterned inner-city schools on private military academies. Throughout the 1990s attempts to establish national standards for knowledge in specific subjects was also a focus of efforts to improve the schools. In the early 2000s most people polled supported such standards. Large majorities also supported using yearly standardized tests to measure students' progress and the quality of schools, another approach President George W. Bush's No Child Left Behind (NCLB) Act put in practice. Obama signed the reauthorization of that program.

But in 2009–12, much of the public and a decisive majority of teachers no longer favored the NCLB. Teachers and students complained that "teaching for tests" had narrowed the curriculum unduly, undermined pedagogic strategies for better learning and made public education anxiety-driven. The public thought the best means of improving the schools were paying teachers better, using more federal money for schools (but letting local districts decide how to use it), and using standardized tests and allowing voucher plans—in that order. The public further indicated that it highly approved of re-introducing the prayers and general religious content that were common in US schools before the 1970s. This mixture of ideas, some commonly advocated by self-identified conservatives and others usually expected from those who call themselves liberals, seemed characteristic of the enduringly controversial and central place of education in American life.

American educational history

The colonial period

Local control over education developed early in America and remains characteristic of its educational institutions. During the colonial period, the British authorities did not provide money for education, so the first schools varied according to the interest local settlers had in education. The common view was that parents were responsible for children's education. In the Southern colonies, schooling often came from a private tutor, if the family could afford one. Each town tried to build a school in colonial New England and Pennsylvania.

The colonists expected the schools to teach religion, and a skill in reading was highly valued because it allowed people to read the Bible. Puritan Massachusetts founded the first American public school under a law entitled the "Old Deluder Satan Act." Reading, writing and arithmetic (the so-called "three Rs") were the core subjects and, through them, pupils prepared for local religious, economic and political life.

Higher education also began early in the colonial period. In 1636 Harvard College was founded, only six years after the Puritan migration to America began. By the Revolutionary War, nine colleges prepared a small elite of men for the ministry and leadership in public life. Although these colleges encouraged religious toleration, rivalry among them was evident, in part because all but two

(Columbia and the University of Pennsylvania) represented one of the major Protestant denominations. At this point, church and state were not separated, and essentially private institutions of higher education regularly received public funding.

Building a society along the frontier also motivated the early development of schools. Because they were few and the wilderness vast, the settlers discovered that law, order and social tradition broke down unless people cooperated to establish the basic institutions of society. Thus, "school-raisings" became as much a standard part of cooperative community building as house- or barn-raisings.

Before the Civil War

Nonetheless, only five of the 13 original states included provisions for public schools in the constitutions they wrote during the War for Independence. In 1830, none offered statewide, free public education. Support for common schools was strong, however. Thomas Jefferson, Benjamin Franklin and other founding fathers insisted that universal public education was essential to produce the informed citizenry on which a democracy depended. In the 1780s the federal government passed laws providing for education and land for schools in the future states of the Great Lakes region.

Jefferson envisioned replacing Europe's aristocracy of birth with a school-bred *meritocracy* of talent. In the 1830s, President Andrew Jackson's Democratic Party opposed that ideal as elitist, and supported public schools as an equalizer that would give every man a chance to rise in society. Around the same time, reformers in the Northeast, such as Horace Mann, publicized the notion that public schools could reduce the growing crime, poverty and vice of the cities by helping to assimilate their growing immigrant population. Towards those ends, Mann led a movement to lengthen the school year, add "practical" subjects, raise teachers' salaries and provide professional teacher-training. By the Civil War, all states accepted the principle of tax-supported, free elementary schools. Every state had such schools in some places, but most teachers were poorly trained, and the quality of the schools was considerably lower in the South and West. Most children went to school sporadically or not at all. In the North only one out of six white children attended public school in 1860. In the South, the figure was one in seven, and it was illegal to give slaves schooling.

At the time, public opinion rejected the idea of mandatory school attendance, mainly because most people still believed parents, rather than governments, should decide matters of education. Moreover, most parents needed their children's work or wages to make ends meet. Public secondary education was available at some 300 "free academies" across the nation, for those who could spare their children's contributions to the family economy.

As the states abolished established religions in the half century after the revolution, church and state became separate. Only gradually, however, did

Protestant instruction disappear from public schools. In the North and Midwest, immigrant groups began to establish parochial (private, church-related) elementary and secondary schools in the 1840s to preserve their ethnic heritage and avoid pressures to assimilate in public schools.

The pattern of higher education was transformed before 1865. The Supreme Court distinguished between public and private colleges in 1819 and freed private institutions of higher learning from state control. Thereafter hundreds of private experiments in higher education appeared, even though public funding dropped to very low levels. During the Civil War, the Morrill Act (or Land-Grant College Act) set a revolutionary precedent by laying the foundation for the state university. The beginning of the federal government's involvement in public higher education, the Act gave each state huge land areas for higher education. The result was dozens of land-grant colleges, which developed into state universities. Equally important, it promoted the higher education of larger numbers of students and called for college-level courses in agriculture and technical and industrial subjects, in order to attract students from the working classes. The first colleges to admit African Americans and women also opened before the Civil War.

Immigration, assimilation and segregation, 1865–1945

The rapid pace of urbanization, industrialization and immigration brought a turning point in American education after 1865. In the popular print media, the immigrant slum child became the symbol of the dangers of these processes, and the public schools were asked to remedy the situation.

Assimilation through the schools seemed increasingly necessary as immigrants from southern and eastern Europe and several Asian nations arrived in large numbers. The schools were expected to Americanize these exotic newcomers by teaching English, the principles of American democracy and the skills needed for the workplace. Just as importantly, the schools would also get immigrant children out of unhealthy tenement housing, off the streets, out of factories and away from gangs. To accomplish these goals, compulsory school attendance laws were soon adopted. By 1880 almost three-quarters of school-aged children were in school.

These laws also applied to racial minorities. After the Civil War, the federal government's Freedmen's Bureau and other Northern organizations founded many schools in the South for the former slaves. But whether African, Asian or Native American, minority students everywhere were placed in separate schools. In 1896 the Supreme Court's *Plessy* v. *Ferguson* ruling gave legal backing to the segregation that already existed.

Politicians quickly put children in school, but they did not as quickly appropriate money for hiring more teachers and erecting new buildings. Overcrowded, poorly maintained schools and staff shortages were typical of American public schools between the 1880s and 1920s. Opening teaching to women (often the daughters of immigrants) provided the new teachers, and "normal schools" to train them grew rapidly in number. Around 1900, public school teaching was not considered a profession. The average annual salary for teachers was lower than that of an unskilled worker, and many teachers had no more than a high school education themselves. Yet real progress was made in teacher preparation in the decades after compulsory attendance laws were passed. States set standards for teaching licenses, which increasingly included a college degree with courses in pedagogy. After the 1920s, "school marms" and "schoolkeepers" (again more often joined by men) were members of a profession called "educators." Salaries for teachers, however, remained low, and the profession was regarded as one of the least prestigious.

In the same period, reformers assigned the schools new priorities and duties. John Dewey and others held that curricula and teaching methods had to be changed. Instead of moralistic piety and rote memorization, the schools had to give pupils practical skills suited to their environment and the habit of discovering knowledge for themselves. "Learning by doing," personal growth, and child-centered rather than subject-centered teaching became the goals.

Public schools were to become community centers and the means of social progress. About this time, progressive education introduced physical education, music and fine arts, and vocational subjects (training in skilled occupations) as electives (optional courses). These educators also developed the after-school extra-curricular activities, such as team sports, that became a typical aspect of American education. In 1917, the federal government offered financial support to any public secondary school that emphasized vocational education. Some immigrant parents criticized progressive education because they felt electives took time away from academic subjects. They also objected to the frequent assumption that immigrant children did not need academic studies, since they would not go on to higher education.

After 1865, private church-related colleges, often founded by European immigrant groups, rapidly increased in number, especially in the Midwest. Coeducational higher education (colleges open to both men and women) became the norm there during the Civil War, when fee-paying women were necessary to replace the men who joined the Union armies. Coeducation continued to spread, and by the 1920s almost half of American college students were women. Further east, however, the so-called Ivy League universities (Harvard and other prestigious schools from the colonial period) remained men's institutions and, hence, benefactors established separate women's colleges in that region. Racial segregation extended to higher education during this period, when colleges for African Americans, such as Howard University and the Hampton Institute, were founded in the South after the Civil War. In 1890 a new Morrill Act provided the region with land for African American public colleges that emphasized manual and industrial education.

After 1900, graduate and professional schools became more common. Advanced degree programs began to transform some well-established universities into research institutions, and engineering schools, business colleges, law and medical schools were founded in growing numbers. For all but a small elite, however, a college degree seemed a luxury. Even in 1940, less than two out of ten college-age people attended institutions of higher learning. Instead, as parents less often had farms, handicrafts or family businesses to pass on, they secured their children's future through further education at vocational, office, secretarial or management schools.

The Second World War and the Cold War

The Second World War was a watershed in American higher education. To ease the return of war veterans to civilian life, Congress passed the Servicemen's Readjustment Act (the so-called "GI Bill") in 1944. Under the Act, the federal government paid tuition and living costs for veterans in higher education and directly funded the expansion of study programs for the first time. Within two years, half the people in college were veterans, many of them from working-class families with little education. More students graduated than ever before, and the typical student ceased to be a member of the upper-middle or upper classes. By 1971, when the program ended, nearly 2.5 million veterans had benefited from its provisions. Higher education in the US had become mass education and was regarded as a right rather than a privilege.

The launching of the Soviet satellite *Sputnik* in 1957 spurred another increase in the federal government's role in public education. Now the schools were enlisted in the Cold War and called on to meet the challenge of Soviet technology. The National Defense Education Act (1958) provided federal money for research and university programs in science and technology, as well as loans to college students. The legislation also allotted federal funds for teaching science, mathematics and foreign languages in high schools.

After 1958, federal money was targeted for college-level foreign-language teaching, the equipping of language laboratories, and eventually for the humanities in general. In the 1950s, state after state required teachers to sign "loyalty oaths" to the US, and Senator Joseph McCarthy (among others) attacked the universities as hotbeds of communism. Education became a patriotic obligation as well as a right.

Race and school desegregation

The Supreme Court's *Brown* v. *Board of Education* decision struck down the principle of separate-but-equal educational facilities for the races in 1954. One year later the court ruled that public school districts all over the nation had to present plans for achieving "racial balance" in their schools. Federal school policy began to show a profound change in national priorities.

PLATE 12.1 Federal paratroopers, sent by President Eisenhower, escort black students to Central High School in Little Rock, Arkansas. This gave notice that the executive-in-chief stood behind the Supreme Court's *Brown* v. *the Bd of Education* ruling that called for the integration of public education across the nation.
(Everett Collection/Rex Features)

For almost 20 years, from 1955 to 1974, the court tried to desegregate America's public schools. It settled on bussing as the most effective way to integrate the schools. Until very recently, one universal rule in America had been that pupils attended the school closest to their homes. Since African Americans and whites lived in different residential sections of US cities, they attended different school districts. Residential segregation produced segregated schools. Therefore, the Supreme Court decided to "bus" students to other districts until "racial balance" in all city schools resulted.

In city after city across the nation, parents, school authorities and politicians of both races protested and resisted, but the court held firm, with the result that whites fled to the suburbs in greater numbers and the small percentage who could afford it sent their children to private schools. Federal authorities decided that bussing plans could produce integrated schools only if they included the "lily-white" suburban schools around major cities. After such plans resulted in white pupils being transported into city schools, the public outcry grew louder. By 1974, the nation's mood had become strongly anti-bussing, and when asked to decide whether a city-and-suburbs bussing plan was constitutional, the Supreme Court backed down, saying no tradition in American public education was more deeply rooted than the local control of schools. Thus bussing stopped being effective for school desegregation.

The trend towards increasing integration of the races in the school slowed, and by the late 1980s the trend had reversed. *Re*segregation of the schools began. By 2006, more than 40 percent of the schools were mostly or entirely African American. An even larger percentage were "racially segregated" if the definition includes schools that were predominantly Latino, Asian and African American. Most of these schools were located in the North, West, or Southwest, because the court integrated Southern schools first and did not support bussing between the suburbs and inner-cities of the North after 1974. Not only the end of bussing, but the continued "white flight" (now to the outer suburbs) and decades of high immigration of non-white, poor Latinos and Asian Americans contributed to the growing resegregation of the schools. As the portion of these minorities who were middle class grew in the first decade of the twenty-first century, however, the diversity of the student body increased in many regions of the country, even in suburban areas.

Affirmative action and the schools

Starting in the 1960s, the federal authorities fought the effects of prejudice and the related problems of poverty through involvement in educational programs. In 1963, Congress began providing money for college and university buildings. In 1964, it decided that federal funding was available only to educational institutions that proved they did not discriminate on the basis of race, religion or national origin. The Higher Education Act of 1965 helped minority and "disadvantaged" students get college loans. State and federal grants to poorer public schools generally came in two ways. First, laws made the income levels in local districts the basis for distributing public funds. "Low income" areas qualified for extra grants and special programs to attract good teachers. Second, governments more than tripled their contribution to the general budgets of cities with social and educational problems.

In general, federal government policy aimed to implement the principle of affirmative action that President Lyndon Johnson expressed in his commencement speech at Howard University in 1965:

> You do not take a person who for years has been hobbled by chains and liberate him, bring him up to the starting line of a race, and then say, "You are free to compete with all the others," and still justly believe that you have been completely fair.

Affirmative action programs to improve women's and minority groups' access to education proliferated during the early 1970s. On the primary and secondary levels of public education, affirmative action first led to a redesigning of teaching programs and textbooks. Discriminatory references to women and minorities were replaced with even-handed treatments or, more often, with "positive role models" and examples of how women and minorities contributed to American history and culture. History and literature books, especially, changed as a result of this effort.

The hiring of staff on all levels was also affected because governments required educational institutions to become equal-opportunity employers. That meant hiring more teachers from minority groups at elementary and secondary schools and more women professors at universities and colleges. By law, educational institutions must encourage minority group members to apply for teaching positions. They must be sought out and interviewed or the school might lose government funding. Finding qualified women and minority group members for positions became somewhat easier after the 1970s because of affirmative action plans for teacher-training programs and the increased number of students from these groups who completed university degrees.

Two affirmative action programs were designed to help "disadvantaged" pupils succeed in primary and secondary schools. Head Start provides preschool tutoring to children in educationally deprived families to help them begin formal schooling at the same level as those in more fortunate families. Upward Bound supplies remedial teaching, private tutoring and work–study programs for older children. While Upward Bound suffered repeated funding reductions, Head Start is considered a success and has continued to receive additional congressional appropriations. It benefits close to a million children today.

Affirmative action programs in education provoked a number of US Supreme Court decisions. These did not call for the end of affirmative action, but changed the methods used to put it into effect. The best-known court cases in this area involved complaints from white males denied admission to university programs, in their opinion, because female and minority group applicants were given preferential treatment. In the *Bakke* decision (1978), for example, the Supreme Court ruled that it is unconstitutional to increase the number of students from racial minorities in university programs by setting numerical quotas. In the 1990s and the first decade of the 2000s voters ended affirmative action programs in several states by supporting propositions at elections to eliminate them. The Supreme Court ruling in cases involving the University of Michigan in this period more strictly limited admissions policies that favored minorities in the interest of recruiting a diverse student body at institutions of higher learning.

Accumulated expectations, disappointments and newer trends

Diane Ravitch, a well-known authority on US schools, has listed the accumulated expectations Americans have for their educational institutions. Education should:

■ reduce social inequality;
■ improve the economy and economic opportunity for individuals;
■ spread the capacity for personal fulfillment;
■ civilize and uplift the nation's cultural life;
■ raise the level of and participation in its political life;
■ lessen alienation, distrust and prejudice by increasing the contact among racial and socio-economic groups.

Perhaps understandably, a mood of disappointment with educational institutions has been evident in the US because most of the social dilemmas the schools were supposed to solve remain serious problems. Bussing was largely abandoned, racial separation grew and the controversial effects of affirmative action led to the curtailing of those programs. In the late 1990s and first decade of the 2000s the public added yet other expectations to its list, expressing support for more public money, national standards, religious values, testing and vouchers to raise the quality of the schools.

Elementary and secondary schools

Local control over schools became traditional during the colonial period. The Constitution makes no mention of education, which reserves power over education to the states or people, according to the Tenth Amendment. All 50 state constitutions have quite specific provisions about education. Generally, these clauses (and state education laws) define the state's role and delegate primary responsibility for schools to local governments. As these are created by the states, their powers over education can be altered by the states.

Local authorities set up independent school districts, whose elected local boards of education make most decisions regarding public elementary and secondary schools. Generally, the districts organize their schools into kindergartens for five-year-olds, elementary schools for six- to 12-year-olds, middle schools (or junior highs) for pupils from 13 to 15 and high schools for students between 16 and 18 years old. The overall structure of education has several variants progressing from kindergarten through to doctoral degrees. See Figure 12.1 for a diagram of the most common of these. In the 2012–13 school year there were some 99,000 elementary and secondary districts with a total enrolment of over 50 million pupils.

Only when specific powers given to the federal government in the Constitution are involved, such as the protection of rights guaranteed in the Bill of Rights, do the federal authorities get directly involved in educational issues. In

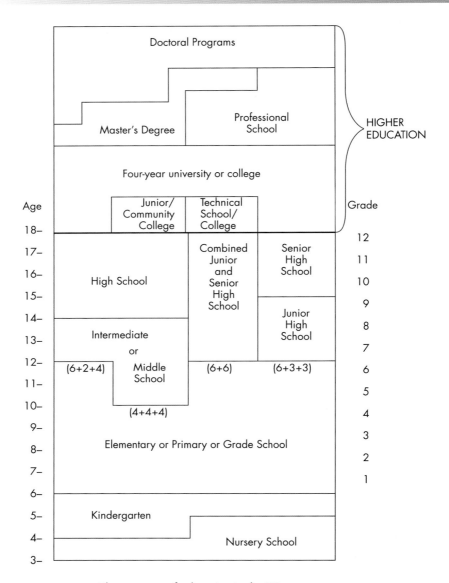

FIGURE 12.1 The structure of education in the US.

practice, the federal government seldom interfered with local schools to protect civil rights until the 1950s. The national government has also provided land for school sites, funds for special educational projects and has influenced local school policy by making federal grants for education dependent on following non-discriminatory practices.

The federal government's involvement in education remains quite limited. Its administrative agency for overseeing and formulating educational policies was formed late and is still understaffed compared to those in other developed countries. Not until the early 1950s did Congress set up a federal Office of Education in the Department of Health, Education and Welfare. A separate Department of Education was not established until 1979. Ronald Reagan received considerable support when he promised to eliminate the department if he was elected. Even today the federal government provides on average only a little over 7 percent of the funding for public primary and secondary schools, despite increases under the NCLB. Until the 1950s almost all state governments limited their involvement in education to two areas: establishing public state universities and setting general guidelines for public primary and secondary education. A state board of education, appointed by the governor, formulated the guidelines, and the state's agency or department of education was to see that they were carried out in local districts. The state Board of Education commonly sets only general minimum standards. It determines the number of days in the school year, the procedures for licensing teachers and administrators, the school-leaving age (usually 16), the "core curriculum" that pupils must complete at each level of school and minimum requirements for academic progress at different grade levels. To graduate from secondary school, for example, students must pass a core

PLATE 12.2 Kindergarten children working with laptops.
(Erik Isakson/Tetra Images/Corbis)

curriculum that usually includes four years of courses in English, three in social studies and two in mathematics and science.

These common requirements serve several purposes. By establishing a degree of uniformity among diverse school districts, they allow educational leaders to keep the schools in line with standards in other states and developments in pedagogy. Hence, the core curriculum also facilitates the evaluation of individual schools and makes it easier for pupils to move from one district or state to another and gain admission to colleges and universities around the nation.

Current trends in public school reform

In recent decades, state boards have increasingly implemented testing programs to make individual districts more accountable for reaching a certain level of academic achievement at specified points in pupils' schooling. The same tests are often used in many states, and the results for districts and states are publicly available. The state board and parents are therefore better able to judge the relative success of the local schools in meeting educational goals. During the 1980s and 1990s, growing numbers of state boards won approval for statewide tests to measure teachers' mastery of core subjects and educational methods.

These trends, the points on the public's agenda in the 1990s that were included in the Bush administration's NCLB education reform package, as well as reactions to it by 2009 have already been outlined. NCLB appropriates more federal money for public education than any such legislation in decades. It involves an unprecedented degree of top-down federal intrusion into state and local control over public schools. It requires the formulation of national and state standards of achievement in core curriculum subjects, greatly increased use of standardized testing of pupils and teachers to hold individual schools accountable to these standards, and a system of sanctions against public schools that do not meet annual targets for improvement. These include vouchers for sending pupils to other schools, including private religious institutions.

Between 2009 and 2012 opposition to NCLB from teachers' core subject organizations, their unions and from state boards of education grew considerably. The Obama administration used executive action rather than new or revised legislation to deal with the mounting dissatisfaction. By mid-2012 Obama and his secretary of education, Arne Duncan, gave 26 states waivers from participating in NCLB. They became free to use a combination of other measures to judge and report the progress of their schools. Many state educational leaders feel relieved that they no longer need to struggle toward unrealistic goals measured through the inadequate means of centrally made quantitative tests alone. As one educator expressed it:

> NCLB "oversimplifies" what is a far more complex process . . . Is it more important (and valuable) to answer a question on an assessment, out of

context, or to apply knowledge and skills successfully in integrated systems (where they will be used to solve higher level problems)?

Localism and public education

There are three important kinds of localism encouraged by the delegation of state authority to local school districts (LEDs). All these forms of localism remain very important in most school districts despite the greater state and federal policy intrusion brought by NCLB. Financial localism generally refers to the delegation of responsibility for funding schools to local districts. In the final decades of the twentieth century, state spending on education increased by as much as 70 percent, and federal contributions to public schools grew significantly as well. Yet, local real-estate taxes still raise around 43 percent of LED budgets. (Half of funds came from the state and the rest from the federal government.) In other words, local money still makes a very significant difference for public schools.

This 43 percent in a rich LED with valuable homes and businesses represents the resources for better teaching salaries, buildings and equipment than those in most other districts. In the smaller school budget of a poor LED, 43 percent represents less money, and that has a proportional effect on resources for its schools. Each district is free to decide how high it wants to set property taxes for education. But even when poor LEDs approve higher tax rates to those of wealthy districts, they raise less money for schools because local property has so little value. Thus, financial localism (in combination with the causes of the great economic differences between school districts) is still the reason for wide variations in the quality of American public schools.

PLATE 12.3   A Local Education District (LED) school board meeting. Sometimes when issues arise that are controversial locally, such as textbooks and teaching methods in sex education, board meetings draw large audiences and heated discussion. Routine matters bring few participants. *(Zuma Wire Service/Alamy)*

State plans to redistribute local property taxes aim to reduce the educational inequality resulting from financial localism. Redistribution plans collect the real-estate taxes in the state and place them in a fund for public education. This money is then distributed to even out the differences in school budgets across the state. Such plans can bring drastic changes in the school budgets of both rich and poor LEDs. Generally, they have taken money for education from the suburbs and given it to inner-city areas. Hence, there has been less money for schools dominated by white pupils and more for schools with many Latinos and African and Asian Americans.

As expected, redistribution plans have met opposition. Some suburban groups have tried to preserve the advantages of their schools through private donations or special local education taxes. At least one state (New Jersey) responded by ruling that any increase in the school budgets of richer LEDs would result in an automatic equal increase in the budgets of poorer LEDs. State courts in several parts of the nation have demanded redistribution programs. Increased state contributions to local school budgets and redistribution plans have given state boards of education greater leverage in enforcing statewide standards. However, state authorities often show a reluctance to use their power. Like the public they serve, they still believe that in a democracy, education should not be imparted by central authorities, but designed by the people in the governments closest to them. Such thinking and the opposition of suburban voters have limited the effects of redistribution plans. The result is that the money spent per pupil in predominantly white suburban schools is commonly two to three times that spent in racially mixed city schools. American traditions of financial localism in education remain strong.

Political localism is chiefly exercised through the members of the LED board of education. They have more power over the schools than members of the state board do and are nearly always elected. Anyone who lives in the district can be a candidate for the board. The majority of those elected are parents, teachers and local business people. It is also common to elect a student to the board. The school system's chief administrator is usually an ex-officio member of the board with no vote but great informal influence over decisions. While some boards have difficulty reaching agreement because members represent opposing political views, often the board as a whole reflects the district's predominant conservative or liberal political attitudes.

The local board is powerful because it makes a range of important decisions. It determines the size and content of the school budget and controls the hiring and firing of teachers and administrators. The choice of subjects, programs and educational goals beyond the state minimums is the board's, as is the definition of school disciplinary rules and routines. It must approve the selection of library and textbooks, and it has the final word on how educational facilities should be designed, constructed and maintained. Local boards make decisions on whether the LED should apply to the state or federal government for aid under specific programs. The boards that are most resourceful in applying for these funds get more help. In practice, that means districts with well-educated populations (and usually higher incomes) often succeed in getting more money from the state and federal governments.

Another important source of political localism is the PTSA (the Parent–Teacher–Student Association). The PTSA is a voluntary organization whose officers are elected by its members. It has no legal authority to make school policy, but its discussions often frame the issues debated and decided by the school board. Moreover, people who have been active in the PTSA are often the local residents who get elected to the board.

The third kind of localism in American education, social localism, refers to the distinctiveness of LEDs' educational priorities and goals that result from differences in their populations' social attitudes. These attitudes generally reflect the local population's dominant socio-economic class and mix of occupations, religions, races and ethnic groups. It can be argued that social localism produces differences in the public schools that are quite as significant as those caused by differences in districts' ability to pay for schooling. School board members and PTSA leaders, who may or may not be representative of the local population, cannot afford to ignore these attitudes and the population characteristics from which they spring.

Social localism is significant because local boards make important policy decisions. It has led to public schools emphasizing agricultural methods, industrial arts, commercial studies or college-level "advanced placement" courses. It has inspired religious, white supremacist and assimilationist policies in some LEDs, and opposing policies in others. Extreme examples of social localism have resulted in replacing evolutionary theory with the biblical story of creation in science courses, removing literary classics from school libraries, sex-education lessons and the presentation of alternative lifestyles and sexual orientations in elementary schools, a district policy of teaching that American society is the world's greatest and decisions to refuse the children of illegal immigrants public schooling. Many such extreme social policies are struck down by judicial rulings or changed after public reactions.

The goal of Americanizing immigrant children has been discarded. Today, after the civil rights movements of the 1960s and 1970s, support for equal educational opportunity and pluralism (the belief in allowing several alternatives) is standard in the rhetoric (although not as often in the practices) of most American school districts. In fact, equal opportunity today means that both state and federal governments sometimes deem it necessary to intervene in the affairs of local school districts to ensure that minority students are given an education fitted to their special needs and problems. Pluralism produces even more various public schools as some local districts tailor their curricula to suit Native American or African as well as Latino and Asian immigrant children and add ethnic studies courses and bilingual education programs.

Pluralism in the public schools has also meant debate over the core curriculum. Led by scholars in college education departments who question the traditional content of required subjects, districts, states and even the federal government have tried to redefine common standards and the canon (accepted principal content) of subjects in recent decades. Committees of recognized experts in many fields have met (sometimes for years) to develop national standards for subjects and a national curriculum. In the US, however, that can only consist of suggested guidelines. NCLB, for example, offers national models for appropriate standards in core subjects at different grade levels, but it bows to the states' constitutional authority over education by leaving it to them to define each state's legal variant of the Act's rules. States still control educational programs. The standards adopted in many LEDs and states to meet the general guidelines of the new law have caused publishers to redesign basic textbooks in several core subjects for all school levels.

Private elementary and secondary schools

Pluralism means not only permitting great variety in the public schools but also allowing a wide variety of private schools. During the 2009–10 academic year, 10 percent of the school-age population attended one of the nation's more than 33,370 private schools. Private educational institutions show even more variety than the public schools. Four out of five are parochial schools (run by religious groups). By far the largest number of these are Catholic institutions, but fundamentalist sects, a range of other Protestant denominations, orthodox Jews, as well as Islamic and Asian religious groups also run parochial schools.

Non-sectarian private schools have a weak religious allegiance or are entirely secular. They are quite diverse but frequently promise a high standard of academic excellence, adherence to a particular theory of education, the ability to instill discipline and maturity, or some combination of these qualities. The Montessori schools offer a specific method of learning. Elite college-preparatory boarding schools (so-called "prep schools") have exceptionally well-qualified faculties whose goal is to help the children of the wealthy gain admission to prestigious universities such as those in the Ivy League, and to eventually take their place in the country's upper class. A variety of military academies specialize in dealing with "problem children" whose parents can afford to reform their habits by subjecting them to the rigors of a regimented life away from home.

Private schools depend heavily on endowments (private donations), investments and income from fee-paying students to meet their expenses. Public funding amounts to less than 10 percent of their budgets. Until very recently, the courts limited the public funding available to parochial schools to programs that benefit school pupils in general, rather than particular institutions. Thus, all children can receive government aid for some medical services, nutrition supplements and transportation to school.

A recent development is that in some areas parents can receive grants (or government vouchers) to pay for tuition at private schools. Especially in the inner cities, where private schools have a better record than nearby public schools, states have for some time operated voucher plans. The NCLB Act now makes this a possibility anywhere a local school repeatedly fails to meet annual improvement goals.

Some private educational institutions offer financial aid to attract students from a variety of social backgrounds, while others follow a restrictive admissions policy to maintain a more homogeneous student body. Exclusivity has always been an important attraction of many private schools. Bussing programs to end segregation contributed to increased enrolment at all-white private institutions. The Supreme Court's ban on group prayers and religious instruction in general in the public schools caused others to turn to private education. Dissatisfaction with the public schools' academic standards, lax discipline, drug abuse or crime convinced yet more parents to pay for private education. These problems are certainly more avoidable in private schools, since the expulsion of pupils who cause them is much simpler for private institutions.

Higher education

High-school graduates enter higher education through a process of mutual selection in a system that is decentralized, diverse and competitive. Colleges and universities select a student body according to criteria set by the individual institution rather than by a central authority. The federal government has only an indirect influence on these standards through equal educational opportunity programs, civil rights laws and constitutional rights. State approval is necessary for institutions of higher learning to operate and grant degrees, but once that is gained, state involvement is usually minimal.

This large degree of institutional independence has encouraged grassroots experiments and innovations in higher education. The resulting diversity is enormous. The public sector includes the national military academies, 50 state university systems and thousands of local technical or "specialty" schools, community colleges and city universities. In the private sector there are also many thousands of institutions, ranging from specialty schools to small church-related colleges to major universities with separate undergraduate, graduate and professional schools.

Thus entrance criteria reflect the particular character of the institution and the competition it faces from institutions of a similar sort. High-school graduates try to gain admission to a school that suits their individual needs. Students' requirements also vary greatly because the population is so heterogeneous and secondary schools so different in type and quality. In such a system, devices are needed to help institutions and students make informed choices in the selection process. There is no battery of nationally designed and evaluated examinations that pupils must pass to receive a high school diploma. That fact and the great variation in the programs and quality of US secondary schools make evaluating applicants' academic achievement difficult for colleges. To provide a basis for comparing pupils' skills, private firms have developed competitive college entrance examinations that are given all over the country on the same day. Almost all colleges and universities require applicants to take the best known of these, the Scholastic Achievement Test (SAT), and many prestigious schools also require pupils to submit their scores on other national tests.

In addition, institutions have admissions departments that visit and evaluate secondary schools, interview applicants and review pupils' application forms. Secondary schools have guidance departments with counselors that evaluate colleges and universities for students and recommend programs suited to their abilities and test scores. Regional organizations called accrediting bodies monitor the quality of secondary schools and institutions of higher education.

A closer look at some of these institutions of higher learning illustrates the choices students have. Post-secondary technical or "specialty" schools offer training for specific occupations, such as accounting, computer programming, laboratory work or business management. These institutions have become particularly numerous since the Second World War because of rapid changes in technology. Today, a few specialty schools are as prestigious as well-known universities. Community colleges give courses covering the usual requirements for the first two years of college, at little or no cost to local residents. After that, students may graduate with an associate in arts (AA degree) or transfer into the third year of a full college or university program and continue toward a bachelor of arts or science (BA or BSc degree). Community colleges are run by local authorities and offer many shorter certificate programs suited to the occupational needs of a local area. As a result, many of their students are mature adults who study part-time.

Community colleges first appeared in the 1930s but did not become common-place until around 1970. One of the more important recent developments in American higher education, community colleges fulfill a number of public expectations. They give reality to the consensus view that a basic college-level education should be available to the general population virtually free of charge. They satisfy the nation's commitment to "lifelong learning," the belief that retraining and continuing education are vital to the individual's and the nation's international competitiveness. Finally, they reflect public opinion that favors local control of education. Community colleges have opened the possibility of almost unlimited local control over courses of study and have also proved particularly adept at organizing cooperative programs with local businesses and trade unions.

Although a clear majority of colleges and universities in the US are private, three-quarters of high-school graduates chose public institutions in 2012. One important reason for this situation is that tuition (the cost of instruction) at city and state universities is often a small fraction of the fee charged at a private institution. Location also reduces the cost. City or state residents pay much lower tuition rates than students who come from other places. Public systems have purposely built campuses in many parts of the city or state so that students can live at home while they study.

Public systems also attract more students because some have open admissions policies and many have minimal acceptance requirements for area residents. The majority of secondary school graduates who have average grades can thus avoid rejection in the intense competition for acceptance at more selective schools. Most of those are private, but city and state systems also have an enormous range of standards and programs. Most states operate two university systems, one of them usually more oriented to applied studies and the other to academic work leading to research and the more prestigious professions. Many outlying "branch" campuses of public universities are much like community colleges, but some concentrate on excellence through advanced courses in a limited number of fields. State university systems usually have a main campus that maintains higher overall standards. The best of these, the Berkeley campus of the University of California and the Madison campus of the University of Wisconsin, for example, have reputations that equal those of such elite private universities as Harvard, Yale, Princeton and Stanford.

Private higher education in the US is typical of American pluralism. The private sector that educates a quarter of university-level students in the US is large compared to that in other western nations. Yet private institutions could expand their size greatly if they wished. On average, private colleges and universities accept only one in ten applicants.

There is no single or simple reason for this restrictive admissions policy. Inability to pay school costs is rarely the main reason for turning down an applicant. Good private institutions have little difficulty finding enough fee-paying students. Stipends, scholarships, low-interest loans, part-time work–study programs or a combination of these are made available to people the institution wants. Private colleges and universities recruit as much as a third of their students among well-qualified poor, minority and foreign groups. Even the most prestigious institutions offer some of these recruits extra help (so-called remedial courses) as a form of affirmative action, because they believe in helping promising students in economic difficulty and think that studying with people of varied backgrounds is a vital part of a good education. As noted in Chapter 4, however, in the last two decades such affirmative action has faced rising opposition in public opinion.

The reasons most private institutions have for remaining relatively small are related to their concept of a quality education. A few concentrate on high academic standards as their single definition of quality. Many more combine that goal with the ideal of a special community of learning. The ideal of community is often served by requiring students to live on campus and by having relatively few students per teacher to encourage the close contacts between students and faculty. A sense of community is also often established by bringing together staff and students who share a religious or ethnic background or socio-political orientation. Most American racial, nationality and religious groups have founded at least one private college or university.

Some institutions are common to both public and private higher education. The four-year liberal arts college, which about two-thirds of American students attend, is the most important of these. One of several units in a university or an independent organization, its purpose is to provide basic courses in a broad range of humanities and sciences. Liberal arts students usually do not specialize until their third year. That "major," the capstone of their undergraduate education, is a requirement for the BA or BSc degree.

A primary goal of the liberal arts college is making its graduates so-called "well-rounded" individuals (generally well-informed and cultured people). By requiring a core curriculum, these colleges help maintain a common culture in the US. Until around 1980 few questioned this canon of study and research, which aimed to expose students to the fundamental values of American and western culture. Since then, the definition of the canon has conflicted with the ideal of pluralism.

Debate over the canon became so intense in the academy and educated public that Americans speak of the "culture wars." Nothing less than a redefinition of American identity or realizing cultural equality has been attempted. By the latter 1990s, many scholars had successfully argued that the canon of many subjects must be widened to include work of women and the non-western cultures of many Americans. Debate continues, but the core curriculum is already much changed.

A liberal arts degree is required before students can enter graduate schools. These may be professional schools, such as law or medical schools, or advanced liberal arts schools that offer masters degrees (the MA or MSc) and doctorates (the PhD). To be admitted to graduate schools, students must normally take a competitive examination, either an entrance test for the professional school or graduate record exams (GREs) in liberal arts subjects. A hallmark of the best universities, America's high-quality graduate schools are internationally famous centers of research and magnets for well-qualified students from abroad.

Taking part in higher education in the US is a competitive struggle. Between 2001 and 2011, when around 20 million people had enrolled at colleges or universities each year, the central problem seemed to be that only half of these students completed a degree. City and state universities normally "weed out" one-third to one-half of the freshman class through tough introductory courses and exams that must be passed if a student is to stay enrolled. Half of those enrolled in a first degree do not graduate. All American institutions of higher education use the system called continuous evaluation. It requires students to take mid-term and end-of-term examinations, write essays and term papers and complete additional tasks the instructor chooses to give. Course grades result from a

PLATE 12.4 Harvard University, founded in 1636 and the oldest of the universities in the "Ivy League."
(Charles Sykes/Rex Features)

weighted average of the student's marks on these assignments. A minimum overall grade average is necessary to continue one's studies.

Recent problems and policy debates

"State of the nation" evaluations have become a regular part of public debate about American education. Presidential candidates, federal commissions and the US secretary of education, associations of the states, organizations of educators and private foundations regularly identify problems and suggest policy changes. Concern over the quality of schooling at all levels has been the common theme in expert reports and public opinion polls in recent decades. Efforts at reform have stabilized falling test scores on national public school tests and college entrance examinations but have not raised them significantly. Average achievement levels in language skills, mathematics and science have remained lower in the US than in many other developed nations, according to comparative studies of secondary pupils, which also show that American students spent less time doing homework.

In the first decade of the 2000s, institutions of higher education in the US found that a large portion of college-age youth were not among the "college ready" (high-school graduates who had completed a minimum of secondary-level courses and scored at least up to a basic level on a national test). In the high school "class of 2010," for example, only 33 percent were college-ready, 30 percent had dropped out earlier and 37 percent who graduated did not have the academic achievements to be accepted at a college. In the fall of that year 36 percent of the class began their college careers. Roughly two-thirds did not go on to higher education because they had not reached the necessary academic level and so were not admitted. Whites and Asian Americans had the highest rates of readiness and attendance, while Latinos, Native Americans and blacks had lower rates.

The causes of unsatisfactory quality in public education have provoked much debate. Some commentators on elementary and secondary schools claim that only the achievement levels of inner-city districts are a problem and that their poor results skew the national averages. There was agreement, however, that continued "white flight" to the suburbs and private schools produced increased racial segregation and inadequate funding in urban areas. Others thought the problem of quality was nearly universal in the public schools.

Polls from 2003 through 2011 showed that the public linked lowered quality most to inadequate financial support, lack of discipline in the classroom and overcrowding, or to schools that were too large to allow students to develop a sense of shared community. The lack of well-qualified teachers or low pay scales for educators came much farther down on the public's list of concerns. In the wake of school shootings from Columbine through Sandy Hook, the schools continue to strive to improve security as they prioritize dealing with the causes of violence, such as problems at home, the availability of guns, violence and the attention given school shootings in the media, teasing and bullying, and the loss of a sense of community that results from how often American families move.

Expert analyses of the causes of decline of school quality focus on curriculum changes. Some critics assert that students neglect basic skills because they are allowed to choose too many excessively vocational or undemanding electives. Such criticisms provoke heated responses, especially when they are linked with allegations that pluralism, the introduction of women's or non-western "multi-cultural" components, has weakened the core curriculum in schools. Revision of the academic canon is ongoing, as many institutions adjust their sense of the essential, learn to function according to newly required state standards under the NCLB Act, and implement stricter standards to meet yearly improvement targets.

Proposals for policy changes in public elementary and secondary schools show the conflicting opinions about decentralization. In Gallup polls, large majorities support requiring local schools to follow a central standardized national curriculum and to conform to national achievement standards. The same polls reveal strong support for school choice programs, which often involve further decentralization. School choice allows families, rather than school authorities, to select the schools their children attend. Choice programs began with the decentralizing of school districts by giving individual schools the autonomy to design their own curricula. The first autonomous public schools were so-called magnet schools in inner cities. These institutions were allowed to specialize in particular subject areas (such as the fine arts or science) and were given the funds and staff that, it was hoped, would bring voluntary desegregation by attracting students from other districts.

By 2000 magnet schools had become commonplace, especially in large urban school systems, and school choice programs now aim to maintain high standards by putting these schools in competition with each other. In increasingly large areas, universal choice completely breaks the connection between a place of residence and the public school a pupil attends. The NCLB institutionalized school choice by allowing parents to choose another school if the one nearest their home failed to reach state standards for improvement.

School choice advocates say the increased number of high-quality programs made available through choice gives students more chances to develop their abilities and point to reductions in racial segregation. Opponents argue that school choice relegates most staff and pupils to institutions that are weaker than ever before because they lack leadership and positive role models. They also criticize the concentration of the best faculty and pupils in magnet schools as an elitist approach that contradicts the ideals of American democracy. In 2008 an estimated 2 million children in the US were being taught at home because their parents had decided to opt out of institutional schooling altogether. The number of children in home schooling had increased by 15–20 percent per year since 2000.

Exercises

Explain and examine the significance of the following names and terms:

meritocracy	Horace Mann	No Child Left Behind Act (NCLB)
Morrill Act	John Dewey	compulsory school attendance laws
GI Bill	*Sputnik*	coeducational education
bussing	affirmative action	progressive education programs
financial localism	political localism	state redistribution plans
Local Education	state board of education	parochial schools
Districts (LEDs)	pluralism	private higher education
social localism	state university	continuous evaluation
community college	graduate school	school choice programs
liberal arts	college admissions policy	school vouchers
magnet schools	school choice	

Write short essays on the following questions:

1. What do you view as major developments in the historical evolution of American education? Defend your views.

2. Debate the advantages and disadvantages of localism in public elementary and secondary education, keeping in mind the limits that have been put on local control.

3. Describe the private sector in American education. Is it good public policy for the US to support alternatives to public schooling?

4. Discuss the issues of current debate in American education. Why are these questions important or difficult in the US?

5. How can entering American higher education be described as a process of mutual selection in a system that is decentralized, diverse and competitive? Discuss the pros and cons of such a system.

Further reading

Cohen, D.K. and Moffitt, S.L. (2009) *The Ordeal of Equality: Did Federal Regulation Fix the Schools?* Cambridge, MA: Harvard University Press.

Department of Education (2012, annual) *Digest of Education Statistics*, Washington, DC: DOE.

Gitlin, T. (1995) *The Twilight of Common Dreams: Why America is Wracked by Culture Wars*, New York: Holt.

Kozol, J. (1991) *Savage Inequalities: Children in America's Schools*, New York: HarperCollins.

Meier, D. and Wood, G. (2004) *Many Children Left Behind: How the No Child Left Behind Act is Damaging Our Children and Our Schools*, Boston, MA: Beacon.

Ravitch, D. (2010) *The Death and Life of the Great American School System: How Testing and Choice Are Undermining Education*, New York: Basic Books.

Sowell, T. (1993) *Inside American Education: The Decline, the Deception, the Dogmas*, New York: Macmillan.

Websites

The National Center for Education Statistics (NCES): www.nces.ed.gov

http://nces.ed.gov/fastfacts

The National Education Association (NEA): www.nea.org

www.gallup.com/poll/indicators/education.asp

www.ed.gov

www.dese.mo.gov

www.nytimes.com/2012/07/06/education/no-child-left-behind-whittled-down-under-obama.html?pagewanted=all&_r=0

www.capenet.org/facts.html

http://exchanges.state.gov
www.usnews.com/education/articles/2009/08/19/dropouts-loom-large-for-schools
www.washingtonpost.com/local/education
http://nces.ed.gov/pubs2009/pesagencies07/findings.asp
http://nces.ed.gov/programs/digest/d12/tables/dt12_00m.asp

Chapter 13

The media

This chapter examines the component parts of the US media and reactions to them. The term "media" includes channels of communication through which people are informed and entertained. In the US, it generally refers to the print media (newspapers, books and magazines); the broadcasting media (television and radio); and new media devices, such as the internet, iPads, computers, e-books, cell phones and smartphones, and social networking sites such as Facebook and Twitter. These last forms are profitable and integral parts of film, video, publishing, telecommunications and multimedia groups, and are developing and changing at a very fast pace. The information industry is a very large US business sector and Veronis Suhler Stevenson forecast that it would grow faster than the US economy as a whole in 2012 (5.6 percent compared with 4.4 percent GDP growth).

The media have evolved from basic methods of production and distribution to their present sophisticated technologies. Communications systems convey words, images and messages to a mass audience, offer diverse consumer choices, cover homes, educational institutions and businesses, and are a powerful, influential and controversial part of daily life.

Americans are conditioned by the media in various ways. The average full-time worker is exposed at home and at work to different forms of the media for some nine hours a day. Average home usage in 2010 for television was 34 hours per week (Nielsen) and 19 access hours per week in 2009 for the internet (Digital Future Report). However, polls suggest that Americans are losing interest in general current affairs and instead are concentrating on specific concerns. They may pick news items from a mixture of network, public and local television, local and national newspapers, commercial and public radio, cable channels and the internet. A NBC/*Wall Street Journal* poll in July 2012 reported that respondents' main sources of political news and information were television (63 percent), internet (44 percent), newspaper (32 percent), radio (23 percent), talking with others (15 percent) and social media, such as Facebook and Twitter. Network TV news and newspapers have declined, while cable, independent radio and television, and online services have grown.

The media may influence public opinion and shape attitudes by deciding what is newsworthy and therefore publishable, although there is resistance to their dominant role. Historically, government has tried to license and muzzle the media (to little real effect after independence in 1776 and the First Amendment guaranteeing freedom of the press in 1791). The press or media are sometimes called the "Fourth Estate." They claim to be guardians of US democracy and argue for equal status with the branches of government established by the Constitution.

However, the media today is subject to considerable criticism and pressure groups of various persuasions attempt to promote reform of media outlets.

More positively, radio and television have minimized cultural and regional differences in the US, and have also reflected social diversity as they search for new markets and profits. Access to power may be gained through media sources, which politicians use to influence voters, particularly at election times. Political life and national and international events have become more immediate for many Americans, although an isolationist thread runs through US media production and culture. The mass of information and images may also confuse and desensitize audiences, leading some to distrust and reject the media.

There are non-commercial media in the US, but most newspapers, magazines, publishers, radio and television stations, and electronic companies are privately owned. They are businesses operating for profit and are tied to commerce, advertising and sponsorship. Companies use the media to persuade consumers to buy their products through nationwide advertising, but critics oppose the alleged negative influence of advertising on media, such as television. Traditional media (such as newspapers) have declined from being the largest source of advertising revenue. According to PWC/IAB research in 2011, network television ($28.6 billion) was in first place, the internet ($26 billion) had climbed to second and newspapers ($22.8 billion) were in third, followed by cable television, radio, directories and magazines. There is now greater diversification and competition among advertisers, with the internet and telecommunications in particular becoming more attractive to commercial companies.

Consumer opinion also influences the media and their agendas. They must respond to the public's wishes for a range of entertainment, information and news, if they are to be profitable. The ratings system for radio and television (statistics on audience approval) and print-media circulation figures are important determinants of success or failure.

Developments in mass communications and entertainment technology, such as computers, CDs, videos, DVDs, iPads, e-books, cable and satellite television, printing advances, interactive formats, the internet and smartphones have expanded the scope of the media society and helped to shape the country's cultural life. The growth of media outlets has increased markets, reduced the dominance of traditional formats (such as newspapers, network television, and videos, CDs and DVDs for rent and sale), appealed to more diverse groups in the population and increased participation by viewers, readers and listeners. The availability of American television, books, periodicals, satellite and cable news programs (such as CNN) and online newspapers has internationalized the US media's influence.

Media history

Books and newspapers were the first media to emerge in early American history due to a public need for news, education and information. Book production increased when a printing press was set up in 1638 in Cambridge, Massachusetts. But presses and the print media were controlled politically by the British colonial authorities through a licensing system. Although the first basic newspaper, Benjamin Harris' *Publick Occcurrences Both Foreign and Domestick*, was published in Boston in 1690, it was banned because it did not have a license.

The eighteenth century

Newspapers developed quickly in the eighteenth century. They gained influence and readership as they fought against licensing control and responded to political events and the demands of a growing population for information and communication. The first, relatively comprehensive newspaper, the Franklins' *New England Courant*, was published in Boston in 1721. Papers were a unifying force in the fight for independence from the British and communicated news of East Coast revolt to Western settlers. After independence, the First Amendment and court decisions bolstered freedom of speech and the press.

Magazines were the last journalistic print media to emerge, expanded more slowly than newspapers and were partly influenced by middle-class wishes for entertainment and education. Andrew Bradford's *American Magazine* was the first magazine, appearing shortly before Benjamin Franklin's *General Magazine* (January 1741).

As the population grew and expanded westwards, the social role of the print media was emphasized. Presses and print shops were established by settlers, who published books of local laws, newspapers and magazines. After the War for Independence, newspapers declined in quality. They became abusive and biased propaganda tools of political parties and vested interests with vehement editorials in support of special causes and political programs. Nevertheless, by 1800 there were some 20 daily papers and about 1,000 weeklies in local areas, which made greater attempts at objectivity in order to gain and retain readers.

Newspapers had also gained the protection of the First Amendment of the Bill of Rights in 1791, which guaranteed freedom of the press. Americans were aware that some papers had supported them against the British before and during the War for Independence. They were determined that Congress and government should not have the power to infringe press freedom. This crucial development formed the basis of "prior restraint" (the doctrine that the authorities cannot muzzle the press before publication).

The nineteenth century

By the mid-nineteenth century, the print media became more influential as social and cultural forces. Literacy rates increased and an expansion of schools and libraries created a mass market of readers. High-speed presses were manufactured to satisfy the demand for news, entertainment, education and information. New magazines and mass newspapers emerged after 1825 (such as New York's *The Sun* in 1833) and the market for novels, textbooks and general books increased as publishers organized the book industry into its modern structure.

There was a strong demand for novels, which sold in large numbers, and many were written by women. Novelists were aided by the introduction of paperback books in 1842. This development is still influential today, because paperbacks are an essential part of publishing firms' structure and are relatively cheap purchases for consumers. They began as supplements to newspapers and were later printed by orthodox book publishers.

Newspapers became a cheap and genuine mass medium and rapidly increased in number. They were mostly owned and edited by powerful and influential individuals who were personally involved in their papers. They introduced new publishing methods and forms of communication. James Gordon Bennett founded the first modern, forward-looking American newspaper, the *New York Herald*, in 1835. He employed reporters to gather news, appointed the first foreign correspondents, developed a Washington press corps and delivered the news before his competitors by using the telegraph and fast transportation.

Bennett was followed by Horace Greeley with his *New York Tribune* (1841), whose editorial page was very influential nationwide, and by Henry Raymond, who published *The New York Times* (1851). These and other owners improved news-gathering methods and developed innovative newspaper structures.

By the end of the nineteenth century, Joseph Pulitzer and William Randolph Hearst, with the *New York World* (1883) and the *New York Journal* (1895) respectively, dominated US newspapers. They were fierce rivals in a struggle for bigger circulation figures, produced papers that mixed sensational news reporting ("yellow journalism") with social crusading and introduced Sunday papers and the comic strip. A significant development occurred when E.W. Scripps founded the first newspaper chain (a collectivist structure under one owner) from 1889. This trend became important in the twentieth century.

Newspapers (about 2,326 dailies by 1900) and other print media were established as the primary means of communication for the population and had very large readerships. But journalism also became big business for some news organizations, which focused less on social crusading and accurate reporting and more on maximizing profits.

The twentieth century

Personal newspaper-ownership continued in the early twentieth century, although the total number of daily newspapers declined from their nineteenth-century high point. Joseph Medill Patterson printed the New York *Daily News* in 1919 (the first modern tabloid) and Robert R. McCormick published the *Chicago Tribune* from 1910.

Owners and editors realized that objective reporting rather than bias attracted more readers. Newspapers also became more conservative because advertising, on which they now depended financially, replaced circulation figures as the main source of income. Advertisers initially aimed at a middle-class market, but later divided the population into all the class and income groups. Different types of newspapers appeared, which reflected varied lifestyles, social status, education, political ideologies and consumption levels. Most newspapers were still concentrated in local areas and cities and were owned by individuals or companies. But economic pressures by the middle of the twentieth century forced many owners to sell their papers or join large chains that then dominated the media business.

Magazines and newspapers were similar in form and content and often embarked on crusading investigative journalism, which President Theodore Roosevelt called "muckraking" (exposing scandal and corruption). Investigative reporting had previously been largely political. But it now also included criticisms of the general social system and attempted to gain public support for specific campaigns. Such investigative journalism became a feature of the print industries and was to spread to radio and television later in the twentieth century.

The print media were challenged first by Hollywood's silent films and later by sound motion pictures, which became the dominant entertainment sources of the 1920s and 1930s and an alternative attraction for audiences. These media forms also had to compete with radio broadcasting in the 1920s. Radio provided a new national and world perspective for many Americans. It unified country and city, minimized rural isolation, contributed greatly to cultural standardization and continues to be significant for news and entertainment.

Commercial television was introduced at the New York World's Fair in 1939, but the Second World War hindered its progress. After the war, television began to dominate the other broadcast and print media. Its information service threatened the news function of newspapers, and its entertainment role challenged magazines, books and films. The other media had to cope with this and later competition (such as the internet).

The twenty-first century

Today, the US has the most varied mass media in the world. They are relatively decentralized and are comprised of newspapers, magazines, radio and television stations, publishers and internet websites, and most are owned by multimedia concerns. US books, dramas, comedies, television soap operas and series, films and music attract a global following. The early twenty-first century also saw great advances for the internet and other electronic/digital media, such as broadband, cell phones, social networking sites such as Facebook and Twitter, smartphones, iPads and a large increase of blogs (independently written websites). The print media have lost circulation as their functions were transferred online either by subscriptions to existing newspapers and magazines or by independent writers on the internet and social networks. These developments are characterized by instant communication, vast audiences, interactive websites and alternative advertising and revenue sources (see Table 13.1).

There is also concern that largely unregulated new media can lead to irresponsibility, abuse and inaccuracy. But the United Nations Human Rights Council passed a resolution in July 2012, supporting freedom of expression on the internet. According to the Pew Internet Center, the question is whether internet companies, in the interests of profit and their financial backers, will support governments that restrict their citizens from freely using the internet. The domestic US debate is also concerned with whether regulation of the First Amendment beyond existing legal and governmental restrictions is necessary, desirable and possible.

PLATE 13.1 The Cloudforce Expo, San Francisco, 2012, at which salesforce.com advertised how new social media tools can boost business productivity.
(Kim Kulish/Corbis)

Freedom of the media

The First Amendment to the Constitution states that Congress shall not make any law that abridges freedom of speech or the press. This freedom from government control and censorship has long been defended. It has enabled the press to serve as a watchdog over official actions, executive abuses and violations of individual rights. Some critics have argued that the freedoms of speech and the press should be distinguished with the former being more absolute than the latter. But the Supreme Court has not distinguished between the two and has dismissed appeals to give the press any greater rights than those of ordinary citizens.

All the media today (not only the press) claim equal treatment under the First Amendment and there is no overt government censorship of content or form. But freedom from prior restraint is not absolute. The Supreme Court has indicated that injunctions preventing publication could be granted if material clearly jeopardized national security and other exceptions have occurred in areas such as school newspapers. There are licensing and anti-monopolistic regulations by the Federal Communications Commission (FCC), which supposedly make the broadcasting media less free than the print media. It is also argued that while the media appear to be constitutionally free, they are in fact subject to and conditioned by advertising, concentrated ownership patterns, economic pressures and consumer opinion.

Attitudes to the freedom of the press are divided. Respondents to an ABC News Nightline poll in January 2003 felt that the right to a free press is essential/very important (38/49 percent) and 59 percent thought that the government should not have the right to control what information the news media can report. But, in a war-time situation, 60 percent argued that the priority was the government's need to keep military secrets, rather than preserving a free press (34 percent); 56 percent thought that the media should support the government (rather than questioning it); and 66 percent felt that the government should have the right to prohibit the media from reporting sensitive military information.

A BBC World Service poll in 2007 found that 66 percent of American respondents thought that freedom of the press was very important to ensure a fair society. Twenty-four percent felt that stability and peace were more important and that controls were sometimes needed. Seventy-four per cent were concerned about the ownership of the private media and believed that concentration of media ownership in a few hands resulted in owners' political views emerging in reports. Although a majority of respondents strongly believed in press freedom, they were critical of the media's honesty and accuracy and only some 29 percent thought that the media did a good job in reporting news accurately.

A 2005 University of Connecticut survey found that 32 percent of high school students felt that the press enjoyed too much freedom; 37 percent said that it had the right amount; and 10 percent thought that it had too little. Thirty-six percent felt that the government should approve newspaper stories before publication, while 51 percent thought that the press should be able to publish freely. Although a large majority of students said that musicians and others should be allowed to express unpopular opinions, 74 percent said that people should not be able to burn or deface the American flag as a political statement.

According to the Worldwide Press Freedom Index 2011–12 compiled by Reporters Without Borders, the US was in 47th place in a list of 169 countries evaluated for their degree of press freedom. This decline from 20th position in 2010–11 was reportedly attributed to alleged police actions against journalists and photographers who had covered protests in the US, such as the "Occupy" movements. It was argued that press freedoms were being eroded.

The media, in pursuing their constitutional rights, have often pursued an adversarial or confrontational line towards public authorities and individuals. They have published official secrets, revealed classified documents and exposed corrupt practices, unethical behavior and injustices in American life. This has led to tension between the media and public authorities.

For example, the *Washington Post* and the *New York Times* published the "Pentagon Papers" in 1971. These classified US Defense papers contained details of the American role in the Vietnam War. After government appeals, the Supreme Court ruled that the newspapers had a constitutional right to publish the information. The *Washington Post* also disclosed the Watergate scandal (that resulted in the resignation of President Nixon). The media revealed the 1968 My Lai massacre by US troops in Vietnam and the 1986 Iran–Contra affair involving secret and illegal dealings by US government officials. Contemporary investigations have probed the activities of politicians, institutions and public figures (such as the Clintons' Whitewater business dealings). In 2001 the White House did not want television networks to broadcast videotaped statements by Osama bin Laden and his associates, although they had already shown another bin Laden tape. The networks agreed not to broadcast such statements again without reviewing them. It was argued that the decision meant that the media was not fulfilling its responsibility to report all of the news.

The question of the media's role, influence and power is controversial and debatable. Critics argue that the media have become too powerful and influential, that their freedom should be curtailed and that they should show more responsibility. The news media are accused of bias, distorted journalism, invasion of privacy, manipulation of events, and actively trying to shape public opinion by setting particular agendas. Legal actions for libel, obscenity, contempt of court (to force the identification of journalists' sources) and injunctions may be used against the media. These can protect individuals, the authorities and organizations and arguably prevent absolute free expression by the media.

There is a close (arguably unhealthy) bond between authorities and the media. Each needs and uses the other to mutual advantage and gains access to sources and policymakers. One example was "embedding" reporters with military units in the 2003 Iraq war. This connection may be thought inappropriate for the media and limits their adversarial role.

The mainstream press has historically tended to ignore the private lives of its political leaders. But this relationship has changed as tabloid newspapers, 24-hour TV news channels, talk radio stations, websites and independent blogs probe the private and official lives of public figures. It is argued that such people have chosen their roles and may be investigated, particularly if their private actions affect their public duties. The internet and interactive talk radio in particular have expanded opportunities for extreme commentary, scandal-mongering and disclosure of classified information. Increasingly, it has been argued that these media are as accountable as more traditional media. Nevertheless, critics feel that a wide dissemination of information is healthier and more democratic than suppression and censorship.

The contemporary print media

The press (newspapers)

In 2010, some 1,397 daily newspapers (mornings and evenings during the week) were published in the US, with a circulation of 46 million. This was a decrease from 2008 and continued a pattern of print decline. The 919 Sunday papers were relatively stable from 2008, but circulation had dropped to 47 million. There were 6,055 weekly, semi-weekly and monthly local newspapers in 2009, a drop from 2005, with a weekly circulation of 45.5 million.

Newspapers cater for different readerships. Some are characterized as "quality" or "serious" papers and have in-depth international and national news and feature coverage. Others are "popular" or "tabloid" publications, which emphasize crime, sports, comic pages, sex and scandal. However, critics argue that many US papers today have pretensions to quality and seriousness rather than ferocious and sensational presentation.

It is often argued that the US does not have a national press or newspapers that are available in all parts of the country on the same morning. This is due partly to the nation's size and different time zones, but also because of a concern with local issues and identity. The one newspaper that is aimed at a national readership and regional distribution by means of satellite technology is the top-selling *USA Today*, which first appeared in 1982. It has brief articles rather than longer stories and a popular tabloid style.

However, most US papers are now available in online and updated format (often by subscription charge) on the internet across the country. The national influence of some large quality metropolitan newspapers, such as the *New York Times*, the *Washington Post*, the *Los Angeles Times* and the *Wall Street Journal* is considerable. These newspapers, and others such as the *Christian Science Monitor*,

TABLE 13.1 Average circulation of main daily newspapers, 2009

Newspaper	Description	Circulation
USA Today	popular	2,113,725
Wall Street Journal	quality	2,082,189
New York Times	quality	1,039,031
Los Angeles Times	quality	723,181
Washington Post	quality	665,383
(New York) Daily News	popular	602,857
New York Post	popular	558,140
Chicago Tribune	quality	501, 202
(Houston) Chronicle	quality	425,138
Arizona Republic	quality	389,701
Denver Post	quality	371,728
(Long Island, NY) Newsday	quality	368,194
(Dallas) Morning News	quality	331,907
Minneapolis Star Tribune	quality	320,076
Chicago Sun-Times	quality	312,141
San Francisco Chronicle	quality	312,118
Boston Globe	quality	302,638

Source: Audit Bureau of Circulations, 2009.

the *Baltimore Sun*, the *St. Louis Post-Dispatch* and the (Milwaukee) *Journal Sentinel* also have international reputations.

Newspapers have experienced fundamental changes and developments in recent decades and have been forced to adapt to changed markets in order to survive. There has been a continuous decline in the sales of most papers since the mass circulation years of the early twentieth century due to news and advertising competition from television, radio and the internet. The number of newspapers has also decreased because of mergers, conversions and closures. Readers have developed new media habits (such as using the internet rather than paper newspapers) and circulation battles between different print formats (such as magazine supplements) have increased. But some smaller dailies and weeklies have nevertheless increased in number and circulation in local areas.

Newspaper decline and amalgamation have been accompanied by a reduction in competition in many (if not all) cities and a lack of variety in publications. The number of cities and towns with competing newspapers has been reduced and many cities now have only a single daily paper. Ownership is held by a few publishers or corporations (media conglomerates) and 75 percent of daily papers are now owned by newspaper chains.

Concentrated ownership of newspapers by large groups supposedly results in economies of size, efficiency and rationalization and gives greater profitability. But it also causes monopolistic conditions, a similarity in content and format and raises questions about objectivity and accuracy. While some quality papers are local monopolies, it is argued that a greater diversity of newspapers would result in the reduction of potential error and bias.

Newspapers have experienced technological changes in recent years, such as automated composing-rooms and the use of computer and electronic technology to process news. Some news is still gathered by individual reporters, but most newspapers and radio and television networks worldwide now obtain their news directly from US-based news agencies, such as Associated Press (AP), Bloomberg LP and United Press International (UPI). They are independently owned and collect national and international news items that are sold to newspapers and other media. A few news sources therefore dominate the US market, resulting in comparatively homogeneous international and national news.

The big American papers still provide some of their own news stories and sell copyrighted news and features to international and national papers. This allows the wide dissemination of news throughout the US and contributes to the influence of the larger papers. Similarly, the articles of independent syndicated columnists appear simultaneously in many newspapers. The stories in the big papers often influence local newspapers and television news programs in their choice and presentation of newsworthy items.

It is argued that, following competition from television, newspapers generally have become more responsible, make their news columns as fair and accurate as possible, attempt to be objective in their reports and try to separate news from opinion (which is usually confined to political- and policy-influenced editorial pages).

Investigative journalism is still a part of the newspaper trade, although costs have reduced its use. Small newspapers concentrate largely on local news, but they may also cover issues such as pollution, nuclear leaks and climate change, and have revealed cases of local political and social corruption and cover-ups, which have wider national ramifications. Some large city papers are the most active in investigative journalism and have the resources for in-depth coverage. However, the amount of investigative reporting carried out by the US media should not be exaggerated. Few journalists engage in such work and many rely on common sources rather than their own independent investigations.

Investigative (and other) journalists argue that they uphold press freedom of speech and promote important social change with their news presentations; maintain that they perform a necessary democratic service; and see themselves as servants of the public rather than officialdom. However, as in the past, some critics oppose vigorous reporting and argue that it constitutes a serious invasion of privacy in many cases, gives newspapers too much social and political influence, and encourages irresponsibility.

Magazines and periodicals

Some 11,000 magazines and periodicals are published in the US at varying times from weekly and monthly to quarterly and half-yearly. About four out of five adults read magazines, which cater for most tastes and interests. Some have small and others large circulations, with the top 100 selling collectively 244 million copies in 2009 and some magazines sell more than 1 million copies each issue. Some of these have international editions or are translated into other languages. Only six magazine companies account for half the total magazine revenue, indicating a high conglomerate concentration and influence. The bestselling (specialist) magazines deal with retirement (*AARP The Magazine* and *AARP The Bulletin*) and have sales of more than 20 million per year. The list in Table 13.2 refers to generalist and specialist popular magazines covering television news, reading, travel, women's interests, news and video-gaming. The income revenue of magazines comes from advertising and circulation/digital subscription, and paper circulation continued to fall in 2010.

Mass-circulation magazines declined from the 1950s because they had to compete for advertising and sales with television and newspapers. Rising costs of production and paper led to smaller formats and fewer magazines. Classic publications such as *Life*, the *Saturday Evening Post* and *Look* did not survive as weeklies. A shift to specialization in specific areas has occurred, as magazines try to establish market positions and profitability.

However, general magazines (such as *Reader's Digest*) are an important element of American cultural life. They were originally designed for entertainment, but they could also be influential in social and political areas. Today, general magazines are mainly informational and are concerned with very varied aspects of social life. They are aimed at readers in specific age, interest or economic groups.

The more specialist magazines are targeted at people with particular professional occupations and interests and serve as an important means of communication among them. In fact, the majority of all magazines and periodicals are "trade" or specialist publications. They cover business, professional, technical, industrial, scientific and scholarly areas.

US news magazines have been successful when compared with those of other countries in this field, but sales have declined significantly since 1999. In 2010, *Time* (with sales per issue of 3,312,484), *Newsweek* (1,610,632) and *US News and World Report* (1,121,618) led the news-magazine market. They sold in the US, had international and internet editions and sold some of their news material to publications worldwide. However, *Newsweek* merged with the *Daily Beast* in 2010 because of declining sales and switched from paper to a digital online publication called *Newsweek Global* in 2012.

Some influential periodicals specialize in coverage of educational, political and cultural topics, such as the *Atlantic Monthly*, *Harvard Educational Review*, *Saturday Review*, the *New Republic*, *National Review*, *Scientific American*, *Foreign*

TABLE 13.2 Leading magazines: average circulation, 2010

Magazine	Paid circulation
AARP The Magazine (special interest)	23,721,626
AARP The Bulletin (specialist)	23,574,328
Better Homes and Gardens (specialist)	7,644,011
Reader's Digest (general interest)	6,112,811
National Geographic (specialist)	4,493,110
Good Housekeeping (women's interest)	4,427,694
Game Informer (specialist, video games)	4,364,170
Woman's Day (women's interest)	3,919,488
Family Circle (women's interest)	3,849,673
Ladies Home Journal (women's interest)	3,831,072
People (celebrity life)	3,553,420
Time (specialist, news)	3,312,484

Source: Audit Bureau of Circulations, 2010.

Affairs, *Smithsonian* and the *New Yorker*. These, together with other specialist professional journals, supply the more serious end of the magazine market, and some of their material is reprinted internationally.

The leisure or hobby end of the market is catered for by magazines which deal with sports, popular pastimes, motoring, fashion and leisure activities. Some, such as *Vogue* (sales per issue of 1,215,027 in 2010) and *Cosmopolitan* (3,046,229), also sell well internationally.

The often significant difference between paid circulation sales and advertising revenue meant that in 2009 the most successful in terms of advertising revenue were (in descending order according to Magazine Publishers of America) *People*, *Better Homes and Gardens*, *Sports Illustrated*, *Good Housekeeping*, *Family Circle*, *Time*, *Woman's Day*, *In Style* and *Ladies' Home Journal*.

Book publishing

There was concern in the twentieth century that radio, film and television might reduce the appeal of reading books. But book purchases did increase and the US led the world in the number of books read per head of population. However, printed book sales declined in 2009 and, according to Nielsen BookScan, dropped by 3 percent to 724 million units with the biggest fall being in adult non-fiction. But it was noted that publishers' net revenue rose, because the average price of books increased.

Although computers, tablets and e-books were supposed to eradicate the paper book industry, it has continued to produce. The Bowker book site estimated that 764,448 titles produced in 2009 included conventional paper books, print-on-demand or self-published titles and electronic editions. E-books had an estimated 3–5 percent of the market in 2009 and this was predicted to rise to 25 percent by 2012. According to the Book Industry Study Group, 25 percent of people who bought e-books in 2010 purchased fewer print books and 15 percent did not normally buy print books. But the future of the paper book is again debated, as anecdotal evidence and sales figures in the US and Britain in 2012 might suggest a rise in paper books and a retreat from electronic versions. This fluid situation is also tied to different forms and sources of reading (see the section on leisure in Chapter 14).

Historically, US schools have generally encouraged reading and a love of books, public libraries have actively sponsored book-usage in local communities nationwide and there are no restrictive laws that control book-selling and prices. There is an open market in new and used books, which are sold in a variety of sales outlets, such as supermarkets, in addition to standard book shops.

American books cover a comprehensive range from fiction to technical works. They are an important leisure, as well as an educational and professional, activity. There are 2,500 major book publishers in the US, with about six conglomerates accounting for more than half of total book revenues. They publish hardcover and paperback books and differ in size and variety of publications. Many thousands of new books are still published each year and a large export trade has contributed to the worldwide influence of American books, especially in the scientific and technological fields.

About a quarter of the publishing structure deals with books intended for a general audience, such as fiction, bestsellers, biography, art books and children's books. Three-quarters of the publishing business is divided among textbooks, reference works, subscription book clubs, and scientific and technical publications.

The contemporary broadcasting media

The broadcasting system (radio and television stations) is characterized by its diversity and division into commercial and non-commercial sectors. The commercial sector is largely financed from businesses that pay to advertise goods or services before, during and after programs, or by subscriptions from cable and satellite users. Advertising is a large and profitable industry and its connection to the media is controversial because of its influence.

The non-commercial radio and television sectors, such as the television Public Broadcasting Service (PBS), do not carry advertising, are largely non-profit-making, educational or cultural in nature and run by bodies such as colleges and universities. They are funded by individual subscriptions, sponsorship, grants from foundations, private bodies, educational sources and the government, but have to survive on relatively limited budgets.

All radio and television stations must be licensed to broadcast by the Federal Communications Commission (FCC). This is an independent federal agency, financed by Congress, whose members are appointed by the president. It controls the stations by granting limited-period licenses to applicants and has a supervisory and regulatory role. The FCC does not control the reception of broadcast programs through the air. This means that there are no license fees in the US for owning equipment such as television sets. Broadcast reception is freely available in most cases, except for cable and decoded satellite services, and underwent a switchover from analog to digital reception in June 2009.

There is no direct government censorship of broadcasting content, but the FCC, with its licensing power, does regulate media-ownership by ensuring that there are no monopolies and that a variety of services, programs and frequencies is provided throughout the country. Its "fairness doctrine" also requires stations to give equal time to opposing views, and commercial stations must show free "public-service" announcements, such as Red Cross blood drives and Alcoholics Anonymous programs.

Television

Television is a popular and controversial medium. In 2010, according to Nielsen Media Research, 114.9 million (or 99 percent of) US households owned at least one television set and 84 percent had two or more. The majority was color and the average viewing time for all viewers was 34.05 hours per week. Surveys suggest that television is an important source of news for Americans, although the network share is declining in competition with online and cable news. It can be influential in forming opinions and consumer choice and may be potentially capable of affecting the outcome of political elections.

The Federal Communications Act of 1934 established local television stations as the bodies legally responsible for all their output, no matter where their programs originated. In 2011, there were about 1,774 television stations in the US, which vary in size, have separate identities and characteristics, and different transmission strengths. Some 392 were non-commercial or educational and 1,382 were commercial stations.

Most commercial television stations are affiliated with and receive many programs from the current Big Four private television networks, which buy most of their material from independent production companies. The Big Four are the American Broadcasting Company (ABC, established in 1943), the National Broadcasting Company (NBC, 1926), the Columbia Broadcasting System (CBS, 1928) and Fox Broadcasting Company (1986). The Fox network broke the dominance of the original Big Three networks, ABC, CBS and NBC.

The networks compete against each other to attract the highest audience ratings and advertising revenue, which are crucial for the survival of individual shows. Most of the programs that 82 percent of those with a TV set watch follow the same formats nationwide, and similar offerings (see Table 13.3) are shown at the same time during "prime time" (8pm to 11pm). This structure traditionally gave the three older networks (ABC, NBC and CBS) great influence. Until the 1980s, they dominated American television, having a combined share of 90 percent of the total television audience.

In addition to an entertainment role, the networks have news-gathering organizations in the US and worldwide. They broadcast nationwide news and current affairs programs throughout the week, and have developed classics such as CBS's *60 Minutes* and NBC's *Meet the Press*. Local commercial television stations also have news teams, reporters and film crews to provide local news programs, but may be parochial and limited in their scope.

However, a large television network (in terms of the number of its member stations) and an alternative to commercial television is the advertising-free PBS. This system was created in 1969 by the Public Broadcasting Act, has 350 stations sharing programs, reaches 73 million people each week and delivers quality and educational programs. The growth of PBS has been considerable, although it has a smaller audience than commercial television. The high standard of its news, entertainment and educational programs (such as children's programs, imported drama series and films) has attracted selective audiences.

The way Americans view television changed significantly in June 2009 when the FCC stipulated that all US-based TV signals must be transmitted digitally. Some 97.5 percent of homes complied with the switchover from analog reception. Americans are also changing the way that they watch television. From 2008–9 more people have watched recorded or "time-shifted television" (DVR) and the major networks attract viewers by providing free episodes of popular shows streamed from their website. Other sites offer advertising-supported episodes from traditional television shows and specially-made internet programs.

Independent, cable and satellite television

Since the 1980s, the power of the original Big Three networks has declined because of competition, such as the Fox network. New challenges have also come from other independent television stations that were originally unaffiliated with the networks and broadcast syndicated programming, comprising mostly repeats of earlier network series. They have built larger audiences nationwide by expanding the quality and range of their services and by using broadcast technology and cable and satellite facilities.

Cable stations originally provided television programs to subscribers in communities that could not receive good reception from air broadcasts because of geographical limitations. In the past 30 years, cable has changed television broadcasting, by attracting a third of the television audience from existing channels and 71 percent of television set owners in 2010 watched cable programs for varying periods of time in an average week. This has split the total television audience, which is now shared by more competitors.

According to Nielsen Media Research, there were 7,853 cable-television systems in 2008 and the number of household subscribers was 104 million in 2010 or 90.6 percent of those households with television sets. Basic cable subscribers increased to 63.7 million in 2008 and digital pay cable reached 40.4 million. The two largest cable providers in 2009 were Comcast Cable Communications and DirecTV and the top cable networks were TBS Superstation (1976), the Discovery Channel (1985), Nickelodeon (1979), the Weather Channel (1982) and CNN/HLN (1980). Fox News is the leading US cable news network.

There are now many different types of cable systems and programs. Companies transmit cable and other network affiliated, independent and public television services. They are financed by advertising and a fee from subscribers for the cable service. Viewers may also pay additional sums for specialist channels and live broadcasts. There has been a big increase in religious and ethnic cable stations and channels nationwide with networks for African, Latino, Jewish, Chinese, Japanese, Portuguese, Greek, Hindi and Korean interests.

Satellite television also undercut the dominance of the original Big Three networks. It initially offered programs to rural populations who could not receive cable systems and now provides an alternative to cable. It gives those people who have a satellite dish and pay subscriptions a wide range of television channels. After a period when there was a variety of satellite providers, many of which went out of business, there are now two main servers, which compete against each other. DirecTV (1994) has national coverage and offers digital-quality and multi-

TABLE 13.3 Top ten favorite prime-time commercial TV programs, 2009–10

Rank	Title	Genre
1	*American Idol* (Wednesday) (Fox)	singing competition
2	*American Idol* (Tuesday) (Fox)	singing competition
3	*Dancing with the Stars* (ABC)	dance competition
4	*NBC Sunday Night Football* (NBC)	sport
5	*Dancing with the Stars – Results* (ABC)	dance competition
6	*NCIS: Los Angeles* (CBS)	naval crime investigation
7	*NCIS* (CBS)	naval crime investigation
=8	*NFL Regular Season* (ESPN)	sport
=8	*Sunday Night NFL Pre-Kick* (NBC)	sport
10	*The Good Wife* (CBS)	legal drama

Source: adapted from Nielsen Media Research, 2009–10.

channel TV programming. Dish Network (1996) operates globally and delivers Direct Broadcast Satellite products. While satellite programming has attracted ethnic communities and minority interests in the US and abroad, it has experienced technological problems, monitoring and regulation issues, and political conflicts on viability.

A further threat to Big Three supremacy was the home-video market, with videos for sale or rent. In 2006 there was at least one video-cassette recorder (VCR) in 85 percent of American homes that had television sets. Video was successfully challenged by huge sales of digital versatile discs (DVDs) and 84 percent of television-owning households had a DVD player in 2006. These forms have now also been partly replaced by videos shown by made-for-internet programs streamed from network and company websites. Monthly time spent watching video online (including both user-generated content and recorded programs) grew by more than 50 percent from 2008 to 2009.

Traditional network television has thus faced severe competition to retain its audience as viewers have changed to other services. Cable, satellite and independent television stations and internet providers are attractive because they offer many different channels and a range of alternative choices. In 2009, television household viewing shares were 24 percent network affiliates, 1 percent for public television, 5 percent for independent and satellite stations, 57 percent for basic cable and 4 percent for pay cable.

Attitudes to commercial television

Commercial television programs have a mixed reputation in the US and abroad. A variety of opinions and criticisms have been leveled by consumers and government authorities.

Commercial television has been attacked for its bias towards commercial and mass-entertainment programs ("reality" shows with huge audiences, talk shows, soap operas and quiz games) that advertise goods and services. Advertising companies and station-owners may also interfere in program content in the pursuit of profit. Some consumers criticize the programming, which is aimed at the lower end of the television market, and argue that companies should develop more quality programs. News broadcasting is also increasingly controversial because it can either appear to trivialize events by its reporting techniques or try to affect public opinion by the biases in its news coverage.

Television is criticized for its portrayal of gratuitous violence and for the alleged impact of such violence, explicit sex, immorality and bad language upon both children and adults. The debate over possible links between violence on television and its imitation in society continues, although such programs are not now shown in the early evening and "v-chip" technology allows parents to censor children's viewing. There is a considerable amount of citizen involvement in other television-related issues, such as groups campaigning for better quality children's television. Minorities and women are also concerned with television programs and object to the representation of ethnic and gender stereotypes.

Commercial television networks and advertising companies are often sensitive to such criticism, since it can affect their profits. It is argued that objections have made commercial television into a more conservative institution, and there are some indications that advertisers and companies may be paying more attention to the public's wishes.

Nevertheless, attitudes to American commercial television are not solely a list of complaints and negative comments. Some situation comedy and drama series are excellent and are very popular worldwide. Television can also perform essential educational and information functions, with high-quality documentaries and in-depth news presentations. It provides live coverage of important events from both domestic and worldwide sources. It has the capacity to closely examine politicians and their policies, so that viewers may make up their own minds about a range of issues. Politicians and advertisers are also very aware of television's power and influence, and this may help to moderate their behavior.

Radio

Radio had a dramatic impact after its commercial introduction to the US in the 1920s. It (and its immediate news function) helped to unify the population of the cities and the countryside, increased the national and world awareness of Americans and informed them about the events of the Second World War. Radio was overtaken by television in the 1940s and has had to develop new markets and emphases to survive. It has become divided into formats that are directed at specific consumer markets and this has increased the diversity of radio offerings. Some 98 percent of American households have at least one radio set, and radio is still popular and important, particularly on the local level, for its news, participatory (talk radio) and entertainment roles. According to Radio Advertising Bureau statistics, 95.3 percent of Americans over the age of 12 listen to radio for an average of three hours and 20 minutes each workday.

The US does not have one national radio station. Instead, cities and local areas have commercial stations and all are regulated by the FCC, which grants them operating licenses. They have different approaches. Town stations carry local interest items and news, and national and international news derived from larger stations. Big cities have a large number of stations and different formats and services to satisfy varied tastes. News, sports and talk stations predominate on medium wave (AM), with music on FM. Subscription satellite and cable radio offers hundreds of stations and has attracted millions of customers. Freedom of expression is guaranteed by the Constitution, and some broadcast outlets give airtime to radical political and religious views. There were 10,997 commercial radio stations in 2010, that obtain their funding mainly from the advertising on their programs, which are purchased from many different sources, although they do also make their own programs. Commercial radio ownership is concentrated in the hands of relatively few conglomerates.

The National Public Radio network (NPR) is an organization of 797 public or non-commercial radio stations and provides quality news, debate and music without advertising. In a 2005 Harris poll, the NPR was voted the most trusted news source in the US. The public radio stations are generally owned and operated by educational institutions and religious groups, with a similar high reputation as PBS for their news, debates and documentaries.

Diversity of choice is the key element of radio in the US and many stations provide 24-hour services to satisfy their customers. Most commercial radio stations are organized around and follow a specific format or genre, which is designed to attract particular audiences. Permission from the FCC is required if a station wishes to change its format.

Some stations consequently only provide music programs (mixed or specialist) such as country, popular music, rock and roll, light classics, classical music and jazz. Others concentrate on news, studio interviews and discussions, talk shows and interviews, phone-ins (audience participation by telephone) and religious programs. Stations with a talk format account for 10 percent of stations and the number of listeners and active participants has increased considerably. Some stations broadcast only news for 24 hours a day, while most others provide five-minute summaries hourly or half-hourly. Others offer a variety or mixture of the above. According to the M. Street Corporation in 2010, the primary formats of the top commercial AM and FM radio stations were country, news/talk, Spanish, sports, oldies, adult contemporary (AC), Top 40, classic rock, hot AC, classic hits, religion and rock.

Online radio began in 1993 and had a simple structure until traditional radio stations began to broadcast online from 1994. Today online radio enjoys great popularity and most major radio stations offer to stream some programs online, free of cost. Internet radio has grown, especially in music stations, and attracted advertising. According to AcuStream Research, internet advertising revenue has expanded hugely and listening hours were 6.6 billion in 2008. AOL's Shoutcast was the most popular internet music station, followed by Clear Channel Online, Yahoo Music, AOL Radio Networks and Pandora.

The internet and new media sources

The infant internet was used by the US Defense Department in 1969 to improve information exchange and communication between government agencies. In the 1980s, the National Science Foundation developed hardware and software that allowed other computer networks to use the government system. Commercial servers, such as America Online, expanded these communications systems and supplied information to more computer users.

In the 1990s, the world wide web also became commercially available; new software increased internet usage; and the Netscape browser allowed users to more easily navigate the net. E-mail broke the monopoly of letter and postal delivery until it was later challenged by mobile phone texting (SMS). SMS declined in 2012 and gave way to smartphones and social networking sites such as Facebook and Twitter. The internet and web have influenced individual and professional lives, are decentralized and largely unregulated.

It is estimated that internet users in the US reached 50 million by 1998 and there was a considerable increase in usage from 2000 to 2010. Nielsen Net Ratings estimated that, in May 2009, monthly computer usage per person was 36 hours at home and 82 hours at work and disparities of gender, age, income, education and race among users had diminished. Individuals and organizations have built their own websites and cyber expansion encouraged the creation of competitive search engine such as Google, Yahoo!, AOL and Bing in the US.

The twenty-first century has seen great advances for the internet and other new forms of electronic/digital media. According to Internet WorldStats.com, 270 million Americans were online in 2011 (78 percent of the population), with 66 percent having broadband access at home. Wireless telecommunications systems had 298 million subscribers in 2009 and smartphones increasingly use a variety of other connected media (such as fax and the internet). Seventy-four percent of Americans use social networks and blogs, and 62 percent were active on the Facebook website in 2010 (Nielsen), with 142 million visitors in June 2010. MySpace had 67 million visitors and Twitter had 23 million (comScore Media Metrix).

Technological growth has made the internet an attractive business medium as a low-cost sales market for producers of goods and services and a platform for online shopping. Ninety-two percent of e-commerce is conducted between many businesses and the internet has increased efficiencies of scale, cut costs and established comparison websites for goods and services. But online shopping by consumers has developed slowly and in 2008 was still a small part of total internet commerce. The US Census Bureau in 2007 reported that most online sales were for retailers, such as Amazon.com and mail order companies, or motor vehicles and parts. The internet is now a major source of US commercial advertising amounting to $55.2 billion in 2010, with a projected increase to $96.8 billion by 2014.

The internet has also been seen as a growing threat to personal privacy and property rights. Databases can be hacked to gain detailed information about usage habits, financial history and contact information and US agencies have tried to protect privacy and combat identity theft online. But the United Nations (2012) and campaign groups support freedom of expression and information on the internet. The data-sharing power of the internet has affected traditional pro-tections for personal information and copyright material. Despite some success in combating swap sites and downloading of popular music, users continue to pirate digital songs, music, games and books through online file-sharing systems. Copyright protection and intellectual property rights on the internet are continuing long-term issues.

The increase in independent blogging in recent years illustrates the positive and negative sides of the internet. These websites usually contain the personal thoughts or views of the site's owner as well as links to other sites of interest and can be a democratic method of spreading ideas and opinions, as well as serving as a campaigning source. But blogs can be abusive with extreme views and personal attacks. An ongoing debate about the internet is concerned with whether and how it should be supervised, controlled and regulated.

Attitudes to the media

The US news media attract different reactions and attitudes. In summing up the effort to gather information in a diverse society, Welch et al. (1995: 244) suggested that:

> The media have to be responsive to the people to make a profit. They present the news they think the people want. Because they believe the majority desire entertainment, or at least diversion, rather than education, they structure the news towards this end. According to a number of studies, they correctly assess their consumers. For the majority who want entertainment, network television provides it. For the minority who want education, the better newspapers and magazines provide it. Public radio, with its hour-and-a-half nightly newscast . . . and public television, with its hour nightly newscast . . . also provide quality coverage. The media offer something for everyone.

American attitudes to the news media may be seen in the context of constitutional freedom of speech and of the press. Of respondents to a State of the First Amendment Survey in July 2009, 39 percent felt that the press had too much freedom to do what it wants, 48 percent thought it had about the right amount, and 7 percent said it had too little. In another First Amendment survey in 2012, only 33 percent of respondents believed that the news media attempted to report news without bias, but 75 percent agreed that it should act as a government watchdog and only 20 percent disagreed. Eighty-one percent of respondents said that the First Amendment does not go too far in the rights it guarantees, while 13 percent said it does.

The news media for their part often argue that their decisions to focus on specific newsworthy items are based on their organization's views, editorial policy and individual journalists' opinions. They insist that they try to be objective, present all sides of a case and use self-censorship in order to avoid overt bias or partiality.

But a Pew Research Center poll in 2000 found that 57 percent of respondents thought that members of the news media often let their political preferences influence the way they report the news, while 32 percent believed that this happened "sometimes." A Gallup poll in September 2003 reported that 45 percent of respondents considered that the news media was too liberal, 14 percent thought it too conservative, and 39 percent felt that the political balance was "about right." A survey by the Roper Organization in 1984 found that 41 percent of respondents thought that the news media were biased against groups, such as business executives, workers, liberals and conservatives. Such findings, which might indicate that the media in fact are doing a neutral job, point to the difficulties in assessing media bias.

However, critics have long argued that there is a clear positive bias towards some established institutions and values in the US news media, although not much partiality for particular political candidates and specific political policies. There appears to be a general media skepticism aimed at all politicians and their policies. The tendency is towards negativism rather than positivism, which influences reporting.

In terms of media behavior, a September 2012 Gallup poll reported that 39 percent of respondents did not have very much confidence in the media to report the news fully, accurately and fairly and 21 percent none at all, while 32 percent had a fair amount of confidence and 8 percent had a great deal. A July 2011 Pew News Interest Index poll found that 34 percent of respondents thought that it was very likely or somewhat likely (38 percent) that the media would intrude into people's private lives by hacking cell phones or private medical and financial records. Only 16 percent felt that it was not too likely.

Prior to the presidential election campaign in 2008, 54 percent of respondents in a March Harris poll said they tended not to trust the press in general (30 percent trusted) and 46 percent said they did not trust television (36 percent trusted). Internet news sites were trusted by 41 percent (34 percent not trusted). Radio tended to do best with 44 percent saying that they tend to trust it (32 percent distrusted). But a Gallup poll in July 2012 found that only 21 percent of respondents had a great deal or quite a lot of confidence in network television news, a drop to a new low since 27 percent in 2011. It now ranked 11th among 16 US institutions and newspapers were in 10th place. Eleven percent of liberals had faith in network television news and moderates were ranked with conservatives at 10 percent.

Gallup, July 10, 2012, considered these results:

> It is not clear precisely why Americans soured so much on television news this year compared with last. Americans' negativity likely reflects the continuation of a broader trend that appeared to enjoy only a brief respite last year. Americans have grown more negative about the media in recent years, as they have about many other US institutions and the direction of the country in general.

Exercises

Explain and examine the significance of the following names and terms:

"yellow journalism"	William Randolph Hearst	ratings
soap operas	circulation	AM/FM
"muckraking"	newspaper chains	networks
New England Courant	advertising	formats
broadband	v-chip technology	NPR
conglomerates	*Washington Post*	Watergate
syndication	cable television	PBS
FCC	bias	UPI
blog	ESPN	injunction
"Fourth Estate"	First Amendment	talk shows

Write short essays on the following questions:

1. Should the freedom of the American news media be curtailed?

2. Analyze the contemporary significance of American newspapers in terms of their historical development and in the light of other alternatives.

3. Discuss the structure and influence of US television.

4. Critically examine the American media in terms of the public opinion polls in this chapter.

Further reading

Alterman, E. (2003) *What Liberal Media? The Truth About Bias and the News*, New York: Basic Books.

Bagdikian, B.H. (2004) *The New Media Monopoly*, Boston, MA: Beacon Press.

Dautrich, K. and Hartley, T.H. (1999) *How the News Media Fail American Voters: Causes, Consequences and Remedies*, New York: Columbia University Press.

Fallows, J. (1996) *Breaking the News: How the Media Undermine American Democracy*, New York: Pantheon Books.

Fuller, J. (1996) *News Values: Ideas for an Information Age*, Chicago, IL: University of Chicago Press.

Garry, P.M. (1994) *Scrambling for Protection: The New Media and the First Amendment*, Pittsburgh, PA: Pittsburgh Press.

Kovach, B. and Rosenstiel, T. (1999) *Warp Speed: America in the Age of Mixed Media*, New York: The Century Foundation.

Krimsky, G.A. and Hamilton, J.M. (1996) *Hold the Press: The Inside Story on Newspapers*, Baton Rouge, LA: Louisiana State University Press.

Kurtz, H. (1998) *Spin Cycle: How the White House and the Media Manipulate the News*, New York: Simon & Schuster.

McChesney, R.W. (2004) *The Problem of the Media: US Communication Politics in the Twenty-First Century*, New York: Monthly Review Press.

Teeter, D. and Le Duc, D.R. (1995) *Law of Mass Communications: Freedom and Control of Print and Broadcast Media*, Westbury, NY: Foundation Press.

The World Almanac and Book of Facts (annual) New York: World Almanac Books.

Welch, S., Gruhl, J., Steinman, M., Comer, J., Ambrosius, M.M. and Rigdon, S. (1995) *Understanding American Government*, St. Paul, MN: West.

Wright, J.W. (general editor) (annual) *The New York Times Almanac*, New York: Penguin.

Websites

First Amendment: www.knightfoundation.org/publications/future-first-amendment-2011
www.firstamendmentcenter.org/sofa
http://infousa.state.gov/media/index.html
FCC: www.fcc.gov
Nielsen Media Research: http://mashable.com/category/nielsen
PBS: www.pbs.org
The Washington Post: www.washingtonpost.com
The New York Times: www.nytimes.com
CNN: www.cnn.com
Time: www.time.com/time/magazine
USA Today: www.usatoday.com

Chapter 14

Arts, sports and leisure cultures

- The arts
- Sports
- Leisure
- *Exercises*
- *Further reading*
- *Websites*

The diversity of US society is reflected in Americans' artistic, sporting and leisure lives. These reveal different cultural habits at all social levels; have professional and amateur dimensions; and include participatory and spectator pastimes. They have varied in popularity over a 400-year-old history, have been influenced by new cultural developments and many still hold to their traditional forms.

There are differences between so-called popular and elite cultures in the US, which have been redefined over time. Popular culture may include mass-interest sports such as baseball, football and basketball; movies; and music such as jazz, rock and roll, and country. Elite cultures were often associated with European visual art, symphony orchestras, opera, art galleries and museums. The elitist has now become more inclusive; music was popularized and commercialized; and sports and the arts generally have been democratized. Cultural activities are dependent for their funding upon private and public donations, sponsorship and advertising, attendance fees and an economic system that responds to demand and the search for profit. There is also a small amount of state and federal funding, such as the National Endowment for the Arts (NEA), the National Endowment for the Humanities (NEH) and congressional appropriations.

There are American aspects in the arts and sports, which now convey distinctive national identities, but which have sometimes been influenced by European and other global influences. Baseball, country, folk music, painting and the musical, arguably derive from non-American sources. "Ethnic" and folklorist expressions, such as slave and settler traditions, Latino music and dance, Jewish and Chinese theatre, Native American art and Asian cinema, reflect their culture of origin rather than a purely American identification.

All have collectively created American cultural identities, and an American-oriented internationalized culture. The latter is resented in some countries which seek to preserve their own artistic integrity and inheritance. Critics (including Americans) also disparage what they see as a US mass market and media that is allegedly directed to the lowest common denominator of taste and quality. But Americans have produced models in the arts, sports and leisure fields to which many people worldwide respond positively, both for their initial inventiveness and strangeness and their later incorporation into a global culture.

A general US work ethic, competitive ethos, ambition and drive for success and achievement also influence sporting, leisure and artistic pursuits. These are often taken very seriously on both professional and amateur levels. Americans who play professional sports do so because they want to win, as well as to achieve the large amounts of money available in many of the professional games. Amateur sports may be similarly driven, beyond a wish for fitness. The arts are part of a competitive business structure and leisure activities for some may have a deliberately planned and goal-oriented context.

American values, such as self-improvement and self-definition, are echoed by those people who go to concerts and the theater or who pursue other artistic activities. They indulge in these not only for fashionable reasons, but often because they feel that the arts are self-improving and that so-called elite culture is an admirable and positive thing in itself. Many Americans also exercise, take part in keep-fit classes and diet, at least initially, to improve themselves by becoming healthier and fitter in body and mind, although these pastimes can sometimes be short-lived fads. But many people are spectators rather than active participants, whether of sports, television and concerts or as visitors to museums and art galleries. Such activities may nevertheless have informational, recreational and entertainment value.

Sports, leisure and the arts are important for many people and central to their lives. This is reflected in the large amounts of money spent by Americans on attendance fees, sports equipment, training, musical instruments, electronic equipment, sports stadiums, concert halls, museums and art galleries. A huge advertising expenditure is normally devoted to them, through newspapers, television and the internet. "Entertainment" (broadly defined) regularly comes near the top of total advertising fees after cars and retailing services. However, research in 2008 by the NEA showed that personal spending on the performing arts, movie theaters and spectator sports declined in the recessionary economic climate of 2007–9 as a proportion of total recreation expenditure. But the purchase of computers and electronic games and software is still a significant share of spending, which suggests that more people are following arts, sport and leisure activities through technology in the home.

American sporting and artistic history have had their darker sides. Discrimination has been widespread, so that African Americans, Native Americans, Jews and women, among other minorities, have experienced considerable racism and exclusion. This applied not only to performers, but also to spectators who were segregated and to sports, which were divided on color and ethnic lines. In the early twentieth century, there was a gulf between America's divided society and its democratic ideals, which forced civil rights on to the political agenda and encouraged attempts to widen equal access to cultural activity.

While overt racism and discrimination have been reduced, they still influence contemporary pursuits. Racial, gender and class stereotyping exist so that, for example, African Americans may find it difficult to advance in professional tennis and golf. Those individuals who do succeed, such as Althea Gibson, Arthur Ashe and the Williams sisters in tennis, are seen as role models. The impact of women in some sports, such as soccer and athletics, increased considerably in the twentieth century and breakthroughs by minorities into the wider US society have often come partly through sports and the arts.

The arts

The development of elite and popular arts in the US has been influenced by European traditions (sometimes brought to America by European immigrants) and distinctive domestic cultures. Historically, there has been a tension between the two traditions and European sophistication was contrasted with American originality. Gradually, suspicion decreased and the two coexisted and intermixed. American painters, sculptors, musicians, dancers and film-makers have developed their own (often controversial) artistic styles as US culture has evolved through a process of innovation, experiment, variety and reaction to earlier art forms. However, the US is still often stereotypically perceived as a society in which television, sports, film and other forms of popular or mass entertainment are more accessible than the "highbrow" arts and "high culture."

Surveys had recently suggested that more Americans of all ages and social groups were attending dance performances, classical or symphonic concerts, music recitals and opera as well as visiting a varied range of quality museums and art galleries. These activities indicated a wider and more acceptable cultural profile for the "elite" arts than in the past. Artistic activity had developed from the 1960s and there has been increased participation by amateur and professional individuals and groups in a wide range of visual arts, music, modern dance, theater, ballet and film. The media, such as some television networks and the Public Broadcasting System (PBS), have helped to establish an interest in and support for the arts through their promotion, sponsorship and coverage of cultural events. However, the arts, sports and leisure were significantly affected by the economic downturn in 2007–9.

Visual arts

American painters and artists in the nineteenth and early twentieth century followed European styles. They continued established naturalist and realist traditions, but gradually adapted these to specific American themes, locations and subject matter as they responded more to America's physical nature in the westward expansion of the population.

After the Second World War, new American painters arrived on the traditional scene with revolutionary and distinctively American concepts, such as cityscapes and gritty urban lifestyles. Modernist, cubist and abstract influences then arrived from Europe, from which developed an American abstract expressionism. This was initially begun by New York artists such as Jackson Pollock, Willem de Kooning and Mark Rothko in the 1940s, who rejected established painting styles and subject matter and organized their work around a fluid use of color, space and texture. These painters attracted international attention and New York increasingly became the center of the art world.

Later generations reacted to abstract expressionism and moved to new styles. Painters in the late 1950s and 1960s such as Robert Rauschenberg and Jasper Johns concentrated on collage-type painting and used a variety of ordinary objects to produce works of mixed media. Other innovators, such as Andy Warhol and Roy Lichtenstein, introduced "pop art." This genre used everyday items of the consumer society and popular culture to reflect and comment on what the artist saw as distinctive features of modern America. In this process, the ordinary became iconic and established concepts of culture and "reality" were challenged.

American painters and sculptors continue to experiment with a wide range of styles and materials and have created a number of exotically named artistic movements, such as "op art," graffiti art and performance art. Their distinguishing features have been change, reaction, variety, new techniques and a refusal to be restricted to specific philosophies, styles, schools or media. They gather their inspiration from many sources and influences. The very definition and existence of art is often ironically challenged in "postmodernist" work.

Music

Interesting as some of these visual art styles have been, a more influential expression of US artistic distinctiveness has been in music (elitist and popular). In previous centuries, American classical music was influenced by European traditions and standards. The breakthrough to a distinctive American voice came with George Gershwin and Aaron Copland in the early twentieth century, who allied domestic elements (such as African American influences, jazz, folk songs and country) with European idioms. This mixture of old and new styles continued through the century. There was also a movement to make classical music less elitist and more accessible to more people as symphony orchestra directors and conductors introduced combined programs of mainstream and new music.

The more immediate and commercial forms of American music historically have been mainstream popular, ragtime, blues, jazz, the musical, country, and rock and roll, which have often mixed with and influenced each other over time. They became domestic American successes, but many have also been exported and greatly affected world cultures.

Mainstream popular music with a distinctive American voice was largely initiated by Stephen Foster in the mid-nineteenth century. He combined European styles with African American rhythms and themes to produce classic American songs. There was also a growth of light operetta shows and popular travelling stage reviews (vaudeville or Variety Theater) that provided songs, dance and comedy. By the end of the nineteenth century, popular music became more commercially successful. Writing and production were centered on New York City and its Tin Pan Alley. Songwriters such as Irving Berlin and Cole Porter created American standards, which have survived to the present day.

A wide range of singers and performers has been associated with the mainstream popular category, each having their own appeal and fan base. A Reuters International/Zogby poll of April 1999 found that respondents thought that Barbra Streisand was the best female singer of the twentieth century and Frank Sinatra was the best male singer. But later polls have chosen other favorite artists who have appealed to different current tastes.

African American composers also wrote and performed popular works in the late nineteenth and early twentieth century. Ragtime was an African American music that was popularized by Scott Joplin and derived partly from the rural blues tradition of often melancholic and fatalistic folk songs and church music that reflected the lives of poor African Americans. Bessie Smith was an early and popular exponent of the blues style and mixed the rural tradition with urban themes.

The blues also inspired jazz at the end of the nineteenth century. It is argued that this is America's most original and native music form. It was first played by African American musicians in the South, derives mainly from African influences and Southern slave culture, combines elements of ragtime, slave songs and brass bands and is a fluid, improvised and rhythmic form of music. Traditionally, New Orleans has been the city of jazz, but it later spread to other parts of the country. Jazz reached the height of its popularity in the 1930s and 1940s. It was then incorporated into big-band music and popularized by artists and band leaders such as Louis Armstrong and Duke Ellington.

Reflecting an American capacity for experiment, jazz developed alternative sounds and rhythms from the 1950s by individualistic artists such as Dave Brubeck. It also influenced music such as pop, rock and roll and American musicals. Today, jazz is popular in the US and overseas, although it has lost its mass audience appeal, and the best jazz is supposedly provided in New York, Chicago and Los Angeles, rather than the South.

American country music has become very popular in the US and worldwide. It was based on the folk-song traditions of early Scottish, Irish and English immigrants. It developed into modern country music in the 1920s and is played on the string guitar, banjo or fiddle. Its typically mournful or melancholic lyrics dealt with love, relationships, loss and poverty and reflected the disadvantaged rural life of poor whites in the South, the Southeast and Appalachia. Modern country music deals with more contemporary concerns and has expanded beyond its origins, but Nashville, Tennessee, is still regarded as its home. According to M. Street Corporation, country was the third-placed commercial radio primary format with 2,006 AM and FM radio stations in 2010, and was fifth-placed in US recorded music sales with 11.9 percent in 2008 (Recording Industry Association of America).

American folk music also has a worldwide audience. It had a working-class, underprivileged and rural emphasis, originating in the mountain regions of North Carolina and West Virginia, and was mainly based on immigrant Scottish, Irish and English folk ballads. It later took on American themes through figures such as Woody Guthrie. In the 1960s, it developed a wider and more commercial appeal through singers such as Judy Collins, Bob Dylan and Joan Baez who also introduced social and political comment into their texts. Dylan then moved from acoustic to electric guitar and blended folk with rock, and other folk music became more commercialized.

Rock and roll developed in the 1950s as distinctively American popular entertainment when jazz was losing its mass audience. Many of its practitioners, such as Elvis Presley and later Jimi Hendrix, Janis Joplin and Bruce Springsteen, combined the traditions of African American rhythm and blues and country, with strong rhythms. It became a popular form of music with young Americans and others worldwide and was associated with a succession of rock icons. Its sounds, rhythm and style dominated the popular music scene and have influenced other forms of pop music, whether in imitation or reaction.

Rock has become very commercialized in recent decades. It was initially centered on live concert performances in huge stadiums or open venues, but these have decreased and rock and its derivatives generally became studio production based on the issue of videos, compact discs (CDs) and DVDs. In 2008, rock was the best-selling genre in US recorded music with a 31.8 percent share of all music sold (Recording Industry Association of America) and also the fourth-placed format in commercial AM and FM radio stations with 1,329 stations in 2010 (M. Street Corporation). But the rock category had amounted to nearly half of all music sales in 1987. Touring and live rock-based shows have also been taken over by foreign musicians. In terms of the North American top-grossing tour lists (1985–2009), European artists were in the top 11 places according to Pollstar, CA, with music acts such as the Rolling Stones (1994, 2005, 2006), U2 (2001, 2005, 2009), Pink Floyd (1994), The Police (2007) and Paul McCartney (2002). Yet US rock in its many fashions manages to re-energize itself and retain its popularity.

Elvis Presley was long considered the greatest rock star of all time, but fashions change and he has been replaced by a succession of other singers in the polls. However, large majorities in historical polls have felt that Presley had a lasting impact on American culture and that this was positive. An NBC News/*Wall Street Journal* poll in April 2002 reported that 41 percent of respondents thought that rock music has had a positive influence on American society, culture and values, while 34 percent thought that its effects have been negative.

Popular offshoots of these musical traditions, whether in reaction or modification, are found in a wide range of contemporary music such as rap and hip-hop; urban-influenced styles which can include R&B, blues, dance, disco, funk, fusion, Motown and soul; reggae with its Caribbean origins; gospel, hymn, Christian, inspirational, spiritual and religious songs; ethnic music; standards; big band; swing; Latin; mood and easy listening genres; electronic; and instrumental.

The modern stage musical is of American origin (although some trace the genre to earlier Italian models and the English music hall/pantomime tradition) and developed in the early twentieth century. Its combination of acting, music and dancing was often allied to escapist plots and exotic shows in glossy theatres. Some later musicals became more serious and socially aware, but the entertainment emphasis continued. The musical has recently fallen on hard times and has had to compete with successful foreign imports, particularly from Britain, that are indebted to the original American format. The longest-running Broadway musical as of March 3, 2013 was Andrew Lloyd Webber's *The Phantom of the Opera* with 10,439 performances, followed by his *Cats* with 7,485 performances. But American musicals such as *Chicago* (6,765), *The Lion King* (6,355) and *A Chorus Line* (6,137) are again becoming popular.

Americans spend billions of dollars on music. According to sales figures collected by the Recording Industry Association of America (2008) and categorized by genre, rock accounted for 31.8 percent; rap/hip-hop for 10.7 percent; R&B/urban for 10.2 percent; country for 11.9 percent; pop for 9.1 percent; religious/gospel for 6.5 percent; jazz for 1.1 percent; classical for 1.9 percent; and other forms, such as children's, oldies, New Age and soundtracks for 14.2 percent. The joint top-selling albums of all time in the US are Michael Jackson's *Thriller* and the Eagles' *Their Greatest Hits 1971–1975*, both with 29 million unit sales.

These statistics show catholic musical tastes, but also declines since 2007 in rock, rap/hip-hop, R&B/urban, jazz and classical, with increases in country, some pop and religious/gospel. They include traditional but also popular, urban-based, "ethnic" and constantly evolving and mixed music, which appeal to an important youth culture in the US. The music business is lucrative and profitable for record companies although they have to cope with illegal downloading, pirated copies, site sharing, competition from other formats and declining sales of videos, CDs and DVDs. The consumer culture has commercialized native forms and American music has capitalized on its global attraction. Americans also attend live music shows and concerts and each form of music has its own musicians, clubs and followers, although some attendance figures have declined.

Dance and ballet

Modern dance developed as a new distinctively American art form in the early twentieth century. Isadora Duncan, one of its first exponents, based her dance styles on Greek classical art and was more successful in Europe than America. Her followers, such as Martha Graham in New York, combined modern dance with developments in American music and ethnic life. They rejected the formal restrictions of classical ballet and improvised expressive, random, and emotional dance movements. Modern (and contemporary) dance in America has developed very successfully and has incorporated different elements such as African American music, video, back-projection, films and African dance movement into many different styles of dance practiced by a large number of professional and amateur dance companies.

US ballet was influenced by visiting European classical ballet companies in the early twentieth century and then by US-based foreign dancers, choreographers and administrators. These created a vibrant ballet presence, more companies were established throughout the country and ballet tried to minimize its elitist tradition by combining classic revivals, original offerings and experimental programs. An NEA survey in 2008 reported that 2.9 percent of adults attended ballet performances while 5.2 percent attended other forms of dance at least once a year. Some 6.6 million adults themselves participated in ballet and 11.7 million in other dance at least once a year.

Film

The film industry and Hollywood have been influential forces on domestic American culture and have been very successful internationally. The film industry started on the East Coast, but later moved to Los Angeles, and Hollywood became the center of American film-making. In the early twentieth century, the motion picture (first silent, then sound) was the most popular and dominant art form. In the 1940s, the Hollywood production studios were releasing some 400 films annually, seen by an estimated 90 million people each week.

Hollywood has always been an entertainment business concerned with selling a product. Its films were originally designed for American audiences and it has reflected American culture in its handling of themes such as the family, romance, individualism, war, heroism, female roles, children and patriotism. These have been used in different film genres in different periods and have reflected changing social conditions and attitudes in the US. Film-makers also strove for financial profits by making films with mass appeal and repeated successful formulas such as Westerns, gangster films, comedies, animation and musicals. But the system also produced classic films, whose appeal has endured, and quality products.

During the decades of Hollywood's golden age in the early to mid-twentieth century, films, movie stars and movie theaters were glittering and grandiose. The film industry sold a package in which the movie-goer was a consumer and the star was a commodity with a lifestyle and image specifically created for public consumption and approval. Other merchandise, such as fan clubs, was tied into this package and sold to a mass audience

Although the celebrity cult continues, the film industry and the star system have changed over the years. They have had to adapt to changing moral, social, economic and industrial climates. The original studio structure altered as a result of a series of mergers. The major companies were effectively taken over by financiers in the 1930s and eight companies (Paramount, MGM, Warner Brothers, RKO, 20th Century Fox, Universal, Columbia and United Artists) were formed. After a prosperous period during the Second World War, the industry was split up by anti-monopolistic legislation. In 2005, Hollywood's last major independent studio, Metro-Goldwyn-Mayer (MGM), negotiated a partner-sale with Japan's

Sony Corporation. MGM was formed in 1924 after a merger with other studios and produced classics such as *Ben-Hur* and *The Wizard of Oz*. The production of movies has declined over the years, but the budgets of big blockbuster films have increased greatly. However, quality films are still made by independent producers and directors.

Table 14.1 is based on ballots sent originally by the American Film Institute (AFI) to respondents in 1997, who were asked to suggest a list of the best movies ever made. The list was updated in 2007, reflected shifting perspectives and showed a mixture of early and later favorites. The AFI stipulated that evaluation criteria should include historical significance, cultural impact, critical recognition, awards and popularity.

It is interesting to compare Table 14.1 with a list of the all-time top-grossing American movies at the box office in the US and Canada 2010 (see Table 14.2), although this has not been adjusted for inflation, and so favors recent film releases.

By the mid-twentieth century, the earlier classical Hollywood, with its powerful studios and business tycoons, was largely finished. Fewer expensive films were made and independent production companies increased. Hollywood was moving away from the studio system and its large-scale productions to a culture of cost considerations. The post-war period saw the making of increasingly different varieties and genres of film, and Disney, for example, became an important source of full-length animated films. Disney is now a very large entertainment group after its 1995 merger with the ABC television network and has continued to develop its theme parks worldwide.

TABLE 14.1 Selection (1–13) from 100 Best American Movies of All Time, 2007

Rank	Title	First released
1	Citizen Kane	1941
2	The Godfather	1972
3	Casablanca	1942
4	Raging Bull	1980
5	Singin' in the Rain	1952
6	Gone with the Wind	1939
7	Lawrence of Arabia	1962
8	Schindler's List	1993
9	Vertigo	1958
10	The Wizard of Oz	1939
11	City Lights	1931
12	The Searchers	1956
13	Star Wars	1977

Source: adapted from American Film Institute, 2007.

TABLE 14.2 Selection (1–13) from All-Time Top-Grossing American Movies, 2010

Rank	Title (original release)	Gross ($ millions)
1	*Avatar* (2009)	749.8
2	*Titanic* (1997)	600.8
3	*The Dark Knight* (2008)	533.3
4	*Star Wars* (1977)	461.0
5	*Shrek 2* (2004)	436.7
6	*E.T. The Extra-Terrestrial* (1982)	435.0
7	*Star Wars: Episode 1 – The Phantom Menace* (1999)	431.1
8	*Pirates of the Caribbean: Dead Man's Chest* (2006)	423.3
9	*Toy Story 3* (2010)	403.8
10	*Spider-Man* (2002)	403.7
11	*Transformers: Revenge of the Fallen* (2009)	402.1
12	*Star Wars: Episode III Revenge of the Sith* (2005)	380.3
13	*The Lord of the Rings: The Return of the King* (2003)	377.0

Source: adapted from Rentrak Corporation, 2010.

The increasing influence of television forced the film industry to redefine itself in order to keep its market share of leisure activities. The number of television sets in the US grew hugely from the early 1950s. Cinema audiences declined and were halved by 1953. Hollywood responded by making films for teenagers (a rapidly increasing consumer market) and Western television series such as *Gunsmoke* and *Cheyenne*. It also introduced some innovations such as Cinerama (wide-screen projection) and 3D (three-dimensional) films, which reappeared successfully in 2010.

Gradually from the 1970s and 1980s Hollywood studios were taken over by conglomerates with diverse business interests such as Gulf & Western, and there was increased competition from independent film-production companies. New technologies such as video developed, and media companies and film studios were increasingly owned by multimedia businesses such as Time Warner Inc. Time Warner merged with the Turner Broadcasting System (which owns the CNN cable-television news channel) in 1995 and with America Online in 2000 to become the world's largest media and entertainment group.

Hollywood has therefore changed considerably as the film, media and entertainment industries developed. It is now a multimedia corporate business system, as well as a film industry, with many commercial tie-ins. Production costs and profits have become crucial, and it is difficult to find finance for new film ideas. The audience has also changed. Young people watch television but also still go to the cinema out of interest and for social reasons. Older people tend to

PLATE 14.1 Meryl Streep won Best Actress Award for *The Iron Lady* at the 84th Annual Academy Awards, 2012.
(Frank Trapper/Corbis)

watch television films and series, videos or DVDs in the home. In 2008, 99 percent of American households had at least one television set, 91 percent had VCRs, 43 percent had CD players, 84 percent had a DVD player and 86 percent received basic cable services (48 percent premium cable). But videos, CDs and DVDs for sale and rent have declining sales as television networks and the internet and smartphones take over their functions by streaming films and shows.

Television series, soap operas and comedy sitcoms have become an important staple diet of the film-production industry and studios rent their feature films to television networks or to internet providers. Blockbuster films with huge budgets and expensive stars are still being made, although more are being filmed on locations outside Hollywood and California, such as New York and Texas as well as abroad, in an effort to cut rising costs as cinema audiences declined from the 1960s and to search for new markets and ideas. However, the US remains the largest producer of films for a world audience, some of which succeed and others fail. American themes are still examined in films, but Hollywood is now both an American institution and part of international popular culture. The top-grossing US movie in 2009 was *Transformers: Revenge of the Fallen* with $402.1 million, while the all-time top-grossing US movie (as of 2010) is *Avatar* with $749.8 million. According to Rentrak Corporation, there were 1,415 million admissions to US movie theaters in 2009, or 27.2 million per week. The average ticket price was $7.50; 677 films were produced; and 588 films were released. In 2010, annual admissions dropped to 1,341 million.

Although the golden age is past, film is still an entertainment medium with huge domestic and international appeal. Instructional films are also being made by the film industry and can be used in business, industry, advertising and training programs. Hollywood and the film industry have consequently had to adapt to changing ownership structures and different social tastes and audiences in order to remain profitable and to develop new markets. In the scramble for entertainment profits based on established themes and successful formulae, the quality of many of Hollywood's commercial films and blockbusters is criticized within the US; the price of ticket admissions is regarded as too high; and an alleged concentration on gratuitous violence and sexual explicitness is opposed.

The arts: performance and participation

The National Endowment for the Arts reported in 2008 that, counting all art forms, 36.2 percent (76 percent in 2002) of US adults (81 .3 million people as against 157 million in 2002) had attended a performance or had participated in at least one activity.

A smaller percentage of adults had therefore attended or participated in arts events than in 2002, with declines in most areas. Museum and art gallery attendance had fallen significantly, as had the proportion of adults visiting parks, historical buildings, craft fairs and visual arts festivals. Fewer adults attended performance arts, such as classical music, jazz, ballet or other dance, Latin or salsa music and opera.

Adults were not creating or performing as much, and only photography, classical music, choir/chorus and painting/drawing showed increased participation. Jazz remained stable, while opera, musical plays, non-musical plays, dance, pottery/ceramics, weaving/sewing and creative writing had seen reduced numbers since 2002.

The survey also suggested that educated Americans were participating less than previously and college-educated and degree-level adults showed lower attendance rates at most arts events. Less educated adults had significantly reduced their already low levels of attendance at art performances or visiting museums and art galleries.

It is argued that the reasons for these declines were the bad economic situation from 2007, the 2008–9 recession, high gas and travel costs and weak consumer spending. This situation may be temporary and an economic improvement might boost the arts scene.

However, interestingly, the number of adults reading literature in 2008 rose from 46.7 percent to 50.2 percent, possibly because this is a less expensive arts activity. Significant numbers of American adults in 2008 enjoyed viewing and listening to the arts on the internet; downloading music, theater or dance performances; viewing paintings, sculpture or photography; and posting their own art or performances. These results indicate an increased role for the electronic and online media in the accessibility and enjoyment of the arts.

The NEA survey found in fact that more adults viewed or listened to broadcasts and recordings of arts events in 2008 than attended live performances, except for live theater. The most popular were classical music broadcasts or recordings, followed by programs about the visual arts, programs about books/ writers, Latin or salsa music, jazz, dance, musical plays, non-musical plays and opera.

The survey also reported that attendees at arts events are becoming older than the average US adult, and since 1982 young adult (18–24-year-old) attendance rates have declined significantly for jazz, classical music, ballet and non-musical plays. This suggests that young people and young adults are finding alternative self-made, group or online entertainment. However, from 2002 to 2008, 45–54 year-olds, who are historically a large component of arts audiences, showed the steepest declines in attendance at most arts events.

Developments in opera companies, orchestras, and ballet and dance companies

The number of nationwide arts-related companies or organizations has increased since the 1960s, although some suffered in the adverse economic conditions from 2007. In 2008 there were major professional organizations in the US, such as 125 opera companies, 50 symphony orchestras, 50 youth orchestras and 108 ballet and dance companies. Many of these have world reputations and international conductors, directors and soloists, and cultural buildings have been built throughout the US, with lavish styles and facilities. There are also many smaller organizations companies, often amateur and semi-professional across the country.

In 2008–9, the most performed composers by symphony orchestras were Beethoven, Mozart, Brahms, Tchaikovsky, Dvorak, Mendelssohn and Ravel. In 2009–10, the most performed works by opera companies were Mozart's *The Marriage of Figaro*, Puccini's *La Bohème*, Bizet's *Carmen* and Puccini's *Tosca* (League of American Orchestras and Opera America.)

Some of these activities are still associated with traditional notions of "high culture." On the other hand, many people are following other more popular art forms, such as film and theater. It seems as though increasing numbers (particularly the young) are returning to these and other cultural pursuits (including electronic forms) in preference to television, which, although still enjoyed by the young, has arguably become the province of older viewers, although films and television productions might now be streamed through the computer.

This cultural development is being carried out with some direct financial support for the arts from federal or state governments. Although their role in supporting, financing and sponsoring the arts increased significantly from 1970, funding and involvement decreased in the 1990s. The NEA was created in 1965 and is an independent federal agency. It encourages and develops artistic activities by bringing them to Americans throughout the country and by helping arts education. It receives federal funding and distributes this to the arts at state and local levels. In its support role, the NEA is the country's largest annual federal funder of the arts ($186.8 million in 2009). National Endowment for the Humanities funding was $134.5 million in 2009 and the states collectively provided $272 million of legislative appropriations in 2011. Although much of the money goes to administrative costs, activities such as music, media, museums, theatre, arts in education, dance, opera, visual arts and literature benefit from this aid. However, orchestras, opera companies and other arts organizations have not historically received much public support.

The arts in the US have traditionally depended for their survival and promotion upon private sources, commercial activities and admission fees. The private financial contributions of individuals, philanthropic foundations (such as Ford and Rockefeller) and corporate bodies are also important for artistic funding. There is tax relief or deductions (tax breaks) on donations to the arts from individuals and companies.

Sports

Sport in the US was until the mid-twentieth century relatively isolated from national and international events. It had a provincial and minority image, except for the major sports of football, baseball, basketball and hockey, which did provide many Americans with team identification and recreation. Sport now reflects the national condition. Issues such as international competition, prestige, drug abuse (particularly in cycling, track and field athletics and baseball), sex discrimination, labor–management relations, the power of television, sponsorship and advertising, racism, gambling and corruption have all been associated at various times with both amateur and professional sport. The billions of dollars spent on contemporary sport and its buildings can lead to an exaggerated image of sport's worth and also reflect adversely on local communities that might have prioritized their spending on other areas of social life. For example, the US Census Bureau projected that sales of sporting goods in 2010 would amount to $75,666 million

US sports are taken very seriously by many people and are large commercial businesses for others. On some levels, Americans are obsessively involved with winning and money, but others may still see sport as a wholesome and positive means of enriching their lives, are highly involved in their sports as participants and spectators, and are dedicated to the success of their particular teams.

American sports divide into the professional and amateur ranks. Professionally, the most popular and favorite spectator-oriented sports have traditionally been National Football League (NFL) games (with their Super Bowl finals), major league (National and American) baseball (with its World Series), basketball, National (Ice) Hockey League, horse-racing and greyhound-racing. The football season begins in early fall, basketball is an indoor winter sport and baseball is played in spring and summer, although there is now some overlap. The strong tradition of American football is reflected in its television and commercial figures. The 2011 Super Bowl attracted some 111 million viewers and the NFL broadcast rights are worth about $5 billion a year.

Some sports have moved up or down in popularity over time. A Harris poll in January 2012 reported that despite some image problems with baseball, the favorite sports in 2011 were professional football (36 percent), professional baseball (13 percent), college football (13 percent), automobile racing (8 percent), professional basketball (5 percent), men's college basketball (5 percent), hockey (5 percent), men's tennis (2 percent), boxing (2 percent), horse-racing (2 percent), swimming (2 percent), men's golf (2 percent), track and field (1 percent), men's soccer (1 percent), bowling (1 percent) and women's tennis (1 percent).

In terms of national representative quality and popularity, it is argued that baseball, football and basketball are uniquely American in their varying combinations of individualism and a teamwork ethos and have been identified with notions of American exceptionalism. Baseball is said to be the nation's premier sport since most Americans have supposedly played it from childhood onwards,

PLATE 14.2 LeBron James, professional basketball player with the Miami Heat. He was also a member of the US men's gold medal winning basketball team at the 2012 London Olympic Games.

(Paul J. Sutton/Duomo/Corbis)

whether as the full game, Little League baseball or the softball variant (mainly for women). Baseball arguably originated in the US before the Civil War as rounders. This is a traditional English children's game played for centuries on the street, or in any open space, where the ball is thrown underarm to the hitter. It is also argued that baseball is more democratic and representative than football and basketball since it can be played by most people.

However, the 2012 Harris poll found that different demographic groups have their own favorite sports. Respondents who indicated that professional football was their favorite sport were African Americans (48 percent), those aged 30–9 years (46 percent) and those with some college education (42 percent). In terms of baseball, respondents aged 50–64 (21 percent), Latinos (19 percent) and Easterners (17 percent) indicated that it was their favorite sport. Respondents with a postgraduate degree (22 percent), college graduates (19 percent) and Midwesterners (18 percent) indicated that college football was their favorite sport.

Traditionally, many children were attracted to the three dominant sports of American football, baseball and basketball. But critics argue that they are now finding alternative sports because football is in decline due to high equipment and insurance costs, and the risk of injury; baseball is apparently too hard and has had ownership and economic problems; and basketball players need to be above-average height.

A central feature of the American sports scene is that since few other countries play baseball, basketball and American football on a professional and large-scale level, competition in them is mainly restricted to the US and there is no international opposition as such in these sports. However, although they are seen as distinctively American sports, they are increasingly being played in other countries and viewed on television internationally.

In other sports, a significant development in April 1996 was the inaugural match in Major League Soccer (MLS), which marked the latest US attempt to introduce a professional soccer league. Earlier ventures had failed, although soccer had been played at various levels in the US since the nineteenth century. Despite widespread familiarity among specific groups, such as college students, until recently most Americans did not see soccer as a spectator option, even if they had played it themselves. It was hoped that the 1994 World Cup held in the US would generate new enthusiasm. It is suggested that the growth of soccer has been America's silent sporting revolution. In 2012, MLS had an average attendance of 5.5 million with teams such as the Seattle Sounders having an average crowd of 43,000 each game. Although MLS is not generally as well-attended as the major leagues of football and baseball, a MLS attendance review in 2010 reported that MLS had higher game attendances than basketball and ice hockey, and attendance and television viewing figures continue to rise. There are some 20 million registered soccer players in the country and surveys indicate that more than 50 million Americans are "soccer literate."

Although soccer has long been played in schools and on college and university campuses, it is now popular with corporate sponsors, schools (with equal number of girls and boys), Latinos and affluent households (50 percent of soccer fans are from households with an income over $60,000). Women account for about 40 percent of all registered players and had 967 soccer teams and 23,650 players in the National Collegiate Athletic Association (NCAA) in 2010 (more representation than males). The US women's national soccer team was ranked first in the world in 2013, has won the World Cup twice (in 1991 and 1999) and won gold at four Olympic Games (1996, 2004, 2008 and 2012). The growth and success of women's soccer at national and international levels have increased general interest in soccer in the US. It also rivals the traditional place of Little League baseball as the sport of young suburban families, although it will probably not overtake American football and baseball in popularity.

However, youth sports organizations have welcomed soccer as a supplement to or a replacement for American football because of the latter's high costs. The senior professional soccer game has yet to attract significant consistent support, and soccer divides American opinion between those who find it tedious and slow and those who seriously support it. However, increased interest may come as more US television networks, such as NBC, pay for the rights to screen European

PLATE 14.3 Roger Staubach, professional football player, making a pass, 1976. He was the Dallas Cowboys quarterback, who led Dallas to two Super Bowl victories in 1972 and 1978. (*Bettmann/Corbis*)

soccer leagues such as the Premier League in England and help to establish soccer as a major sport in the US.

Although some professional and college sports such as football, ice hockey and boxing are tough action games, American sports do not suffer the same amount of spectator violence as some other countries' sports. Events such as baseball and football can still be family outings. They have a carnival atmosphere and a large element of show-business, including cheerleaders who orchestrate the crowds and marching bands that provide additional entertainment.

There is extensive media coverage of sports by newspapers and television, which reflects the popularity and commercial standing of sports in the US. Sports programs are an integral part of television and radio programming and attract large audience figures as the networks and other stations fight for a market share. Some cable stations (such as ESPN, the Entertainment and Sports Programming Network) are devoted exclusively to sports events, report for 24 hours a day and attract very large audiences. The various media, particularly television, have created a profitable, audience-based industry and also made sport accessible to many more people, who are unable either to attend or afford live events.

The media popularization of sports has led to increasing commercialization. The television networks and cable stations compete to obtain financially rewarding contracts from the professional sports bodies which allow the stations to televise sports events. Advertisers are attracted by the mass audiences and pay the television stations to advertise mainly male-oriented products on their programs. Advertisers benefit from the resulting sales of products and the sports bodies receive fees and funding from their broadcasting rights contracts. Some, such as the NFL, receive much of their revenue from the networks and cable companies.

Professional baseball, basketball and football are big business in which team-owners virtually control the players and realize their assets, investments and profits as players are bought and sold. In the case of baseball, the previous restrictive rules have been changed to allow players greater freedom and they (and other professionals) now earn huge salaries. Disputes between the players' union and owners have sometimes interrupted baseball seasons and fans have become more dissatisfied with baseball and other professional sports because of strikes, high ticket prices, players' huge financial rewards and the big business ethos.

The commercialization of American professional sports can affect an athlete's career. Success and financial rewards are connected not only to the person's ability and competitive skills, but also to the marketability of the athlete, who must have agents to act on his or her behalf, take part in publicity campaigns, endorse and promote products such as sportswear and attract sponsorship by corporate advertisers.

American sports are very competitive. As they have become more profit-oriented, success has become paramount and the importance of winning for participants and owners at all levels is considerable. Critics feel that this attitude has detracted from the traditional spirit of teamwork and the pleasure of playing sport, and fans can react negatively.

Increased commercialization of college (and even school) sports has also occurred. High schools and colleges provide a wide variety of sports activities as well as practice and match facilities for both male and female students. These are highly organized and competitive and generally receive substantial local publicity and support. The sports include American football, basketball, baseball, tennis, wrestling, gymnastics, athletics (track and field), cross-country running, soccer, swimming, volleyball, fencing, softball and golf.

Outstanding high-school athletes receive scholarships to enable them to go to college or university, where sports are an essential part of the educational program. College sports are supposed to be amateur, but have become very competitive and commercialized. College sports teams contribute finance (through television rights and ticket sales) to, as well as publicity for, their institutions and are given considerable local community support. Football and basketball are the most financially rewarding college sports and the top college teams can attract large amounts of money. The emphasis on recruiting top high-school athletes can affect the college's overall reputation, because college sports stars have traditionally been recruited to play their sport, to earn profits for the college and possibly to move on to the higher professional ranks, rather than to gain an academic education.

The apparent popularity of professional and amateur sports would seem to suggest that a large majority of Americans are avid and committed sports fans with a tribal affection for certain games and teams. A Marist poll in March 2012 asked respondents whether they would describe themselves as sports fans or not. A majority of 58 percent said they would and 42 percent said they would not. A Gallup poll in December 2011 asked respondents whether they were fans of professional football or not. Forty-eight percent said they were, 6 percent said they were somewhat, while 46 percent said they were not. Such replies do not seem to represent overwhelming interest in or support for sport.

These figures suggest that changes (possibly temporary) had occurred in Americans' attitudes to organized sport, particularly at the professional level. Fans have experienced a period of disillusionment resulting from strikes, high ticket prices, drug abuse, gambling scandals, excessive salaries of players, the behavior of club-owners and an apparent disrespect for fans by both owners and players. Many have indicated that they prefer to watch college games rather than the professional ones.

However, the US Census Bureau reported that 270 million Americans in 2009 participated in sports activities more than once a year. The most popular activities were in descending order: exercise walking, exercising with equipment, camping, swimming, bowling, bicycle riding, weightlifting, hiking, aerobic exercising, fishing and running/jogging.

Leisure

According to a Harris poll in December 2008, the median number of hours that adults (aged 18 and over) worked per week (paid work, housekeeping and studying) was 46 hours in 2008, up from 45 hours in 2007, at a time of economic difficulties and unemployment. However, the number of median hours available for leisure activities per week was an all-time low of 16 hours (as opposed to 20 hours in 2007). The one-hour increase in work and the four-hour loss in leisure were arguably due to worries over possible unemployment, which led workers to spend more time checking in to their jobs and being present at their place of work.

Nevertheless, adult Americans in 2008 enjoyed a wide range of leisure activities at varying rates of frequency. They included individual and collective physical and sporting pursuits, a range of more passive, spectator pastimes, and other participatory forms of entertainment (see Table 14.3). A Gallup/*USA Today* poll in December 2010 reported that 65 percent of respondents were satisfied with the amount of leisure time they had and 33 percent were dissatisfied. US Census Bureau statistics reported that total personal expenditure on recreation and leisure in 2009 was $897.1 billion, a reduction from $916 billion in 2008.

However, it seems that participation in physical exercise is in decline. Interest in this area increased from the 1960s and coincided with the new popularity of health fads, diet and exercise. In part, this was a reaction to research studies that showed that Americans smoked too many cigarettes and were becoming increasingly overweight, obese and sedentary in their lifestyles. Fitness was promoted by doctors and the government for health reasons, but was also allied to national prestige and vitality. Running (jogging), aerobic exercises, dancing, racquetball (an American form of squash played in a four-walled court by two or four people using a short-handed racket), swimming, bicycling, tennis, golf, skiing, basketball and fast-paced walking were encouraged and gained acceptance and popularity. It became fashionable for people of all ages and both genders to exercise, to take part in sport, to be physically fit and to place an emphasis on nutrition and diet.

However, annual Gallup polls on Americans' exercise habits suggest that sedentary habits continue, that participation in exercise has not changed in recent years, and in some cases has declined. About 51.6 percent of respondents reported that they had exercised on three or more days of the week in 2011, compared with 51.8 percent in 2008, 49.9 percent in 2009 and 51.4 in 2010. In 2011, 18.8 percent said that they had exercised one to two days per week and 29.7 percent had not exercised at all.

Updated figures in 2012 from the US Census Bureau, Statistical Abstract of the United States reported that, in terms of passive/sedentary activity by the adult population of 224.8 million, 53.3 million attended the movies and 30.6 million attended sports events. However, 52.9 million said they exercised, 26.3 million played sports, 28.2 million enjoyed physical outdoor activities and 41.2 million engaged in gardening. These respondents may have pursued more than one of these activities.

Some Americans can be obsessive about fitness and health. Although spending on sports/exercise products and related services decreased in 2009 compared with 2008 according to the US Bureau of Economic Analysis, significant numbers of individuals still buy the latest training equipment, clothes, books and videos, and feel that fitness is glamorous and connected to an ideal of healthy, young and lean bodies. Joggers and runners can be seen in many locations, aerobic exercises and weight-training are popular with men and women, health clubs have gradually increased in number and there are public and private organizations that provide facilities for those who want to keep fit or play sports. Some of these are provided free by local communities or by commercial businesses for their employees. Others are private clubs for those who can afford to pay for their services.

Commercial businesses have taken advantage of these developments and supply stylish sporting clothes and equipment, reaping large profits. Book publishers, magazines and television programs dealing with health and fitness concerns have also fed the market. Health companies produce supposedly beneficial products, as do food and beverage businesses. Affluent Americans may spend substantial sums of money to achieve a slim and fit effect. Some go to extreme and even dangerous limits to achieve individual fitness. Even those who cannot afford high prices for equipment and clothes might indulge in some exercise.

However, in spite of the facilities, good intentions and television debates about diets and exercise, 2009–10 data from the Department of Health and Human Services and the Food Research and Action Center showed that despite a slight decline from 2007, 68.8 percent of adult Americans were either overweight or obese with 35.7 percent (or some 80.2 million adult Americans) being obese. Women were more likely to be obese than men. Some 31.8 percent of children and adolescents were overweight, with 16.9 percent of these being obese. The figures contrast with those from the 1970s when only a quarter of the country's adult population was officially regarded as overweight. These medical conditions can lead to serious health complications and rising medical costs for US society.

This situation is arguably due to eating more wrong food and exercising less. The Center for Disease Prevention and Control in 2007 revealed that between 80 and 90 percent of Americans considered themselves to be unfit and lacking in exercise, one in four admitted to being completely sedentary, 40 percent rarely exercised, 23 percent smoked, 20 percent suffered from high cholesterol and 80 percent said that their efforts to improve fitness and diet did not last long. Their condition was made worse by fast-food eating, a lack of home-made food, employment stress and fatty food. However, Americans are now more tolerant of overweight people and no longer equate this with unattractiveness.

Americans have a wide range of leisure pursuits, some of which have a surprising prominence. A Harris poll in 2008 (Table 14.3) reported that the top activities were reading, watching TV and spending time with family and friends. Thirty-five percent cited reading in 2004, but in 2008 this had decreased to 30 percent. TV watching increased from 18 percent in 2007 to 24 percent in 2008. Spending time with friends and family increased from 14 percent in 2007 to 17 percent in 2008. Significantly, exercise (aerobics and weights) climbed up the list from 5 percent in 2007 to 8 percent in 2008.

Computing activities decreased from 9 percent in 2007 to 7 percent. Going to the movies dropped from 7 per cent to 6 per cent. The least-favored activities in the overall list outside the top 23 are exercise-related, such as running (2 percent), bowling (2 percent), swimming (2 percent), bicycling (2 percent), hiking

TABLE 14.3 Selected Top 23 favorite leisure-time activities, 2008

Rank	Activity	%
1	Reading	30
2	TV watching	24
3	Spending time with family/friends	17
4	Exercise (aerobics, weights)	8
5	Computer activities	7
6	Fishing	7
7	Going to the movies	6
8	Golf	6
9	Walking	6
10	Gardening	5
11	Playing team sports	5
12	Renting movies	5
13	Church/church activities	4
14	Outdoor activities	4
15	Relaxing	4
16	Watching sporting events	4
17	Socializing with friends/neighbors	4
18	Hunting	4
19	Shopping	3
20	Travelling	3
21	Playing music	3
22	Entertaining	3
23	Eating out/Dining out	3

Source: adapted from Harris Interactive, 2008.

Note: Some respondents took part in more than one activity.

(2 percent), camping (1 percent), boating (1 percent), horseback riding (1 percent), skiing (1 percent) and tennis (1 percent).

The top place of reading in the leisure list is interesting and shows a lead over television-viewing in recent years. According to the book trade tracker Bowker, 328,259 new print titles and editions were published in 2010 which was an increase of 5 percent over 2009, despite a fall in fiction titles and the competition with e-books. Actual book sales (724 million units books sold in 2009) had declined by some 3 percent.

Books have also historically been associated with libraries. According to the *American Library Directory 2011–12*, there are an estimated 121,785 libraries in the US, which include 9,225 public libraries, 3,689 academic libraries, 99,180 school libraries, 8,313 special libraries, 280 armed forces libraries and 1,098 government libraries. The Harris Interactive poll in 2008 showed the hold that books and libraries have traditionally had and (perhaps surprisingly) continue to have on the American public. Sixty-eight percent of Americans had a library card (those aged 18–31, women, Hispanics, Midwesterners and Democrats are more likely to have one), 76 percent of card-holders visited their libraries in the past year and 41 per cent visited online. More than 35 percent used a library between one and five times in the past year and 15 percent used it more than 25 times. Most people use libraries for borrowing books. Others use them for borrowing CDs, videos and computer software, to connect to the internet or to access reference materials.

Americans had opinions about their local library, whether they used it or not. Ninety-two percent viewed the library as an important education resource, 72 percent agreed that it is a pillar of the community, 71 percent saw it as a community center, 70 percent as a family destination and 69 percent as a cultural center. People were satisfied with their libraries and among those with a library card 68 percent said that they are extremely or very satisfied. Despite competing electronic sources, online services and computers, a Gallup poll in 1998 had reported that nine out of ten respondents expected libraries and books to exist in the future.

The state of reading in the US as a leisure and formal activity has been recently examined in the light of reports about its decline at all age levels. An NEA survey in 2004 (see Further reading, below) reported that there had been a decline of 10 percent in literary readers from 1982 to 2002, particularly in the 18–24 age group. The term "literary" included print fiction, such as novels, short stories or plays, but excluded biography and history.

A later NEA report in 2007 examined all varieties of reading, such as fiction and non-fiction genres in books, magazines, newspapers and online reading. It found that teenagers and young adults read less often and for shorter amounts of time compared with other age groups. Reading scores had worsened, especially among teenagers and young males. By contrast, the average reading score of nine-year-olds had improved.

A new NEA survey in January 2009 reported that for the first time in more than 25 years, American adults were reading more literature, with an overall increase of 7 percent. Since 2002, the biggest increases (9 percent) and most rapid rate increases (21 percent) were among young adults aged 18–24. Reading had increased among Latinos (20 percent), African Americans (15 percent) and whites (8 percent). The survey examined "literary reading" and noted that fiction (novels and short stories) accounted most for the new growth in adult literary readers, poetry and drama continued to decline, and some 15 percent of all US adults read literature online in 2008 or as downloads. The survey reported that a majority of adults (50.2 percent) now read books (119 million) in any format and argued that the improvement was due to the growth of public and private reading programs.

Other critics argue that surveys should consider all forms of reading, that younger children should also be represented, that young readers should be examined on leisure and formal (school and homework) criteria, and that the diverse examples of contemporary youth behavior should be fully explored in order to gauge the extent of reading proficiency. For example, a Gallup poll in 2004 had found that 90 percent of US teenagers aged 13–17 had watched television; 77 percent had listened to music on the radio; 76 percent had listened to music on CDs/MP3s; 60 percent had used the internet; 37 percent had played computer games; 33 percent had read a book (unspecified) for pleasure (not homework); 29 percent had read a magazine; 28 percent had read a newspaper; and 7 percent had read a comic book. Since these findings in 2004, more people pursue several activities simultaneously. Although the electronic media are a dominant influence in young people's worlds, they arguably read in the widest sense, whether it is a print or online novel, an e-book, a non-literary book, a technical manual, game instructions, a newspaper, magazine or school homework.

Exercises

Explain and examine the significance of the following terms:

NFL	NCAA	vaudeville
Hollywood	modern dance	tax breaks
baseball	ragtime	PSB
"pop art"	banjo	college football
aerobics	racquetball	bowling
softball	elitist	abstract expressionism
NEA	the musical	rounders
blockbuster	country	studio system

paperbacks	Super Bowl	jogger
fads	sedentary	obese

Write short essays on the following questions:

1. To what extent are some sports and films uniquely American?

2. Discuss the role of advertising and television in American sports, arts and leisure.

3. Critically examine the opinion polls on the arts, sports and leisure. What do these indicate about the diversity of American society?

Further reading

Balio, T. (1990) *Hollywood in the Age of Television*, Cambridge, MA: Unwin Hyman.

Cullen, J. (ed.) (2001) *Popular Culture in American History*, Oxford: Blackwell.

Davies, R.O. (1994) *America's Obsession: Sport and Society Since 1945*, New York: Harcourt Brace.

Gabler, N. (1988) *An Empire of Their Own: How the Jews Invented Hollywood*, New York: Crown.

Gabler, N. (1998) *Life the Movie: How Entertainment Conquered Reality*, New York: Vintage.

Higgs, R. (1995) *God in the Stadium: Sports and Religion in America*, Lexington, KY: University of Kentucky Press.

Hills, P. (2000) *Modern Art in the USA: Issues and Controversies of the 20th Century*, New Jersey: Prentice Hall.

Mandelbaum, M. (2005) *The Meaning of Sports*, New York: PublicAffairs.

Morgan, W. (1994) *Leftist Theories of Sport: A Critique and Reconstruction*, Urbana, IL: University of Illinois Press.

National Endowment for the Arts (2004) *Reading at Risk: A Survey of Literary Reading in America*, Research Division Report no. 46, Washington, DC: NEA.

National Endowment for the Arts (2007) *To Read or Not to Read*, Research Report no. 47, Washington, DC: NEA.

National Endowment for the Arts (2009) *Arts Participation 2008: Highlights from a National Survey*, Washington, DC: NEA.

National Endowment for the Arts (2009) *Reading on the Rise: A New Chapter in American Literacy*, Washington, DC: NEA.

The New York Times Almanac (annual) New York: Penguin Books.

Petracca, M. and Sorapure, M. (eds) (1995) *Reading and Writing about American Popular Culture*, Englewood Cliffs, NJ: Prentice Hall.

Schatz, T. (1981) *Hollywood Genres: Formulas, Filmmaking and the Studio System*, New York: Random House.

Schlosser, E. (2002) *Fast Food Nation*, New York: Perennial.

The World Almanac and Book of Facts (annual) New York: World Almanac Books

Websites

infousa.state.gov/life/life_artsent.html
National Gallery of Art: www.nga.gov
National Football League: www.nfl.com
National Hockey League: www.nhl.com
National Archives: www.nara.gov
National Endowment for the Arts: www.arts.gov
Library of Congress: www.loc.gov
Harvard Library: lib.harvard.edu

Appendices

Declaration of Independence in Congress, July 4, 1776

The unanimous declaration of the thirteen United States of America

When, in the course of human events, it becomes necessary for one people to dissolve the political bonds which have connected them with another, and to assume, among the powers of the earth, the separate and equal station to which the laws of nature and of nature's God entitle them, a decent respect to the Opinions of mankind requires that they should declare the causes which impel them to the separation.

We hold these truths to be self-evident: That all men are created equal; that they are endowed by their Creator with certain unalienable rights; that among these are life, liberty and the pursuit of happiness; that, to secure these rights, governments are instituted among men, deriving their just powers from the consent of the governed; that whenever any form of government becomes destructive of these ends, it is the right of the people to alter or to abolish it, and to institute new government, laying its foundation on such principles, and organize its powers in such form, as to them shall seem most likely to effect their safety and happiness. Prudence, indeed, will dictate that government long established should not be changed for light and transient causes; and accordingly all experience hath shown that mankind are more disposed to suffer, while evils are sufferable, than to right themselves by abolishing the forms to which they are accustomed. But when a long train of abuses and usurpation, pursuing invariably the same object, evinces a design to reduce them under absolute despotism, it is their right, it is their duty, to throw off such government, and to provide new guards for their future security. Such has been the patient sufferage of these colonies; and such is now the necessity which constrains them to alter their former systems of government. The history of the present King of Great Britain is history of repeated injuries and usurpations, all having in direct object the establishment of an absolute tyranny over these states. To prove this, let facts be submitted to a candid world.

He has refused his assent to laws, the most wholesome and necessary for the public good.

He has forbidden his governors to pass laws of immediate and pressing importance, unless suspended in their operation till his assent should be obtained; and, when so suspended, he has utterly neglected to attend to them.

He has refused to pass other laws for the accommodation of large districts of people, unless those people would relinquish the right of representation in the legislature, a right inestimable to them, and formidable to tyrants only.

He has called together legislative bodies at places unusual, uncomfortable, and distant from the depository of their public records, for the sole purpose of fatiguing them into compliance with his measures.

He has dissolved representative houses repeatedly, for opposing, with manly firmness, his invasions on the rights of the people.

He has refused for a long time, after such dissolutions, to cause others to be elected; whereby the legislative powers, incapable of annihilation, have returned to the people at large for their exercise; the state remaining, in the meantime, exposed to all the dangers of invasions from without and convulsions within.

He has endeavoured to prevent the population of these states; for that purpose obstructing the laws for naturalization of foreigners; refusing to pass others to encourage their migration hither, and raising the conditions of new appropriations of lands.

He has obstructed the administration of justice, by refusing his assent to laws for establishing judiciary powers.

He has made judges dependent on his will alone, for the tenure of their offices, and the amount and payment of their salaries.

He has erected a multitude of new offices, and sent hither swarms of officers to harass our people and eat out their substance.

He has kept among us, in times of peace, standing armies without the consent of our legislatures.

He has affected to render the military independent of, and superior to, the civil power.

He has combined with others to subject us to a jurisdiction foreign to our constitution, and unacknowledged by our laws, giving his assent to their acts of pretended legislation:

For quartering large bodies of armed troops among us;

For protecting them, by a mock trial, from punishment for any murders which they should commit on the inhabitants of these states;

For cutting off our trade with all parts of the world;

For imposing taxes on us without our consent;

For depriving us, in many cases, of the benefits of trial by jury;

For transporting us beyond seas, to be tried for pretended offences;

For abolishing the free system of English laws in a neighbouring province, establishing therein an arbitrary government, and enlarging its boundaries, so as to render it at once an example and fit instrument for introducing the same absolute rule into these colonies;

For taking away our charters, abolishing our most valuable laws, and altering fundamentally the forms of our governments;

For suspending our legislatures, and declaring themselves invested with power to legislate for us in all cases whatsoever.

He has abdicated government here, by declaring us out of his protection and waging war against us.

He has plundered our seas, ravaged our coasts, burned our towns, and destroyed the lives of our people.

He is at this time transporting large armies of foreign mercenaries to complete the works of death, desolation, and tyranny already begun with the circumstances of cruelty and perfidy scarcely paralleled in the most barbarous ages, and totally unworthy the head of a civilized nation.

He has constrained our fellow-citizens, taken captive on the high seas, to bear arms against their country, to become the executioners of their friends and brethren, or to fall themselves by their hands.

He has excited domestic insurrection among us; and has endeavoured to bring on the inhabitants of our frontiers the merciless Indian savages, whose known rule of warfare is an undistinguished destruction of all ages, sexes, and conditions.

In every stage of these oppressions we have petitioned for redress in the most humble terms; our repeated petitions have been answered only by repeated injury. A prince, whose character is thus marked by every act which may define a tyrant, is unfit to be the ruler of a free people.

Nor have we been wanting in our attentions to our British brethren. We have warned them, from time to time, of attempts by their legislature to extend a unwarrantable jurisdiction over us. We have reminded them of the circumstances of our emigration and settlement here. We have appealed to their native justice and magnanimity; and we have conjured them, by the ties of our common kindred, to disavow these usurpations, which would inevitably interrupt our connections and correspondence. They, too, have been deaf to the voice of justice and of consanguinity. We must, therefore, acquiesce in the necessity which denounces our separation, and hold them, as we hold the rest of mankind, enemies in war, in peace friends.

We, therefore, the representatives of the United States of America, in General Congress assembled, appealing to the Supreme Judge of the world for the rectitude of our intentions, do, in the name and by the authority of the good people of these colonies, solemnly publish and declare, that these United Colonies are, and of right ought to be, FREE AND INDEPENDENT STATES; that they are absolved from all allegiance to the British Crown, and that all political connection between them and the state of Great Britain is, and ought to be, totally dissolved; and that, as free and independent states, they have full power to levy war, conclude peace, contract alliances, establish commerce, and do all other acts and things which independent states may of right do. And for the support of this declaration, with a firm reliance on the protection of Divine Providence, we mutually pledge to each other our lives, our fortunes, and our sacred honour.

John Hancock and
fifty-five others

Constitution of the United States of America and Amendments

(Passages no longer in effect are printed in italic type.) Brief identifications of the content of provisions are underlined in parentheses.

PREAMBLE (The people establish the Constitution)

We the people of the United States, in order to form a more perfect union, establish justice, insure domestic tranquillity, provide for the common defense, promote the general welfare, and secure the blessings of liberty to ourselves and our posterity, do ordain and establish this Constitution for the United States of America.

ARTICLE I (Congress, the legislative branch)

Section 1 All legislative powers herein granted shall be vested in a Congress of the United States, which shall consist of a Senate and a House of Representatives. (Bicameralism)

Section 2 The House of Representatives shall be composed of members chosen every second year by the people of the several States, and the electors in each State shall have the qualifications requisite for electors of the most numerous branch of the State Legislature. (Qualifications for voters)

No person shall be a Representative who shall not have attained to the age of twenty-five years, and been seven years a citizen of the United States, and who shall not, when elected, be an inhabitant of that State in which he shall be chosen. (Qualifications for members)

Representative and direct taxes shall be apportioned among the several States which may be included within this Union, according to their respective numbers, *which shall be determined by adding to the whole number of free persons, including those bound to service for a term of years and excluding Indians not taxed, three-fifths of all other persons.* The actual enumeration shall be within three years after the first meeting of the Congress of the United States, and within every subsequent term of ten years, in such manners as they shall by law direct. The number of Representatives shall not exceed one for every thirty thousand, but each State shall have at least one Representative; *and until such enumeration shall be made, the State of New Hampshire shall be entitled to choose three, Massachusetts eight, Rhode Island and Providence Plantations one, Connecticut five, New York six, New Jersey four, Pennsylvania eight, Delaware one, Maryland six, Virginia ten, North Carolina five, South Carolina five, and Georgia three.* (Apportionment according to the census)

When vacancies happen in the representation from any State, the Executive authority thereof shall issue writs of election to fill such vacancies.

The House of Representatives shall choose their Speaker and other officers; and shall have the sole power of impeachment. (Impeachment)

Section 3 The Senate of the United States shall be composed of two Senators from each State, *chosen by the legislature thereof,* for six years; each Senator shall have one vote.

Immediately after they shall be assembled in consequence of the first election, they shall be divided as equally as may be into three classes. The seats of the Senators of the first class shall be vacated at the expiration of the second year, of the second class at the expiration of the fourth year, and of the third class at the expiration of the sixth year, so that one-third may be chosen every second year; *and if vacancies happen by resignation or otherwise, during the recess of the legislature of any State, the Executive thereof may make temporary appointments until the next meeting of the legislature, which shall then fill such vacancies.* (Staggered Senate elections)

No person shall be a Senator who shall not have attained to the age thirty years, and been nine years a citizen of the United States, and who shall not, when elected, be an inhabitant of that State for which he shall be chosen. (Qualifications)

The Vice-President of the United States shall be President of the Senate, but shall have no vote, unless they be equally divided.

The Senate shall choose their other officers, and also a President *pro tempore,* in the absence of the Vice-President or when he shall exercise the office of President of the United States. (President pro tempore)

The Senate shall have the sole power to try all impeachments. When sitting for that purpose, they shall be on oath or affirmation. When the President of the United States is tried, the Chief Justice shall preside; and no person shall be convicted without the concurrence of two-thirds of the members present. (Impeachment)

Judgement in cases of impeachment shall not extend further than to removal from the office, and disqualification to hold and enjoy any office of honour, trust or profit under the United States; but the party convicted shall nevertheless be liable to indictment, trial, judgement and punishment, according to law. (Judgement regulations in cases of impeachment)

Section 4 The times, places and manner of holding elections for Senators and Representatives shall be prescribed in each State by the legislature thereof; but the Congress may at any time by law make or alter such regulations, except as to the places of choosing Senators. (Rules for congressional elections)

The Congress shall assemble at least once in every year, and such meeting *shall be on the first Monday in December, unless they shall by law appoint a different day.*

Section 5 Each house shall be the judge of the elections, returns and qualifications of its own members, and a majority of each shall constitute a quorum to do business; but a smaller number may adjourn from day to day, and may be authorized to compel attendance of absent members, in such manner, and under such penalties, as each house may provide. (Qualifications)

Each house may determine the rules of its proceedings, punish its members for disorderly behaviour, and with the concurrence of two-thirds, expel a member. (Expulsion)

Each house shall keep a journal of its proceedings, and from time to time publish the same, excepting such parts as may in their judgement require secrecy; and the yeas and nays of the members of either house on any question shall, at the desire of one-fifth of those present, be entered on the journal. (Required congressional record)

Neither house, during the session of Congress, shall, without the consent of the other, adjourn for more than three days, nor to any other place than that in which the two houses shall be sitting. (Adjournment regulations)

Section 6 The Senators and Representatives shall receive a compensation for their services, to be ascertained by law and paid out of the treasury of the United States. They shall in all cases except treason, felony and breach of the peace, be privileged from arrest during their attendance at the session of their respective houses, and in going to and returning from the same; and for any speech or debate in either house, they shall not be questioned in any other place. (Pay and immunity)

No Senator or Representative shall, during the time for which he was elected, be appointed to any civil office under the authority of the United States, which shall have been created, or emoluments whereof shall have been increased, during such time; and no person holding any office under the United States shall be a member of either house during his continuance in office. (Limitation related to civil officers)

Section 7 All bills for raising revenue shall originate in the House of Representatives; but the Senate may propose or concur with amendments as on other bills. (The right to tax)

Every bill which shall have passed the House of Representatives and the Senate, shall, before it becomes a law, be presented to the President of the United

States; if he approve he shall sign it, but if not he shall return it with objections to that house in which it originated, who shall enter the objections at large on their journal, and proceed to reconsider it. If after such reconsideration two-thirds of that house shall agree to pass the bill, it shall be sent, together with the objections, to the other house, by which it shall likewise be reconsidered, and, if approved by two-thirds of that house, it shall become a law. But in all such cases the vote of both houses shall be determined by yeas and nays, and the names of the persons voting for and against the bill shall be entered on the journal of each house respectively. If any bill shall not be returned by the President within ten days (Sundays excepted) after it shall have been presented to him, the same shall be a law, in like manner as if he had signed it, unless Congress by their adjournment prevent its return, in which case it shall not be a law. (<u>Procedure of bills, veto power of the President</u>)

Every order, resolution, or vote to which the concurrence of the Senate and House of Representatives may be necessary (except on a question of adjournment) shall be presented to the President of the United States; and before the same shall take effect, shall be approved by him, or being disapproved by him, shall be repassed by two-thirds of the Senate and House of Representatives, according to the rules and limitations prescribed in the case of a bill. (<u>Presidential approval</u>)

Section 8 (<u>Enumerated [specified] powers of Congress</u>)

The Congress shall have power

To lay and collect taxes, duties, imposts, and excises, to pay the debts and provide for the common defense and general welfare of the United States; but all duties, imposts and excises shall be uniform throughout the United States;

To borrow money on the credit of the United States;

To regulate commerce with foreign nations, and among the several States, and with the Indian tribes;

To establish an uniform rule of naturalization, and uniform laws on the subject of bankruptcies throughout the United States;

To coin money, regulate the value thereof, and of foreign coin, and fix the standard of weights and measures;

To provide for the punishment of counterfeiting the securities and current coin of the United States;

To establish post offices and post roads;

To promote the progress of science and useful arts by securing for limited times to authors and inventors the exclusive right to their respective writings and discoveries;

To constitute tribunals inferior to the Supreme Court;

To define and punish piracies and felonies committed on the high seas and offences against the law of nations;

To declare war, grant letters of marque and reprisal, and make rules concerning captures on land and water;

To raise and support armies, but no appropriation of money to that shall be for a longer term than two years;

To provide and maintain a navy;

To make rules for the government and regulation of the land and naval forces;

To provide for calling forth the militia to execute the laws of the Union, supress insurrections, and repel invasions;

To provide for organizing, arming, and disciplining the militia, and for governing such part of them as may be employed in the service of the United States, reserving to the States respectively the appointment of the officers, and the authority of training the militia according to the discipline prescribed by Congress;

To exercise exclusive legislation in all cases whatsoever, over such district (not exceeding ten miles square) as may, by cession of particular States, and the acceptance of Congress, become the seat of government of the United States, and to exercise like authority over all places purchased by the consent of the legislature of the State, in which the same shall be, for erection of forts, magazines, arsenals, dock-yards, and other needful buildings; – and

To make all laws which shall be necessary and proper for carrying into execution the foregoing powers, and all other powers vested by this Constitution in the government of the United States, or in any department or officer thereof. (The "necessary and proper" clause, implied powers of Congress)

Section 9 *The migration or importation of such persons as any of the States now existing shall think proper to admit shall not be prohibited by the Congress prior to the year 1808; but a tax or duty may be imposed on such importation, not exceeding 10 dollars for each person.* (Slave import and limited powers)

The privilege of the writ of habeas corpus shall not be suspended, unless when in cases of rebellion or invasion the public safety may require it. (Habeas corpus)

No bill of attainder or *ex post facto* shall be passed.

No capitation, or other direct, tax shall be laid, unless in proportion to the census or enumeration herein before directed to be taken.

No tax or duty shall be laid on articles exported from any State.

No preference shall be given by any regulation of commerce or revenue to the ports of one State over those of another; nor shall vessels bound to, or from, one State, be obliged to enter, clear, or pay duties in another.

No money shall be drawn from the treasury, but in consequence of appropriations made by law; and a regular statement and account of the receipts and expenditures of all public money shall be published from time to time.

No title or nobility shall be granted by the United States; and no person holding any office of profit or trust under them, shall, without consent of the Congress, accept of any present, emolument, office, or title, of any kind whatever, from any king, prince, or foreign state.

Section 10 No State shall enter into any treaty, alliance, or confederation; grant letters of marque and reprisal; coin money; emit bills of credit; make anything but gold and silver coin a tender in payment of debts; pass any bill of attainder, *ex post facto* law, or law impairing the obligation of contracts, or grant any title of nobility. (Restrictions on powers of the states)

No State shall, without the consent of Congress, lay any imposts or duties on imports or exports, except what may be absolutely necessary for executing its inspection laws; and the net produce of all duties and imposts, laid by any State on imports and exports, shall be for the use of the treasury of the United States; and all such laws shall be subject to the revision and control of the Congress.

No State shall, without the consent of Congress, lay any duty of tonnage, keep troops or ships of war in time of peace, enter into any agreement or compact with another State, or with a foreign power, or engage in war, unless actually invaded, or in such imminent danger as will not admit of delay.

ARTICLE II (The President, the executive branch)

Section 1 The executive power shall be vested in a President of the United States. He shall hold his office during the term of four years, and, together with the Vice-President, chosen for the same term, be elected as follows:

Each State shall appoint, in such manner as the legislature thereof may direct, a number of electors, equal to the whole number of Senators and Representatives to which the State may be entitled in the Congress; but no Senator or Representative, or person holding an office of trust or profit under the United States, shall be appointed an elector.

The electors shall meet in their respective States, and vote by ballot for two persons, of whom one at least shall not be an inhabitant of the same State with themselves. And they shall make a list of all the persons voted for, and of the number of votes for each; which list they shall sign and certify, and transmit sealed to the seat of government of the United States, directed to the President of the Senate. The President of the Senate shall, in the presence of the Senate and House of Representatives, open all the certificates, and the votes shall be counted. The person having the greatest number of votes shall be President, if such number be a majority of the whole number of electors appointed; and if there be more than one who have such majority, and have an equal number of votes, then the House of Representatives shall immediately choose by ballot one of them for President; and if no person have a majority, then from the five highest on the list said house shall in like manner choose the President. But in choosing the President the votes shall be taken by States, the representation from each State having one vote; a quorum for this purpose shall consist of member or members from two-thirds of the States, and a majority of all the States shall be necessary to a choice. In every case, after the choice of the President, the person having the greatest number of votes of the electors shall be the Vice-President. But if there should remain two or more who have equal votes, the Senate shall choose from them by ballot the Vice-President. (Electors)

The Congress may determine the time of choosing the electors and the day on which they shall give their votes; which day shall be the same throughout the United States.

No person except a natural-born citizen, *or a citizen of the United States at the time of the adoption of this Constitution*, shall be eligible to the office of President, neither shall any person be eligible to that office who shall not have attained to the age of thirty-five years, and been fourteen years a resident within the United States. (<u>Qualifications for President</u>)

In case of the removal of the President from office or of his death, resignation, or inability to discharge the powers and duties of the said office, the same shall devolve on the Vice-President, and the Congress may by law provide for the case of removal, death, resignation, or inability, both of the President and Vice-President, declaring what officer shall then act as President, and such officer shall act accordingly, until the disability be removed, or a President shall be elected. (<u>Presidential succession</u>)

The President shall, at stated times, receive for his services a compensation, which shall neither be increased nor diminished during the period for which he shall have been elected, and he shall not receive within that period any other emolument from the United States, or any of them. (<u>Presidential compensation</u>)

Before he enter on the execution of his office, he shall take the following oath or affirmation:- 'I do solemnly swear (or affirm) that I will faithfully execute the office of the President for the United States, and will to the best of my ability preserve, protect and defend the Constitution of the United States.' (<u>Presidential oath of office</u>)

Section 2 The President shall be commander-in-chief of the army and navy of the United States, and of the militia of the several States, when called into the actual service of the United States; he may require the opinion, in writing, of the principal officer in each of the executive departments, upon any subject relating to the duties of their respective offices, and he shall have power to grant reprieves and pardons for offences against the United States, except in cases of impeachment. (<u>Powers of President</u>)

He shall have power, by and with the advice and consent of the Senate, to make treaties, provided two-thirds of the Senators present concur; and he shall nominate, and by and with the advice and consent of the Senate, shall appoint ambassadors, other public ministers and consuls, judges of the Supreme Court, and all other officers of the United States, whose appointments are not herein otherwise provided for, and which shall be established by law; but Congress may by law vest the appointment of such inferior officers, as they think proper, in the President alone, in the courts of law, or in the heads of departments.

The President shall have the power to fill up all vacancies that may happen during the recess of the Senate, by granting commissions which shall expire at the end of their next session.

Section 3 The President shall from time to time give to the Congress information of the state of the Union, and recommend to their consideration such measures as he shall judge necessary and expedient; he may, on extraordinary occasions, convene both houses, or either of them, and in case of disagreement between them, with respect to the time of adjournment, he may adjourn them to such time as he shall think proper; he shall receive ambassadors and other public ministers; he shall take care that the laws be faithfully executed, and shall commission all the officers of the United States. (State of the Union message)

Section 4 The President, the Vice-President and the civil officers of the United States shall be removed from office on impeachment for, and or convictions of, treason, bribery, or other high crimes and misdemeanours. (Impeachment)

ARTICLE III (The Supreme Court, the judiciary branch)

Section 1 The judicial power of the United States shall be vested in one Supreme Court, and in such inferior courts as the Congress may from time to time ordain and establish. The judges, both of the Supreme and inferior courts, shall hold their offices during good behaviour, and shall, at stated times, receive for their services a compensation which shall not be diminished during their continuance in office.

Section 2 The judicial power shall extend to all cases, in law and equity, arising under this Constitution, the laws of the United States, and treaties made, or which shall be made, under their authority; to all cases affecting ambassadors, other public ministers and consuls; to all cases of admiralty and maritime jurisdiction; to controversies to which the United States shall be a party; to controversies between two or more States; *between a State and citizen of another State*; between citizens of different States; between citizens of the same State claiming land under grants of different States, and between a State, or the citizens thereof, and foreign states, citizens or subjects. (Jurisdiction)

In all cases affecting ambassadors, other public ministers and consuls, and those in which a State shall be party, the Supreme Court shall have original jurisdiction. In all the other cases before mentioned, the Supreme Court shall have appellate jurisdiction, both as to law and fact, with such exceptions, and under such regulations, as the Congress shall make.

The trial of all crimes, except in cases of impeachment, shall be by jury; and such trial shall be held in the State where said crimes shall have been committed; but when not committed within any State, the trial shall be at such place or places as the Congress may by law have directed. (Jury trial)

Section 3 Treason against the United States shall consist only in levying war against them, or in adhering to their enemies, giving them aid and comfort. No person shall be convicted of treason unless on the testimony of two witnesses to the same overt act, or on confession in open court.

The Congress shall have power to declare the punishment of treason, but no attainder of treason shall work corruption of blood, or forfeiture except during the life of the person attainted.

ARTICLE IV (The states)

Section 1 Full faith and credit shall be given in each State to the public acts, records, and judicial proceedings of every other State. And the Congress may by general laws prescribe the manner in which such acts, records, and proceedings shall be proved, and the effect thereof.

Section 2 The citizens of each State shall be entitled to all privileges and immunities of citizens in the several States.

A person charged in any State with treason, felony, or other crime, who shall flee from justice, and be found in another State, shall on demand of the executive authority of the State from which he fled, be delivered up, to be removed to the State having jurisdiction of the crime. (Privileges)

No person held to serve or labor in one State, under the laws thereof, escaping into another, shall, in consequence of any law or regulation therein, be discharged from such service or labor, but shall be delivered up on claim of the party to whom such service or labor may be due. (Fugitive slaves)

Section 3 New States may be admitted by the Congress into this Union; but no new State shall be formed or erected within the jurisdiction of any other State; nor any State be formed by the junction of two or more States, or parts of States, without the consent of the legislatures of the States concerned as well as of the Congress. (New states)

The Congress shall have power to dispose of and make all needful rules and regulations respecting the territory or other property belonging to the United States; and nothing in this Constitution shall be so construed as to prejudice any claims of the United States, or of any particular State.

Section 4 The United States shall guarantee to every State in this Union a republican form of government, and shall protect each of them against invasion; and on application of the legislature, or of the executive (when the legislature cannot be convened), against domestic violence. (Promises to states)

ARTICLE V (Amendments)

The Congress, whenever two-thirds of both houses shall deem it necessary, shall propose amendments to this Constitution, or, on the application of the legislatures of two-thirds of the several States, shall call a convention for proposing amendments, which, in either case, shall be valid to all intents and purposes, as part of this Constitution, when ratified by the legislatures of three-fourths of the several States, or by conventions in three-fourths thereof, as the one or the other mode of ratification may be proposed by the Congress; provided *that no amendments which may be made prior to the year one thousand eight hundred and eight shall in any manner affect the first and fourth clauses in the ninth section of the first article;* and that no State, without its consent, shall be deprived of its equal suffrage in the Senate. (Ratification)

ARTICLE VI (Effects of Constitution)

All debts contracted and engagements entered into, before the adoption of this Constitution, shall be as valid against the United States under this Constitution, as under the Confederation.

    This Constitution, and the laws of the United States which shall be made in pursuance thereof; and all treaties made, or which shall be made, under the authority of the United States, shall be the supreme law of the land; and the judges in every State shall be bound thereby, anything in the Constitution or laws of any State to the contrary notwithstanding. (Supremacy clause)

    The Senators and Representatives before mentioned, and the members of the several State legislatures, and all executive and judicial officers, both of the United States and of the several States, shall be bound by oath or affirmation to support this Constitution; but no religious test shall ever be required as a qualification to any office or public trust under the United States. (No religious test)

ARTICLE VII (Ratification)

The ratification of the conventions of nine States shall be sufficient for the establishment of this Constitution between the States so ratifying the same.

    Done in Convention by the unanimous consent of the States present, the seventeenth day of September in the year of our Lord one thousand seven hundred and eighty-seven and of the Independence of the United States of America the twelfth. In witness whereof we have hereunto subscribed our names.

George Washington and thirty-seven others

The Bill of Rights (The first ten Amendments)

AMENDMENT I (1791) (Basic freedoms; separation of church and state)

Congress shall make no law respecting an establishment of religion, or prohibiting the free exercise thereof; or abridging the freedom of speech, or of the press; or the right of the people peaceably to assemble, and to petition the government for a redress of grievances.

AMENDMENT II (1791) (The right to bear arms)

A well-regulated militia being necessary to the security of a free State, the right of the people to keep and bear arms shall not be infringed.

AMENDMENT III (1791) (Quartering of soldiers)

No soldier shall, in time of peace, be quartered in any house without the consent of the owner, nor in time of war, but in a manner to be prescribed by law.

AMENDMENT IV (1791) (Search and seizure)

The right of the people to be secure in their persons, houses, papers, and effects, against unreasonable searches and seizures, shall not be violated, and no warrants shall issue but upon probable cause, supported by oath or affirmation, and particularly described, the place to be searched, and the persons or things to be seized.

AMENDMENT V (1791) (Rights in court cases)

No person shall be held to answer for a capital, or otherwise infamous crime, unless on a presentment or indictment of a grand jury, except in cases arising in the land or naval forces, or in the militia, when in actual service in time of war or public danger; nor shall any person be subject for the same offence to be twice put in jeopardy of life or limb; nor shall be compelled in any criminal case to be a witness against himself, nor be deprived of life, liberty, or property, without due process of law; nor shall private property be taken for public use without just compensation.

AMENDMENT VI (1791) (Rights of the accused)

In all criminal prosecutions, the accused shall enjoy the right to a speedy and public trial, by an impartial jury of the State and district wherein the crime shall have been committed, which district shall have been previously ascertained by law, and to be informed of the nature and cause of the accusation; to be confronted with the witnesses against him; to have compulsory process for obtaining witnesses in his favour, and to have the assistance of counsel for his defence.

AMENDMENT VII (1791) (The right to a trial by jury)

In suits at common law, where the value in controversy shall exceed twenty dollars, the right of trial by jury shall be preserved, and no fact tried by a jury shall be otherwise reexamined in any court of the United States, than according to the rules of the common law.

AMENDMENT VIII (1791) (Bail; cruel and unusual punishment)

Excessive bail shall not be required, nor excessive fines imposed, nor cruel and unusual punishment inflicted.

AMENDMENT IX (1791) (Rights retained by the people)

The enumeration in the Constitution, of certain rights, shall not be construed to deny or disparage others retained by the people.

AMENDMENT X (1791) (Reserved powers)

The powers not delegated to the United States by the Constitution, nor prohibited by it to the States, are reserved to the States respectively, or to the people.

LATER AMENDMENTS

AMENDMENT XI (1798) (Law suits against states)

The judicial power of the United States shall not be construed to extend to any suit in law or equity, commenced or prosecuted against one of the United States by a citizen of another State, or by citizens or subjects of any foreign state.

AMENDMENT XII (1804) (Electoral votes)

The electors shall meet in their respective States, and vote by ballot for President and Vice-President, one of whom, at least, shall not be an inhabitant of the same State with themselves; they shall name in their ballots the person voted for as President, and in distinct ballots the person voted for as Vice-President, and they shall make distinct lists of all persons voted for as President, and of all persons voted for as Vice-President, and of the number of votes for each, which lists they shall sign and certify, and transmit sealed to the seat of government of the United States, directed to the President of the Senate; – the President of the Senate shall, in the presence of the Senate and House of Representatives, open all the certificates and the votes shall then be counted; – the person having the greatest number of votes for President shall be the President if such number be a majority of the whole number of electors appointed, and if no person have a majority, then from the persons having the highest numbers not exceeding three on the list of those voted for as President, the House of Representatives shall choose immediately, by ballot, the President. But in choosing the President, the votes shall be taken by States, the representation from each State having one vote; a quorum for this purpose shall consist of a member or members from two-thirds of the States, and a majority of all the States shall be necessary to a choice. And if the House of Representatives shall not choose a President whenever the right of choice shall devolve upon them, before *the fourth day of March* next following, then the Vice-President shall act as President, as in the case of death or other constitutional disability of the President.

The person having the greatest number of votes as Vice-President shall be the Vice-President, if such number be a majority of the whole number of electors appointed; and if no person have a majority, then from the two highest numbers on the list the Senate shall choose the Vice-President; a quorum for the purpose shall consist of two-thirds of the whole number of Senators, and a majority of the whole number shall be necessary to a choice. But no person constitutionally ineligible to the office of President shall be eligible to that of Vice-President of the United States.

AMENDMENT XIII (1865) (Abolition of slavery)

Section 1 Neither slavery nor involuntary servitude, except as a punishment for crime whereof the party shall have been duly convicted, shall exist within the United States, or any place subject to their jurisdiction.

Section 2 Congress shall have the power to enforce this article by appropriate legislation.

AMENDMENT XIV (1868) (Citizenship for former slaves; due process and equal protection clauses)

Section 1 All persons born or naturalized in the United States, and subject to the jurisdiction thereof, are citizens of the United States and of the State wherein they reside. No State shall make or enforce any law which shall abridge the privileges or immunities of citizens of the United States; nor shall any State deprive any person of life, liberty, or property, without due process of law; nor deny to any person within its jurisdiction the equal protection of the laws.

Section 2 Representatives shall be appointed among the several States according to their respective numbers, counting the whole number of persons in each State, excluding Indians not taxed. But when the right to vote at any election for the choice of Electors for President and Vice-President of the United States, Representatives in Congress, the executive and judicial officers of a State, or the members of the legislature thereof, is denied to any of the male inhabitants of such State, being twenty-one years of age and citizens of the United States, or in any way abridged, except for participation in rebellion, or other crime, the basis of representation therein shall be reduced in the proportion which the number of such male citizens shall bear to the whole number of male citizens twenty-one years of age in such State. (Apportionment)

Section 3 No person shall be a Senator or Representative in Congress, or Elector of President and Vice-President, or hold any office, civil or military, under the United States, or under any State, who, having previously taken an oath, as a member of Congress, or as an officer of the United States, or as a member of any State legislature, or as an executive or judicial officer of any State, to support the Constitution of the United States, shall have engaged in insurrection or rebellion against the same, or given aid or comfort to the enemies thereof. Congress may, by a vote of two-thirds of each house, remove such disability.

Section 4 The validity of the public debt of the United States, authorized by law, including debts incurred for payment of pensions and bounties for services in suppressing insurrection or rebellion, shall not be questioned. But neither the United States nor any State shall assume or pay any debt or obligation incurred in aid of insurrection or rebellion against the United States, or any claim for the loss of emancipation of any slave; but all such debts, obligations, and claims shall be held illegal and void.

Section 5 The Congress shall have power to enforce, by appropriate legislature, the provisions of this article.

AMENDMENT XV (1870) (Voting rights for freed male slaves)

Section 1 The right of citizens of the United States to vote shall not be denied or abridged by the United States or by any State on account of race, colour, or previous condition of servitude.

Section 2 The Congress shall have power to enforce this article by appropriate legislature.

AMENDMENT XVI (1913) (Federal income tax)

The Congress shall have power to lay and collect taxes on incomes, from whatever source derived, without apportionment among the several States, and without regard to any census or enumeration.

AMENDMENT XVII (1913) (The direct election of Senators)

Section 1 The Senate of the United States shall be composed of two Senators from each State, elected by the people thereof, for six years; and each Senator shall have one vote. The electors in each State shall have the qualifications requisite for electors of (voters for) the most numerous branch of the State legislatures.

Section 2 When vacancies happen in the representation of any State in the Senate, the executive authority of such State shall issue writs of election to fill such vacancies: Provided, that the legislature of any State may empower the executive thereof to make temporary appointments until the people fill vacancies by election as the legislature may direct.

Section 3 This amendment shall not be so construed as to affect the election or term of any Senator chosen before it becomes valid as part of the Constitution.

AMENDMENT XVIII (1919, repealed 1933) (Prohibition)

Section 1 *After one year from the ratification of this article the manufacture, sale, or transportation of intoxicating liquors within, the importation thereof into, or the exportation thereof from the United States, and all territory subject to the jurisdiction thereof, for beverage purposes, is hereby prohibited.*

Section 2 *The Congress and the several States shall have concurrent power to enforce this article by appropriate legislation.*

Section 3 *This article shall be inoperative unless it shall have been ratified as an amendment to the Constitution by the legislatures of the several States, as provided by the Constitution, within seven years from the date of the submission thereof to the States by the Congress.*

AMENDMENT XIX (1920) (Voting rights for women)

Section 1 The right of citizens of the United States to vote shall not be denied or abridged by the United States or by any State on account of sex.

Section 2 The Congress shall have the power to enforce this article by appropriate legislation.

AMENDMENT XX (1933) (The President's term of office)

Section 1 The terms of the President and the Vice-President shall end at noon on the 20th day of January, and the terms of Senators and Representatives at noon on the 3rd day of January, of the year in which such terms would have ended if this article had not been ratified; and the terms of their successors shall then begin.

(The start of sessions of Congress)

Section 2 The Congress shall assemble at least once in every year, and such meeting shall begin at noon on the 3rd day of January, unless they shall by law appoint a different day.

(Presidential succession)

Section 3 If, at the time fixed for the beginning of the term of the President, the President-elect shall have died, the Vice-President-elect shall become President. If a President shall not have been chosen before the time fixed for the beginning of his term, or if the President-elect shall have failed to qualify, then the Vice-President-elect shall act as President until a President shall have qualified; and the Congress may by law provide for the case wherein neither a President-elect nor a Vice-President-elect shall have qualified, declaring who shall then act as President, or the manner in which one who is to act shall be selected, and such persons shall act accordingly until a President or Vice-President shall have qualified.

Section 4 The Congress may by law provide for the case of the death of any of the persons from whom the House of Representatives may choose a President whenever the right of choice shall have devolved upon them, and for the case of the death of any of the persons from whom the Senate may choose a Vice-President whenever the right of choice shall have devolved upon them.

Section 5 Sections 1 and 2 shall take effect on the 15th day of October following the ratification of this article.

Section 6 This article shall be inoperative unless it shall have been ratified as an amendment to the Constitution by the legislatures of three-quarters of the several States within seven years from the date of its submission.

AMENDMENT XXI (1933) (Repeal of prohibition)

Section 1 The eighteenth article of amendment to the Constitution of the United States is hereby repealed.

Section 2 The transportation or importation into any State, Territory, or Possession of the United States for delivery or use therein of intoxicating liquors, in violation of the laws thereof, is hereby prohibited.

Section 3 This article shall be inoperative unless it shall have been ratified as an amendment to the Constitution by conventions in the several States, as provided in the Constitution, within seven years from the date of submission thereof to the States by the Congress.

AMENDMENT XXII (1951) (Term limits for the President, 2 terms or 10 years)

Section 1 No person shall be elected to the office of President more than twice, and no person who has held the office of President, or acted as President, for more than two years of a term to which some other person was elected President shall be elected to the office of President more than once. But this article shall not apply to any person holding the office of President when this article was proposed by the Congress, and shall not prevent any person who may be holding the office of President, or acting as President, during the term within which this article becomes operative from holding the office of President or acting as President during the remainder of such term.

Section 2 This article shall be inoperative unless it shall have been ratified as an amendment to the Constitution by the legislatures of three-quarters of the several States within seven years from the date of its submission to the States by the Congress.

AMENDMENT XXIII (1961) (Electoral College votes for the District of Columbia)

Section 1 The District constituting the seat of Government of the United States shall appoint in such manner as the Congress may direct:

A number of electors of President and Vice-President equal to the whole number of Senators and Representatives in Congress to which the District would be entitled if it were a State, but in no event more than the least populous State; they shall be in addition to those appointed by the States, but they shall be considered for the purposes of the election of President and Vice-President, to be electors appointed by a State; and they shall meet in the District and perform such duties as provided by the twelfth article of amendment.

Section 2 The Congress shall have the power to enforce this article by appropriate legislation.

AMENDMENT XXIV (1964) (Prohibition of poll taxes)

Section 1 The right of citizens of the United States to vote in any primary or other election for President or Vice-President, for electors for President or Vice-President, or for Senator or Representative in Congress, shall not be denied or abridged by the United States or any State by reason of failure to pay any poll tax or other tax.

Section 2 The Congress shall have the power to enforce this article by appropriate legislation.

AMENDMENT XXV (1967) (Presidential succession)

Section 1 In the case of the removal of the President from office or of his death or resignation, the Vice-President shall become President.

Section 2 Whenever there is a vacancy in the office of the Vice-President, the President shall nominate a Vice-President who shall take office upon confirmation by a majority vote of both Houses of Congress.

Section 3 Whenever the President transmits to the President *pro tempore* of the Senate and the Speaker of the House of Representatives his written declaration that he is unable to discharge the powers and duties of this office, and until he transmits to them a written declaration to the contrary, such powers and duties shall be discharged by the Vice-President as Acting President.

Section 4 Whenever the Vice-President and a majority of either the principal officers of the executive departments or of such other body as Congress may by law provide, transmit to the President *pro tempore* of the Senate and the Speaker of the House of Representatives their written declaration that the President is unable to discharge the powers and duties of his office, the Vice-President shall immediately assume the powers and duties of the office as Acting President.

Thereafter, when the President transmits to the President *pro tempore* of the Senate and the Speaker of the House of Representatives his written declaration that no inability exists, he shall resume the powers and duties of his office unless the Vice-President and a majority of either the principal officers of the executive department(s) or of such other body as Congress may by law provide, transmit within four days to the President *pro tempore* of the Senate and the Speaker of the House of Representatives their written declaration that the President is unable to discharge the powers and duties of his office. Thereupon Congress shall decide the issue, assembling within forty-eight hours for that purpose if not in session. If the Congress, within twenty-one days after receipt of the latter written declaration, or, if Congress is not in session, within twenty-one days after Congress is required to assemble, determines by two-thirds vote of both Houses that the President is unable to discharge the powers and duties of his office, the Vice-President shall continue to discharge the same as Acting President; otherwise, the President shall resume the powers and duties of his office.

AMENDMENT XXVI (1971) (Voting rights for young people)

Section 1 The right of citizens of the United States, who are eighteen years of age or older, to vote shall not be denied or abridged by the United States or by any State on account of age.

Section 2 The Congress shall have the power to enforce this article by appropriate legislation.

AMENDMENT XXVII (1992) (Timing of congressional pay raises)

No law varying the compensation for the service of Senators and Representatives shall take effect until an election of Representatives shall have intervened.

Index

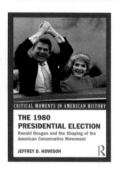

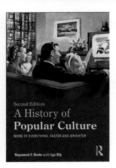